Administration of Schools for Young Children

FOURTH EDITION

Administration of Schools for Young Children

FOURTH EDITION

PHYLLIS M. CLICK

Delmar Publishers

I(T)P An International Thomson Publishing Company

Albany • Bonn • Boston • Cincinnati • Detroit • London • Madrid
Melbourne • Mexico City • New York • Pacific Grove • Paris • San Francisco
Singapore • Tokyo • Toronto • Washington

NOTICE TO THE READER

Cover Design: Synergy Art & Design
Delmar Staff
  Publisher: Diane McOscar
  Administrative Editor: Jay Whitney
  Associate Editor: Erin J. O'Connor
  Production Coordinator: James Zayicek
  Art & Design Coordinator: Timothy J. Conners

Copyright © 1996
By Delmar Publishers
a division of International Thomson Publishing, Inc.

The ITP logo is a trademark under license.

Printed in the United States of America

For more information, contact:

Delmar Publishers
3 Columbia Circle, Box 15015
Albany, New York 12212-5015

International Thomson Publishing Europe
Berkshire House 168–173
High Holborn
London WC1 V7AA
England

Thomas Nelson Australia
102 Dodds Street
South Melbourne, 3205
Victoria, Australia

Nelson Canada
1120 Birchmount Road
Scarborough, Ontario
Canada M1K 5G4

International Thomson Editores
Campos Eliseos 385, Piso 7
Col Polanco
11560 Mexico D F Mexico

International Thomson Publishing GmbH
Königswinterer Strasse 418
53227 Bonn
Germany

International Thomson Publishing Asia
221 Henderson Road
#05–10 Henderson Building
Singapore 0315

International Thomson Publishing –Japan
Hirakawacho Kyowa Building, 3P
Chiyoda-ku, Tokyo 102
Japan

    2 3 4 5 6 7 8 9 10 XXX 01 00 99 98 97 96
Library of Congress Cataloging-in-Publication Data
Click, Phyllis.
    Administration of schools for young children / Phyllis M. Click,
  Donald W. Click. — 4th ed.
        p.   cm.
      Includes bibliographical references and index.
      ISBN 0-8273-5876-8
      1. Nursery schools—United States—Administration.   2. Day care
  centers—United States—Administration. 3. Early childhood
  education—United States.   I. Title
LB2822.7.C55   1995   95-4185
372'.21—dc20   CIP

CONTENTS

Preface   ix
Acknowledgments   xi

PART I **Administration** **1**

Chapter 1   The Director: A Broad View   2
              Director Skills and Characteristics   3
              The Director as Manager   4
              The Director as Organizer   9
              The Director as Communicator   13
              The Director's Evaluation   16
              The Director's Relation to Boards of Directors   17
Chapter 2   Choices: Schools and Programs   25
              Types of Programs   26
              Types of Programs—Characteristics   30
Chapter 3   Beginnings: A New School/A New Year   45
              Location   45
              Finances   51
              Staff Selection   57
              Working Checklist   58
              The New Year   58
              Enrollment   59
              Parents   65
              The New School Year   68

PART II **Program** **75**

Chapter 4   Setting Goals: Planning and Evaluating   76
              Philosophy   77
              Formulating Goals   79
              Developing Objectives   82
              Implementing Goals and Objectives   86
              Evaluating Outcomes   88
Chapter 5   Planning: The Preschool   96
              Preschool Development   97
              Characteristics of a Developmentally
                 Appropriate Program   101
              Other Considerations   112
Chapter 6   Planning: Infants and Toddlers   119
              Infant/Toddler Development   119
              Characteristics of a Developmentally Appropriate
                 Infant/Toddler Program   123
              Suggested Activities for an Infant/Toddler Program   132

Chapter 7   Planning: School-Age Children   137
                   Developmental Characteristics   137
                   Characteristics of a Developmentally
                        Appropriate Program   142
                   Favorite Activities for School-Age Children   145
                   Characteristics of Teacher/Caregiver   146

PART III   Staff   151
Chapter 8   Staff Selection/Personnel Policies   152
                   Staff Qualifications   152
                   Staff Recruitment   155
                   Application Information   157
                   Selection Process   157
                   Notification of Employment or Nonselection   162
                   Personnel Practices   163
                   Personnel Records   168
Chapter 9   Staff Supervision and Training   173
                   Supervision of Staff   174
                   Evaluation of Staff Performance   176
                   The Evaluation Process   177
                   Methods of Evaluation   179
                   Use of Evaluations   181
                   Staff Development   182
                   Purpose of Training   182
                   Planning Staff Development   183
                   Popular Training Methods   187
                   Format for Training Sessions   191
                   Staff Relationships   192
                   Burnout   193
Chapter 10   Student Teachers/Volunteers   199
                   Characteristics of Student Teachers   199
                   Role of the Director   200
                   Choice of a Master Teacher   202
                   Orientation of Student Teachers   203
                   Responsibilities of the Master Teacher   205
                   Reactions of Student Teachers   205
                   Volunteers   207
                   A Plan for Volunteer Services   207
                   Recruitment of Volunteers   208
                   Selection of Volunteers   210
                   Orientation of Volunteers   210

	Handbook for Volunteers	211
	Supervision of Volunteers	212
	Recognition of Volunteers	212
	Records of Volunteer Service	213

PART IV Management 217

Chapter 11	Budget	218
	Development of the Budget	218
	Expenses—Personnel	219
	Expenses—Controllable	220
	Expenses—Fixed	221
	Income	222
	Trial Budget	224
	Summary of Budget Cycle	226
	Budget Analysis	229
	Implementing the Final Budget	230
	Keeping Budget Records	230
Chapter 12	Maintenance, Health, and Safety	234
	Maintenance or Operations?	234
	Inventory	238
	Safety	239
	Health	245
	Health Goals	246
Chapter 13	Food and Nutrition Services	262
	Caregiver's Role	262
	Menu Planning	263
	Guidelines for Menu Planning	265
	Parents	268
	Food Service for Children	270
	Cooking Experiences for Children	273
	Mechanics of Food Service	274

PART V Environment 281

Chapter 14	Space: The Preschool	282
	General Considerations for Organizing Space	282
	Specific Areas	290
	Adaptation for Children with Special Needs	299
Chapter 15	Space: Infants and Toddlers	305
	General Considerations for Infants and Toddlers	305
	Routine Areas	312
	Cognitive Area	314
	Fine-Motor Area	315

		Large-Motor Area	315
		Language Area	317
		Psychosocial Area	317
		Adaptations for Special Needs Infants and Toddlers	318
Chapter 16	Space: School-Age Children		322
		General Considerations	322
		Specific Areas for School-Age Children	327

PART VI Beyond the School Itself   339

Chapter 17	Parent Involvement, Education, and Public Relations	340
	Changing Roles	340
	Parent Involvement	341
	Parent Education	349
	The School and the Public	354
Chapter 18	Regulations and Child Abuse Laws	364
	Regulation Through Licensing	365
	Upgrade the Quality of Programs	368
	Child Abuse	370
	Laws Pertaining to Child Care Settings	376
Appendix A		381
Appendix B		387
References and Additional Resources		392
Glossary		398
Index		403

Preface

This Fourth Edition of *Administration of Schools for Young Children* is designed to help directors and prospective directors of early childhood centers. The need for this new edition is apparent, given the rapid increase in the numbers, and types of schools in operation today. Directors and managers must have new skills and knowledge.

This edition looks at many of the same topics that were covered in the previous editions. Part 1 (*Administration*) includes the general responsibilities of a director, discusses the different kinds of schools, and outlines the process for starting a new school or a new year in an existing school. Part 2 (*Program*) takes you through the process of developing goals and planning programs for children from infancy through the school-age period. Part 3 (*Staff*) discusses staff: selection, personnel policies, supervision, and evaluation. Part 3 also includes a chapter on student teachers and volunteers. In part 4 (*Management*), the budget process, maintenance, and food services are delineated. Part 5 (*Planning Space*) provides guidelines for planning space for infants, preschoolers, and older children. Part 6 (*Beyond the School*) covers influences outside of the school. Parent involvement and education are included, as are suggestions for developing a good public relations process. A portion of this part is devoted to the regulation of schools through laws and licensing procedures.

New Feature

A new feature in this edition is an **FYI** (*For Your Information*) in each chapter. These are bits of statistical information of ideas that pertain to the topic of that chapter. They are designed to spark your interest or evoke your thoughts.

New Topics

Changes in this edition reflect the subjects of political debate, new knowledge gained through research, and the needs of an increasingly diverse population. Each presents new challenges to those who plan and operate new programs for young children.

AIDS has been the topic of political discussion for nearly a decade, but primarily as it affected adults. There is a growing number of children with AIDS, some of whom are enrolled in child care centers or family day care homes. Teachers and directors must become educated about the causes of AIDS and how to prevent its spread. Therefore, this edition contains a section on general precautions to prevent the spread of infectious diseases, and also, special procedures for managing children with AIDS. Included is a sample of one school's policy on infectious diseases that is given to all parents.

Research studies indicate that the quality of programs for all young children can profoundly affect how well, or how poorly, they develop. Quality is determined by the developmental appropriateness for the children involved. Expanded sections in this edition focus on planning programs and environments for infants/toddlers and school-age children that specifically meet their developmental needs.

The growing multiformity of the population in the United States forces us to reexamine how we bring multicultural aspects into the classroom. In addition, the word "diversity" is used more often than "multicultural," signifying a broader meaning.

Diversity now encompasses recognition and acceptance of differences and similarities between genders: this is reflected in the "anti-bias" curriculum. This new edition contains suggestions for bringing these ideas into the classroom.

Diversity also applies to children who are differently abled. The passage of the Americans With Disabilities Act in 1990 reemphasizes the importance of providing an optimum environment for children with special needs. Many schools, child care centers, and family day care homes have already, or will be, including children with disabilities in their programs. This edition includes sections on making adaptations to the program, or to the environment, in order to include these children.

Lastly, this edition upgrades information concerning computerized data management. Since the last edition there has been a proliferation of software programs written specifically for early childhood centers. Directors recognize that if they are to efficiently manage billing, enrollment records, personnel information, and financial data, a computer and appropriate software are a necessity. Appendix A contains a review of the software programs currently available. In addition, there are suggestions of questions to ask a vendor before choosing either hardware or software for your school.

About the Author

Phyllis Click has been involved in early childhood education since receiving a Master's Degree from the University of California, Berkeley, more than forty years ago. She has been both a teacher and a director in a variety of preschool and elementary school settings. She has designed and administered federally funded programs for training day care personnel and licensing workers. As a college and university teacher, she has spent many hours with students, parents, and directors of schools. She is currently retired, but remains involved in early childhood education through consulting and conducting parent-education workshops.

Acknowledgments

I wish to thank Michaelyn Straub for the new photographs for this edition. Michaelyn is a free-lance professional photographer whose work has appeared in other early childhood publications.

Lastly, my thanks to Delmar staff members Jay Whitney and Chris Anzalone. As always, they encouraged me, offered suggestions, and provided needed support.

Part 1

Administration

1

The Director: A Broad View

You probably have had the experience of visiting a child development center in which, soon after you entered, you said to yourself, "This is a good place for children, parents, and teachers." You may also have had the opposite reaction in another school, and thought to yourself, "I am not comfortable here. If I were a parent, I would not want my child to be here." When you try to analyze what it is that makes one school so different from another, you may not be able to be specific: it is a feeling, or the atmosphere. Many components go into making a child development center either a welcoming place or one that make you feel uneasy. The attitudes, beliefs, values, and personalities of everyone involved all contribute to the total ambience. It is the director who brings all these parts together to form a harmonious whole.

Although directors want to create a caring, nurturing work environment, it is sometimes a difficult and frustrating task because of the numerous skills that are required. On any given day, a director performs a wide variety of tasks, yet at the end of the day, wonders what has been accomplished. Let us look at some of the daily occurrences that require a director's attention. He or she may:

- Greet parents and children as they arrive.
- Help some children separate from their parents.
- Find a substitute for a teacher who is ill.
- Talk to teachers about their schedule because it is raining.
- Call the roofers to repair a leak.
- Arrange a conference with a parent to discuss a problem.
- Talk to two teachers who are having difficulty getting along with each other.
- Show a new parent and child around the school.
- Order supplies for the kitchen and the classrooms.
- Arrange for a bus to take children on a field trip.
- Write an agenda for the next staff meeting.
- Begin a report for the next board of trustees meeting.

There are added demands on directors as well. Today's directors are under pressure to use efficient business methods in order to control costs. This may mean that they must take business courses or learn to use a computer. Additional burdens are present in early childhood centers that are part of a corporation. Directors must learn to work with a board or within a corporate structure. In some communities, the early childhood center may be part of the local school system, administered through a central office and housed on school grounds. In this case, the director must work with central office personnel and cooperate with staff members at the local school.

DIRECTOR SKILLS AND CHARACTERISTICS

From the above description of what a director does, it is obvious that a variety of skills and personal characteristics are required. *Management skill* is probably the most important. To manage means to coordinate all the parts of an organization to meet common goals. Other words that describe management processes are directing, commanding, conducting, or overseeing. To be an effective director, you have to organize the resources of your school, develop short-term as well as long-range plans, make decisions, lead, and delegate responsibilities. These skills can be acquired through work experience or through courses in management principles. Many schools now require their directors to have a background both in business management and early childhood education.

Many directors say that teaching seems easy compared to the job of directing. When they were teachers, they often worked alone in their classrooms or had to supervise only an assistant teacher. The focus was on the children, not on adults. On the other hand, as a director you must work with all the adults in the school, dealing with their many differences. Many times you have to delegate responsibilities to others. At times you have to be more iron-handed that you would be in the classroom. Often when you make decisions, some people will be dissatisfied, and will protest.

In addition to management and teaching skills, you should have the ability to *organize*. This means coordinating the various school activities. The bus schedule has to fit the parents' needs as well as get the children to school on time. The daily schedule for each classroom has to allow use of the playground without overcrowding. Evening meetings have to be scheduled so they don't interfere with the cleaning service. Organizing also means making the best use of your own time. You have to plan your day so that essential tasks get done, nonessential tasks can be started, and emergencies don't throw you into a panic.

As director you create the climate in which others work so you have to be a *leader*. That means being out in front, helping others become better at their jobs and inspiring them to meet new challenges. You must be able to encourage staff members to try new ideas, learn new skills, and take on new tasks. As a leader, you set an example for others to follow but you must continue to upgrade your own skills. Teacher and director burnout is a problem, especially in year-round schools. When you and your staff continue to grow professionally, job fatigue should be lessened.

To be a director, you have to like *interacting with people*. Unfortunately, some directors find doing paperwork much easier and tend to avoid people interactions. To be effective, you have to spend much of your day talking to parents, teachers, children, repair people, food and equipment vendors, and school board members or corporation personnel. You have to be able to listen without judging and maintain a respect for the other person's feelings. Sometimes you have to listen to complaints without feeling threatened. Most importantly, you have to know when and how to respond.

You need to have *self-confidence* because you do your job without a lot of help. Probably the most difficult part of being a director of a school is the isolation from others doing the same tasks. Teachers in a school have each other to talk to, complain to, and work with to solve problems. Although some schools have an assistant director, in most schools you work alone. If you are truly professional, you won't discuss administrative problems with teachers. In some situations, such as in the multisite corporation school, other directors are available by telephone when the going is rough. In other kinds of schools, opportunities to meet with fellow directors have to be arranged.

THE DIRECTOR AS MANAGER

Management Style

Your management style will affect everyone who works with you. When you are people oriented, you will see each adult and child as an individual with specific needs. When their needs are met, at least most of the time, staff, parents, and children are happy. Working parents are often under pressure and express their irritations to staff in indirect ways. If you are empathic, you will understand and let the parents know their feelings are important, too.

The director has general responsibilities:

Determines requirements that must be met regarding licensing, health, and safety regulations from the state and local regulatory agencies.

Serves as an *ex officio* member of the board of directors and attends committee meetings as necessary.

Provides leadership for setting overall goals for the school—to be used as a basis for curriculum objectives.

Plans reports on school as required by board or corporation.

Evaluates own work as a director and plans for continuing professional growth.

The director has enrollment duties:

Enrolls children and keeps an accurate waiting list.

Interviews prospective parents, giving information about the school.

Plans orientation for new parents.

Knows the changing needs of the community in order to maintain full enrollment.

The director supervises curriculum:

Provides direction to staff in setting curriculum objectives appropriate to the school goals.

Works with staff to implement and maintain goals and objectives.

Provides leadership in evaluating curriculum.

The director is responsible for the physical plant and equipment:

Plans, allocates, and uses space effectively.

Maintains the physical plant by providing custodial care and repair services.

Plans for the future needs of the school for space and equipment.

Keeps records such as inventories, repair schedules, and purchase information.

Manages supplies, reordering as needed.

Monitors the health and safety aspects of the environment.

The director is in charge of finances:

Sets up a budget.

Controls budget expenditures.

Collects fees and tuition.

Manages disbursements for payroll, equipment, and supplies.

Keeps adequate records of income and expenditures.

Handles petty cash disbursements.

Prepares monthly reports on expenditures to date.

Prepares a year-end analysis of budget and expenditures.

Reports to board or corporation.

Figure 1-1 Responsibilities of a director.

The director is concerned with staff relationships:

    Recruits and hires staff.

    Prepares job descriptions for each position.

    Formulates and implements personnel policies.

    Assists staff in implementing school goals.

    Provides a continuing assessment of staff development needs.

    Plans with staff for in-service training.

    Encourages staff involvement in community activities.

    Meets with staff members to resolve problems.

    Prepares a staff handbook and keeps it current.

    Keeps personnel records.

The director provides leadership in parent involvement and education:

    Communicates goals of the school to parents.

    Plans and implements parent education activities.

    Confers with parents regarding their child's progress.

    Encourages a variety of ways for parents to be involved in school activities.

    Keeps adequate records of parent involvement and education activities.

The director must plan for health and safety:

    Maintains an adequate health program for the school.

    Keeps health records on all children enrolled.

    Keeps staff informed concerning the health status of each child.

    Confers with parents as needed about child's health and nutritional status.

    Refers families to community agencies for special help when necessary.

    Continues to be informed regarding legal responsibilities of the school in relation to safety.

    Plans activities for staff and children to teach safety.

The director builds and maintains good community relations:

    Interprets the school and its goals to visitors.

    Maintains an effective public relations and advertising process.

    Represents the school at community functions.

    Establishes contacts with community agencies.

    Involves self and staff in professional and legislative activities.

Figure 1-1   Responsibilities of a director (*continued*).

Realistically, not every day can be smooth and free of problems. Some days seem filled with emergencies such as a sick teacher and no substitute, children with problems, or an angry parent. But the way in which you meet these problems and eventually resolve them sets the tone for how others react. The director who can realize that tomorrow will probably be a better day will be a model for others. A sense of humor helps on such days.

If you openly value the competence of your employees it will help them feel confident in their own abilities. You should know the strengths and weaknesses of each teacher on your staff. When difficulties arise, encourage faculty members individually or jointly to find a solution. It might be easier and quicker to jump in and offer a solution, but letting them find their own way is more helpful in the long run.

Management Methods

Each director has a management style. Some directors are consistent and use one method most of the time. Others use one method in some situations but change to another when confronted with a different situation. Management methods may be classified as authoritarian, laissez-faire, or democratic. *Authoritarian managers* make the decisions and determine policies. These people tell others what is to be done and allow no choices. *Laissez-faire managers* remain passive, leaving decisions and policy making to others. These managers may give suggestions but do not participate or provide leadership. *Democratic managers* involve others in decisions and policy-making processes.

Authoritarian managers usually believe they have greater knowledge and experience and, therefore, have the responsibility for making decisions for others. They

Figure 1-2 The director is organizer, manager, and communicator.

set goals for the school, tell staff how to implement them, and devise a schedule for each day's activities. They purchase materials and equipment to support goals and conduct all parent activities. This style of management does not take into account the needs of others, but decisions are made on the basis of what seems "right" to the person making the choice.

In an authoritarian environment staff members have little opportunity to gain new skills or to attempt new ways of doing their jobs. For some teachers, this kind of setting is easy and comforting. When they are told what to do, they are relieved of any responsibility for trying new things. For others, this kind of atmosphere is stifling and leads to early teacher burnout or boredom.

The laissez-faire manager takes a less active role than either of the other two types. This kind of manager may allow teachers to do whatever they want in their own classrooms without any concern for an overall cohesiveness of goals for the school. Teachers may do a lot of the purchasing for their own classrooms, again without concern for the good of the whole school. Parent education activities and conferencing may be done totally by the teacher.

Strong, experienced teachers usually can function well and be quite happy under a laissez-faire manager. They know what to do and carry out their jobs without needing support or leadership. In fact, some teachers prefer to have as little interference from a director as possible. On the other hand, inexperienced or unsure teachers may find they need more direction and support. They need a director who will give them new ideas for classroom activities or help them deal with a difficult child. Inexperienced teachers often have a great deal of difficulty working with parents and need a director who will guide them or who will take some of the responsibility.

The democratic director involves staff members in many aspects of the operation of the school. Staff may take part in developing or revising goals for the school. They may plan curriculum together and jointly decide on large purchases of equipment. Teachers may do a lot of parent education work, help in writing a newsletter, participate in parent meetings, and conduct parent conferences. The democratic style of management is the most people-oriented, but it is also the most difficult and time consuming.

FYI

On average, center directors earn $24,430 per year and have 15 years' experience. Forty-seven percent of directors have a graduate degree, many in early childhood education.

SOURCE: 1990 briefing report to the chairman of the Committee on Labor and Human Resources of the U.S. Senate.

Newer Approaches

There has been a great deal of research on management theory in the last few years. A good deal of thinking has been based on the X and Y theories codified by Professor Douglas McGregor of the Massachusetts Institute of Technology.

McGregor split employee behavior into two groups or types. The X type represents traditional thinking about the employee and is sometimes called "conventional wisdom." Here, people dislike work and will do almost anything to avoid it. The chief motivating factors are fear, threats, coercion, and punishment. The X person lacks ambition, is irresponsible, and needs constant supervision.

On the other hand, the Y employee finds work as natural as play or rest. If goal-directed, this person needs minimal supervision after job orientation. The employee accepts responsibility readily and shows imagination, initiative, and ingenuity. Unfortunately, this potential is often untapped.

The difficulty with the X theory is that it is often a self-fulfilling prophecy. The employer expects the worst and often gets it. By treating employees in an authoritarian or dictatorial manner, the worst comes to the surface. This becomes "circular" behavior and the boss ends with a feeling of "I told you so."

Of course, most directors do not embrace either a pure X or Y theory. Many do tend rather strongly in one direction or the other. Examine your own beliefs. Are you an X or Y believer? Those beliefs will strongly color your staff relations.

Another current approach to management includes a heightened awareness of the importance of participation by everyone involved. In "Workplace 2000," Boyett and Conn see the workplace of the future as a caring community. They point to the importance of finding the right "fit" between employer and employee and then helping each person fulfill his or her potential. They expect that the "I just work here" syndrome will no longer exist when all workers feel they are a part of the organization and are contributing to its success. They also point to the importance of information sharing in helping employees understand decisions. Without that information there tends to be distrust and suspicion, or employees may misinterpret management decisions. On the other hand, when employees know why decisions have been made, they are empowered and motivated.

THE DIRECTOR AS ORGANIZER

Delegating Responsibility

In order to accomplish the many tasks required of you as director, you must be a good organizer. This means that you must make the best possible use of the resources available to you. The first step is to learn to delegate responsibilities to others. By doing so, you will not only be able to do more work yourself, but you will achieve greater participation from your staff members. Many directors find it difficult to delegate responsibility to others, feeling that either it puts an unnecessary burden on their staff or that they cannot be sure the job will be done right. In

"The Early Childhood Super Director," Sue Baldwin cites the following reasons directors reported for not being able to delegate:

- Unable to let go of control.
- Staff does not measure up to expectations.
- Fear of repercussions if delegating occurs.
- Perfectionist.
- Concerned about the quality of the job to be delegated.
- Staff perception that the director may be pushing work onto the staff.
- Caretaking personality.
- Fear of imposing on people.
- Because of the director's position, staff will not say "no" to any requests.
- Not being able to explain why others should do the tasks.
- Lack of organization to get help in time.

If you are directing an all-day school, you probably have an assistant director to whom you already delegate some administrative tasks.

You and your assistant must share the long hours of the day, for neither of you can, or should, work ten or twelve hours. One may be responsible for the opening of school in the morning, getting schedules set for the day, and dealing with parents as they drop off their children. The other may be there at the end of the day to close the school and help parents and children reunite after the long day. In between, you can divide the other numerous tasks.

Divide tasks so that each of you can use your skills and interests to the maximum. Some people like to do the myriad paperwork jobs that are necessary in the day-to-day conduct of a school; others like to interact with the people involved in a school operation. The two of you should decide which jobs each does best and is most comfortable with. Each will have primary responsibility for those tasks. Once primary responsibility is assigned, your assistant should be free to do the job relatively free of interference. You still bear ultimate responsibility for the functioning of your assistant, however: therefore, communication between you is important. If the relationship is built on trust and respect, a minimal amount of supervision will be necessary.

Responsibilities can be delegated to other staff members as well. The cook can order supplies, compile information on new equipment to be purchased, or plan schedules for serving snacks and meals. The maintenance person can set up the cleaning schedule, or be asked to suggest ways to recycle or reuse throwaway materials. A secretary may assume responsibility for scheduling classroom field trips that have been suggested by teachers, or call a qualified substitute from an approved list.

Take the time to decide which person can best accomplish the task. This requires that you assess the skills that are needed and then find the best person to carry it out. Remember that the person who will do the task needs to gain something from doing it. No one should be asked to perform extra duties just to help you with your administrative functions. Remember, too, that having delegated a task does not mean you can just forget about it and expect it to be done. You will need to set up a schedule and procedure for maintaining overall supervision of delegated responsibilities. This may mean meeting with the staff person once a week or once a month, or just having that person keep you informed through written information.

When you first attempt to delegate responsibilities, you will probably find it takes more time than if you had done the job yourself. However, as your employees learn and gain confidence, you will find that your time is freed for administrative tasks that only you can do. You will discover from repeated experiences that both you and your staff will benefit immeasurably from the team effort.

Organizing Time

Time is a precious commodity to a busy director. You will find that you accomplish much more each day if you *set priorities*. Make a list starting with either jobs that must be done immediately or jobs that must be done each day; these should take top priority. Next come jobs that should be done as soon as possible or need to be done once a week. Last are the jobs that you would like to do or only have to do infrequently.

Set aside a specific time to do jobs that have to be done every day. Sometimes it helps, for instance, to get to work a half-hour earlier so that certain jobs can be done before the rush of the day. Some of the daily jobs can be done later in the day. It may be difficult to hold to your own schedule for doing the tasks, but if you persist and don't allow nonemergency interruptions, other staff members will begin to honor your commitment.

Schedule one day a week or specific days during the month to do tasks that need to be completed less frequently. Ordering materials, compiling financial reports, and writing a newsletter are examples. Mark the day on your calendar and block out some time. Go into your office, close the door, and get to work. You will be surprised at how quickly it will be finished when you don't have any interruptions.

Also plan for those tasks you would "like to do when I have time." Reading professional materials, writing an article, or making long-range plans for the school may fall in this category. You should not feel guilty if you set aside an afternoon each month to accomplish any of these.

Emergencies will arise—by definition, at the most inopportune times—but if you are prepared you can usually manage to cope with them. What kinds of emergencies come up in a school for young children? The same kinds that happen in a busy household: the plumbing stops working or leaks occur; your licensing worker is coming to visit and two teachers call in sick; a child falls and is bleeding from a cut on his forehead. You won't panic at any of these if you have procedures that you have thought out ahead of time.

For possible building and equipment emergencies, keep an up-to-date list of repair persons. When you buy new equipment, put repair information on the list immediately. For staff emergencies, develop a list of substitutes you can rely on. You can often find women in your neighborhood by advertising in a local newspaper. Students may be found through the local community college or university. When a desirable teacher applies for a position at your school and you have no opening, make it known that a substitute list is available. You should have a written procedure to care for children's injuries. It should be posted in a prominent place so that any staff member can follow the correct procedure. In addition, several staff members should know first aid—Red Cross certified, if possible. Other kinds of emergencies arise, depending upon the area of the country you live in. In southern California, schools are required to have an earthquake disaster plan. In some hillside areas, schools have also developed a plan for evacuating children in case of a brush fire. A tornado drill for schools in the midwest is appropriate.

A *computer* will save you an incredible amount of time. Although it takes time to learn to use one and to input data, it will be an enormously useful tool. You can keep financial records and budgets up to date along with records from previous years. A quick comparison of this year's income and expenses is also at your fingertips. Many personnel records can be kept on a computer file: dates of employment, attendance, and additional academic work are a few examples. A computer word processing program will make any secretarial task faster and easier. All correspondence, newsletters, memos, and notices can be done faster and with greater possibility for interesting variations such as graphics. Programs that will allow you to develop address lists are available. Ample data bases are useful for lists of addresses of parents, staff, community organizations, food and equipment vendors, or persons who have visited the school. Within the last few years, some software manufacturers have developed programs specifically for preschool management. These programs and systems vary considerably in quality and price. Although specific references to computers appear in later chapters, Appendix A contains a lengthy discussion. Once you start using a computer, you will wonder how you ever got along without one. You may even find uses for the computer in the instructional program.

Planning

Faced with the pressures of everyday activities, it is easy to overlook any kind of planning, and yet it is an essential part of managing a child care center. Each day is filled with so many occurrences that must be dealt with immediately that it is difficult to find time to focus on what should happen the next day, let alone the next month. However, both short- and long-term planning are necessary for the smooth operation of your facility. Short-term planning ensures the smooth running of each day and provides contingency plans when the unexpected occurs. At the beginning of each day and each week, know what has to be done. Then see that those tasks are finished. Be prepared, however, to meet the inevitable emergencies. Think ahead about the kinds of emergencies that have occurred in the past and are likely to happen again, then develop backup plans. You certainly will not avoid temporary disruptions caused by emergencies, but you will find that they are easier to manage.

Long-term planning will help you to provide the kind of environment and services that are set forth in the goals for your center. Decide which goals should be addressed at a particular time, then set a schedule for implementation. For example, one of your program goals might be that The Child Learning Center will offer a variety of experiences designed to help children acquire the skills needed for kindergarten entrance. To implement that goal, your staff members need to know which skills are included, when it is developmentally appropriate to introduce experiences to teach those skills, and how to evaluate children's progress. Carefully plan a series of learning experiences to inform your teachers. This kind of in-service may take place over several months or even a year.

The most effective planning will involve your staff as much as possible. Be sure that everyone has a copy of daily and weekly schedules as well as changes for rainy days. In addition, ask them to identify long-term goals to work toward during a particular period of time. Solicit their suggestions for implementing the goals and provide a method for obtaining feedback to evaluate progress.

THE DIRECTOR AS COMMUNICATOR

Much of your day as director is spent talking to people. It is important to develop your communication skills to prevent problems as well as to provide a model for other staff members. All of us experience some difficulty in communicating clearly with others. We know what we mean, and we are sure the other person understands clearly. Often, though, we are surprised at how others interpret what we have said. We think, "How could they have gotten that meaning out of what I said?"

Verbal Messages

Words are a coding system and the means by which our thoughts are conveyed to others. Although each word in a language has a meaning, coloration of that meaning comes from our own experiences. One of the problems is that we cannot all share the same experiences. Words may have different meanings to each of us based on our past. When we use words, what we mean comes from our own experiences. People hearing our words bring their own interpretations. As a result, the message being conveyed may be misunderstood.

Sometimes a particular word triggers an emotional response based on a past experience or association. This causes us to stop listening to the rest of the communication and focus on that one word. The speaker's tone of voice or the emphasis on one word may result in a similar response. "How are you today?" can convey a variety of messages depending on the way it is uttered. It can be merely a polite contact, a real concern, or an irritated inquiry meaning "Are you really all right today since so often you are not?"

Nonverbal Messages

Another reason for problems in communication lies in the fact that we communicate nonverbally as well as verbally. Nonverbal messages are the facial expressions, movements, and posture we use while speaking. In addition, we maintain eye contact or we look away. We sit or stand close to the listener or we maintain a distance between us. Each of these behaviors communicates a meaning and we are not always aware that our words are saying one thing and our behavior something quite different. (It is interesting to note that different cultures also interpret these behaviors differently.) Not everyone notices these subtle expressions but others see them clearly and react accordingly. The nonverbal message gets in the way of their hearing our verbal message clearly.

Preventing Problems in Communication

Since so much of our work as a director is done through communications with others, it is important to develop methods that avoid as many problems as possible. The first step is to decide *what* you want to relay. Are you merely giving information and do not expect a response? "There will be two prospective parents visiting your classroom today." Are you stating a problem and expect a response from the listener? "I'm wondering if you have any suggestions about how we can make cleaning up the playground at the end of the day any easier?"

Second, consider *when* to convey your message. If what you have to say is important, do not do it when your listener is busy and cannot give full attention. This means do not tell a teacher something important when she is busy in the classroom. Wait until the children are gone or when the teacher can take a few minutes away from the children.

Third, allow *enough time* so you can get some feedback. "Words said on the run" are likely to be misunderstood. If your message is not grasped, your listener can ask for clarification or you can question whether your message was clear.

Fourth, decide *where* a message should be conveyed. When you talk to a teacher in your office with the door closed, you convey an atmosphere of confidentiality or perhaps seriousness. When the conversation takes place on the playground or in the staff lounge, the message will seem more casual. Each place may be appropriate for different kinds of communications, so choose the one that best suits your message.

Fifth, decide *how* you want to present your message. Is it something that can or should be written? Sometimes it is important for others to see something stated clearly in written form. When information needs to be distributed to all staff members, this may be the most efficient way. Remember, though, the written message does not allow for immediate feedback so statements have to be clear. A written communication is always impersonal.

It is often necessary to *follow up* on a message. It is apparent that a teacher has misunderstood what you have said or is still confused because you did not get the response you expected. It will help if you first consider the way in which you conveyed your message. Was it because your body language said one thing while your words said another? Would it help if you changed your position or moved closer to, or farther away from, the listener? Is there another way you can state your message? Did you use words that might have caused an emotional reaction? Finally, ask for feedback. "You still seem confused. What is it you do not understand about what I have said?" or "Let me say it in a different way. What I meant was . . ." If you have created an atmosphere that encourages open discussion, staff members themselves will likely ask for further clarification when they do not understand. A healthy give-and-take discussion usually clears the air. This can go a long way toward preventing misunderstanding.

Listening

Part of being an effective communicator is the ability to listen while others speak. Sometimes we only partly listen, letting our minds wander to other topics that seem more urgent. At times, we listen only until there is a point at which we can respond with information, sympathy, a solution, or a denial. One of the most important communication skills you can develop as a director is to really listen to what others have to say and to allow them to express their thoughts fully before you respond. Here are some suggestions that will help you to become a better listener.

1. Stop talking. That sounds redundant, but it is often forgotten. Do not interrupt.
2. Be mentally ready to listen. Put other thoughts out of your mind and give your full attention to the speaker.
3. Listen to the content of the message. Do not get distracted by the speaker's method of delivery or his or her appearance.
4. Use body language that conveys your interest. Maintain eye contact and assume an attentive posture.
5. Try to determine the speaker's intent. Why is the speaker telling you this? If you can answer that question it will help you to focus on what you hear.
6. Listen for the main ideas. What are the most important concepts or pieces of information, and which are irrelevant?
7. Listen for what is *not* said. You can sometimes learn a great deal from what the speaker leaves out or avoids.
8. Give feedback. Nonverbal feedback, such as a nod or a smile, encourages the speaker to continue. You can also use encouraging phrases. Some examples are "go on, tell me more," or "I understand."
9. Check your own understanding of the message. "I hear you saying . . . Am I hearing you correctly?"
10. Summarize the message. "So the main points of what you have been telling me are . . ."

When you have developed both your speaking and listening skills, you will find that your interactions with people will change. You will gain in your understanding of others and will demonstrate that you are truly interested in their concerns or problems. Your relationships with staff members, parents, and even children will be enhanced. Problems will not disappear, but be more easily resolved because each party has a greater understanding of what is involved.

Written Reports

It is sometimes difficult to decide when to convey a message orally and when to write a note or report. If the message is so important that it gives you pause to decide, err on the side of writing. It is permanent and far less likely to be misunderstood.

There is a rule of thumb regarding written reports of almost all types. They should be frequent enough to convey needed information and satisfy normal questions and curiosity, but they should not be so frequent as to be overwhelming, redundant, and burdensome.

In practice, this rule is very difficult to follow. One thing is certain: financial reports or any reports containing arithmetical presentations should be written. Everyone can recall the treasurer's oral report of dozens of items of income and expenditure, followed almost immediately by the question, "How much money do we have?" Not only should this type of report—budget, child/teacher ratio, salary—be written, but it should also appear at stated intervals. Very few items can so upset a board of trustees, parents, teachers, or any interested persons as an abrupt statement announcing that "We are out of money!" Trustees, in particular, should set the schedule for the appearance of budget updates, preliminaries, and final acceptances. They may want a monthly statement of cash flow—something difficult to do manually, but relatively easy to do if the school is using a computerized budget program. Definitely keep a calendar of when reportable financial items are due and stick to it tenaciously.

The same practice is also advised concerning major developments in the total program, especially when changes are contemplated. Remember that almost everyone hates unpleasant surprises. They can be avoided if periodic reports are given in writing. It is best to plan just which reports will be issued and when. Consult with your staff, your parents, and your trustees or corporate supervisor. In the latter case, you may be given a schedule of when reports are due. Follow it without fail.

THE DIRECTOR'S EVALUATION

Assessing Strengths and Weaknesses

If you are conscientious, you will want to know how well you are doing your job. You need to know what your strengths and weaknesses are so you can do a better job. In some schools, a board will do this for you once a year. In corporate schools, you will likely be evaluated by your supervisor. But if you are not in either of these kinds of situations, you will want to do a self-evaluation.

Obviously, trying to look at yourself objectively is difficult, but you can try. Sit down with a piece of paper and list what you feel you do well. Then list those things you would like to do better. Take another look at the list of things you want to do better. Try to define specifically what it is you do or do not do. For instance, you feel you haven't done enough to encourage staff to increase their skills. Try to figure out why not; was it time? Was it a lack of knowledge on your part? Once you decide what it is that prevents you from doing the kind of job you want to do, you will be on the way to finding a solution.

You might also want to list the goals you accomplished for the year. What are the things you set out to accomplish and actually achieved? The list should then include those things you wanted to do and didn't get to. Your assessment of the list will include thinking about why you failed to do some things you planned at the beginning of the year. Was it your own lack of skills that prevented it or some other reason? Your honest answers will give you valuable information about what to do to change.

Self-Evaluation Tools

You can also use written evaluation tools to analyze the kind of job you have been doing. These will be similar to those used to evaluate other staff members. There are basically two types: an evaluation sheet containing a list of questions and a rating scale.

The *evaluation sheet* asks questions about specific areas of your job. It should be based on either your job description or the goals you have set for yourself for that particular year. It will ask, "Have I . . .?"

Some sample questions are the following:

- Have I created an open climate for discussion among staff members?
- Have I used my time efficiently?
- Have my contacts with parents sufficiently conveyed my understanding of their problems and pressures?

You can also use a *rating scale*. It addresses specific skills such as organization, planning, or initiative. It also includes a way of rating the skills comparatively, such as good versus unsatisfactory, or on the frequency of occurrence. It might look like the following example:

I show consideration for the feeling of my employees.	Often	Sometimes	Never
I try to praise rather than criticize.	Often	Sometimes	Never
I welcome suggestions from others.	Often	Sometimes	Never

A *numerical scale* might ask you to rate your own abilities on a scale of 1 to 5, with 1 being the highest. It might look like this:

Schedule and organize work	1	2	3	4	5
Plan for future needs of the school	1	2	3	4	5
Communicate clearly with staff	1	2	3	4	5
Resourceful in resolving problems	1	2	3	4	5

Either of these scales may help you appraise yourself.

A more recent trend is *peer rating*, where you are evaluated by your teachers. In any event, it is imperative that you be honest with yourself.

THE DIRECTOR'S RELATION TO BOARDS OF DIRECTORS

Boards of Directors

You may be hired by an existing early childhood program that is administered by a board of directors or to help set up a new center that is mandated to have a board.

In the past, the largest number of board-governed schools were nonprofit ones sponsored by churches, community organizations, or social agencies. Also in this category are the programs funded by some level of government: Head Start, migrant worker centers, day care centers, and facilities for children with special needs. More recently, there has been a significant rise in the number of profit-making corporation schools governed by a board. These are the multisite enterprises that operate as few as ten schools or more than a thousand. In addition, corporate businesses now operate on-site child care centers or participate in a consortium that is set up as a corporation. In order to work effectively in any of these settings, it is necessary for you to understand the function of boards and their makeup.

Basically, there are two kinds of boards: governing and advisory. A *governing board* makes and enforces policy that is then implemented by the program administrator. An *advisory board* has no power to enforce; instead it suggests policies and procedures or provides information to those who administer a program. The bylaws of an organization should clearly state the purpose and functions of a board of directors.

The composition of a board will vary according to the type of center it administers. A nonprofit board will include members who are chosen from the population it represents. In many cases, these will be parents of the children who attend the school or are members of the sponsoring church. In addition, the board may include professionals in early childhood education and community leaders. A great deal of consideration is usually given to making the board diverse, based on the members' backgrounds, occupation, ethnic groups, ages, gender, and points of view. Board members may be appointed or elected and membership is contingent upon the individual's willingness to serve.

The board of directors of a for-profit corporation are selected by the shareholders or investors. This type of board usually consists of persons who have business expertise, but may also include others. In some situations, parents may also be shareholders and therefore eligible for board membership. The board may decide to include nonshareholder parents, early childhood professionals, or community representatives.

There is no ideal number for a board of directors, although some state laws specify a required number. Some boards have as few as three to five members while others have twenty to twenty-five. A small board is more manageable, and makes it easier for members to get to know each other and to learn to work together effectively, but there are fewer people to carry out the tasks that may be needed. On the other hand, a larger board may be unwieldy but provides greater diversity of ideas and expertise. In addition, there are more people to assign to committees.

Board members may serve terms of one to three years. One year may not allow an individual enough time to become a fully functioning participant. However, some persons may not be able or willing to serve for a longer period. Many boards choose to have three-year terms in order to maintain continuity. This is particularly effective on large boards where terms can be staggered. At all times, a portion of the board has seasoned members while the remainder are newcomers.

The number of times a board member can be reelected or reappointed should be stated in the bylaws. When vacancies need to be filled, there should also be a clear statement of the method to be used. Some provision should be made to remove board members. Sometimes individuals no longer wish to participate, but removal can also be requested by center personnel, parents, or fellow board members.

Board Duties

One of the first duties of a new board of trustees is to research, draft, and publish an appropriate set of bylaws. In an existing school, bylaws should be periodically reviewed to determine if changes or updates need to be made. The bylaws constitute the basic charter of the school and should include:
- Official name of the school.
- Purpose.
- Composition of the board.
- Terms of office, and procedure for selection or replacement.
- Officers, and procedure for selection.
- Participation by staff members.
- Board duties.
- Standing committees and their duties.
- Guidelines for regular or special meetings.
- Procedures for amending bylaws.

A typical set of bylaws is shown in Figure 1-3. Some programs may require additional items to be added.

When the bylaws have been completed, the work of the board can begin. Its first task should be to state the philosophy of the program. Philosophy is discussed in a later chapter, but basically it is a condensed version of the ideas, beliefs, and values held by those formulating the statement. The philosophy statement is used as the foundation for all policies. Policies are general instructions for future actions and should be broad enough to allow personnel to make day-to-day decisions. Broad statements will allow the center director to develop procedures for implementation that fit new or unpredicted situations. When policies are too limited, the director may have to request policy changes at frequent intervals. Most directors would balk at that kind of restriction.

Standing committees usually are charged with the responsibility of developing policies that must then be approved by the entire board. Members of these committees are appointed by the board chairman and are selected because of their interest or expertise. They should also provide a balanced representation of the board membership in terms of gender, race, and points of view. Although the types of standing committees may vary from one program to another, there are some that appear most frequently. They are:

Executive committee: comprised of officers plus the program administrator as ex officio member. Meets more often than the full board as emergencies arise or as changes need to be made.

Finance committee: responsible for the budget and soliciting funding sources. The committee may meet with the center director to gather information for budget preparation, but may also merely approve a budget prepared by the director.

Personnel committee: hires the director, but may also help in the preparation of job descriptions for all staff members. It participates in interviewing job candidates and makes final recommendations to the board.

Program committee: responsible for the children's program, staff in-service, and parent education activities. Frequently, the center director and staff determine the specifics, but the committee formulates overall policies regarding these areas. It may also make recommendations to the director.

Building committee: finds a building appropriate for the type of program and plans for future additions or remodeling as needed. It also oversees maintenance, plans preventative measures, and approves emergency repairs.

Nominating committee: screens potential new members and prepares a slate for election by the board. This committee may also plan and conduct orientation activities for new members.

Communication with Boards of Directors

Responsibility for the operation of an early childhood center is shared by the board and the center director. Effective communication between the two levels is essential to achieve a sense of unity. Ineffective communication can lead to distrust, disagreements, and unresolved problems. It may be necessary to provide training so everyone involved can learn to express their ideas clearly and discuss problems in a way that is nonthreatening and leads to solutions.

Communication has to be two-way, from the board to the director and from the director to the board. The board must inform the director of policy changes and provide reasons for making those changes. A well-functioning board will even seek information from the director before suggesting policy changes. The director must keep the board informed as well. There should be open sharing of problems that arise at the center that might require personnel changes or revisions of job descriptions. The board needs to be informed when parents or staff request changes or additions to the center's program. The board must also be aware of changing community needs that could be addressed by additional services. Communication can take place either through direct contact or by written reports. Both have their place. Often, directors keep closest direct contact with the chairman of the board of trustees, either through frequent telephone conversations or by scheduled meetings. Sometimes a great deal can be accomplished over a lunch away from the distractions of administrative responsibilities. As an ex officio member of the board, the director also attends board meetings and at that time can present information, discuss problems, or make suggestions. Periodic written reports to the board are also required: enrollment reports, personnel changes, and budget information are examples.

The Corporation

In some corporate settings the director does not have direct contact with a board. In national corporate chains such as Children's World Learning Centers or Kinder

Care, communications go first to an area supervisor. That person will send the information to the next administrative level. It gets passed on from that level until it finally reaches the person who takes it to the board. Correspondingly, in business settings, the director usually works with an executive such as the director of personnel or a vice president. Some directors find this kind of structure frustrating and impersonal. Others accept the challenge, even finding it easier to be responsible to one person rather than several. Working with a supervisor or business executive

---

(Official Name and Address of School)

Article I. Board of Trustees

Section 1.   The board of trustees shall consist of not less than _____ nor more than _____ persons.

Section 2.   Members of the board of trustees shall be elected at the membership meeting in _____ (month) and such trustees shall be elected for terms as hereafter provided.

Section 3.   The terms of office shall be for _____ years, beginning _____.

Section 4.   The board of trustees shall meet at least _____ times a year. A special meeting may be called at any time by _____.

Section 5.   A quorum shall be constituted by _____ of the membership.

Section 6.   A vacancy on the board may be filled by the board, pending the next meeting of the membership.

Article II. Officers

Section 1.   The officers shall consist of _____.

Section 2.   All officers shall be elected for a term of _____.

Section 3.   Officers shall be elected at the membership meeting in ___ (month).

Section 4.   The chairman shall have the following duties _____.

Section 5.   The vice chairman shall have the following duties _____.

Section 6.   The treasurer shall have the following duties _____.

Section 7.   The following officers may be elected if desired _____.

Section 8.   The director of the school will serve as an *ex officio* member of the board.

Article III. Standing Committees

Section 1.   The following standing committees shall be appointed by the _____.

Section 2.   The function of the (curriculum, finance, personnel, building, etc.) committees shall be _____.

Article IV. Membership Meetings

Section 1.   The regular annual meeting of the membership may be held during the month of _____.

Section 2.   Special meetings of the membership may be called by _____.

Article V. Amendments

These bylaws shall be subject to amendment by _____ vote of the membership.

Figure 1-3   Sample board by-laws.

takes practice, but it can be done. It is important that both of you have similar goals and philosophy, and that each respect the other's competency. Here again, communication skills are absolutely essential! You have to be able to state your ideas clearly, discuss problems openly, and give concise information when required. You must be able to write complete and easily understood reports. In this kind of setting, written information takes on added importance since it may be your primary means to gain access to the board. Being part of a large corporation or business has many positive benefits. You can call on resources that are not usually available in single schools. You can profit from the experience and knowledge of experts who plan curricula. There are others to help you resolve problems with staff or parents. Even more importantly, there are often opportunities to move to higher levels of management. In national child care chains, you can advance to area supervisor, specialist, or consultant. In these corporations, or in businesses, there is the possibility of becoming an executive.

Throughout this chapter we have reviewed the characteristics of an effective director, and discussed the wide variety of skills and knowledge that are needed. If you choose to be a director, you will find the job challenging, and one that has many rewards. The rewards are different from those of teaching but retain some similarities. The following chapters will explore the similarities and the differences. While you are reading them, try to decide if you would make an effective director. Nothing less than our best efforts are necessary for this responsibility.

SUMMARY

Many components go into making a child development center a welcoming place: the attitudes, beliefs, values, and personalities of everyone involved. It is the director of the center who brings these parts together to form a harmonious whole.

There are many demands made upon directors. During any day, they perform a wide variety of tasks requiring many different skills. Added to this are the pressures to use efficient business methods. Additional pressures come from having to work with others outside of the school: boards of trustees, corporate executives, and school district personnel.

A director needs some specific skills to be successful. Management ability is probably the most important. These can be learned either through work experience or business courses. In addition to managing, many directors must be teachers. This is true in small schools, parent cooperatives, or in home-based day care. A director must be able to organize, program activities, and utilize resources and time.

Certain personal characteristics are necessary for the effective director: ability to lead others, a liking for interacting with people, and self-confidence.

Each director has a management style: authoritarian, laissez-faire, or democratic. Some use one method all of the time, while others use one in some situations and another when it is appropriate. Newer approaches to management include the X and Y theory and a heightened awareness of the importance of participation by employees in decision-making processes.

Delegating responsibility to others is part of being organized. Some directors find delegating difficult for a variety of reasons: unable to let go of control, fear of imposing on people, and the inability to get organized in time.

Responsibilities can be delegated to all staff members: assistant director, teachers, and nonteaching staff. It is well to remember that when you first start delegating, it may take more time. As your employees become more competent, you will have more time to devote to tasks that only you can do.

SELECTED FURTHER READING

Baldwin, S. 1991. *The Early Childhood Super Director*. Mt. Rainier, MD: Redleaf Press.
Boyett, J., and Coon, H. 1991. *Workplace 2000: The Revolution Reshaping American Business*. New York: Penguin Books USA Inc.
Decker, A., and Decker J. 1992. *Planning and Administering Early Childhood Programs*, 5th ed. New York: Macmillan Publishing Co.

STUDENT ACTIVITIES

1. Visit a school for young children. With permission, follow the director for an hour or so. Count the number of people spoken to and note any follow-up actions.
2. Describe the method your school uses to distribute materials. Suggest how to better control waste.
3. Think of your most flagrant failure in communicating with someone. What caused it? Is such failure common? How can it be remedied?
4. Who has the ultimate authority at your school? How does this power most often make itself felt? Suggest improvements.
5. Visit a board meeting or an advisory committee. What was discussed? How could this time have been better spent?

REVIEW

1. Compare a laissez-faire management style with a democratic style. How does each affect teachers?
2. Describe the workplace of the future as envisioned by the authors of "Workplace 2000."
3. List five reasons directors cite for not delegating responsibility to others.
4. In what ways can a busy director organize time so that necessary tasks are completed?

5. Why are verbal messages often misinterpreted by the listener?
6. List things you can do to prevent problems in communicating.
7. Part of being a good communicator is the ability to listen. State five sugges-
    tions for being a better listener.
8. Describe two methods directors can use to evaluate themselves.
9. Compare membership on a board of a nonprofit early childhood center
    with one that is part of a profit-making enterprise.
10. Standing committees develop policies that are then approved by the full
    board of directors. List the committees and briefly describe their functions.

GLOSSARY

Authoritarian manager   those administrators who make decisions and determine
policies for others.

Democratic manager   those administrators who involve others in decisions and
policy-making processes.

Laissez-faire managers   those administrators who remain passive, often leaving
decisions to others.

Management skill   ability to coordinate all the parts of an organization to meet
common goals.

Nonverbal messages   facial expressions, movements, and posture.

2

Choices:
Schools and Programs

OBJECTIVES

After studying this chapter, the student should be able to:

- State the differences between a half-day school and one that is in session all day.
- Describe the characteristics for each type of private and publicly funded program.
- Discuss the advantages and disadvantages of each type of program.

In the United States today, more than half the mothers of children under the age of thirteen work outside the home. A report published by The Children's Defense Fund titled *The State of America's Children 1991* projects that by 1995, there will be 14.6 million children younger than six years whose mothers are in the work force. There will also be 34.4 million children between the ages of six to seventeen. Children younger than five years are often cared for by relatives; almost half of working families have this arrangement. Six percent have a nonrelative care-giver in the child's home. Twenty-two percent attend day care homes, while twenty-five percent are in centers or preschools. Older children often care for themselves after school, but an increasing number are being enrolled in group programs. Boys and girls clubs, recreation programs, and community organizations offer some excellent before- and after-school activities for these older children. Early childhood centers are extending their offerings to include activities for children's out-of-school hours, including special summer sessions.

The quality of care given to children not only determines whether these children are safe and well-cared for each day, but also has some long-term effects as well.

Studies show that children who have been in quality programs tend to have fewer behavior problems, get along better with their peers, and have better academic skills. Quality care can be provided by individuals who care for a single child in a home or by a family day care provider with a small group of children. However, because of the knowledge and expense required to design and operate a quality program, it is more often found in group-based settings. Later chapters in this text include extensive information concerning the components of quality child care. A summary is outlined below.

Quality child care includes:

- A well-trained staff able to provide interactions with children that meet their developmental needs.
- Low staff turnover so children can maintain consistent relationships with care-givers.
- Health and nutrition practices that promote good health.
- A physical environment that is safe, well-maintained, and adequately supervised.
- Activities that are developmentally appropriate for the age level of the children.
- Inclusion of parents through open access and sharing of decisions that affect their children.
- Sensitivity to cultural differences and a commitment to preserve each child's cultural uniqueness.

As a director, it is important to know the possibilities or limitations of the various types of child care arrangements. Although all share many common attributes, each type has some unique features. The characteristics are determined by the hours of operation each day, by the philosophy upon which their goals are based, and by the sponsorship of each program.

TYPES OF PROGRAMS

Half-Day Schools

Half-day schools have sessions of four hours or less. Their primary purpose is to provide an enriched educational experience for children before they are old enough to attend elementary school. They are called preschools, learning centers, or early childhood education centers. They usually serve children between the ages of two and six years. Some schools have extended their offerings to include infants and toddlers.

Fewer half-day schools are available now than in the past. There are basically two reasons for the decline in their number: (1) Parents need all-day care for their children, and (2) the expense of operating a school cannot be met with a half-day session. Among those that are left are church preschools that function as an adjunct to the church's educational program. Cost of space and some services are covered by the church. Cooperative schools with their decreased cost due to high parent participation are usually half-day programs. Colleges or universities may operate a half-day school as part of their early childhood education curriculum. Private proprietary schools may meet expenses if they schedule a morning class and an afternoon class. Head Start, which does not depend upon tuition for income, has always offered two half-day sessions each day.

A good preschool will provide for all parts of the child's development: social, emotional, cognitive, and physical. There are many opportunities for interaction with both adults and children so the child can develop social skills and language. Responsive adults encourage independence, self-confidence, and control of impulses. Learning centers or individualized activities allow the child to explore and develop cognitive skills. Outdoor play with wheel toys, climbing equipment, sandboxes, and large blocks will develop large muscles. Cutting, painting, and manipulative materials indoors help the child develop fine muscle coordination.

Since the primary focus of this type of school is the education of the child, the staff should have an especially strong background in early childhood curriculum.

Teachers should have knowledge to plan stimulating activities for children and take advantage of the many spontaneous learning experiences available in the environment. Both the director and staff will be motivated to continue to learn by attending workshops and special classes.

All-Day Schools

All-day schools are in session for more than four hours each day, many as long as ten or twelve hours. Their primary purpose is to provide safe care for children while their parents work and are called day care or child care centers. They operate twelve months of the year, closing only for a few holidays. A large proportion of child care centers are operated by profit-making corporations, some of which have schools throughout the United States. The largest, Kinder-Care Learning Centers, Inc., has over one thousand, while La Petite Academy, Inc., and Children's World Learning Centers have over five hundred. Other corporations have been established within the last few years, some with as few as ten sites, and others with fifty or more. Individually owned "for profit" schools also offer child care, providing space for infants as well as preschool and school-age children. Churches and community organizations may also provide all-day care. Many businesses, hospitals, and governmental agencies have begun to offer child care for their employees.

The daily schedule of the child care center must meet the total developmental needs of the child since a large portion of the day will be spent there. Time must be allowed for the same kinds of enriched learning activities that take place in a half-day school. But, in addition, enough time must be allowed for the child to take care of his own health needs: brushing his teeth, getting enough rest, and eating a nutritious diet. The child must be encouraged to develop independence and language skills. A good day care program allows time for a child to be by himself and to be involved in activities that can be done alone. The pace of a day in child care should be slower than in a half-day school, alternating quiet times with active times to avoid overstimulation and fatigue.

FYI

*In 1987, the primary child care arrangement for children under the age
of five whose mothers worked full-time was:*
* *39 percent by relatives.*
* *6 percent by nonrelative in the child's home.*
* *25 percent by family day care homes.*
* *30 percent by child care centers or preschools.*

SOURCE: The State of America's Children, 1991. *Children's Defense
Fund.*

As the director of a day care center, you will have different management problems
than the director of a half-day school. Since you cannot possibly be present
during all the hours your school is open, you will need an assistant to share administrative tasks. This can be either a separate position, or a head teacher who shares
administrative tasks when not teaching. You may work an early shift, from the opening of the school until early afternoon. Your assistant will share the middle of the day
time with you and assume responsibility for the late afternoon to closing time.

An all-day school needs additional staff. Each group of children will have two
shifts of teachers, some who arrive early in the morning and others who stay until
closing. Most all-day schools have at least a part-time person who works in the
kitchen. Many hire drivers to pick up children at home or at their elementary
schools. A secretary and a bookkeeper might also be on the staff.

Staff members in an all-day school should have special qualities that help make
school a secure and happy place for children. Each person should like being with
children. The cook who welcomes children into the kitchen or makes sure that
good cooking smells permeate the school does a lot to create a pleasant atmosphere. Since drivers often must help children separate from home, they should be
warm and reassuring people. Even a secretary will have contact with children and
should be able to respond appropriately. Teachers should be able to allow children
to develop at their own pace, not rushing them to perform at unrealistic levels.
They also should be nurturing and responsive to children's needs. Everyone involved in an all-day school should have good health and lots of energy.

Communication becomes extremely important in an all-day school when so
many people are involved. You and your assistant have to talk to each other every
day. The morning teacher must let the afternoon teacher know about anything
unusual that happened. The cook, driver, and secretary all need to be a part of the
"communication loop," focusing on what is happening to children. Parents, too,
want to know what their children did at school during the day and should be
encouraged to let the school know about home occurrences.

One of the biggest problems for the staff in a day care center is fatigue. The long
hours with children with few days off can put a tremendous burden on the staff. This
results in low morale or, in the extreme, burnout. If you are sensitive to the needs of

adults, you will provide time for teachers to be away from children each day. Vary responsibilities for planning outdoor supervision and for naptime duty to help overcome fatigue. Staff meetings at which teachers can air problems and find solutions will also help. Schedule social activities to promote staff cohesiveness.

Figure 2–1 A private proprietary school.

TYPES OF PROGRAMS—CHARACTERISTICS

Private For Profit Schools

PRIVATE FOR PROFIT SCHOOL

The private for profit or proprietary school is owned by one or more individuals and is established to provide a community service while also making a profit for the owners. Tuition is the primary source of income and must be adequate to meet expenses and allow a profit margin. Many times the owner, or owners, are active participants, alternating administrative tasks with teaching a group of children. These schools can be half-day programs, but increasing numbers are offering a full-day session.

Two factors will be important to you as the director/owner of this kind of school. First, you have the freedom to initiate a program based on your own ideas. You can design a program that emphasizes cognitive development of children, or you can focus on the child's creative expression. You might want to develop a program using the Montessori method and materials. The opportunity to have "the kind of school you've always wanted" has great appeal to a lot of people.

The second factor is a disadvantage. You are likely to have a constant financial worry about making "ends meet." Each school is licensed for a specific number of children, so the amount of possible income is limited. Day care is expensive, and it is difficult to keep tuitions high enough to pay expenses but not so high that parents cannot pay. Many schools meet this challenge by adding programs. You can add before- and after-school care of older children, filling in the time slots when enrollment of other children may be less. If most of your preschoolers do not arrive until 8:30 or 9:00, you can have a group of elementary children before they go off to school. The same will be true at the end of the day when some of the younger children have already gone home. The additional outlay for materials and staff can be outweighed by the additional income generated. Having children who come two or three days a week can also add income. The total income from two part-time tuitions can be greater than that gained from one child five days a week.

In the current economic climate, directing a for profit school must be approached as would any small business. Costs must be controlled as far as possible without jeopardizing quality. Income must cover all expenses and allow for a profit. However, many director/owners do not expect to make a profit beyond their own salary. If they own the building that houses their school, additional compensation may come from equity in the real estate.

FAMILY DAY CARE HOME

Another form of for profit program is the family child care home. These are also called family day care, home-based child care, or in-home child care, and are usually licensed for six to twelve children. Some states do not require a license, but when they do, certification is done through the same agency responsible for child care centers. However, guidelines for this type of care will not be the same as for a group setting. Tuition is the primary source of income.

The advantage of this kind of program is that you can earn an income while staying home with your own children. You are also free to design your own curriculum. The disadvantage of this kind of setting is that you are separated from any kind of professional stimulation. There is little time to take courses or attend meetings where you might increase your skills. In addition to the isolation, the workload is heavy. You do bookkeeping, order the materials, cook, clean, and provide educational activities for the children.

Many parents choose family day care because they like the home-like atmosphere and the small group size. This kind of setting is especially suited to the needs of infants or toddlers. A family day care setting can offer the same kind of stimulating environment that a center might offer. The small group, though, will allow greater interaction between child and adult, more individual attention, and less need for restrictive rules. The day's schedule is likely to be more flexible to meet the needs of an individual child. Another advantage is that a family day care home can usually be found near the parent's work or residence. In addition, when a child is only slightly ill, the home can often provide care while at a center the child would be excluded. The disadvantage for the parent may lie in the fact that there is little supervision of the program. Licensing visits are made only once a year, if that often. During the rest of the time, the operator is free of any kind of monitoring.

Corporate Schools

As a business, corporate schools operate multiple facilities at many different sites, often in different states. Income comes primarily from tuition. The corporate school functions like any big business with a board and a chief executive officer. Ideas may or may not be developed at corporate headquarters, in some cases resulting in a great deal of similarity from one school to another. Building, curriculum, and teacher training may be the same in a school in Oregon as in a school in Georgia. In others, much more local autonomy is allowed. General guidelines may be proposed by corporate headquarters, but implementation may be done at the discretion of director and staff at each center.

The thinking behind these corporations is the traditional aim of selling a trusted product to the public. They spend effort and money to create a recognizable image, either a name or symbol. The originator of Kinder-Care's red tower has said he wanted that symbol to be as familiar as the McDonald's arches.

There are advantages to you as director of a corporate school. Financial problems for an individual school are lessened because of the greater resources of the corporation. When one school is under-enrolled for a period of time, there is financial support until enrollment increases. More money for materials and equipment is available since the company purchases in large quantities. Maintenance and repair people are often available. Area supervisors provide extra support. They help you plan in-service training, resolve problems, and develop recruitment strategies. Other corporate directors in your area are available by telephone to share ideas, problems, substitute teachers, and even materials. Directors of these schools are sometimes able to move to another school within the corporation if they change their residence. For many, the greatest advantage is the ability to move up the "corporate ladder." Advancing to area supervisor, and then into other positions within the corporation, is a possibility.

You will also find some disadvantages. Directors in these schools report there is a tremendous amount of necessary paperwork; everything has to be accounted for, sometimes minutely. You may find some constraint on planning curriculum if this is preplanned at the corporate office. A business orientation and making a profit for the corporation are stressed. Costs must be kept within specified budget limits. This can have a definite influence on salaries.

EMPLOYER-SPONSORED PROGRAMS

Employer-sponsored programs have proliferated in recent years in response to the needs of working families. Only a few companies offer direct assistance and those that do often focus on care for very young children. However, a wider focus is emerging. Some companies now extend their work/family coverage to include elder care, special activities for school-age children and adolescents, and care for children who are mildly ill. Diane Harris, in a 1993 article in *Working Woman* magazine, states that only one-tenth of one percent of companies offer these kinds of direct care, but the ranks swell to 60 percent when counting corporations that offer indirect services. These include free access to child care information services, tax breaks, and time off to take care of family needs. Today, work/family issues are very much a part of the workplace.

In 1993, about 600 companies in the United States supported *on-site* or *near-site centers*. If you add hospitals, the number increases to 1,400. These centers are open during hours that meet the needs of the employees. The primary advantage is location at the work site, or near enough, to eliminate transportation time.

Another advantage is that parents can drop in any time. Parents can visit their child at lunch time or breaks during the day. Parents are also accessible if a child needs some extra comfort. A director of this kind of center may find this advantage can also have some problems. One director said, "The eyes of the whole company are looking at us all the time." She related that a parent may come to visit a child and observe a teacher trying to manage a problem with someone else's child. When that parent goes back to a work station, the incident might be reported with a possibility for misunderstanding. For some directors without business experience, another disadvantage is having to work within a hierarchy.

A company may use family day care homes as *satellites* to a center program. The homes are usually located near the business or near elementary schools. The operators of the homes may receive some salary support and benefits from the company. A few companies have a staff person who works with the home operators to provide training or a toy loan service.

Some companies support child care without operating a center by using indirect methods. In 1980, Merck & Co. in New Jersey *provided a grant* to start a center in a nearby community. The center was run by a local group as a nonprofit enterprise. Space was made available for infants and preschoolers of Merck employees. Continued income for the center comes from tuition, fund-raising activities, and in-kind services. A similar kind of arrangement is the *voucher* whereby some companies allow their employees to use the day care setting of their choice. The company pays part of the tuition. A variation of the grant method is being tried by some companies. Several form a *consortium* to provide funds to build a child care center.

The *resource and referral service*, a more attractive alternative, has been instituted by some companies. Either a person within the company or someone outside the company establishes an information service for parents seeking child care. Xerox Corporation has contracted with Work/Family Directions, a community-based agency, to provide this service to its employees throughout the United States. The service allows parents a wide variety of child care options from which to choose. An agency employee visits each of the approved day care centers or family day care homes before it is placed in the directory. Parents are given guidelines to help them in choosing the appropriate care setting for their child. A list of baby-sitters, especially those who can be available to care for a sick child, is often included in the directory. In addition to information about child care, some companies offer *flexible benefit plans* in which a parent can choose support for child care over dental coverage, for instance.

Care for a *sick child* is of such importance to working parents that companies are becoming aware of the benefits of helping to resolve the problem. In 1987, about

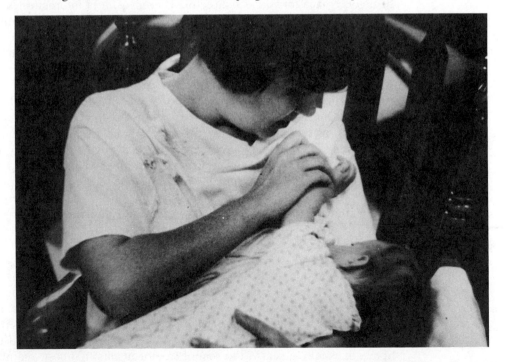

Figure 2–2 At an on-site center, a mother can still nurse her baby.

eighty employers had made some provision for care of sick children. An example, Levi Strauss & Co. funded an infirmary that is attached to an independent day care center in San Jose, California. At the San Juan Batista Child Development Center, Levi Strauss reserves space for its employees at a reduced cost to the parents.

Nonprofit Schools

COOPERATIVE SCHOOL

The cooperative school is privately owned but operated as a nonprofit enterprise. These schools usually have half-day sessions. A co-op, as it is often called, is owned by all the parents who currently have children enrolled in the school. Ownership ends when school enrollment ends. These schools may be incorporated and have a board of trustees elected by the members. Tuition is the primary source of income; additional income may come from fund-raising activities. Tuition is usually lower than in profit-making schools.

The co-op employs a teacher/director with dual responsibilities for teaching and directing. Parents perform many of the administrative tasks such as purchasing supplies and overseeing finances. Parents also assist in the classroom on a regular basis. The number of co-op schools has decreased in the last decade because few working parents can spare the time necessary for participation.

If you like working with adults as well as children, the cooperative school would be a good place for you as a director. There is a lot of interaction with parents on a daily basis as they participate in the classroom. This provides many opportunities for parent education activities. In addition to time in the classroom, parents often spend time building and maintaining equipment, or making materials for the school. As director, you will spend a lot of time in meetings, discussing administrative matters and conducting parent education activities. One director of a co-op reported that the children in her school often "played meetings" because that was what their mothers did. The children got dressed up in high heels and long dresses, took their purses, paper, and pencils, and sat at a table "having a meeting."

You may find that having to share administrative and teaching responsibilities with parents is a disadvantage. It is difficult at times to mediate all the differences of opinions and ideas. Also, there is limited income to purchase equipment or materials. Few co-ops can afford their own building, so you may be housed in a community center, a church building, or a park. Facilities for storage may be minimal.

CHURCH-SPONSORED SCHOOLS

Many churches sponsor a half-day preschool, a kindergarten, or an all-day center. These are set up as an extension of the church educational program or as a service to its members. Enrollment might be limited to church member families or be open to the community. These schools are expected to pay for their own expenses with income from tuitions, although some costs may be shared by the church. Space is usually given to the school free or at minimal cost, maintenance service may be provided, and insurance may be covered through the church policy.

General policies for the school are determined by the church board or a committee appointed by the board. When you direct this kind of school, you have to work cooperatively with the board or committee members. They may specify the inclusion of religious teaching along with the traditional preschool and kindergarten activities. It is then up to you to decide how that policy will be implemented in the day-to-day program. They may give you guidelines for hiring staff or setting up a budget. You are free to decide how you carry out those guidelines.

You may be faced with some other special challenges. The school often has to share space with church activities during the week or on weekends. The classroom may be used for Sunday school or social functions. You and your staff will have to develop creative ways to use space or to store equipment at the end of a school day.

LABORATORY SCHOOLS

Colleges and universities often operate laboratory schools as part of their instructional program in early childhood education, teacher training, or psychology. Most often these schools are half-day sessions accepting children either from the campus community alone or from the wider community. Although tuition is charged, operational expenses are supplemented by one or several departments of the college or university.

The laboratory school has several purposes. It is designed to demonstrate to students the materials and techniques appropriate for working with young children. It provides a setting for students to do practice teaching under the supervision of a master teacher. The school often is a site for research studies conducted by campus

Figure 2–3 Mother and child in a co-op school. (*Jack Lasek*)

personnel in various disciplines. Lastly, the school might serve as a model for other programs in the community.

Because they serve as models, lab schools usually have high standards, well-planned facilities, and a wide variety of materials and equipment. The curriculum will vary from school to school, often based on a particular philosophy. Some schools may use a Piagetian approach, allowing children a great deal of freedom to explore. Another school might use a behaviorist approach with emphasis on more structured learning with a system of rewards for reinforcement. Still another might be based on the ideas of Maria Montessori and use the materials developed by her.

As director of a laboratory school, you have at least two distinct responsibilities. One is to the instructional program of the college or university. This means that the adult students are your primary focus. Their needs for learning experiences must be met. The children's program has to allow students to plan activities, implement them in a day's schedule, and have an opportunity to evaluate their lessons. Your second focus is to foster and maintain a good educational program for the children. This means a delicate balance between the adult students' needs for experimentation with activities, and what is acceptable and appropriate for the children.

It is also important to become part of the campus community. You have to learn to work within the campus administrative structure. Sometimes this means selling your program to either administrators or faculty to maintain or increase your budget. You should be active in the wider community, participating in conferences, speaking to groups, and generally informing others of your program. These activities are essential to recruiting new students.

Publicly Funded Schools

CHILD CARE CENTERS

Child care centers are sponsored by public agencies and maintained primarily to meet the needs of working mothers or one-parent families with limited incomes. Today's centers are an outgrowth of the day care centers started during World War II to care for the children of women working in the war industries. They are all-day programs, open ten or twelve hours a day, five or six days a week. Funding comes from federal, state, county, or city sources or a combination of these. Tuition may be charged on a sliding scale according to family income. Responsibility for operating the school usually rests with the local school district. The centers are often housed on the school grounds and are sometimes referred to as child development centers.

Hired by the local school board, the director of a child care center carries out the policies of the board. Guidelines and regulations for parent fees, curriculum, staff qualifications, salary scales, purchasing, facility plan, and maintenance procedures may all be covered by board policy. Federal and state guidelines may include additional restrictions on administrative procedures and program requirements.

When you are the director of this kind of center, you are part of the school district and as such must work within the "system." A distinct advantage is that

Figure 2–4   A father brings his child to day care.

income does not depend upon tuition; therefore, there is usually more money for materials and equipment. Standards for teachers may be higher than in other schools, and salaries may be proportional. You also have available to you all the resources of the school district. You can call upon psychologists, nutritionists, and curriculum specialists as needed. A disadvantage may be that you are not totally free to design your own curriculum but must implement the guidelines that come with the funding source. For some people, the restrictions of working within a public school system may be difficult.

HEAD START

Head Start is one of the compensatory educational programs begun in 1965 by the Office of Economic Opportunity. It was the outgrowth of political and social decisions to break the cycle of poverty by providing a comprehensive preschool program for young children. It is now administered by the Administration for Children, Youth and Families, Office of Human Development in the U.S. Department of Health and Human Services. Funds go directly to an agency that operates the various centers or to a delegate agency that disburses funds to nonprofit organizations who then operate centers. Head Start programs are half-day, and no tuition is charged the families of children who are enrolled.

Head Start has several clearly defined program goals as stated in their Performance Standard guidelines (DHHS Publication No. 84-31131):

The overall goal of the Head Start program is to bring about a greater degree of social competence in children of low-income families.

To accomplish this goal, Head Start objectives and performance standards provide for:

1. The improvement of the child's health and physical abilities, including the family's attitude toward future health care.
2. The encouragement of self-confidence, spontaneity, curiosity, and self-discipline, all of which will assist in the development of the child's social and emotional health.
3. The enhancement of the child's mental processes and skills with particular attention to conceptual and communication skills.
4. The establishment of patterns and expectations of success for the child, which will create a climate of confidence for present and future learning efforts and overall development.
5. An increase in the ability of the child and the family to relate to each other and to others.
6. The enhancement of the sense of dignity and self-worth within the child and his family.

Figure 2–5   In day care, rest time is needed.

Head Start achieves its goals through providing a wide variety of medical and social services to families and through requiring active involvement of parents in the functions of the centers. Parents serve on policy boards, assist in the classroom, and are active in a variety of support committees. In addition to fostering parent participation, Head Start encourages staff to upgrade their skills constantly. Teachers receive financial support to attend classes at local colleges or universities. Some go through a structured training program leading to a Child Development Associate credential administered by the National Association for the Education of Young Children.

Since many Head Start centers are single-classroom schools, a Head Teacher is in charge of the center. This person supervises all other staff in addition to teaching. Responsibilities include coordinating all activities at the center, receiving and distributing information from the Head Start office, ordering supplies, and setting up staff meetings. This position is not the same as that of director in other kinds of schools, but does offer a good opportunity for someone with a background in early childhood education.

If you are the Head Teacher in one of these centers, you will need to be sensitive to the needs and interests of the community you serve. You should be able to work with families of diverse ethnic and cultural backgrounds. It helps if you can speak the language of the parents, but is not a requirement of employment. An advantage to working in this kind of program is a higher pay level than you would find in private schools. Staff also enjoy benefits such as health coverage and retirement. One of the most noteworthy disadvantages is the tremendous amount of paperwork required; records must be kept and reports submitted on all aspects of the center's functioning. Guidelines for curriculum are fairly specific and must be followed, although how you and your staff implement them is left to you.

Each preschool or day care setting has its own characteristics, advantages, and disadvantages. As shown in Figure 2-6, there is a very great variation between types of schools. Directors must understand the differences. They must know the characteristics of the specific school in which they serve to be effective leaders. Knowledge of the differences may also allow prospective directors to choose the kind of program best suited to their particular personality, interests, and experience.

SUMMARY

Children who are younger than age five are most often cared for by a relative. The remainder are cared for by a nonrelative in the home or go to child care settings. Increasing numbers of school-age children are enrolled in before- and after-school programs.

The quality of care given to the children keeps them safe, and also has long-term effects. Children who have been in quality programs have fewer behavior problems, get along better with their peers, and have better academic skills.

Half-day schools are in session for four hours or less. Their primary purpose is the education of the child.

TYPE	SPONSORSHIP	INCOME	CHARACTERISTICS
Private Schools			
For Profit	One or more individuals	Tuition	Profitmaking. Freedom to initiate programs. Limited resources for income. Must use good business practices.
Family Day Care Home	Individual	Tuition	Same as for profit school. **Advantages:** Small number of children. Home-like atmosphere. Suited to infants. **Disadvantages:** Operator works alone. Infrequent monitoring.
Corporate	Group of people	Tuition	Goals set by corporation. Director must be business oriented. **Advantages:** Shared resources for purchasing, maintenance. Financial problems shared. Support from area supervisors. Director can be promoted to other jobs. **Disadvantages:** Many aspects preplanned at corporate headquarters. Need to show a profit. May pay lower salaries.
Employer-Supported	Business, hospital, government agency, building developer	Tuition	Set up as fringe benefit for employees. Close to parents' work. **Advantages:** Parents can visit during day. Parents nearby if needed by child. **Disadvantages:** Must work within business hierarchy. "Eyes" of company may be on school.
Nonprofit Schools			
Cooperative	Member families	Tuition Fund-raising	Intense parent involvement. Less costly to operate. **Advantages:** Opportunity for parent education. Opportunity to work with adults as well as children. **Disadvantages:** Work with untrained staff. Lots of meetings. Have to share administrative tasks with parents. Limited income. May not have own building.
Church	Church	Tuition Fund-raising Supplements	Policies determined by church board. Share church facilities. Is part of church educational program. **Advantage:** Support from the church. **Disadvantages:** Must work with church board. Share space with other church programs.

Figure 2–6 Types of schools.

TYPE	SPONSORSHIP	INCOME	CHARACTERISTICS
Laboratory	College or university	Tuition Supplements	Model program design. Used for practice teaching placements. **Advantages:** Well-planned facility. Good equipment. **Disadvantages:** Must balance needs of children and adult students. Must work within administrative structure of college or university.

Publicly Funded Schools

TYPE	SPONSORSHIP	INCOME	CHARACTERISTICS
Child Care Centers	Local school district	Government funds Tuition– sliding scale	Director hired by school district. School board sets policy guidelines. **Advantages:** Not dependent on tuition. More money for equipment and materials. Standards for teachers high; salaries better. Resources of school district available. **Disadvantages:** Not totally free to design own curriculum. For some, working within school district is restrictive.
Head Start	Public or private nonprofit agencies	Government funds	Designed to prepare child for school. Parent involvement. Community participation. Director must be sensitive to diverse ethnic and cultural backgrounds. **Advantages:** Higher pay levels. Opportunity to work with parents. **Disadvantages:** Lots of recordkeeping necessary.

Figure 2–6 (*continued*)   Types of schools.

All-day schools function more than four hours per day. They must provide for the full care of the child. Different management problems are encountered. Additional staffing is also necessary. Communication must be complete for the school to function successfully.

A private, for profit school is owned by one or more individuals and is expected to show a profit. This type of school has the freedom to experiment and the constraint to operate efficiently.

A family day care home is usually licensed to supervise six to twelve children. This environment is especially suitable for infants and toddlers and probably has a flexible schedule.

Corporate schools are relatively new. They are expected to show a profit and have many different locations. They are marked by some similarities with each other, a recognizable "style," and often an interchangeable curriculum. Advantages are their financial strength and increased resources and your opportunity to advance professionally.

Employer-sponsored schools are increasing in number. The parent company may furnish a building and/or capital for an on-site child care center. Some employers support satellite programs near the workplace or where employees live.

Other companies offer a voucher program where employees are given a fixed amount for child care. Another form of support is a resource and referral service where parents seeking child care may get reliable information.

The cooperative school, an enterprise somewhat on the decline, is operated as a nonprofit center. The director is also the teacher. Parents fill in as staff, and coordination emerges as a major factor.

Churches characteristically offer a half-day program. It may or may not be religiously oriented. Most of these must be self-supporting, with little or no help from the larger organization. Space may be a problem here as the school often shares facilities with other church-related functions.

Many colleges and universities operate laboratory schools. These serve at least two functions: training and demonstration, and research. Various orientations may be found; standards are generally high.

Child care centers are often publicly funded and are usually adjuncts to the local school system. They have the many strengths and weaknesses of public education, including bureaucratic rules, but offer relatively higher salaries and adequate funding.

Head Start is a federal program begun in 1965 primarily for the disadvantaged child. It is generally a single-classroom school aimed at bringing the child up to grade level before entering elementary grades. It has been generally successful.

SELECTED FURTHER READING

Children's Defense Fund. 1991. *The State of America's Children 1991*. Washington, DC, author.

Galinsky, E. 1989. "Update on Employer-Supported Child Care." *Young Children*, 44 (6) 2, 75–77.

Harris, D. June 1993. "A Blueprint for Reform." *Working Woman*, 54–55.

Harris, D. June 1993. "Big Business Takes on Child Care." *Working Woman*, 50–51, 56.

Kegan, S., and Newton, J. 1989. "For-Profit and Nonprofit Child Care: Similarities and Differences." *Young Children*, 45 (1) 4–10.

Shuster, C., Finn-Stevenson, M., and Ward, P. 1992. "Family Day Care Support Systems: An Emerging Infrastructure." *Young Children*, 47 (5) 29–35.

Waxman, P. 1991. "Children in the World of Adults—OnSite Child Care." *Young Children*, 46 (5) 16–21.

Willer, B. 1992. "An Overview of Demand and Supply of Child Care in 1990." *Young Children*, 47 (2) 19–22.

STUDENT ACTIVITIES

1. Visit a half-day school and a full-day school. Return to the full-day school at the end of a day. Observe the similarities and differences during the morning hours of each of the schools. What happens at the end of a day at the all-day school? Report your findings to the class.
2. Make an appointment to visit a family day care home. Choose a time when the operator will be able to talk to you. Observe the number of children, the kinds of activities that are provided, and the routine of the day. Talk to the operator about the satisfactions and difficulties of conducting this kind of program.
3. Meet with the director of a corporate school. Before the meeting, prepare a list of questions to ask. After the visit, summarize your findings and report to the class. Some suggested questions are the following:
   a. How is your school budget prepared?
   b. Is there someone within the corporation you can call on when you have problems?
   c. How is the curriculum of your school planned?
   d. What is the process for hiring new staff members? Are you free to determine the salary for that person?
   e. What are the advantages for you in working in this kind of school?
   f. What have you found difficult about working for a corporate school?
4. Visit two other different types of schools. Do you observe differences in the character of the job of director in each? Ask the directors to describe the most important aspects of their job. Are they different or the same in each school? Is the role of a director the same or different from what you expected before your visit?

REVIEW

1. According to the Children's Defense Fund report *The State of America's Children 1991*, who are the caregivers of the greatest number of children under the age of six?
2. List the components of quality child care.
3. Although an all-day program offers many of the same activities you would find in a half-day program, there are differences. What are they?
4. What is the primary source of income for a for profit school? In what ways can income be increased?
5. What are the advantages and disadvantages of operating a home-based child care?
6. Discuss the advantages and disadvantages of directing a school that is part of a national corporation.
7. List the types of work/family services businesses are offering to their employees.

8. The laboratory school has several purposes that are usually not found in other programs. What are they?

9. What are the advantages and disadvantages of being the director of a child care center that is part of a public school district?

10. The overall goal of Head Start programs was cited in this chapter. What is it?

GLOSSARY

Church-sponsored school   a child care center or preschool organized as an extension of the educational program of the church.

Cooperative school   nonprofit enterprise, owned by all the parents who currently have children enrolled in the school.

Corporate school   business corporation operating multiple schools at different sites.

Employer-sponsored programs   on-site or off-site child care facilities supported by a company or business.

Family child care home   child care service provided in a private residence.

For profit proprietary school   school owned by one or more individuals, established to provide a community service but also to make a profit for the owners.

Laboratory school   early childhood center that is part of the instructional program of a college or university.

Resource and referral service   information service for parents seeking child care.

3

Beginnings:
A New School/A New Year

OBJECTIVES

After studying this chapter, the student should be able to:

- Discuss factors affecting the location of a school.
- Discuss costs of starting a new school.
- Identify additional requirements a school should meet before beginning operation.
- Develop procedures to facilitate routine opening of school tasks.
- Identify tasks that are necessary to begin a school year.

Operating a child care facility requires a long-term commitment to provide services to families and their children. The decision should not be made lightly, and requires a great deal of thought and planning. It may take as long as a year to research the issues that will affect your operation. Before you make the investment of time and money, assess the current needs of your community, then put together a realistic plan for start-up and operating expenses. Gain as much knowledge as you can about the business side of child care management, since you will exist for only a short time if you operate at a deficit. Even a nonprofit center must use prudent business practices so supporters are not overburdened with fund raising. This chapter outlines the steps necessary to open a new early childhood facility. You will also learn what is necessary at the beginning of a school year when your school closes during the summer and reopens in the fall.

LOCATION

Community Survey

The best way to determine the need for an early childhood center is to survey the community it is intended to serve. This involves collecting information on the number of families with children, income level of parents, number of working parents, transportation available to families, and number of child care facilities already in the neighborhood. Some of this information can be obtained from U.S. Census data, labor and employment statistics, school district counts, and child care organizations. Directors of existing schools may be willing to tell you whether their schools are full or if there seems to be a need for additional places for children. Your local public library can help you find census and employment data.

You can survey a community with a *needs assessment questionnaire*. On a college campus you can place an article in the campus newspaper, with a request for reply by telephone or in written form. Within a business, send out a questionnaire to all employees. In an apartment complex or densely populated residential area, you can do door-to-door canvassing to determine the need for a school.

In general, the questionnaire should be as simple as possible, yet it should ask all the questions you need answered. The sample company assessment questionnaire on the next page may give you a beginning.

This preliminary information should tell you whether there is a need for another school. It will probably also help you consider the kind of school to plan. If there are more school-age children than younger ones, then an after-school program with provision for summer and holiday care for children may be needed. If there are more infants, toddlers, and preschoolers, a preschool with an infant room should be successful. A large number of working parents will probably rule out the possibility of a co-op and tell you that an all-day school is necessary.

Licensing and Zoning Requirements

Obtain a copy of the licensing regulations for your area before you begin the search for a site for your school. In most states, the health and welfare agency or department of social services is responsible for setting guidelines and regulating child care centers, preschools, and family day care homes. Regulations are based mainly on size and safety aspects of the physical facility. You must show evidence that you have met all requirements before receiving your license. Therefore, know your needs before you look at possible sites. Look first at the amount of usable space in a potential building.

Licensing requirements specify the number of square feet needed both indoors and outdoors. This will limit your school to certain communities where you can have a building and outdoor space large enough to accommodate the required footage. In some states, 35 square feet per child is a minimum recommendation for indoor space. To provide for maximum play space and freedom of movement, 40 to 60 square feet per child is preferable. Space used by children usually constitutes 60 percent of a school's total area, with an additional 40 percent needed for storage, kitchen, offices, bathroom, and so on. A fenced-in yard containing 75 to 100 square feet per child is recommended for outdoors.

In some states, preschools cannot be operated on the second floor of a building, setting further limits on your search for space. A ground floor school is safer since young children have difficulty managing stairs. They should have easy access to

COMMUNITY HOSPITAL
5329 Center Way
Emerson, PA 16112

In response to a request by employees, we are assessing the need for a child care center on the premises of Community Hospital. It may become part of your work/family benefit package. Please complete the questionnaire and return it to your supervisor before December 15.

Name _____ Employee Number _____

Department _____ Location _____ Shift _____

Number and ages of your children _____

Do you have a child who needs special care? _____

Describe his/her special needs _____

Where are your children cared for now?

      Preschool or child care center: cost/hr _____   per week _____

      Caregiver in your home: cost/hr_____   per week _____

      Family day care home: cost/hr_____   per week _____

      Relative's home _____ Home alone_____

What kind of child care service to you need?

      Part time____(hrs)   Full time _____ (hrs)

      Evening____ (hrs)   Weekend _____(hrs)

Would you enroll your child in a quality child care center on our premises?

Please rank (1-most, 2-next, 3-least) the following benefits in importance to you and your family.

     *Prepaid medical and dental_____   *Child care _____

     *Elder care _____   *Maternity/family leave _____

Comments:

_____

_____

*These items may need to be altered to fit specific benefit packages.

outdoor play areas. Meeting requirements for bathroom facilities also can be a challenge when you are looking for space for a day care center. The bathroom should be close to the classrooms, and there should be enough toilets and basins for the number of children anticipated. Specifications for the number of windows and the kind of heating, kitchen equipment, drinking fountains, and so on, may all affect your decisions.

Figure 3–1   A well-planned outdoor environment.

Your building will be subject to other requirements as well. Before you can be licensed to operate at a particular location, the city will send individual representatives from the building, fire, and sanitation departments. Familiarize yourself with their regulations, including any special requirements for children with disabilities. The cost of bringing a building up to the required standards should figure in any choice of site for your center. Remember that it usually is less expensive to choose a building that is already, or almost, up to standard than to make costly renovations. However, allow for some renovation costs when you put together your start-up budget.

Zoning regulations determine the kind of community in which a school can operate, usually in a commercial zone. Therefore, before deciding on the location of your school, drive through the neighborhood where you want your school. Ask yourself if you, as a parent, would want to bring your child there. Does it have the kind of atmosphere you want for your school? Check to see if the site is easily visible to street traffic since your sign and school building will be your best advertising. Determine whether there are any barriers preventing easy access to the school entrance. Lastly, consider whether this is a safe place for children to spend their day.

Buy, Build, Remodel, or Rent?

After you research licensing and zoning requirements and look at your community, you are ready to consider the choices available.

Building a school on a convenient lot is a dream of many potential owners. It is probably the only way you can have most of the things you want in your school. But as costs of both land and building have increased in the last few years, this option is less and less feasible. If you can find a school that has been built recently, find out what it cost to build. If you cannot find that out, then talk to builders or architects about building costs in your area. They should be able to estimate the cost of building based on your approximate size. Realtors can tell you the cost of purchasing land.

If building your own school is a hopeless dream, consider the other options available. Many attractive schools for young children are housed in *renovated residences*. If you can find a large, older house at a reasonable price, this may be a good choice. Unfortunately, some communities prohibit schools in residential areas. In addition, the cost of renovation is often very high unless you can do some of it yourself. Usually, you must install additional bathrooms and bathroom fixtures. Hallways, stairs, porches, heating equipment, outdoor fences, and gates that meet safety standards also add to the cost.

Another possibility is to *rent unused classrooms in a public school*. In Simi Valley, California, THE FAMILY CONNECTION, sponsored by Simi Adventist Hospital, rents rooms in a public school building that is not currently needed by the school district. Adapting the space for use by infants, toddlers, and preschoolers has been a challenge to staff members. Bathrooms were far away from the rooms, there was no office space included, and walls could not be changed in any way. Staff members working over several years have managed to make a pleasant and functioning school for themselves and the children despite the difficulties.

Churches often provide space for preschool programs as part of their own educational program. Sometimes they will rent space to a separate organization. Laws do not allow renting for profit-making purposes, but they do allow rental to nonprofit organizations. The main disadvantage of this kind of arrangement is having to share space with church functions. In addition, church space that was planned for religious classes may not have the kind of outdoor area needed by a preschool. Often, though, there is enough space on the church grounds where a playground can be installed.

Storefronts have been used for early childhood programs. In the author's community there are currently three child care centers in shopping centers. Each has a large playground enclosed by a six-foot wall behind the school. In areas that cannot accommodate an attached playground, storefront schools use nearby parks where the children go for outings. An advantage to this type of site is the high visibility of the center as people come to shop. That in itself may provide sufficient publicity to attract initial enrollees, and to maintain enrollment. A disadvantage may be the cost of installing bathrooms, dividing indoor space, and building a playground.

Industrial sites such as a factory or warehouse can also be used as a school when a little imagination is applied. These sites may be near where parents work, allowing them to visit during the day. The rent may also be low. A factory, with its high ceilings, might be converted with a two-level design, allowing for climbing, delineation of spaces, and nooks or corners in which children can be alone. On the nega-

Figure 3–2   Making good use of cramped quarters.

tive side, industrial areas are sometimes noisy and may be subject to various kinds of pollutants. THE GREAT PACIFIC IRON WORKS Child Development Center in Ventura, California, had to spend thousands of dollars removing soil beneath a playground when the soil was thought to be polluted by toxic wastes from a previous industrial tenant. Take care to ensure that the surrounding environment is safe for children.

If you already own some land, putting *pre-fab buildings* on the site may be the best solution. One California school in Santa Monica used two "temporary" bungalows unused by a school district. The buildings were attached, then divided inside to make two classrooms, offices, bathrooms, and a conference room. This choice is somewhat limiting because of the adjoining walls and the structure of the buildings, but it is possible to use the space creatively.

A final possibility is to *buy an existing school.* Each year some schools change hands for one reason or another. Watch real estate ads, let directors in your area know you are interested, and talk to realtors. Chances are a school will come up for sale. Check carefully, though, as to why the school is being sold. Is it because the area already has too many schools or just that the owners no longer want to run a school? Investigate the building just as you would when buying a house, finding out all the things that will need to be repaired when you take over. Buying a school may be a good decision especially for a profit-making school since it can be seen as a real estate investment as well as a business investment.

Now you are ready to *set some priorities* to help you decide where to house your school. List the advantages and disadvantages of each proposed site, remembering that few schools have ideal environments. Most school personnel learn to make creative adaptations of the space they have. Start-up costs will certainly figure in your decision. Remember, though, the least expensive may not always be the best choice, for minimal facilities may make a poor and unsuccessful school.

As soon as you have purchased or leased a building, you should begin preparations to comply with licensing requirements. Allow ample time because it can take two to six months to complete. Familiarize yourself with the guidelines, then make a list of obvious building changes that need to be done. When the initial renovations are completed, schedule visits from inspectors from the departments involved. There may still be things that need to be done to bring your building up to code. However, some items might be negotiable with an allowance for an extension of time before completion. This will allow you to budget for expensive renovations over a period of time. Remember that your license will not be issued until all inspections are completed and approved. When all the inspections have been completed, fill out the application form, then send it with any accompanying documents and the fee to the appropriate licensing agent.

FYI

As the number of full-time equivalent children enrolled in a center increases, the cost per child decreases. A ten percent increase in center size results in an increase of only eight percent in total cost when all other factors remain the same. If a center of 50 children enrolled five additional children, the cost per child would go from $4,500 to $4,418.

The results must be interpreted with care. A large center size may result in additional administrative burdens requiring higher salaries or decrease in the quality of the educational program.

SOURCE: Early Childhood Education: What Are the Costs of High-Quality Programs? *United States General Accounting Office, 1990.*

FINANCES

Start-Up Costs

Consider the finances of operating a school when making a decision to open a new school. Figure start-up costs for the possible space choices you have selected. These costs include any money to be spent during the initial stages of planning a new school. They can be considerable for a large school, since the cost per child can run from $1,000 to $5,000 (see Figure 3-3).

Capital costs include the purchase of land and an existing school or a building to be renovated. If you purchase property, the down payment must be considered in start-up cost. Repayment of the loan is then amortized over the ensuing years and included in each following year's budget. Even if you are renting a building, an initial outlay will include the first and last month's rent and any security deposit required.

TYPICAL START-UP REQUIREMENTS	
Capacity: 70 children	
Building: 4,800 square feet Purchased building	
Start-up personnel costs	
Director $30,000/yr. 2 months	$5,000
3 Teachers $18,000/yr. 2 weeks	2,076
2 Asst. teachers $10,500/yr. 2 weeks	808
Secretary $12,000/yr. 1 month	1,000
Maintenance $10,000/yr. 2 weeks	384
Subtotal	9,268
Employee Benefits (Estimated 15 percent)	1,390
Total Personnel Cost	$10,658
Renovation/Construction (exclusive of land costs)	$30,000
Contract services and consultants	
Architect	$2,000
Lawyer 3 hours @ $250/hr.	750
Renovations, contractor 10 hours @ $30/hr.	300
Supplies (office, classroom, cleaning, food, 1st month)	2,500
Advertising (phone book, flyers, newspaper)	500
Occupancy	
Down payment on building	75,000
Utilities	1,000
Furniture, equipment, vehicles	45,000
Other	
License fee	500
Insurance (quarterly payment)	1,000
Miscellaneous	1,000
Payment into cash reserve	32,000
TOTAL START-UP COSTS	$201,708
START-UP COST PER CHILD	$2,882

Figure 3–3 Typical start-up requirements.

You also need to purchase equipment and supplies necessary to begin operation of the school. Kitchen equipment, playground equipment, and classroom and office furniture all entail a fairly large investment. Some equipment supply companies can help you to estimate the cost of equipping a classroom, office, or kitchen. Some will send a representative out to your school to help. Lakeshore Curriculum Materials Company publishes a booklet listing equipment needed. In 1987 they estimated the cost of equipping classrooms for 100 children, including infants and toddlers, at $61,489. Not all schools are that large, and not all schools start out with ideal environments. You can make many things yourself, purchase used furniture, and plan to add to your equipment once the school gets started. Teachers are also notorious scroungers and creative "make-doers."

Allocate money to cover the probability that your enrollment will not be filled immediately after opening the school. You may not achieve full enrollment for several months or even a year. During that time, your expenses will not be decreased proportionately. California licensing laws require three months operating expenses to be set aside before a license is issued. Even if your state does not have that requirement, providing a "cushion" to fall back on during the early stages of getting a school started is a good idea.

Personnel costs have to be considered as well, when figuring start-up costs. Someone has to go through the lengthy process of obtaining a license; in urban areas, this can take as much as six months. You have to order materials and equipment and then unpack them after delivery. The building has to be readied, and any renovations must be made. Anyone who has done house remodeling knows how long that can take. We recommend that the director be on salary full time at least two months before opening. A part-time secretary during this time can help to get paperwork done.

Hire a core staff before the opening of your school and the remainder of your staff as enrollment requires it. The core staff members should be on salary at least two weeks before the opening day. During that time you can have an orientation/ training session. This time together helps staff to develop a good working relationship. Teachers can also set up their rooms and plan their curriculum for the first few weeks. Figure costs for salaries during this time in your start-up budget.

Some of these personnel expenses can be met through in-kind contributions. If you own the school, you may wish to forego a salary while you get the school started. In other situations, a parent who has time and energy may take on some of the start-up tasks. Teachers may also be willing to volunteer a day or so getting their rooms set up. Some equipment cost can be decreased through renovations done by a skilled volunteer or donations. But proceed with caution when expecting people to work without pay. Take care not to exploit those who are willing or who need to have a job.

Some expenses can be amortized over the first year of operation. You can delay paying some bills until tuition fees begin to arrive. Renovation costs can sometimes be handled in the same way. If your landlord in a rental property does improvements for you, you may be able to pay off the cost over the first year.

Remember, though, to add these costs into your operating budget and be sure that your income will be able to sustain them.

Contract services and consultants may be necessary in some settings. Be sure to obtain legal advice when two or more people own a school. When organized as a simple partnership, either partner is liable for all partnership debts. The private assets of either one may be charged for payment of indebtedness. When the school is set up as a corporation, the corporation assumes responsibility for any debts. The individual is protected from personal liability.

Although attorneys are expensive, they are indispensable in drawing up incorporation papers or assisting in the establishment of partnerships. It is better to have sound legal advice early than to flounder in indecision later. Legal requirements vary from state to state, so find out what the laws are in your state. Consider the advantages of incorporation over a partnership at tax time and in relation to liability for debts.

You might wish to have an architect draw up renovation plans needed for building-safety approval or for zoning. You may want an accountant to help you set up your bookkeeping system. You may also call upon a pediatrician or child development specialist when planning an infant classroom. All these services are expensive, costing upwards of $100 per hour. Some of these services may be provided free of charge by a parent or a friend. Low-cost legal services can be obtained sometimes from a legal services agency.

Advertising and publicity are essential to a new school. Families with children have to know about your school, and you want to fill your enrollment as soon as possible. Some methods are relatively expensive for the start-up period, but there are others that cost little. One form, without cost, is an article in your *local newspaper*. Contact a reporter and describe some unique feature of your program. You may be able to spark enough interest to warrant some publicity. *Telephone* advertising is excellent since parents often look there first when trying to find child care. The timing may not always fit your need during start-up, however, since telephone books are printed only once a year. Listing is included in the cost of service installation, but a display ad can cost close to a hundred dollars a month. Next to advertising in the Yellow Pages, the radio seems to be the most effective way to publicize child care. Check with your *local radio station* about running ads during morning drive times when parents might be listening. Cost of an ad will vary depending on the time the promotion is aired.

Consider *purchasing a mailing list* of prospects for your center. Look in the Yellow Pages under "Mailing Lists" for companies that supply lists. You can specify a geographic area, residences in which there are children, and those in which the parents earn a certain income. For a fee of about fifty dollars, the company will send you a list that you can use on a one-time basis, and may even send you address labels. They will also rent you the list for a one-year period. Compare prices from various companies to be sure that you have secured the one that will provide the best service for the least cost. Design an eye-catching *flyer* for your mailer to announce the opening of your school and invite recipients to come for a visit.

An *attractive brochure* is an effective tool for selling your school. However, it can be expensive if the layout includes photographs or it is printed on heavy paper. You might want to employ some of the methods described above during your start-up period but develop a brochure that you can use for continuing recruitment once your center has opened. The contents and makeup of a brochure are discussed in a later chapter.

Another form of advertising that will help you to recruit students is *an attractive sign* outside your school. It should be in keeping with the neighborhood but should be clearly visible from the street. Once your school is in operation, the outside of your school and the playground will help sell it to prospective families. The appearance of your school is an ever-visible advertisement to any parent driving by on the way to work.

You will probably divide *insurance* costs between your start-up costs and your first-year budget. Usually, you must pay a portion of your insurance even before the school opens and pay the balance during the year. Insurance for schools has become a problem in recent years because the cost has gone up astronomically. Check around for the best price; even try talking to other directors about their insurance carriers. The National Association for the Education of Young Children offers a good insurance package. You can write to them for information. Most schools have the following kinds of insurance:

- Liability and property damage—to provide legal protection for the owner/operator of the school.
- Fire damage—to cover buildings and contents.
- Fire, extended coverage—to protect against vandalism and malicious mischief.
- Automobile—for any vehicles used in transporting children.
- Accident—for children and staff.
- Workmen's compensation (required by law if ten or more persons are employed)—to cover on-the-job injuries.

You might also want to consider the following kinds of insurance:

- Burglary and robbery—on the contents of the building.
- Business interruption—payment for lost income while damaged property is being repaired.
- Fidelity bond—to protect against theft by employees.

Ongoing Costs

Before going further in your decision-making process, make a tentative estimate of ongoing costs. Budget is discussed in detail in a later chapter, but at this point you need to compare potential income with expected costs of operating your school.

Determine your *potential income* by the number of children enrolled in your school. You can judge that figure by dividing the total amount of indoor space in a building by the requirements set by your state's licensing agency. Next, find out the amount of tuition being charged by other schools in your area. Set your tuition near that amount. It would seem, then, that all you need to do is multiply the number of children by the amount of tuition. This is not true! You seldom will have 100 percent enrollment, even after your school has been established for a period of time. Most successful, established schools average 95 percent capacity. During your first year, allowing for a slow first few months, you may not reach more than 60 to 75 percent capacity. It is better to figure low than to find you have anticipated more income during the year than you actually take in. After your first year, you will have a better base of information with which to make your second-year budget.

Tuition income may be less than expected for another reason. During some months, children tend to become ill more frequently than others. Parents see no reason to pay for school when the child is not attending. Your expenses go on, though, despite decreased attendance. If you establish a policy stating that tuitions are payable even when children are ill for short periods of time, you will decrease these low-income times. Most schools excuse tuition payments only when a child is ill for several weeks or more.

Another factor that affects your ability to project income is that you will always have uncollectible tuitions. For one reason or another, families fall behind in payment of fees; some even leave the school without paying. Allow 10 to 15 percent of your expected income as uncollectible. Your own procedures for following up on late fee payments will eventually decrease that amount.

Estimate your *costs* by starting with salaries since that will take the largest proportion of total revenue. Salaries may take 50 to 75 percent of your total income. Figure the number of staff members you will need during the times when you will have the most children. In an all-day school, peak hours of enrollment may be from 8:00 in the morning until 4:00 in the afternoon. Figure the number of teachers you need to maintain the ratio of adults to children required by licensing. Estimate the number of children and teachers needed to cover the times before and after the peak times. Until you actually start enrolling children, you will not know how many children you will have before 8:00 A.M. and after 4:00 P.M. For your budget estimate, you can only guess. It helps to make a chart of the number of children anticipated and staff needed, as seen in Figure 3–4.

The cost of your building will probably be the next largest budget expenditure. This usually takes about 15 percent of your total income but it should not exceed 25 percent. This expenditure includes the cost of repaying a loan to purchase property and renovate or of making the ongoing rental payments on your property. In 1990, the U.S. General Accounting Office (GAO) issued a report titled "Report on Early Childhood Education: What Are the Costs of High-Quality Programs?" That report offered guidelines for determining the real costs of providing quality early childhood programs. The estimates of costs show that personnel costs are the largest portion of a budget.

All personnel	65%
Rent or mortgage	11%
Other	24%

The breakdown of nonpersonnel budget items in the GAO report are as follows:

Rent or mortgage	27%
Food	20%
Educational materials/ equipment	8%
Other*	45%

*Other includes telephone and utilities, repair, maintenance, office supplies and equipment, insurance, health and social services, and other miscellaneous costs.

Figure 3–4 Sample teacher assignment chart.

STAFF SELECTION

The entire process of staff selection is discussed more fully in a later chapter. However, some guidelines for staffing the new school are helpful here.

Recruit staff through advertisements in your local newspapers or flyers sent to teacher organizations and local colleges and universities. In many programs you must follow affirmative action guidelines. State the education and experience required for the position and the method of application. If time is short, you may request replies be made by telephone. However, if you have the time, ask for written applications returned by mail.

Choose your first teachers carefully since during the first year the reputation of your school is being formed. Teachers are an important part of that process. Be sure that your teachers know the goals of your school and that you have time to help them implement the goals.

WORKING CHECKLIST

Each of the tasks necessary for opening a new school may entail many weeks of work. You may encounter delays when you try to meet licensing requirements. Bad weather may delay building or renovation plans. Allow a realistic amount of time and add extra time for unforeseen events. A checklist of tasks with a time line will help you to feel you are making progress and to be sure that everything is getting done. An example is seen in Figure 3–5

THE NEW YEAR

Plan the opening of your school for a time that will fit the needs of your community or your situation. In an employer-sponsored program, for instance, the time will

Task	Expected Completion Date	Date Completed
1. Prepare needs assessment		
2. Contact licensing and zoning agencies		
3. Seek legal advice if needed		
4. Survey available sites		
5. Figure start-up costs		
6. Choose building or decide to build		
7. Start licensing process		
8. Establish a bank account		
9. Obtain insurance		
10. Prepare first-year budget		
11. Order supplies and equipment		
12. Prepare a brochure		
13. Advertise for students		
14. Write job descriptions		
15. Advertise for staff		
16. Interview and select staff		
17. Set personnel policies		
18. Prepare forms for children's files		
19. Meet with children and parents		
20. Conduct orientation for staff		
21. Conduct orientation for parents		
22. Prepare for opening day		

Figure 3–5   Checklist of tasks needed to open a new school.

probably not be important. But if you are opening a private school in your community, think about the optimum time to open your doors. Traditionally, families make plans for their children's education during the summer. Changes in child care arrangements are often made at this time. A September opening that coincides with the school calendar often works best. Allow at least two months before your opening date to complete all the preparations necessary.

Existing programs, too, find that changes often take place during the summer. Families move or children go on to elementary school. After summer vacation is the time many families decide to make a change in child care arrangements. So even if you manage an existing year-round school, you will have some of the same tasks as the director of a new school.

At the beginning of a new year, schools receive a flurry of telephone calls from parents frantically looking for places for their children. During this time, you have to order materials and prepare the classrooms. The playground may need new sand, and equipment must be inspected for safety. If you can develop organized procedures for managing all these tasks, life will certainly be easier.

ENROLLMENT

During the several weeks before opening day, your most important task is to enroll children. Parents usually make their first contact by telephone. It is important to keep a record of each call and to have a procedure for follow up. Printed cards or a report form will provide an organized method of getting information. Figure 3–6 shows a form that can be used to record inquiries about the school. Follow each call with a mailed brochure or information sheet about your school. Even if the parents do not enroll their child, they may pass the information on to other families. Send an application packet including the application form, brochure, fee schedule, and medical forms to those parents who seem ready to enroll.

If you are fortunate enough to have a computer, this is an excellent example of where it will come in handy. Put the names and addresses of anyone inquiring about the school in a data base. When new programs or changes that would affect these inquiries are added to the school, notify these people. Write a form letter and then personalize it with the name of each person on your list. Update this list periodically.

Before finalizing any application, meet with the parent and child. Some parents want to visit the school even before sending in an application. Others already know about the school and schedule a visit after they send in their application. Figure 3–7 shows a sample application form. Whichever order is chosen for the visit, it is important for you and the family to have a chance for a leisurely visit. No child should be enrolled without it. In fact, some states require visits as a part of licensing. These visits usually take half an hour or longer so do not schedule them too close together.

The purpose of these visits is to provide information to both you and the parent. If possible, the visit should take place in the classroom where the child will be placed after enrolling. When you can, have the teacher present. Put some toys out for the child to play with while you and the parents talk. This is an opportunity for

```
┌──────────────────────────────────────────────────────────────────┐
│                          INQUIRY REPORT                            │
│                                                                    │
│   NAME_____  DATE_____          │
│                                                                    │
│   ADDRESS_____ PHONE_____         │
│                                                                    │
│           _____                        │
│                                                                    │
│   Child's Birthdate _____                       │
│                          month-day-year                            │
│                                                                    │
│   How did you hear about our school?_____      │
│                                                                    │
│   Brochure sent _____                     │
│                              Date                                  │
│                                                                    │
│   Application packet sent _____             │
│                                   Date                             │
│                                                                    │
│   Additional comments: _____      │
│                                                                    │
│        _____      │
│                                                                    │
│        _____      │
└──────────────────────────────────────────────────────────────────┘
```

Figure 3–6   Sample inquiry report form.

you to observe the child informally and to get an impression of the parent/child relationship. The parents will be able to ask questions about your school and express any concerns about the child's adjustment. If the parents decide to enroll the child, take time to get some of the forms filled out for the child's file.

Enrollment Decisions

The maximum number of children your center can accommodate will be determined by the size of your physical space and specified on your license. You can enroll every applicant up to the maximum allowed or decide to limit the number of children you accept. The total number of children must then be divided into manageable groups. Group size will vary depending on the skill of the teacher, the age of the children, and the licensing specifications in your state.

As you place children in groups, you will also have to make another decision: should the children in each group be approximately the *same age*, or should the groups have a *range of age* level? The first method is called a *peer group* and includes children who are near the same age, usually with about a six-month to one-year difference. The second method is called a *family group* and includes children with a wide age span. Children in this group may differ in age as much as several years. Teachers and administrators who prefer peer grouping point to the advantage when planning curriculum activities. It is easier to include materials that most of the children will be able to use successfully. Those who like the family

---

APPLICATION FOR ENROLLMENT

Village Child Care Center

Name of Child _____ Date of Birth _____

Home Address _____ Phone _____

Mother (or guardian) _____

Father (or guardian) _____

Parents employment: Mother _____

_____

Father _____

_____

Days requested: (Circle)   Mon   Tues   Wed   Thu   Fri

Hours requested: From _____ to _____

Beginning Date: _____

A registration fee of $_____ must accompany this application. Paid $ _____

Signed _____
(parent's signature)

Date _____

Figure 3–7   Sample application form.

group will extol the advantage of children learning from others who are older or younger than themselves. They also feel that, especially in child care settings, this kind of group more closely resembles the home and, therefore, is more familiar to the children. You have to decide what suits your school, goals, and teachers.

Another important consideration is the inclusion of *children with special needs*. Under the Americans with Disabilities Act (the ADA) enacted in 1990, discrimination against persons with disabilities is prohibited. This measure has an impact on early childhood education programs since it requires all public and private schools, child care centers, and family child care providers to make reasonable accommodations to include special-needs children. Each child's needs must be evaluated on an individual basis and then an equal, nonsegregated educational program provided. A primary legal reason for refusing admission to a child with special needs is that doing so would place an undue burden on the provider and that there is no reasonable alternative. An additional reason for denial of admission is that the child's condition would pose a direct threat to the health or safety of that child, other children, or staff members.

There are many other questions that you will probably want answered in relation to accepting children with special needs into your school. Look for community resources such as a "Health Hot-Line." California has one with a toll-free number: 800-333-3212. Your local resource and referral agency may provide information and materials. Ask them for a copy of *Caring for Our Children, National Health and Safety Standards: Guidelines for Out-of-Home Child Care Programs*, a joint project of the American Public Health Association and the American Academy of Pediatrics. The California Child Care Law Center publishes *Caring for Children with Special Needs: The Americans with Disabilities Act and Child Care*. The booklet covers legal concerns, insurance, and taxes. The Law Center's address is 22 Second Street, San Francisco, CA 94105.

Make an *attendance chart* showing the days and hours each child will be attending school. Most children will attend on the same days and at the same hours fairly consistently. Some schools give parents the option of choosing to send a child two or three days a week instead of five. Attendance may vary more radically, for instance, in the case of the parent who works changing shifts. It will be important to record this so teachers will know which children to include in their plan.

Prepare an overall *schedule* for the school. This means planning where each group will be during specified periods of time during the day. This prevents all the children from being on the playground at once and allows teachers periodic use of additional spaces in the school building. A daily schedule should allow for snack and meal times, toileting and handwashing, naps, and large blocks of time both indoors and out. The day should have a leisurely pace so that children do not feel they are constantly being rushed from one activity to another. This is especially important in an all-day school since children are there for many hours.

Establish a file for each child enrolled in the school. Each file should contain:

- Application form.
- Medical evaluation.
- Dietary restrictions, if any.
- Emergency information (see Figure 3–8).
- Permission form for medical treatment (see Figure 3–8).
- Permission form for field trips (see Figure 3–9).
- Financial agreements (see Figure 3–10).

In addition to the foregoing information, California currently requires a form signed and dated by the parents acknowledging receipt of a *child abuse prevention* pamphlet. If the parents refuse to sign the form, the director must note their refusal in the child's record file.

You must follow up to see that each file is complete, using a system that works for you. Some directors use a running checklist that shows at a glance what is still needed in a file. Another system is to put the completed files in one place, leaving

IDENTIFICATION AND EMERGENCY INFORMATION
To Be Completed by Parent or Guardian

Child's Name _____ Date of Birth _____

Address _____
Street Address

_____

City   Zip   Phone

Mother or guardian _____

    Business Telephone _____ Hours _____

Father or guardian _____

    Business Telephone _____ Hours _____

Additional persons who may be called in an emergency:

Name	Address	Phone	Relationship

Physician to be called in an emergency:

Name _____ Phone _____

Address _____

If physician cannot be reached, what action should be taken? _____

    Call emergency hospital _____

    Other _____

Names of persons authorized to take child from the facility:

Name	Relationship

Time child will be called for_____

Signature of parent or guardian   Date

_____   _____

Figure 3–8   Sample identification and emergency information form.

PERMISSION

I hereby give permission for _____
child's name

to participate in the following activities at _____ School.

_____ Field trip with the class. I understand that I will be notified prior to a
scheduled trip and will be given information regarding transportation,
destination, lunch or other food, and arrival and departure time.

_____ Pictures taken of my child to be used for educational purposes, teacher
training, or school use. I understand my child's name will not be used at
any time.

_____ Distribution of my address and/or telephone number to other parents of a
child enrolled in this school. (Addresses will not be given out for any commercial purposes.)

Signature of parent _____

Date _____

Figure 3–9 Sample permission form.

FINANCIAL AGREEMENT

I agree to pay $_____ per month, payable in advance for tuition for my child. I
understand there is no tuition allowance for absences unless my child is ill for more
than two weeks.

I also agree to notify the school two weeks in advance of withdrawal, should that be
necessary. I understand that without notification, I am obligated for two weeks'
tuition or until the place is filled.

I have read the Parents' Handbook and understand the school's policies regarding
tuition payment.

Signed _____
Mother or guardian

Signed _____
Father or guardian

Date _____

Figure 3–10 Financial agreement.

the incomplete ones in another place until finished. Whatever the system, it is important to see that the task of getting all needed forms on file is accomplished as quickly as possible at the beginning of the school year.

Develop a procedure for *checking children in and out* so you have a written record of attendance plus arrival and departure times. A few teachers have had panic-stricken moments when they find a child missing and don t know if the parent has picked up the child. One school has a sign at the checkout: "Make certain you only have your own child." They had experienced children slipping out with other parents before anyone realized they were gone. A sign-in-and-out sheet or book posted at the entrance of the school or at each classroom will serve this purpose.

Make a place for *parent messages*. A bulletin board in the reception area will serve for general notices. When you want to send notes to individual parents, use some other method. Some schools use something like a shoe bag that hangs on the wall outside each classroom. There are pockets for each family. Others have pigeonhole slots in a cabinet at the entrance to the school. Teachers can use these to send messages to parents about the child's day or some special occurrence that might be important for the parent to know. Some schools use a HappyGram form; others just use an informal note.

If your school has a before- and after-school program for older children, you may need to arrange for *bus service*. You can rent the buses from school bus companies or buy your own vehicles and employ a driver. List the children who will be using the service to pick them up from home and take them to school, or pick them up after school. List their addresses and approximate times that fit in with parents' schedules and the school schedules. Use a map to chart a route for the bus driver.

Once you have a route and schedule set, send your driver on a trial run during the hours that would ordinarily be used. That is the only way you will be able to see if the schedule is realistic in terms of the traffic and the distances traveled. You may find you have to make some adjustments.

PARENTS

A *parent handbook* helps parents become oriented as quickly as possible to their new experience in your school. It also can serve as a reference for information they may need during the year. A parent handbook should contain the following information:

- *Philosophy*—a statement of the program's philosophy.
- *Arrival and departure*—times and procedures for signing in and out.
- *Health policies*—guidelines for inclusion or exclusion of children who are ill.
- *Safety*—what the school will do when a child is injured or needs medical help.
- *Food*—what kind of food can be brought from home; foods that will be served at school.
- *Special occasions*—how the parent can make a birthday a special occasion for the child and his or her class; how the school will celebrate special occasions.
- *Home toys*—what the child can bring to school.
- *Clothing*—what is appropriate for school activities.
- *Parent visits*—how to be a good visitor.

In addition, many parent handbooks contain general information to help parents understand their child's school experience better, and make the adjustment easier. These kinds of information are:

- *Developmental characteristics*—brief profiles of expected behavior of children at different age levels.
- *Separation*—suggestions for making separation between parent and child easier for both.
- *Progress reports*—methods staff will use to report the child's progress to parents.
- *Information*—the kinds of information parents can provide teachers.
- *Parent involvement*—ways in which parents can be involved in school activities.

A parent handbook should be a useful and attractive tool to both parents and staff; therefore, a lot of thought should go into its writing and composition. The following suggestions may help:

- Think about whether some information will vary from one year to the next or if it will always be the same. Be sure that variable information is on a separate page. If changes are needed, choose a loose-leaf or stapled binding for the book so pages can be inserted as needed.
- Arrange information logically, with a table of contents. Try printing each section on a different color paper so that it is easily identifiable. You can also cut each section wider or longer than the previous one, providing a tab for ease in locating.
- Information should be concise. Remember that some parents will never read the whole document. Make it possible for them to get specific kinds of information without a lot of searching.
- The writing should be clear and free of poor grammar or misspelled words. Sentences should be easy to understand; they should not contain any professional jargon.
- Make the handbook attractive so that parents are invited to explore its contents. A computer will allow you to vary the print font, add drawings, or alter the format.
- Cost will probably be a consideration, especially if you have it typeset and printed professionally. Get several estimates before deciding to use this method. If it is too expensive, consider using a copier and collating it yourself.

Parent Orientation

It is a good idea to schedule *orientation meetings* with parents before the opening of school or within the first few weeks. These are relaxed meetings that are a convenient way to introduce parents to staff members, and to each other. They can provide time for informal discussions of concerns or questions parents may still have about their child starting school. It is at these meetings that the relationship between parents and the school is established. They will set the tone for future interactions.

Some schools plan one orientation night; parents meet with the teachers of their child's group in the child's assigned classroom. With so many parents working, many schools are finding that this arrangement does not work. Parents do not want to come out again to a meeting after putting in a full day on the job, so attendance suffers. Some schools have found innovative ways of managing orientation by scheduling a series of meetings. These are held either early in the morning over breakfast or immediately after the end of the school day. Care is provided for the children while parents and staff meet briefly. Five or six parents is a good number to work with at a time. This kind of arrangement may take more staff time and effort, but it will probably repay with greater parent involvement in school activities.

If you have an infant and toddler program, it is important to *plan with parents* for care of their children at school. This can be done at orientation meetings or individually. Parents of infants are probably going to be anxious about placing their child in day care for the first time. Understandably, they want to know the child will receive care that is similar to that which he or she receives at home. Teachers should know when the children eat and how much, when they usually sleep, and any other pertinent information about each child's temperament. Parents of toddlers can help staff to plan for the child's toileting and daily schedule.

It is important that parents can communicate to staff about the infant or toddler's activities before coming to school. Many schools ask parents to fill out a *daily information sheet*. Similar information about the child's day at school is provided for the parents at the end of the day.

Figure 3–11 The director includes staff in planning.

THE NEW SCHOOL YEAR

Staff

It is important that all staff members work one or two weeks before the opening of school. This is a time when each classroom *environment* is prepared. Teachers should have time to:

- Do last minute room cleaning.
- Clean and organize supply cupboards.
- Put away new materials.
- Rearrange their classroom furniture.
- Set up a schedule for general classroom maintenance.

Staff should have time to review *curriculum materials* available in their classrooms and in the general storage areas. They should also have time to:

- Order last-minute items as needed.
- Prepare curriculum materials for first week of school.

The time before school is an important one for the establishment of *relationships among staff members*. Use this time to set the tone for your working partnership with staff. It is a time when you can:

- Give teachers a list of the children in their classes.
- Make children's files available.

Figure 3–12   Staff chooses equipment, too.

- Discuss group schedules.
- Review sign-in procedures to be used by parents.
- Review emergency procedures for safety of children.
- Encourage teachers to schedule and complete home visits.
- Plan procedures for the first day of school.

Supplies

The beginning of a school year is a good time to do an inventory of supplies and equipment on hand. This can be very detailed or cover only items that are most used. For instance, you may not need to know how many pencils you have on hand, but you certainly need to know if there will be enough paint for the teachers to use.

Paint is an example of an *expendable* supply, things that get used up and have to be replaced. Also included are paper, glue, paper towels, toilet paper, and cleaning supplies. Bikes are *nonexpendable* items for they last a long time before they need to be replaced. Office equipment, outdoor equipment, and many toys are also considered nonexpendable.

Divide your inventory into these two categories. Complete your count of what you have on hand and order what will be needed. Remember that ordering in large quantities often decreases the cost. Be sure to allow enough time for delivery. Many times it will take up to six weeks for an order to arrive.

Consider setting up a petty-cash fund for each classroom as an additional way of providing supplies. Budget a specified amount for the year for each room and allow teachers to purchase things they need. This can relieve you of some of the responsibility and can also give teachers greater freedom to buy what they need.

Finances

Only a few schools can afford the luxury of a bookkeeper. Therefore, you will have to assume that job. Before school begins each year is a good time to review

Name _____		No. of days per week _____			
Address _____		Tuition Amt. _____			
Telephone _____					
Date	Item	Amt. Due	Amt. Paid	Credit	Balance

Figure 3–13   Sample individual ledger sheet form.

CASH RECEIPTS RECORD				
Date	Item	Cash	Check Number	Amount

Figure 3–14   Sample cash receipts record form.

EXPENDITURES RECORD				
Date	Item	Check Number	Amount	From Account

Figure 3–15   Sample expenditures record form.

MONTHLY BUDGET SUMMARY					
Date	Item	Budget Amt.	This Month (last day)	Year to Date	Balance

Figure 3–16   Sample monthly budget summary form.

whether your procedures for collecting tuitions, recording income, and paying bills is efficient. You may find you want to make some changes. The following suggestions may be helpful:

- Collect tuition payments promptly each month on the same date.
- Accumulate checks for a few days at a time, then alphabetize them and post them on individual ledger sheets for each child.
- When you receive cash, issue a duplicate receipt—one for the parent, and one for the school.
- Record all checks and cash in the cash receipts record.
- At a specified time, usually ten days, check individual ledgers to see if tuitions have been paid. Notify all families who have not paid the tuition.
- Record expenditures as they are made and summarize them each month.

Almost all these procedures can be assisted by use of a computer and computerized methods.

Facility

The final task before the beginning of the school year is to check the overall appearance of your school. You want to be sure that it is clean and attractive. Often parents say the first thing they look for in a school is cleanliness. Remember, then, that parents' first impressions will be formed by how your school looks. Is the entrance to your school appealing? Is there a bulletin board that will interest parents? Does the environment welcome parents as well as children?

Make sure the playground also looks inviting. Often this is what people see as they approach your school. It should look like a place that is safe for children and that children will enjoy. If there are any garden areas around the school, have they been cared for? Is lighting adequate for dark mornings or late afternoons? You might even try driving up to your school in the morning as though you had never before seen it. Look at it as a parent would. Does it have "curb appeal?" Is it a place you would want to stop to investigate as a place for your own child? If your answer is "yes," then your school is ready for another year!

SUMMARY

The decision to open an early childhood center must be carefully thought out, for it entails many choices and a variety of tasks. Begin with a *needs assessment* to determine whether there is a pool of prospective clients. Consult census information about the community to determine whether it will support another child care center.

There are several possibilities for *housing* a school. You can build anew, remodel a residence, rent unused public school classrooms, use space in a church, renovate a storefront or industrial building, use pre-fab buildings, or buy an existing school.

Determine the *start-up costs* of opening a center. The cost of the land and buildings, equipment and materials, and personnel will comprise the major portion.

Additional expenses will include fees for consultant or legal services, advertising, and insurance.

Before going any further in your decision-making process, make an estimate of *on-going costs*. Potential income will be determined by the number of children your facility will support. There are some suggested ranges of fixed costs that may help you. If the site you have chosen will accommodate enough children to cover your expenses, you are ready to go to the next step.

Plan the opening of your school for a time that fits the needs of your community. Often the optimum time is at the end of summer. Develop *enrollment procedures* that ensure careful attention to each inquiry. Once you begin receiving applications, you will need to make enrollment decisions: the total number to accept, whether to group children in peer or family groups, and how to incorporate children with special needs into the program. There are additional tasks that must be completed. Make attendance charts, prepare an overall schedule for the school, establish and complete files for each child, and organize a place for parent messages. If you will enroll school-age children, you may need to prepare a bus schedule to take children to and from their schools.

Prepare a handbook to distribute to each new parent. Include information about the philosophy of your school and specific information about rules and procedures. Also plan a parent orientation before school begins, or within the first few weeks. Informal meetings allow time for questions, and for a relationship between parents and teachers to be established. Staff members should be working at least two weeks before opening day. This is a time for preparation of their room environments and to review curriculum materials.

There are a few additional tasks to be completed before you are ready to open your doors. Order supplies, set up procedures for collecting tuitions, and give your facility a *final inspection*. Make sure the appearance of your school is clean and inviting.

SELECTED FURTHER READING

Baker, A. 1993. "New frontiers in family day care: Integrating children with ADHD." *Young Children,* 48 (5) 69–73.

Saifer, S. 1990. *Practical Solutions for Practically Every Problem: The Early Childhood Teacher's Manual.* St. Paul, MN: Redleaf Press.

Surr, J. 1992. "Early childhood programs and the Americans with Disabilities Act (ADA)." *Young Children,* 47 (5) 18–21.

What Are the High Costs of High-Quality Programs? 1990. General Accounting Office (P.O. Box 6015), Gaithersburg, MD.

Willer, B. ed. 1990. *Reaching the Full Cost of Quality in Early Childhood Programs* Washington, DC: National Association for the Education of Young Children.

STUDENT ACTIVITIES

1. Visit your local zoning agency. Ask for zoning requirements for a child care center and a home-based center. If there are differences, ask about the reasoning behind them.

2. Obtain a copy of the licensing requirements for your area. Determine the following:
    a. What is the maximum size for a group of toddlers?
    b. What is the teacher/child ratio for a group of four-year-olds?
    c. Are there any regulations pertaining to school-age children?
    d. What are the minimum qualifications for staff members?

3. Invite a director of a child care center to visit your class. Ask him or her to discuss which sections of the licensing code make a director's job easier. Ask also if there are items in the regulations that should be changed.

4. Collect parent handbooks from several child care centers. Compare them and determine:
    a. If they contain the same kinds of information.
    b. In what ways they differ.
    c. If the information is easy to understand.
    d. If you think essential information has been omitted.

REVIEW

1. What information should be included in a community survey to determine whether a community can support another child care center?

2. List the possible types of housing for an early childhood center.

3. Discuss the advantages and disadvantages of using the following space for a child care center: a church building, a factory, an existing school.

4. Differentiate between start-up and on-going costs.

5. List the categories of expenses that are included in a start-up budget.

6. Which expenditure comprises the largest percentage of on-going costs?

7. What is meant by the terms *peer group* and *family group*?

8. List the completed forms that should be included in a child's enrollment file.

9. What is the purpose of a parent handbook? What kinds of information should it contain?

10. What is meant by expendable and nonexpendable supplies?

GLOSSARY

Start-up costs   expenses incurred before a new school can open.

On-going costs   expected costs of operating a school.

Peer group   children who are close to the same age.

Family group   children whose ages vary, sometimes by several years.

Expendable supplies   items that are used up and have to be replaced.

Nonexpendable items   equipment and toys that last a long time.

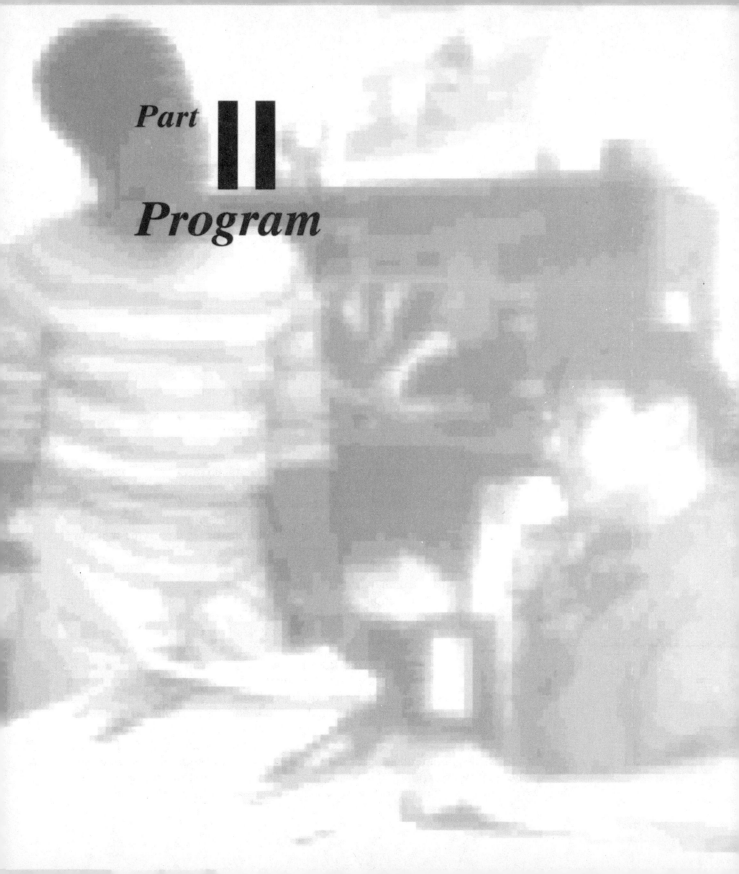

Part II

Program

4

Setting Goals: Planning and Evaluating

OBJECTIVES
After studying this chapter, the student should be able to:
- Tell what is meant by the philosophy of a school.
- Distinguish between goals and objectives.
- Discuss how goals are developed.
- List methods of evaluating program goals.

Every early childhood center has its own unique characteristics based on the ideas of the original developers, refined by each of the succeeding directors, and implemented by current staff members. At the core are a philosophy and a set of goals that are used for planning and implementing all aspects of the school's operations: the facility design, hiring policies, equipment purchases, and activities that are offered. There is wide variation from one school to the next, for there is no consensus as to what is best for the children who attend these centers. Our ideas about what should be included change as research studies reveal more about how children learn, as social conditions change, as the needs of the children change, and even as political forces exert pressures. Some of the resulting changes are not always based on knowledge of the developmental needs of young children.

Attempts have been made by the National Association for the Education of Young Children to articulate guidelines for quality early childhood education. In 1984, a commission was created for the purpose of developing a statement on *appropriate educational practices* for young children. The result of the commission's deliberations was first published in 1986, and then expanded in 1987 as *Developmentally Appropriate Practice in Early Childhood Programs Serving Children From Birth Through Age 8*. The statement has been widely read, and the concept of developmental appropriateness has become a frequently used measure of the quality of early childhood programs. Developmental appropriateness has two dimensions: an understanding of the universal sequences of growth and change that occur in children, and the recognition that each child is unique with an individual pattern and timing of growth.

As the director of an early childhood program, it is your responsibility to see that the *philosophy* and *goals* of the center are implemented effectively. In an ongoing program, someone else would already have developed the philosophy and set of goals. These should be compatible with your own professional and personal beliefs and values. In a new facility, it will be your responsibility to work with others to develop a philosophy statement, and then, a set of goals.

PHILOSOPHY

The need to formulate a *philosophy statement* for a new school is intimidating to some directors and teachers; however, it should not be. A philosophy is a distillation of ideas, beliefs, and values held by a group or organization. There are three areas that are reflected in a philosophy statement: assumptions about how children learn, values held by program planners and parents of the children involved, and ideas about education and the function of a school. Remember that you will never get a consensus on these areas, but discussions will engender a great deal of thought about the importance of each.

Begin with an exploration of assumptions about how children learn:

- Do you believe that children learn best when they are given extrinsic motivations in the form of rewards such as tokens or gold stars? This is called the *environmental approach*. What the child learns is determined by adults and can be observed or measured. The behaviorists Thorndike, Skinner, and Watson are associated with this approach.
- Do you believe that there is an inner force that activates cognitive systems as children grow and mature? When children are *developmentally ready*, they will choose activities and experiences that they can accomplish. Their satisfaction at mastering tasks provides intrinsic rewards. Gesell is the theorist most often associated with this approach.
- Do you believe that learning results from an *interaction* between the child and his environment? Children construct their own knowledge through repeated interactions with people and objects. They experiment, test their errors or misconceptions, arrive at new conclusions, and thus, construct new knowledge. Piaget is the theorist associated with this approach.

Consider next the values held by those involved in planning the program of your center: board members, administrative personnel, teaching staff, and parents. The basic question here is which is more important, social/emotional, or cognitive development of children? Ask the following:

- Which is more important, children's self-esteem or what they learn?
- Should children develop autonomy in order to enable them to participate fully in a free society, or should they learn to obey adults?
- Do children have a right to make their own choices, or should they accept adult decisions?

- Should families be more a part of school activities, or should school be the exclusive domain of professionals?

Nearly everyone has ideas about education and the function of the school. A thorough exploration of this area must be a part of developing a philosophy statement. Consider the following thoughts about education and a school:

- A preschool center should prepare children for kindergarten.
- A school should teach children to be better disciplined.
- The environment of a school should be nurturing and protective.
- School should prepare children for life, not just for the next phase of education.
- The teaching of moral values should be left to parents.
- The school curriculum should provide an opportunity for students to retain aspects of their own cultural background.

As you discuss the beliefs and issues outlined above, you will probably find many more ideas and thoughts to include. Compile a list for each of the three areas and distribute to committee members. Ask them to rank the items in order of importance. A lot of discussion and negotiation will take place during this process, but debate helps each member to clarify thinking and refine ideas. The dialogue will probably take many weeks. At the end of the process, you should have a statement of philosophy. You are now ready to develop a set of goals for your school. The following are examples of philosophy statements.

EXAMPLE 1

The curriculum of the Child Learning Center is based on the belief that children learn best when they are rewarded for their accomplishments. For the youngest children, rewards are concrete and specific. As children grow, the emphasis shifts to encouraging children to take pride in their own accomplishments without expecting extrinsic rewards. The Child Learning Center also teaches children discipline and a respect for authority in preparation for later experiences in life. Staff members are expected to be positive role models for children.

EXAMPLE 2

Each activity at Golden Preschool is carefully matched to coincide with universal stages in all areas of children's development; physical, cognitive, social/emotional, and creative. Therefore, when children move to new levels of ability, there are always experiences they can choose in order to gain new mastery. There are many opportunities for children to practice physical skills, learn problem-solving, gain knowledge of their environment, and practice interacting more effectively with others. We also believe that parents are an important part of children's learning experiences and are partners in the education and care of the children.

EXAMPLE 3

Basic to the philosophy of Green Oaks School is the recognition that children are continually learning, both in school and out. Children are given many opportunities to choose their own activities and to explore their own interests. All classroom experiences actively involve children in their own learning process.

We also believe that their educational development extends beyond the class-room and is influenced by what happens in their home and their neighborhood. Although the school has primary responsibility for the child's academic training, the support and cooperation of parents and others outside the school are necessary in creating an environment in which children can reach their full potential.

FORMULATING GOALS

What Are They?

You must clearly distinguish between goals and objectives even though many peo-ple use these words interchangeably. Both a goal and an objective can be defined as a change at the end of a specified period of time. However, a *goal* indicates changes that take place over a long period of time. A month and a school year are the typical periods that are specified. When doing overall planning for a school, goals may even extend over several years. Use of the word "objective" is appropri-ate when referring to short-term changes. A day or a week may be the time period for the attainment of an objective. Teachers use objectives as the basis for daily lesson plans. A director might set an objective of accomplishing a specific task dur-ing a particular week.

When discussing goals, people frequently confuse which kind of goal is appro-priate: overall, curriculum, or individual. Teachers sometimes make the mistake of thinking only in terms of overall school goals when planning curriculum. A typical overall goal might read "The Child Learning Center will provide a stimulating en-vironment in which children are free to explore." That kind of goal does not say anything about what happens to the child. A curriculum goal should reflect the expected change in the child. This is discussed in greater detail later in this chapter.

Who Sets Them?

Although every director does not have an opportunity to develop goals, you should still understand the process. Many schools already have their goals; your responsibility as director is to see that they are implemented. In other schools, one of your first tasks will be to set new goals for the school.

Goals can be developed by individuals or groups. The process is largely determined by the kind of school for which the goals are formulated. In a singly owned school, such as the private proprietary school referred to in Chapter 2, the owner usually decides goals. In a corporate school, goals often come from the corporate office.

As can be seen, overall goal setting starts at the top of an administrative structure. One person sets down a list of goals. School personnel are expected to use these goals to plan and implement all parts of the program. This method of goal formula-tion has the advantage that it is usually accomplished quickly. Its disadvantage is that those who are responsible for implementing them may not understand or be commit-ted to those goals. At an extreme, teachers may be unaware of their existence.

FYI

As of August 1993, more than 2,700 programs have received accreditation through NAEYC, and 8,000 more programs are enrolled in self-study. Texas has the greatest number of accredited centers with 296; California is in second place with 284. Outside the United States, Germany, Iceland, Japan, South Korea, and Turkey have accredited centers with yet others enrolled in self-study.

A preferred method of setting overall goals uses a committee or group of people. Director, parents, teachers, and even community representatives may be involved. This method is likely to be used in nonprofit schools such as cooperatives or church schools. The decided advantage in this method of goal determination is that users of the goals are more likely to implement them. With input comes an inducement to implement those goals. On the other hand, the committee method often takes a long time to produce results. The diverse opinions of each member must be discussed and then negotiated until the final product satisfies all members.

Directors can use a third method of setting overall goals. They can circulate a list of goals among staff and then gather opinions, changes, and further suggestions at staff meetings. From these, they can formulate a new list. That list, too, may be subject to revision until all staff members are reasonably satisfied with the results.

A final method might be to use a set of existing goals from another source. Goals can be found in many books and pamphlets. One of the best sources is the National Association for the Education of Young Children. The association has developed a set of goals for high-quality early childhood programs to be used by schools and day care centers as the basis for a voluntary accreditation system. A kit for self-study is available through the National Academy of Early Childhood Programs, 1834 Connecticut Avenue, NW, Washington, DC 20009-5786.

Writing Goals

Before you begin to write goals, there are several considerations to keep in mind. First, it is better to have a few goals that can realistically be accomplished than a long list that can never be attained. Five to ten goals are a reasonable number. Second, you may wish to categorize goals into the areas of a child's development: physical, social/emotional, and cognitive. Lastly, state goals in terms of changes that will occur in children as a result of their school experiences.

Underline key words in your philosophy statement to use as the starting point for your goals. In Example 3, key words might be the following:

1. *Choose their own activities and explore their own interests.*
2. *Involve children actively in their own learning process.*
3. *Development is influenced by what happens in their home and neighborhood.*
4. *Environment in which children can reach their full potential.*

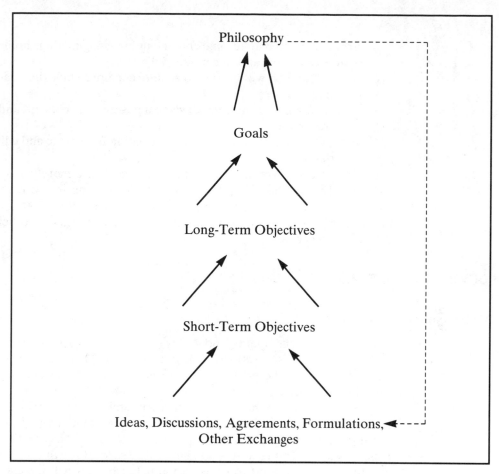

Figure 4–1 A chart for idea development.

Based on the first two statements, a goal might be:

> Children will choose their own learning experiences in order to stimulate their curiosity about the world and develop confidence in their own abilities as learners.

The third statement might refer to the fact that children today live in neighborhoods where violence is a daily occurrence. A goal for a school might be:

> Children will learn to resolve problems without resorting to violence and will acquire techniques for mediating disputes.

The fourth statement might yield the following goal:

> Children will learn to appreciate their own unique characteristics and abilities and strive to reach their own level of excellence.

Goals are sometimes categorized by the areas of children's development. Example 2 of the philosophy statements speaks of children gaining mastery in all areas of their development. Those writing goals for this preschool might categorize them.

Physical: Children will become competent in managing their bodies and acquire basic gross motor and fine motor skills.

Cognitive: Children will be able to acquire cognitive skills that lead to life-long learning.

Social/emotional: Children will develop a positive self-concept and a genuine concern for others.

Creative: Children will develop an appreciation for artistic and cultural experiences.

As you can see from the above examples, goals are merely statements of what we hope the children will achieve as a result of being in a preschool, school, or child care center. Each facility will have its own separate and unique goals. There are many variations, but each goal represents a commitment to help children "be the best they can be."

DEVELOPING OBJECTIVES

From Goals to Objectives

Goals are broad statements, and it may seem difficult to get from there to the daily activities of a school. Actually, it is not too hard. Think of objectives as paths or steps that lead to the goals. You can pursue many directions or many different steps before reaching the final goal.

Write down the end-behavior, attitudes, or abilities that will indicate the achievement of a goal. It is easier to describe this for goals that are about actions. You can observe them. You can probably picture the kind of behavior that will tell you a child has achieved the ability to choose and carry through an activity. It is more difficult when you need to envision the behavior that will indicate to you a child has a positive self-image.

An example will help to illustrate how to go about this task.

EXAMPLE

GOAL: The child will be able to choose, carry through, and take pride in a variety of learning experiences.

What observable behavior would lead a teacher to decide that a particular child had indeed achieved this objective? Many situations could be used, but a child's use of blocks is a good example. The teacher might observe the following incident:

When free choice time is announced, John goes to the block shelf and begins taking down a pile of long blocks. He lays them out in a square, goes back to the shelf, and chooses four more blocks the same size. He continues in this manner until he has a structure that is three blocks high. He looks around to find suitable materials for a roof. He decides against using blocks and chooses a square piece of plywood. It fits.

John now tries to park some small cars on the roof of the building. To get the cars up on the roof, he attempts to build a long ramp with several inclines and square blocks to lift the inclines to the right height. It is a difficult problem, but after several tries, he does it. As he drives the first cars up the ramp and parks them, he sits back with a look of pleasure on his face. At snack time, he asks his teacher if his building can be saved to show his mother when she comes to pick him up.

John has chosen his own activity without any help from the teacher. He solved the problems that arose as he carried his project to the end. His pride in his accomplishment was indicated by his request to save it to show to his mother.

What steps were necessary to reach this end result? There would have been many over a long period of time. A few will serve to illustrate the process. As you will see from the examples, a series of carefully planned challenges led John to the achievement of this goal.

CHOOSING

When the teacher suggests an activity, John willingly takes part.
When three activities are suggested, John is able to choose one of them.
When told that it is free-choice time, John is able to choose an activity without help from the teacher.

CARRY THROUGH

John is able to complete a fifteen-piece puzzle with some help from the teacher.
John is able to put together a twenty-piece puzzle by himself.

TAKE PRIDE

John complains to the teacher that he cannot build a garage for his cars and wants some help. His teacher shows him how to start, and he continues to build.
John is able to start his building but gets frustrated when he cannot figure out how to make a ramp for the cars. He knocks down the building and goes off to paint. His teacher suggests that next time he could ask for help in solving his problem rather than knocking down the whole building.
John is able to build the kind of structure he wants and asks to save it for his mother to see.

Each of these already described behaviors is a step leading to the achievement of the goal. The same kind of steps might have been observed in art activities, outdoor play, or any number of situations during the school day. They all were paths leading to the achievement of the goal. If you have in mind what the end behavior will be, you will be able to observe it in many situations.

It is a little more difficult to describe the end behavior when the goal involves feelings or attitudes. Take the goal: "The child will have a positive self-concept, valuing her- or himself as a unique individual." Each person will probably have different ideas about how a child will show those characteristics. So *you* have to decide what evidence suggests that a child has a positive self-concept. You may consider some of the following attitudes and behaviors:

- The child is clear about being a boy or a girl.
- The child walks with an appearance of self-confidence.
- The child enters the room in the morning saying, "Well, here I am, Teacher."
- The child says, "I have brown hair, and my sister has blonde hair."
- The child often says, "I don't need any help. I can do it."

You will be able to add many more to your own list. Some may be ways in which most children show how they feel about themselves. Others may be specific to individual children. But each will constitute a step or path that leads to the attainment of the goal of a positive self-concept.

Figure 4–2 It's fun to learn and play at the same time.

Figure 4–2 (*continued*)   It's fun to learn and play at the same time.

Behavioral Objectives

Once you have outlined the steps leading to the achievement of a goal, you can state some behavioral objectives. There are traditional ways in which this is done. An outline should give you further help:

- State the objective in terms of the child's behavior.
- Include the conditions for learning in specific terms.
- Verify that the behavior is observable.
- State the amount or extent of expected behavior.

Certain words are helpful in clarifying objectives.

TO DESCRIBE CONDITIONS FOR LEARNING
When asked . . .
When shown . . .
When completed . . .
Having used . . .

TO DESCRIBE OBSERVABLE BEHAVIOR
The child will select . . .
The child will place . . .
The child will express . . .
The child will return . . .
The child will identify . . .
The child will match . . .

Another example of a goal and the behavioral objectives that might lead to its attainment should help you to understand the process.

GOAL: The child will be able to attend to and appreciate music, poetry, and stories.

BEHAVIORAL OBJECTIVES:

- When read a list of six words, the child will be able to say correctly a word that rhymes with three of them.
- When read three lines of a four-line poem, the child will be able to state the final line.
- When hearing the sound of six hidden objects, the child will be able to identify five of them correctly.
- When hearing a recording of "Peter and the Wolf," the child will be able to name three of the instruments correctly.
- When alone with the teacher, the child will be able to attend to and identify 60 percent of the objects in a picture book.
- In a group story time, the child will be able to listen to a short and simple story book.

Each step reflects weekly or monthly objectives. There will be many more than those listed here. The teacher carefully plans the kinds of activities and experiences that the child needs from the beginning of the school year to the end. Daily, weekly, and monthly activities are not haphazardly put together but are put together in an organized manner.

IMPLEMENTING GOALS AND OBJECTIVES

General Principles

After you formulate objectives for each goal, take steps to implement them. Do this by following some general principles.

Implementing objectives begins with setting up the environment. The teacher organizes the environment and structures the learning experiences in ways that stimulate the kind of reaction desired in the children. When implementing the goal of developing their ability to make choices, the classroom must be set up so that this is possible. A variety of activities and materials should be available. Children should be free to choose whatever they wish.

The child must have opportunities to practice the kind of behavior implied by the objective. Changes in behavior are achieved slowly. Therefore, for any objective, the children must have many experiences in which they can meet this objective. Often this means repeating the same activity many times. Young children will build up a tower of blocks and knock it down many times. Others will paint ten pictures, each time experimenting with brush strokes or mixing colors. Each of these experiences provides an opportunity to practice a skill, leading eventually to the achievement of an objective.

The child must gain a feeling of satisfaction from carrying on the behavior expected to result from the experience. Each learning experience should give the children satisfaction from having participated in it. Unpleasant experiences will cause children to avoid the same or similar experiences in the future.

The child must be able to achieve the behavior expected to result from the learning experience. Teachers must have a good knowledge of child development. With that knowledge, they are less likely to set unrealistic expectations for children. When a learning experience is designed to produce behavior in children that is far beyond their level of functioning, they become discouraged. If the experience is far below their level, they will not be challenged.

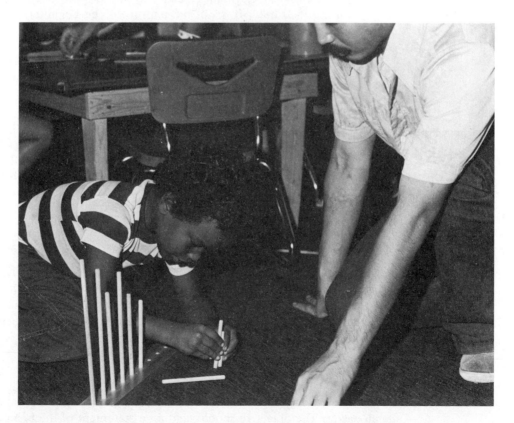

Figure 4–3 Preparation for kindergarten. *(Joseph Tardi Associates.)*

The child should have a choice of experiences that can result in the desired behavior. Any group of children will have a wide range of interests and abilities. Even individual children will vary from one time to another. Choices will allow alternate ways of achieving an objective.

The child should be able to repeat familiar activities in order to achieve the desired behavior. Every learning activity has many possible outcomes as children change. At age three, children use clay to explore how it feels or how it changes under different conditions. They will cut it, roll it, pound it, and squeeze it. By age five, children use clay to express an idea. They may make a figure, a rocketship, or an animal, for example.

Many teachers get bored with the same activities or materials. With freedom to explore, children seldom do. At each age level, children find new possibilities in the use of familiar materials.

Curriculum Design

It may be difficult for a beginning teacher to put into practice the guidelines that have been outlined here. It might be helpful for the beginner to start with one short-term objective and fill in experiences for a week. Figure 4–4 provides a suggested form to use.

It is also helpful to keep a log of learning activities offered each day. Include any comments about how the children responded to the experiences or any variations they might have brought to them. Children often think of new ways to use materials that teachers have never considered.

The log notes may also include suggestions for setting up the activity in another way. With a different presentation, the objective may be achieved more easily. Over a period of months, the record of activities and reactions related to a particular objective will yield a great deal of information. It should certainly help in planning for other objectives.

EVALUATING OUTCOMES

To determine whether goals are being met, evaluate them continually. Evaluation of a director was discussed in Chapter 1, and evaluation of teachers appears in Chapter 8. The NAEYC accreditation process has its own method of evaluating the overall program of a school or child care center. This section focuses on assessing curriculum goals.

Evaluation process

If you have clearly stated objectives, the process of evaluating outcomes will be much easier. The objective should contain a statement of the behavior that is expected. Some examples are:

GOAL: The child will develop habits and attitudes that promote and maintain his physical health and well-being.					
Behavioral Objective: When presented with a new food, the child will taste it.					
Activity	Monday	Tuesday	Wednesday	Thursday	Friday
Learning Centers	Vegetable Lotto Game	Taped reading of *Carrot Seed*	Video cassette on food and nutrition	Categorize foods—cut and paste pictures	Seed collage
Story	*Carrot Seed*		*Stone Soup*		
Play Activity	Prepare carrot and raisin salad for lunch		Cut up vegetables for lunch soup		
Lunch	Throughout the week, the children will set the table and serve their own portions from serving dishes.				
Outside	Throughout the week, the children will be getting soil ready and then planting a vegetable garden.				

Figure 4–4   Sample plan for a week.

- The child completes a puzzle.
- The child shares a toy.
- The child unbuttons the sweater.
- The child returns the books to the shelf.

When the behavior is clear, the next step is to set up standards for judging an acceptable level of performance. Should the child perform the expected behavior all the time or only part of the time? Must the child be able to complete a series of tasks or only part of them? Some illustrations of this kind of statement follow:

- Shown five name cards, the child will correctly pick out his own name 75 percent of the time.
- Shown the colors yellow, red, and blue, the child will correctly name each of them.

The evaluation process should also include a determination of where to look for evidence that the objective has been met. This is especially true of the social areas of the child's development. Look for these in situations where children are interacting, not during times when children are alone. List the possible situations in which the expected behavior is likely to occur.

Methods of Evaluation

Methods of evaluation are the ways in which the achievement of objectives is tested or judged. Regardless of the method teachers use, evaluation will yield valuable information. As teachers focus on each child, they will become more aware of all children's abilities. The resulting information may force teachers to change their curriculum or the ways they present materials. Evaluation also helps teachers plan more effectively for individual children. When a particular child's strengths and weaknesses are known, teachers can plan to foster or increase them. Finally, if teachers thoroughly understand a child's capabilities, they will be able to report more accurately to parents. Most parents want to know how their child is doing. Specific information is more helpful than generalities.

Remember, that although some methods of evaluation may be valuable, they may not be practical for daily use. Teachers simply may not have time to carry through complex testing methods with each child and to do it well. In this case, it is better not to do it at all since the results will not be accurate. Find methods that suit your particular school and the staff available.

Observation

The most frequently used evaluation method in preschools is the *observation* or *anecdotal record*. Basically, these are notes made by teachers as they observe children's behavior. Teachers often keep these records on index cards or in a log. What is written down is what teachers choose as being important. They usually include what the child does and says. Sometimes teachers add their own conclusions about the behavior.

Many teachers choose to record information about each child on a weekly basis. Others find it is easier to focus on part of the group one week and the other the following week. In the conduct of a busy day, teachers often have little time to sit back, watch, and then record what is happening. Less frequent observations may still yield plenty of information. However, guard against coming to any conclusions about a child based on only one observation.

The difficulty with anecdotal records is that only a small portion of what the child is doing or saying can be recorded. Therefore, what teachers actually write may present a skewed picture of the child's behavior. It is also true that two people looking at the same situation may see two entirely different actions. Still, with practice, teachers can learn to be more accurate in their reporting and can choose what is important.

The anecdotal record is only one form of observation that can help teachers. A video camera, tape recorder, or movie camera can provide more permanent records of what children are doing. These methods might be especially helpful when considering how to help a child who is having some difficulty. Rather than trying to deal with the child and observe at the same time, teachers can look at what happened during leisure time. Also, having more than one person look at the record may yield further information.

Commercial Tests

Today, tests that have been developed specifically for use in assessing young children's development are available. If they have been developed by experts, they usually have been tested with children of varying backgrounds. Choose only standardized tests from reputable companies. Follow the directions for administration and interpretation.

Unfortunately, these ready-made tests have some drawbacks. First, administration can be time-consuming and inconvenient. Teachers seldom have the time to spend an hour alone with each child. Some of these tests require the administrator to have special training or to be a psychologist. Few schools have that type of person on the staff or can afford to hire one.

An even more serious problem with commercial tests is the question of quality. Many tests are biased in favor of white, middle-class children and, therefore, are inappropriate to use in all situations. Children who come from poor families or who are bilingual will not be assessed accurately.

Before using commercial tests, get as much information as possible. Try to find personnel from another school who have used the test and ask how they would rate it. Check with college or university staff in your community to find out if they know of the particular test. If you are part of a school district, the school psychologist can probably help you.

Checklists

Checklists are a quick and fairly easy way of assessing a child's capabilities. They can be constructed to cover almost any aspect of development. They can also be designed to match specific objectives. A checklist may have items that can be merely checked off, or it may include a rating scale indicating degree or frequency of accomplishment.

An example from one of the goals already discussed should help to clarify the process.

GOAL: The child will choose, carry through, and take pride in a variety of learning experiences.
From the behavioral objectives listed for the attainment of the particular goal, the following checklist could be developed.

ACTIVITY	Usually	Sometimes	Never	No Opportunity to Observe
Chooses one of three activities				
Initiates own activity				
Completes fifteen-piece puzzle with help				
Completes twenty-piece puzzle with no help				
Uses words to express pride				
Shows completed task to others				

Figure 4–5 Children choose their own activity.

Develop the kind of checklist you use in your school to suit your set of goals. It does help to gather similar lists from other schools to give you ideas, but your list should be specifically fitted to what you are trying to accomplish.

Another word of caution: Do not make a checklist so long that the evaluator begins to guess at items. It is easier to try to observe and then check off a short list than to do one of thirty or forty items. You can do several short lists during a school year in order to get an idea of a child's progress.

Parent Interviews

Parent interviews are probably one of the best ways of collecting information about a child. Parents today are vitally interested in their child's school progress and can give you a great deal of information. Some interviews may be in written form such as a short questionnaire.

A face-to-face interview with the parent, parents, or guardian will provide you with even more information. During a conference you have an opportunity to compare the way the child behaves both at home and at school. Children are very often quite different in the two situations. The disparities can help you to understand more about the child's functioning and characteristics.

Remember that talking to the child is also a form of interview. Conversations can reveal information about the child's feelings, knowledge, and relationships.

Time Samplings

Sometimes, time-interval sampling of the presence or absence of behavior is helpful in understanding a child. This is a record taken at periodic intervals. The kinds of behavior that lend themselves to time sampling are language development, interest span, and incidences of aggression. If you want to know how long a child stays at an activity, do a time sampling every five minutes, say for half- or three-quarters of an hour. During that time, you will be able to see how often the child changes activities. It will give you a better picture of the child's interest span than trying to record the number of minutes spent at each activity.

Collection of End Products

Elementary school teachers use homework and seatwork papers to judge how well children are doing. In preschools, a similar technique can be employed. Save the child's artwork over a period of time. Take pictures of the kinds of block buildings he or she does. Each of these will give you an overview of the progress the child has made in those particular situations.

Assessment Information Summary

When you have gathered a sufficient amount of information about a child, put it together in an organized form. This is usually called a *profile* and is a picture of the child's development at a particular time.

Organize the profile according to your goals. If you have categorized goals into the three areas—physical, cognitive, social/emotional—these may be the broad areas. Summarize the information gathered from all sources supporting the child's achievement of each goal or area. Use this information to plan further for each child.

Clear goals and objectives, along with an effective evaluation process, can make your school a model for others to follow. However, neither goals nor objectives may be formulated or achieved in a short space of time. Both take thought, planning, and cooperation to reach worthwhile ends.

SUMMARY

Every early childhood center has its own characteristics that are articulated in its philosophy and goals. A philosophy is a distillation of ideas, beliefs, and values held by an individual, a group, or an organization. There are three areas that are reflected in a philosophy statement: assumptions about how children learn; values held by program planners and parents; and ideas about education and the function of a school.

Although the words *goals* and *objectives* are often used interchangeably, there is a difference. Goal is used to indicate changes that take place over a long period of time; a month or even a year. Objective is used to describe changes that take place during a short period of time; a day, a week, or a month. Goals may be formulated by individuals, a group, or a committee. Begin the process of writing goals by underlining key statements in your philosophy statement. Use these as the basis for a goal that indicates changes in children's behavior as a result of their school experience.

Objectives are used by teachers to plan daily activities for children. Think of objectives as steps or paths that lead to the eventual achievement of goals. Write down the end behavior and then list all the steps that will lead to the goal. These become your objectives.

Once objectives are specified, you can implement them by:
• Organizing the environment in ways that stimulate the expected reaction.
• Giving children ample opportunity to practice.
• Allowing children to feel satisfaction.
• Determine that the child is developmentally able to achieve the objective.
• Provide a choice of experiences.
• Allow children to repeat familiar experiences.

An evaluation process is facilitated when a standard for judging achievement is established. Methods of evaluation include: observation, commercial tests, checklists, parent interviews, time samplings, and collection of end products.

Summarize goal achievement for each child by compiling a profile, a picture of the child's development at a particular time. This can be used for planning individualized instruction for each child.

SUGGESTED FURTHER READING

Bredekamp, S. ed.. 1987. *Developmentally Appropriate Practice in Early Childhood Programs Serving Children from Birth Through Age 8* (ex. ed.). Washington, DC: National Association for the Education of Young Children.

Eisner, E. 1990. "Who Decides What Schools Teach?" *Phi Delta Kappan*, 71 (7) 523–526.

Gordon, A., and Browne, K.W. 1993. *Beginnings and Beyond*, 3rd ed. Albany, NY: Delmar Publishers, Inc.

Kamii, C., ed. 1990. *Achievement Testing in Early Childhood Education: The Games Grown-Ups Play*. Washington, DC: National Association for the Education of Young Children.

National Association for the Education of Young Children. 1988. "Position Statement on Standardized Testing of Young Children 3 Through 8 Years of Age." *Young Children*, 43 (3) 42–47.

National Association for the Education of Young Children. 1991. "Guidelines for Appropriate Curriculum Content and Assessment in Programs Serving Children Ages 3 Through 8." *Young Children*, 46 (3) 21–38.

STUDENT ACTIVITIES

1. Review Example 1 of the philosophy statement for the Child Learning Center. Write three curriculum goals for this school. Remember to state them in terms of what happens to children.
2. Write to, or visit, three different kinds of schools: a corporate school, a privately owned center, a Head Start unit, and a business-sponsored child care center. Ask for a list of their goals and inquire as to how they were formulated. Are there similarities, or are they all different? What accounts for any differences?
3. State one goal for a group of four-year-olds. Write three behavioral objectives that would lead to achievement of that goal.
4. Use one objective to plan five activities that lead to its achievement.
5. Discuss your beliefs regarding parents' roles in setting goals for a school.

REVIEW

1. Define philosophy.
2. How does a goal differ from an objective?
3. Three methods for setting goals were discussed in this chapter. What are they?
4. How many goals are considered a reasonable number?
5. List the six general principles for implementing goals and objectives.
6. What is the most frequently used method of evaluating goal achievement?
7. State the drawbacks of using a commercial test to evaluate children's progress.
8. What kind of information about a child's progress can be obtained from a parent interview?
9. Describe a time sampling.
10. What is a profile? What information should be included?

GLOSSARY

Developmental appropriateness   based on a knowledge of universal sequences of growth and change and of each child's individual pattern and timing.

Goal   expected long-term changes in a child's behavior.

Objective   expected short-term changes in a child's behavior.

Philosophy   a distillation of ideas, beliefs, and values held by an individual, a group, or an organization.

5

Planning: The Preschool

OBJECTIVES

After studying this chapter, the student should be able to:

- Describe the major developmental characteristics of three- and four-year-old children.
- State the components of developmentally appropriate practices in an early childhood program.
- Discuss the use of computers in a preschool.
- Discuss the inclusion of children with special needs in an early childhood program.

As the administrator of an early childhood center, it is your responsibility to help staff provide an optimum setting in which children can develop physically, socially, emotionally, and intellectually. The best preschool programs provide developmentally appropriate experiences for the children they serve. This means, simply, that learning experiences are based on a knowledge of what most children are capable of doing and where their interests lie. Therefore, this chapter gives you a brief overview of the development of children in the preschool years, then some guidelines for planning your curriculum.

Note that when speaking of staff in this chapter and in other chapters in this text, two words are used: "teacher" and "caregiver." "Teacher" has long been understood by nearly everyone to designate a person who teaches or instructs. More recently, with the proliferation of child care settings, "caregiver" has appeared in the vocabularies of early childhood professionals. It is most often used to describe adults who care for infants and toddlers but may also designate an adult in after-school care. The use of this term implies nurturing and concern for the physical well-being of the children. The two terms are sometimes used interchangeably since a teacher also cares for children while a caregiver also teaches children. A teacher should not be seen as more valuable than a caregiver. Each has an important function in furthering children's development.

PRESCHOOL DEVELOPMENT

"Preschool period" designates the years before a child enters elementary school. Some people include children two to five; others term three- to six-year-olds as preschoolers. In the context of this chapter, "preschooler" means three- and four-year-olds. Two-year-olds are discussed in the next chapter on infant/toddler development. Five-year-olds are usually in a prekindergarten or kindergarten program and, therefore, are not included.

Three- and four-year-olds each have their distinct characteristics that must be considered when planning an appropriate program for them. The threes are no longer toddlers, but they often have some of the same characteristics. At other times, they show the motor skills and language abilities that are usually seen in four-year-olds. Similarly, four-year-olds sometimes function at the level of the previous age period. At other times, they display abilities to learn, think, and reason that would be expected of kindergarten children. Preschool teachers and caregivers must understand the continuum from toddlerhood to school age and judge each child's development accordingly. Although the scope of this chapter cannot present a highly defined differentiation between these two age levels, where appropriate, the distinction will be made.

During the preschool years, physical growth slows down. By two, most children have achieved adult body proportions. That is, the percentage of their height apportioned to the head, the torso, and the legs is similar to that of an adult. Two-year-olds look like children rather than round, roly-poly babies. This development continues in the preschool years, but the physical changes are less noticeable because they are slower. If you had not seen a three-year-old for several months, you would probably not detect changes in physical appearance. This slowdown in growth is important because it means children need fewer calories per pound of body weight than they did in the previous years since birth. As a result, their appetites are noticeably smaller.

Along with changes in body height and weight, changes are taking place in the brain. By age five, most children have attained about 90 percent of their full brain weight. As the brain matures, specialization of function takes place. During this period, children must have the opportunity to maximize these functions as well as increase the coordination between functions.

During the preschool period, children have an extremely high activity level. This is a period in which children are mastering their gross motor skills. They recklessly practice running, climbing, jumping, and so on. They test out what they can do and attempt to overcome fears of new activities. It can be a time when the accident rate is high unless preventive measures are taken.

Three- and four-year-olds are perfecting their fine motor skills as well. Threes have great difficulty managing complex tasks such as cutting with scissors or tying their shoelaces. They still tend to use their whole hands and cannot manipulate objects easily with their separate fingers. By age four, most children have mastered scissors, and many can tie their own shoes. Fours can use their fingers to pick up and manipulate small objects.

The difference between the physical development of boys and girls during this period is minimal. Boys may be slightly taller and more muscular. Girls may mature a little more rapidly. Their bone age may be ahead of boys, and they lose their baby teeth sooner. However, these physical differences do not seem to cause differences in abilities. The amount of practice children engage in has a greater impact on differences in abilities.

Children's play changes in the preschool years. During infancy and toddler-hood, play allows children to use all their senses and motor abilities to explore their environment. In the preschool period, children use play to master new skills. Block building provides an opportunity to learn how to control the hands while placing one block on top of another. Riding bicycles outdoors allows children to develop the ability to control their legs and arms.

Although three-year-old boys and girls often play together, by age four there is a decided preference for same-sex playmates and a difference in choice of play activi-ties. Researchers explain this by suggesting that the innate biological differences become more prevalent, causing this disparity. Others suggest that the explanation lies with the impact of how parents and culture shape children's gender identity, and therefore, their play preferences. Whatever the cause, a decided shift to same-sex playmates at age four accompanies a corresponding preference for certain kinds of play activities.

Dramatic play becomes an important part of children's play during this period. In this kind of play, children act out familiar or fantasy scenes. Most children employ standard plots. Three-year-olds typically play out scenes reminiscent of home experiences. There may be a "mommy," a "daddy," and a "baby." The sce-nario includes all the experiences that are part of a child's day at home, from eat-ing to going to bed, from administering punishment to giving rewards. On the other hand, four-year-olds branch out to characters and situations outside the home. They may play out scenes involving favorite TV people or people they see in their neighborhood. They become the current TV "monster" or the neighbor-hood gas station attendant or firefighter.

Through dramatic play, children have an opportunity to test out what it might be like to be the person portrayed. This kind of play also provides them with an opportunity to perfect physical skills as they carry out the tasks assigned to each role. To be included in others' dramatic play, children must develop social skills and learn to cooperate to prolong the play. Finally, dramatic play allows children a chance to work out feelings they may have about their own experiences. Children who give "shots" with glee to other children during "doctor" play are reliving what it felt like to have an injection themselves.

Aggressive acts become more frequent during children's play in the preschool years. Two-year-olds often bite other children. This kind of aggression is not really directed toward the other child but is a way of expressing frustrations. During the preschool period, deliberate aggressive acts begin to appear. Children learn to hit when they are angry or to shove children who are in their way. These should be seen as a healthy sign of assertiveness. Gradually, four-year-olds learn to use language to express their feelings, and then physical acts of aggression tend to lessen.

Children are able to fantasize but may also develop fears during the preschool period. By age three and later, children are able to imagine but may still have difficulty knowing what is real and what is not real. Some children develop elaborate constructions of a fantasy friend who is with them throughout the day. They talk to the friend, include the friend at the dinner table, and blame the friend for any transgressions. Other children develop fears. A typical example is fear of dogs, even though there has never been an unpleasant encounter with one. Some children have nightmares. Each of these developments comes from the ability to think about things that cannot be seen or may not have been experienced directly. Because children's understanding is still limited, some of their thoughts may frighten or overwhelm them. Both a fantasy friend and fears or nightmares, are normal for this age level. With support from adults, most children manage to move beyond this stage.

Figure 5–1   Independence comes in preschool years.

During the preschool years, children are trying to define their self-concept. They begin to understand some of their own characteristics but have unrealistic ideas about others. They develop quite general and usually positive impressions of themselves. But they also have unrealistic ideas about what they are capable of doing. They may think they can build the biggest block building or run faster than anybody. This is vastly different from the elementary school child who will tell you he is "good" in reading, but is "terrible" in math.

Preschoolers are trying to solidify their understanding of gender. At about age three, most children become aware of differences. They are curious about other children's bodies and explore their own. Gradually, they begin to understand "I am a girl" or "I am a boy." But not until close to the age of five do children know gender is irreversible, that they will always be the same. Until that time, they sometimes believe changing clothes or hair styles will also change their gender.

Self-concept in the preschooler also depends on what Erik Erikson called "initiative." Because of higher activity levels, children are eager to initiate new experiences. Children enthusiastically enter into new play activities and try new things. When these efforts end in failure or criticism, children may feel guilt or that they are worthless. A certain amount of guilt is necessary to learn to control impulses and behaviors that interfere with others, but too much paralyzes children's ability to function to their fullest.

As children develop their own sense of self, they also begin to have a greater awareness of others. This enables them to give up some of their strong attachment to their parents and to begin to move out into their wider environment. They begin to see that not everyone has the same needs, thoughts, and feelings that they and their families do. With help, they can learn to accept and appreciate those differences.

Children's thinking changes during the preschool years. The ability to imagine and think symbolically begins to emerge at about age two. Two-year-olds can pretend to play out scenes from their own experiences but require concrete objects to support their play. With a tiny cup in hand, they can feed their doll or Teddy bear. By age three, children can pretend without props or can use any object to represent what they want. If a car is not at hand to add to their block play, they can pretend that a particular block is one. If they do not have an airplane, they use their hand and appropriate sounds to simulate a plane flying over their building.

Their ability to think has some limitations, however. They tend to be egocentric, being able to see things only from their own point of view. They cannot imagine reversing processes. As an example, children may understand that 3 plus 1 is 4 but will not be able to see that 4 minus 1 is 3. This kind of thinking interferes with their ability to think through processes in a logical way.

Language develops rapidly during this preschool period. Some children will learn as many as ten new words a day, usually following a predictable sequence. Nouns seem to be learned most easily by all children. They seem to have some understanding of grammar, but often apply the rules incorrectly. For instance, children learn that adding an "s" makes a noun plural. They may say "foots" until they learn the correct plural form. Similarly, they learn that adding "ed" to words makes them past tense. They will say "he goed" instead of "he went." During this period, many children also try out the power of words. They learn that certain words bring intense responses from adults or other children.

Differences in language skills are often evident during these preschool years. Girls, first-borns, and single-borns, tend to be more proficient in language than boys, later-borns, and twins. Middle-class children often have more advanced communication skills than lower-class children. Family communication patterns also affect children's language skills. Parents who talk to children, listen to their children's communications, and encourage further conversation, produce children with greater ability in language skills.

A good preschool or day care center can foster optimum growth in all areas of children's development. Environment, activities, and adult/child interactions must be based on a firm knowledge of what children are like at this stage of their development. In addition, you must understand the characteristics of a good program, then adapt these ideas to fit the needs of your particular school.

CHARACTERISTICS OF A DEVELOPMENTALLY APPROPRIATE PROGRAM

Grouping Children

Imagine being a child in a classroom full of other children, materials, and strange adults. In addition, imagine a lot of noise, confusion, and people moving around. All, but the most independent child, might be overwhelmed. In order to facilitate each child's adjustment to a group setting, you must keep group sizes manageable. The National Association for the Education of Young Children recommends that a group for three- and four-year-olds be no larger than sixteen, and should be staffed by two adults. When staff members are highly qualified, groups can contain up to twenty children with a teacher/child ratio of 1:10. However, group size and teacher/child ratio are also affected by other factors.

Licensing requirements usually specify the number of children allowed in a particular physical space. The regulations typically state that you must have 35 to 50 square feet per child in indoor space. So the size of the classrooms will tell you how many children can be accommodated there. You can choose to have fewer children but not to exceed that limit.

The *philosophy and goals* of your school may also dictate the number of children you place in each group. Some people believe that children do best when they have the opportunity to develop close, interactive relationships with adults. This requires a small group of children so that teachers or caregivers can develop a close bond with children. Others believe that children do best when they work independently of adults. In this kind of situation, a larger group of children can be managed.

The *needs of children* may dictate the best group size. When a group contains children who have special needs, consideration should be given to limiting the total number of children, and decreasing the teacher/child ratio. Children who have any of the disabilities discussed later in this chapter may require additional time and attention. In some situations, this can best be accomplished in smaller groups.

You must also decide what *ages* of children to put together in each group. The most frequent grouping puts children who are close in age in the same group. This is called peer or chronological grouping. Many directors and teachers feel this configuration allows for better programming. They can plan materials and activities more easily when children are close together in age. An alternate way of grouping children is in "family groups." Here, children may differ in age as much as two or three years. A typical group might have a few two-year-olds, some threes and fours, and possibly even some five-year-olds. Rationale for this kind of group is that children can help each other and learn from each other. Another argument points to the closer resemblance to a family.

Staff qualifications may also determine the size of preschool groups. When staff members are highly qualified and have had experience planning and implementing programs, they can usually manage a larger group. Preprofessionals who are in the process of learning to be qualified teachers should either be under the supervision of experienced teachers, or be assigned to a limited number of children. (Specific staff qualifications are discussed extensively in later chapters.)

Schedule

Your daily schedule should allow alternate periods of quiet and active experiences. There should be a pattern that minimizes the possibility that children will become overstimulated or overtired. If quiet times are interspersed with others that allow children to move around vigorously, children will not become exhausted.

The schedule should provide what is best for the group as well as the needs of individual children. Many children benefit from the stimulation of group activities. Others cannot stay with a group for long periods and should be allowed to leave and go to something else. Some children get engrossed in an activity and deeply resent having to leave to go on to something else. Others want to spend a longer time at a particular activity, and whenever possible, should be allowed to do so.

Balance child-initiated activities with teacher-directed ones. Schedule large blocks of time in which children can choose from a variety of activities or even do nothing if they wish. At other times, offer group learning activities led by the teacher. Children need to develop both the ability to be self-directed as well as function in a teacher-structured situation.

The schedule of a day should provide for both indoor and outdoor play. Some schools have an open indoor/outdoor program in which children can move freely from one to the other. This requires an adequate number of staff to supervise, and a mild climate. Other schools set times when all children in a group move outdoors and then back inside again. This is the more usual approach since it allows more than one group of children to use the outdoor space. In areas where winter weather prevents children from being outside, plan plenty of opportunities for them to engage in active play. Indoor climbing equipment, active games, or music activities can substitute for outdoor play.

FYI

In late 1989, President Bush and the nation's governors established six educational goals to guide the nation's schools. Goal one states that by the year 2000, all children will start school ready to learn. Three objectives are included in the goal:
1. *All disadvantaged and disabled children will be able to participate in high-quality, and developmentally appropriate programs.*
2. *Every parent will have access to the training and support they need to help their preschool children improve learning skills.*
3. *All children will receive adequate health and nutrition care in order to arrive at school ready to learn.*

Prepared Environment

Only a brief note about the environment is appropriate here, since Chapter 14 covers planning preschool space. A good program begins with a well-planned environment. Both indoor and outdoor space should invite children to participate in the activities available. Offer a variety of choices from which children can select those that fit their own needs or interests. Set up materials so that a minimum of adult help and supervision is required. Children should be able to explore freely. In general, the environment must help children to feel successful and competent.

Goals

Goals provide the framework for designing a developmentally appropriate preschool program. In its publication *Accreditation Criteria & Procedures*, NAEYC recommends that staff provide activities and materials that help children to achieve the following goals:

- Foster positive self-concept.
- Develop social skills.
- Encourage children to think, reason, question, and experiment.
- Encourage language development.
- Enhance physical development and skills.
- Encourage and demonstrate sound health, safety, and nutritional practices.
- Encourage creative expression and appreciation for the arts.
- Respect cultural diversity.

Assessment

A program for three- and four-year-olds should be realistic, that is, based on an assessment of what children are capable of doing. The most frequently used assessment tool is observation. Watch the children to find out what they can do. You can also use simple tests to evaluate children's abilities. Games that require physical agility can become tests for those abilities. Checklists are an easy way to assess other abilities. In addition, find out individual or group interests. Listen to the questions children ask or what they talk about. These will give you clues to their interests.

Once you know children's capabilities and interests, you can design developmentally appropriate learning experiences. Materials and learning activities should fit the age of the children. Some should be easy for most of the children so they will have a feeling of competence. Include, as well, some experiences that will challenge children to move to a new level of functioning.

Plan activities that fit the needs and interests of the gender makeup of the group. As indicated in the overview of development at the beginning of this chapter, a group of three-year-olds seldom divides along gender lines. But by age four, children show decided sex preferences in playmates and play activities. You should provide for those differences and encourage children to cross strict gender lines in their play.

Variety

Provide a wide variety of materials and activities so children can select their own experiences. This fosters the development of initiative and also allows children to choose what is best for them. Some classrooms have a selection of materials available on shelves at all times. There may be puzzles, manipulatives, art materials, construction kits, and block accessories. Children are free to take down what they want, use it, and then replace it before moving on to another area. In other classrooms, teachers select a variety of materials to put out each day and allow children to move from one to the other. The first method allows children a wider choice, but requires a lot of storage space for the materials. Another drawback is that occasionally teachers fail to change or add to the selection, and the children become bored. The second method allows children a smaller number of choices each day, but may offer more choices in the long run.

Cognitive Development

The preschool program should be designed to foster children's cognitive development through the use of *concrete materials* that children can touch, taste, smell, hear, and see. There should be blocks, cars, trucks, and planes for building. Include dolls, dishes, and dressup clothes for dramatic play. Add puzzles, Legos™, and other small manipulative materials. Provide real tools for real tasks such as cooking. Children can manage knives for cutting food and blenders or frying pans for preparing food. All materials should be relevant to the children's own lives, things they either know about or have previously experienced. In this way, each new experience builds on the base of previous experiences.

Materials and activities should *foster children's self-confidence and independence*. One typical way in which this is accomplished is through learning centers. In specific areas of the room, teachers set up materials that children can explore either with a few friends or by themselves. The activity must be designed so children can participate with a minimum of help and supervision from adults. The best learning centers are set up so that children can immediately see what might be done there and can proceed entirely on their own.

Cognitive activities should *encourage children to think, question, and experiment.* Open-ended activities that have more than one answer do this. An example is a collection of spoons for children to categorize. Include in the collection small and large spoons; silver, plastic, and wooden ones; and soup ladles, stirring spoons, and teaspoons. Children can categorize this collection according to size, material used to make the spoon, and use for the spoon. There may even be additional categories such as color, kind of decorations on the spoons, and slotted or unslotted.

Cognitive activities should *encourage children's language skills.* Children should be able to add new words to their vocabularies through their play activities. They should have many opportunities to practice language to explain what they have learned, to ask questions, or to solve problems. Gradually, the development of language skills may include the ability to recognize some written words. Children learn to recognize their own names during the preschool period, some as early as age three. A few children learn to read other words during this period.

Cognitive activities should *emphasize the development of physical skills.* There should be ample opportunities to enhance both large- and small-muscle development. Scissors, paint brushes, collage materials, and puzzles are some examples of materials that require small-muscle coordination. Music and movement activities

Figure 5–2 Work is play for children.

Figure 5–2 (*continued*)   Work is play for children.

and outdoor play encourage children to use their large muscles. Both are necessary for the development of preschool children.

Creativity

The preschool program should provide children opportunities to be *creative*. Although there may be many perceptions of what creativity is, in the context of this chapter it means a unique way of reacting to a situation, not just imitating what others have done. Unique ways of reacting call for behaviors that include intuition, originality, divergent thinking, and flexibility.

Opportunities for creativity can be provided in many of the activities of the preschool. The one that is thought of first is art. Provide materials that children can use to do whatever they want. Patterns and prepared models stifle creativity. Have on hand selections of paint, paper, brushes, collage materials, scissors, marking pens, and so on. From these tools, children can use their imaginations to produce whatever they want.

Creativity can be fostered in the dramatic play area of a classroom. The kind and variety of props that are available to the children will dictate the subject for their play activities. So offer a selection of clothes, jewelry, hats, shoes, brushes, combs, hair curlers, razors (without blades), etc. Anything children may have in their own homes will encourage play in this area.

Figure 5–3   Building takes practice.

Diversity

Early childhood professionals stress the importance of including *concepts concerning diversity* in the early childhood curriculum. Two terms are used to describe these ideas. *Multiculturalism* is the most widely used, and its focus is on introducing children to the similarities and differences among different cultures and ethnic groups. The goal of a multicultural program is to provide opportunities for children to develop a positive self-concept, including an acceptance of their own differences, and the differences of others. *Anti-bias* is the term used to describe a broader approach that includes not only cultural aspects, but also gender and physical ability differences. Those using this approach stress the importance of freeing children from gender stereotyping, and preventing the development of biased attitudes toward persons who are differently abled. The additional goal of an anti-bias curriculum is to encourage children to develop critical thinking skills that will enable them to counteract injustices that are directed toward themselves or others.

Whichever approach you choose, all activities should be part of an integrated curriculum, not just added onto the existing curriculum. Too often, an attempt to introduce diversity into an early childhood program becomes what Louise Derman-Sparks writing in *Anti-Bias Curriculum* labels the "tourist" curriculum.

Figure 5–3 (*continued*)   Building takes practice.

Cultural concepts are introduced through holiday celebrations such as Chinese New Year, or Cinco de Mayo. When this is done, children learn only about the more exotic aspects of a culture. She recommends that children learn about the everyday aspects of life in other countries. She also suggests that children should "be free to ask questions about any subject, to engage in real dialogue with adults, to make choices, and to have some say in their daily school life. If we are to facilitate children's sense of self-esteem, critical thinking, and ability to 'stand up' for themselves, then our methodology must allow them to experience their intelligence and power as having a constructive effect on their world."

Some materials you can use to create a diverse environment are:

- Images of people of different color; women and men doing work in the home or outside the home, elderly people, differently abled people, different family configurations.
- Books that show a diversity of gender roles, people from different cultures or backgrounds doing ordinary tasks, various families.
- Dramatic play materials that reflect a variety of gender roles, including every day objects used in different cultures, tools and equipment used by people with special needs (crutches, canes, etc.).

- Art materials that include a wide variety of skin-tone colors, papers and fabrics that suggest different cultures, paintings or sculptures done by artists from different backgrounds.
- Records that reflect various cultures, opportunities for children to sing or dance to ethnic music.
- Dolls that represent ethnic groups, both male and female dolls, dolls that reflect different kinds of disabilities.

Figure 5–4   Friendship develops early.

Staff

Staff interactions with children should convey warmth and acceptance of each child's worth and uniqueness. Teachers and caregivers do this by touching and holding children and by speaking to them at eye level. This is especially important at the beginning of a day when children may be feeling anxious about separation from their parents. A warm good-bye at the end of the day will also help to bridge the gap to the following day.

Staff should use positive methods of guiding or changing children's behavior. These techniques might include redirection or positive reinforcement. Anticipating problems and suggesting alternative behaviors are more effective than trying to stop unacceptable behaviors. Encouraging children rather than fostering competition also works well. Consistent, clear rules that are explained and then gently enforced help children develop inner control.

Staff interactions with children should foster the development of self-esteem. Certain behaviors in children such as messiness, crying, resistance, and aggression are part of normal development. Adults should accept these behaviors as indications of the child's developmental stage while guiding them to more acceptable behaviors. Adults must never respond to children in ways that will destroy or decrease their self-esteem. This includes yelling in anger, blaming, teasing, accusing, insulting, threatening, or humiliating children.

Staff should encourage children to be as independent as they are capable of being at each stage of their development. Three-year-olds can work with an adult to put away some of their toys and to wipe up spills at snack time. A reminder will encourage them to care for their personal belongings and wash their hands after toileting. Four-year-olds will probably be able to do some of these tasks without reminders and adult help. Fours take pride in getting out their own materials and in putting them away at the end of a play period. They can participate in preparing snacks, serving them, and then cleaning up afterward. Four-year-olds are pretty independent in caring for their own personal needs. They can manage their clothes in the bathroom and put on their own jackets.

Staff should be responsive to children, ready to listen as children communicate their ideas, thoughts, and feelings. They should encourage children to share their experiences. All adults should allow children to put their feelings into words, to talk about things that make them angry or frightened. Each communication from children to adults should be treated with respect. Children's thoughts and feelings should not be belittled or passed off as unimportant. In this way, children learn to understand themselves better and to accept their own feelings.

Parents

Children learn more effectively when parents participate in the school. A good preschool program includes parents whenever possible. Parent involvement begins with an orientation process in which parents learn about the goals of the school and its operating procedures. Schedule preenrollment visits of parents and children. Ask parents to stay with their child during the first few days of school. Involve parents in plans for bringing about separation from their child.

Once separation has taken place, keep parents informed about their child's progress. Frequent informal reports as well as parent conferences let parents know what is happening at school. Daily written communications are an established procedure in many schools. Newsletters, telephone calls, and bulletin boards also keep parents informed.

Encourage parents to visit whenever possible. In some situations, parents can have lunch with their child or visit briefly at the beginning of naptime. At other times, some parents can volunteer time in the classroom. If parents cannot be involved because of working hours, encourage other family members to be a part of the school activities. Grandparents or older siblings may stand in for parents.

Figure 5–5 Making peanut butter is hard work.

Peer Relationships

A good preschool should foster the development of friendships between children. The group makeup should allow most children to find someone on their own level with whom they can talk and play. This usually means having a mix of ages, gender, and abilities. A group of fourteen boys and one girl will not work as well as one in which gender is more evenly distributed. A group of fifteen three-year-olds may not offer a counterpart for a capable four-year-old.

Design activities to encourage social interactions among children. When some learning centers are set up, they should accommodate more than one child working there at a time. Double-sided easels allow two children to work in close proximity, possibly encouraging interaction. Activities that are set out on tables should accommodate several children at a time so that they can talk about what they are doing.

Staff interactions with children should foster relationships and cooperation. Children should be encouraged to play together and to talk to each other. They should be allowed to work out their own problems whenever possible without undue adult interference. When adults do step in, it should be to help children find their own solutions.

OTHER CONSIDERATIONS

When planning an early childhood education program, you will want to keep in mind two other considerations. One is the *addition of computers* to the classroom materials. Today's generation of children will probably need skills to manage many kinds of technology when they become working adults. Therefore, perhaps it is appropriate to begin children's education early. The second consideration is how best to *incorporate children with special needs* into the regular activities of an early childhood environment. The answers are not easy to find, and cannot be thoroughly explored within the scope of this text. A brief discussion follows, but you and your staff will need to do additional research, reading, and discuss theories before making program decisions.

Computers

The use of computers in early childhood classrooms is still the topic of a great deal of controversy. Many professionals question the appropriateness of including computer activities in the early childhood curriculum. They point to the belief that children learn best by hands-on experiences with concrete objects. They ask, "if children learn best what a square is by handling a square object, can they really learn the same concept by drawing one on a computer screen?" The answer that seems to be emerging from research is that it depends on the type of software programs that are used. Open-ended programs do help children to make significant gains in several areas: intelligence, nonverbal skills, structural knowledge, long-term memory, complex manual dexterity, and self-esteem (Haugland, 1992).

There are some specific areas in which computers are particularly effective. When preschool children have plenty of time to practice, computers can aid them in increasing prereading or reading skills. This requires the use of an easy-to-use word processor program, not just sight-reading practice programs. In order to integrate computer work into a whole-language approach, children should be encouraged to work together to plan stories, revise them as needed, discuss how the story is presented, and consider the spelling of words before using the spell-checker. Children can take risks when putting their thoughts into words because the text can be so easily revised on the computer.

Open-ended programs such as LOGO™ can also increase children's problem-solving skills. Research studies show that preschool and primary-grade children can use LOGO to perform some higher-level thinking tasks (Nastasi, Clements, & Battista, 1990). They learn to understand problems and find ways to resolve them by questioning and experimenting.

Computers can be an important tool for children with disabilities. Word processing programs can increase the motivation and writing ability of children with learning disabilities. Minor alterations to input equipment can allow children with limited mobility to experiment with LOGO's problem-solving activities. Voice synthesizers make computers accessible to children with limited visual ability. Probably most important, however, is that these children gain in self-esteem as they learn to control the computer.

Children with Special Needs

With the passage of P.L. 101-476, the Individuals With Disabilities Education Amendment of 1990, the question for early childhood administrators is no longer one of accepting, or not accepting, children with special needs. The question now is "How can we best meet the needs of these children in our program?" The law requires that an individual education plan (IEP) be prepared for each child. In most cases, a multidimensional assessment is done by a team made up of physicians, psychologists, teachers, child care workers, parents or guardians, and the child. This should provide information needed to develop a comprehensive intervention plan. There are also some general guidelines you can use to help these children.

ATTENTION DEFICIT DISORDER

Description. A condition characterized by an inability to sustain attention, lack of perseverance, impulsivity, inability to suppress inappropriate behavior, over activity, and excessive talking.

Teaching Methods. These children do best in a loosely structured environment in which they can be actively involved. It is also important to provide materials and activities that are developmentally appropriate. Behavioral treatment should include giving rewards for appropriate behavior, providing brief and specific directions, and being consistent in methods of discipline used.

DEVELOPMENTAL DELAY

Description. Levels of delay are often determined by testing, but teachers should use their own observational abilities to further assess children's abilities. Look at motor, language, and social abilities. Notice how much help is required from adults or how much the children can do themselves. Note attention span and comprehension of concepts.

Teaching Methods. Low staff/child ratios will provide maximum individualized attention that will be needed. Break tasks down into small components and allow for many repetitions. Use a lot of positive reinforcement. Be consistent in routines and presentation of experiences.

PHYSICAL IMPAIRMENTS

Description. Physical impairment may range from poor coordination to severe limitations of mobility. Some children show difficulty when attempting tasks that require fine motor skills and become easily frustrated. Other children have trouble climbing, riding bikes, or doing other large muscle activities.

Teaching Methods. Provide easy access ramps in all areas of the physical environment. Provide a wide variety of activities requiring physical skills and encourage children to participate. Investigate innovative materials that will enhance physical skills. Offer positive reinforcement for successes.

HEARING IMPAIRMENTS

Description. Limited communication is a frequently seen result of hearing impairment. In addition, these children often do not understand or respond when others talk to them. They may be inattentive at group times.

Teaching Methods. Face hearing-impaired children when talking to them and articulate clearly. In group times, seat these children close to the adult. Talk to these children to provide language stimulation and use tapes for additional listening opportunities.

SPEECH AND LANGUAGE IMPAIRMENTS

Description. Many children exhibit articulation problems as they develop language. Some children continue to have difficulties beyond the expected period of time. They may omit, substitute, and distort sounds of words and letters. Other children exhibit language problems by using gestures or only single words when you might expect them to use sentences.

Teaching Methods. Teachers and caregivers can assist children in developing language by using simple phrases or short sentences. In addition, daily activities that include singing, talking, and word games provide help. Listening activities such as stories read by the adult or on a tape allow children to hear the use of correct language. Above all, adults should listen and respond to children's attempts at communcation.

EMOTIONAL OR BEHAVIORAL PROBLEMS

Description. In preschools, teachers often see either overly aggressive children, or those who are extremely passive. The overly aggressive children are competitive, hostile, defiant of authority, and combative. They are easily distracted and often disrupt classroom activities. Passive children are often forgotten in a classroom, for they are withdrawn, afraid, seldom talk to others, and frequently do not even look at other people.

Teaching Methods. Both passive and aggressive children may benefit from an atmosphere in which they can receive individualized attention. Both need help in verbalizing their feelings. Most important to these children's development is consistency in routines, in what is expected of them, and in how adults respond to their behaviors.

VISUAL IMPAIRMENT

Description. Children who have been diagnosed as having visual impairment may be categorized as either partially sighted or blind. Children who have visual problems may be observed rubbing their eyes, squinting, and blinking. They may also hold objects far away or too close. Their heads may tilt when they try to focus. A few will complain of headaches or dizziness.

Teaching Methods. Provide a variety of materials and activities that require the use of other senses. Foster children's independent movement in the classroom by orienting them to where things are, and then keeping the arrangement constant. Sometimes other children can be encouraged to help by offering guidance when needed, and by stimulating social interactions.

Providing a quality, developmentally appropriate program for the children you serve is one of your most important tasks. Not only will it benefit the children by allowing for maximum development, but also makes good business sense. Your school will build a reputation for "being a good place for children and their families." You may not have parents "pounding on your door to enroll their children," but it should make it easier to fill your classes. Probably an added bonus is that your staff members will take pride in their jobs. That should lessen staff turnover. All of these advantages will certainly be worth the time and effort it will take to work with staff to create a good program.

SUMMARY

The best early childhood centers provide developmentally appropriate experiences that are based on a knowledge of the capabilities and interests of most children. In order to do this, staff members must understand the characteristics of children during the preschool years.

Growth slows down, changing the size and shape of children's bodies. Along with changes in body height and weight, changes are also taking place in the brain. By age five, most children have attained about 90 percent of their full brain weight. During the preschool period, children have a high-activity level as they practice both large- and small-muscle skills. There is little difference between the physical development of boys and girls during the period before school, although boys may be more muscular, and the bone age of girls may be slightly advanced. Their physical abilities are similar.

Play changes as children use playtimes to master new skills. Three-year-old boys and girls often play together, but by age four, there is a decided shift to same-sex playmates. Dramatic play content imitates home situations or is based on children's fantasies. Aggressive acts become more frequent during play, but gradually, children learn to use words to resolve conflicts. The ability to fantasize increases; however, this may lead to an increase in fears. With support from adults, most children manage to master their fears.

During the preschool period, children try to define their self-concept. At first, their perception of themselves is unrealistic, but as they near school age, they are able to assess themselves more realistically.

There are changes in the way children think, and they begin to demonstrate ability to think symbolically. They still remain egocentric, however, and are able to see things only from their own points of view. Language develops rapidly during this period.

A developmentally appropriate program for preschool children should include some specific practices:

- Group size should be limited to no more than twenty children, with two qualified teachers.
- The daily schedule should allow alternate periods of quiet and active experiences.
- The environment should be planned carefully so that children want to participate in the available activities.
- Goals should be used to provide activities and materials that help children reach their optimum development.
- Assessment of three- and four-year-old children should be realistic.
- There should be a wide variety of materials and activities so children can select their own experiences.
- The program should be designed to foster children's cognitive development.
- There should be opportunities for children to be creative.
- The program should be multicultural and anti-bias.
- Activities should encourage social interactions among children, and foster the development of friendships.
- Staff interactions with children should convey warmth and acceptance of each child's worth, and include positive methods of guiding behavior.
- Parent involvement should be an integral part of the children's experience.

Program planners should also consider the inclusion of computers in the early childhood classroom. Recent research points to the effectiveness of open-ended software programs to help children develop cognitive skills.

Early childhood professionals must also gain more knowledge about the characteristics of children with special needs, and how to incorporate them into the preschool environment.

SELECTED FURTHER READING

Charlesworth, R. 1992. *Understanding Child Development,* 3rd ed. Albany, NY: Delmar Publishers, Inc.

Davidson, J. 1989. *Children & Computers Together in the Early Childhood Classroom.* Albany, NY: Delmar Publishers, Inc.

Derman-Sparks, L. 1989. *Anti-Bias Curriculum Tools for Empowering Young Children.* Washington, DC: National Association for the Education of Young Children.

National Association for the Education of Young Children, 1991. *Facility Design for Early Childhood Programs*. Washington, DC.

Haugland, S.W. 1992. "The Effect of Computer Software on Preschool Children's Developmental Gains." *Journal of Computing in Childhood Education*, 3 (1) 15–30.

Holder-Brown, L., and Parette, Jr., H. 1992. "Children with Disabilities Who Use Assistive Technology: Ethical Considerations." *Young Children,* 47 (6) 73–77.

Morris, L.R., and Schulz, L. 1989. *Creative Play Activities for Children with Disabilities,* 2nd ed. Champaign, IL: Human Kinetics Books.

Neugebauer, B., ed. 1992. *Alike and Different: Exploring Our Humanity with Young Children*. Washington, DC: National Association for the Education of Young Children.

Saracho, O., and Spodek, B., eds. 1983. *Understanding the Multicultural Experience in Early Childhood Education*. Washington, DC: National Association for the Education of Young Children.

"Research into Action: The Effects of Group Size, Ratios, and Staff Training on Child Care Quality." 1993. *Young Children,* 48 (2) 65–67.

STUDENT ACTIVITIES

1. Write three goals for the physical development of a three-year-old group.
2. Visit a preschool. Observe a play area for at least a half-hour. Observe the activities of two boys and two girls. Guess their ages as either three or four and write down what they do. Try to find a common thread of behavior. Confirm their ages with the teacher.
3. Collect a number of lesson plans. Analyze each to find whether they agree with the developmental level of the children for whom they were written.
4. If possible, watch a child use the computer program LOGO. What skills are being taught? Is there any cognitive gain? Compare LOGO to a typical computer game. Which is better? Why?

REVIEW

1. What is meant by the term "developmentally appropriate practice?"
2. Unless preventive measures are taken, the accident rate among preschool children can be high. Why?
3. In what ways does children's play change during the period between three and five years?
4. At what age do most children become aware of gender differences?
5. As children develop language skills, they sometimes apply the rules of grammar incorrectly. Indicate how children might configure the following:
   a. change *go* to the past tense
   b. make *goose* plural

6. What is the maximum group size recommended by the National Association for the Education of Young Children?
7. NAEYC recommends that staff provide materials and activities that help children achieve some specific goals. List the goals.
8. List some strategies schools can use to involve parents.
9. Justify the use of computers in an early childhood classroom.
10. What are the significant characteristics of a child with attention deficit disorder?

GLOSSARY

Anti-bias curriculum   an approach to planning curriculum that includes not only cultural aspects, but also gender and physical ability differences.

Concrete materials   objects that children can touch, taste, smell, hear, and see.

Creativity   a unique way of reacting to a situation, not just imitating what others have done.

Egocentric   children's inability to see things from more than one point of view.

Multicultural   a curriculum that introduces children to the similarities and differences among different cultures and ethnic groups.

Preschool period   the years before a child enters elementary school, either from two to five years, or three to six years.

Self-concept   children's understanding of their own characteristics.

6

Planning: Infants and Toddlers

OBJECTIVES

After studying this chapter, the student should be able to:
- Describe the more important steps in human development occurring between birth and two years.
- Describe a developmentally appropriate program for infants and toddlers.
- State the characteristics of a caregiver for infants and toddlers.

An increasing number of infants and toddlers are placed in child care while their parents work to support the family. In addition, more single women and teenagers are having babies. The growing need for places to care for all young children is acute and the supply is limited. Even more scarce are quality programs that are designed specifically to meet the needs of infants and toddlers and are not just adaptations of preschool practices. In order to plan the best infant/toddler addition to your school, you must have an understanding of the characteristics of children under the age of two. This chapter will present an overview of developmental stages, then discuss appropriate programs.

INFANT/TODDLER DEVELOPMENT

Most children go through universal patterns of development in a predictable way. Children crawl before they walk and understand some words long before they speak a single one. So if you know the pattern, you will know what a child will probably be doing at some future time.

That does not mean that all children are going to follow an exact pattern. They do not. So along with understanding the universal characteristics, you must be aware of each child's uniqueness. Children have their own timing of growth so they go through the stages at different rates. They have different ways of approaching new experiences and different ways of interacting with others. Each may have special needs that have to be addressed when planning a program.

The period between birth and age two is a time of startling change, probably more rapid than in any other stage of children's development. During these two short years, they reach half their adult height and move from a state of helplessness to being able to walk around freely. Once totally dependent on others for all their care, they learn to do things for themselves. They start to communicate their needs, thoughts, and feelings. Through exploration, they develop an understanding of the world around them. The following overview of developmental characteristics will help to remind you of these changes.

Children under the age of two learn by experiencing their environment with all their senses. They taste, touch, look at, listen to, and smell whatever they contact. Piaget called this stage the sensorimotor period. Even infants, who cannot move around, use their senses to absorb the world around them. They can stare at objects for long periods of time, attend to an adult's voice, and even wave their

Figure 6–1   Infants explore the world through their senses.

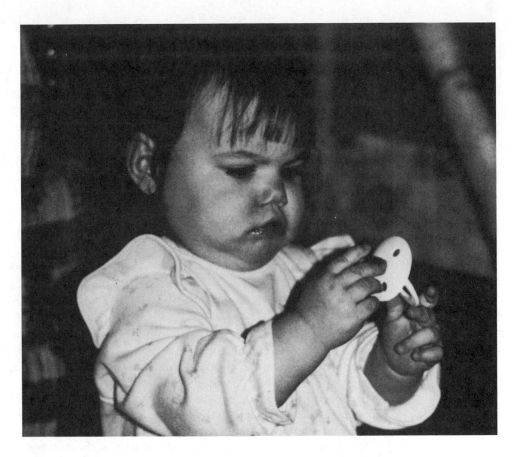

Figure 6–1 (*continued*)   Infants explore the world through their senses.

arms to touch things within their reach. As they begin to crawl—somewhere between five and twelve months—their explorations become broader.

Mobile toddlers continue their active exploration of their environment using their senses, but a new dimension is added. They can also think symbolically. They are able to combine their sensory experiences and come to new conclusions about what they have learned. They remember some past events, can imitate previous experiences, and even think ahead to what will happen next. In this way, they begin to accumulate and organize information about their world.

Motor skills develop quickly and in an orderly sequence. In the first few months, babies are able to lift their heads, then roll over. Gradually they can sit, then crawl. Most children take their first steps at about age one and can walk and run well by age two. Their ability to use their arms, fingers, and hands progresses through several steps as well. At first, movement of their arms is random, then can be controlled to touch an object. When they first grasp something, they do it awkwardly, for they use their whole hand. Later, they can use their fingers to manipulate or pick up small objects.

Infants are learning to trust themselves and others. Erik Erikson called this stage in an infant's development *trust versus mistrust*. Erikson observed that through repeated experiences babies learn that adults will be there when needed and that they will provide food, warmth, and comfort. This results in a feeling of trust in the world outside themselves. When adults are not always available, or do not respond consistently to infants' needs, babies develop a sense of mistrust. They perceive others to be unreliable and cannot be depended on to provide their needs.

Along with developing trust in others, babies develop a secure sense of self. "If my needs are met fairly often, then I must be a worthy person." This is the beginning of later self-confidence and a positive self-image. As they move into the toddler stage, a secure sense of self allows them to act independently at times, but seek comfort from adults when they are tired or frightened.

Infants and toddlers are developing strong attachments to others. It was once thought that babies could develop this kind of relationship only with the mother. More recent research shows that babies are capable of forming strong attachments to several people. However, the strongest attachments are to the parents. Attachment is a vital part of children's development. It provides them a safe haven from which to go out and explore their environment. Those with the strongest attachments to parents or caregivers are the most comfortable in moving away from their caregiver, while still returning at intervals for reassurance.

At around nine months, many infants express some anxiety over separation from their parents. They cry and cling when they are left with the caregiver. During the next year or so, one of the primary tasks is to find ways to manage separation anxiety. Reaction to separation is not always consistent. Sometimes infants or toddlers separate easily from their parents. A few weeks or a month later, they may cry or cling desperately when left. Eventually, by about age three, most children are able to manage separation more easily.

Along with this separation from others comes an awakening awareness of themselves. They realize they are not a part of others, but separate with certain skills and capabilities of their own. They learn the power that comes from being able to get others to respond to them. They gradually find out they can do things on their own. All these things combined form their sense of self. This begins a lifelong process of developing and refining an identity.

Competence and independence are acquired during the first two years. As children's ability to control their bodies increases, they have a growing sense of mastery. The more they can do, the more competent they feel. Typically, toddlers go through a time of "I can do it myself." This is their way of saying they want to be capable and to be less dependent on others for help. They often get so engrossed in perfecting their skills that they resent any attempts to direct their energies elsewhere.

Part of the striving toward independence involves learning to control their body eliminations. During the second year, toddlers become more aware of what is happening to their bodies; they begin anticipating the need to urinate or defecate. Soon, they are able to control their sphincter muscles long enough to get to the toilet. When they are able to do this, they usually have a tremendous feeling of power.

Language begins to appear during the second year and develops rapidly. Infants can communicate by crying or fussing. Parents and caregivers learn to interpret the cries, though some adults are more adept at this than others. But the ability to tell others exactly what is needed does not develop until the second year. With the advent of words, children can begin to say what they mean. At the same time, they find that words have tremendous power; they love to test out their effect on others. An example of this is a toddler's frequent use of "No." With that one word, they can often control what happens to them, and sometimes, control what others do.

Infants and toddlers are learning how to get along with other children. Put two babies on the floor together, and they will look at each other intently. When they are mobile, they may move toward each other, then investigate with pokes and pats. It takes a long while for them to learn that the other "object" is another person who has feelings or may react. As they near the age of two, they begin to play together for brief periods of time. Still, the ability to share and play cooperatively will not be fully developed for another year or so.

CHARACTERISTICS OF A DEVELOPMENTALLY APPROPRIATE INFANT/TODDLER PROGRAM

Goals

A developmentally appropriate infant/toddler program is based on knowledge of the physical, emotional, social, and cognitive abilities of the children served. Program planners use this knowledge to develop goals that form the basis for planning for this age level. Goals are guidelines for choosing activities that allow children to explore their environment freely and use all of their senses to absorb information. Goals imply the kinds of caregiver/child interactions that promote trust and attachment. Goals should also address the development of language and opportunities to learn to interact well with others. Guidelines for developing goals were discussed in Chapter 4. Some additional considerations that must be kept in mind when writing goals for an infant/toddler program follow:

> Do the goals reflect current research on development at this age level? New information is being disseminated each year as more is learned about the earliest years.
>
> Are the goals developmentally appropriate for this age level? Often, goals for infants and toddlers are a diluted version of preschool goals and may not be appropriate.
>
> Do the goals take into account the unique ways that infants and toddlers learn? Goals should allow children to explore using all their senses while developing their gross and fine motor skills.

Interactions with Caregivers

A developmentally appropriate program for infants and toddlers should allow for maximum interactions between children and caregivers. During the early months of life, children are learning about themselves and others. They learn through their interactions with the people who care for them. To allow time for this kind of interaction, keep the teacher/child ratio low. The typical number is four children to one adult. Three children, or even two to one, is a better ratio. This level of staffing will add to the expense of your infant/toddler program, but it will ensure quality care.

It also helps to assign primary responsibility for two or three children to each caregiver. That person is the first to care for those children's needs. When the primary caregiver is occupied with feeding or diapering one child, other adults can share responsibility for the remaining members of the group. The pace of each day should be slow and based on the children's requirements, not the adults'. There should be time to hold babies and get to know each infant's way of expressing distress. A leisurely, flexible schedule will allow infants to explore their environment at their own pace. In addition, there should be time for babies to adjust slowly to new situations and gradually learn to anticipate the next step.

The way caregivers respond to infants is important. Sometimes the word "synchrony" is used to describe the coordination between infants and their parents or caregivers. It means simply a back-and-forth interaction that is responsive to the baby's needs. The baby coos; the adult responds. The adult tickles the baby; the baby laughs. The baby turns away; the adult waits quietly for a return of interest before responding again. From these kinds of play, babies learn about relationships, how to sustain them, or when to withdraw if they become overwhelming. They also learn how they can get a response from others when they wish, and how to respond themselves.

Toddlers develop feelings of competence and independence as their interactions with caregivers change. They move away from their caregivers at times to explore their environment, although they may return at intervals for comfort or encouragement. They test their new abilities by attempting tasks on their own, sometimes even angrily rejecting adult help. Frequently heard words during this period are

"No" and "Do it myself." However, they also want the security of knowing that adults will "set limits" when their behavior overwhelms them or becomes dangerous.

Routines

A large portion of caregivers' time will be spent on routines: changing diapers, washing, dressing, and feeding. Each of these should be perceived as an integral part of the curriculum, as they are just as important to infants and toddlers as examining a toy, building with blocks, or looking at a book. When caregivers give their undivided attention to children during routine functions, they are satisfying babies' needs for security, attention, and closeness. When adults talk to infants during diapering about what is happening, or what might happen next, they are teaching concepts of present and future. When caregivers quietly wait while one-year-old toddlers struggle to get food into their mouths, they are teaching the children to do things for themselves.

Sometimes caregivers' needs interfere with understanding babies' needs. While concentrating on their own needs for a response, caregivers may not recognize that babies sometimes are getting too much stimulation. At other times, caregivers want freedom from the demands of the children in their care and again, fail to recognize what the demands mean. A typical example is feeding a fussy baby because it is fretting, while what the baby really needs is some comforting. It helps if caregivers take time to listen, to look, and to try to feel what babies are communicating. This sets up a two-way communication pattern.

Routines can be used by caregivers to judge children's development. For instance, resistance to diapering or to using the toilet may be a sign of growth, a push toward independence. Children's ability to anticipate and cooperate in a routine can show the development of a cognitive ability. When children can anticipate the next step, they are beginning a long process that eventually leads to logical thinking.

Parent Involvement

Most parents are anxious about placing their infant in child care. Some experience overwhelming feelings of guilt while others are afraid their babies will no longer be as strongly attached to them. They also worry that others will not be as responsive to their babies' needs as they are. They frequently experience strong separation anxieties.

Parents are sometimes faced with other disturbing feelings. If their babies seem to get along well in day care and don't fuss much when they are left, parents feel left out. If, on the other hand, the babies cry when left, parents feel just as terrible. In either situation, there is a possibility for jealousy and competition with the caregiver. If left unrecognized, these may turn into complaints and dissatisfactions.

Many of these problems can be prevented or alleviated when parents and caregivers work together. Good parent/caregiver relationships are based initially on an understanding of the importance of each in the child's life. Then both must work together in a spirit of cooperation for the optimal development of the children.

This happens when:
- Caregivers recognize that parents are the most important people in children's lives.
- Child care staff create an open environment in which parents feel welcome and included.
- Procedures are established for frequent communications between parents and caregivers through daily conversations or notes, telephone calls, conferences, or meetings.
- Parents and staff members discuss and mutually determine ways to manage major changes in children's development, such as toilet training, weaning, and sleeping patterns.

Attachment and Separation

A good infant/toddler program should foster the development of attachment to caregivers and the resolution of separation problems. Developing attachment and managing separation are primary tasks of children during the first three years. Attachment develops when caregivers are consistent and predictable. This means that infants should have one or two caregivers who are there every day. These adults help to develop feelings of trust by responding in ways that meet the babies' needs. In return, babies learn to seek out their caregivers, to respond in ways that evoke further response from the adult. What results is a mutually satisfying relationship between infants and caregivers.

It is difficult for parents, and sometimes for caregivers, to realize that children who are expressing separation distress are behaving quite normally. Teachers and caregivers sometimes feel this kind of behavior indicates poor parenting skills. Instead of condemning the behavior, help parents manage separations more easily.

Some procedures that facilitate both parent and child adjustment are:
- Discuss the separation process with parents before the child enters the program.
- Greet parent and child upon arrival.
- Encourage parent to stay all or part of the first day, then part of the next few days.
- Allow child to have a favorite object: Teddy bear, blanket, or Mom's purse.
- Be sensitive to the needs of each child. This may mean rocking a baby or allowing a toddler to play alone.
- Maintain close communication with parent. Telephone at work during the day if necessary, or report on child's progress at the end of the day.
- Be empathetic to parents' feelings about leaving their child.
- Encourage friendships among the parents. Introduce them to each other, or plan social activities.
- Remember that children's separation anxieties may be greater at naptime or when they are tired.

Records

Good recordkeeping is essential to an infant/toddler program. Daily notes kept by both parent and caregivers provide a record of children's development during this period of rapid change.

Caregivers should keep daily notes of the routine activities of each child as well as any pertinent comments about behavior or development. These should be kept in a specific place so they are accessible to each caregiver who shares responsibility for the child during the day. Guard confidentiality so that these notes are not available to anyone who is not concerned with the child.

Consistent contact with parents is necessary so that caregivers know of any changes in the children that occur at home. Caregivers should know about babies' sleeping, eating, and eliminating patterns. Any changes in behavior such as fussiness or lassitude should also be shared with caregivers. Information that is shared should also include changes that indicate babies are moving to a new stage of development. Signs of greater acceptance of solid foods or drinking from a cup are examples.

Caregivers should provide parents with a record of children's eating, sleeping, and eliminating behaviors during the day. Information for parents may also include new things the children are learning. Be cautious, though, about telling

---

DAILY INFORMATION SHEET FOR CAREGIVERS
To be Filled Out Each Day by Parents

Date _____

Child's Name _____

When was child last fed? _____ What? _____
(Time) (Type of food)

How much did child eat? _____

How long did child sleep last night? _____

When did child awaken this morning? _____

Did child sleep well? _____ If not, what seemed to be the problem? _____

_____

Did child have a nap before arriving today? If so, please note the time.

From _____ To _____

Has child had a bowel movement today? Yes _____ No _____

What is child's general mood today? _____

_____

Is there any other information that will help us take better care of your child today?

_____

_____

Figure 6–2 Sample daily information sheet for caregivers.

parents about important milestones such as first steps or first words. Sometimes it is best to let parents find out these things for themselves at home.

With good records, parents and caregivers can make better plans for each child. Decisions about when to introduce solid foods, when to start toilet training, or when to introduce new challenges to the children are more solidly based.

Environment

The environment of an infant/toddler program should be safe while allowing the maximum possibility for exploration. Provide distinct areas for the various activities that take place—diapering, eating, sleeping, and playing. There should be open

---

DAILY INFORMATION SHEET FOR PARENTS
To Be Filled Out Each Day by Caregivers

Parent's Name _____

Child's Name _____ Date _____

                          Time   Amount/Type of Food

Your child ate _____   _____

                  _____   _____

                  _____   _____

                  _____   _____

                  _____   _____

Your child slept   From _____   To _____

                     From _____   To _____

                     From _____   To _____

                     From _____   To _____

Your child had a bowel movement.   Yes _____ No _____

Medication was given to your child at _____

                  _____

                  _____

Caregiver who administered medicine was_____

Other information about your child's day that might be of interest: _____

_____

_____

Figure 6–3   Sample daily information sheet for parents.

areas where children can move about without restriction. Traffic patterns should allow places where children can sleep without being disturbed or be by themselves if they wish.

A variety of surfaces—soft, hard, warm, and cold—adds to the interest. There should be open areas where babies can crawl and areas where specific activities take place. A variety of developmentally appropriate play materials should be available.

Freedom to move about their environment allows children to venture out to unexplored areas, but also allows them to retreat to places that offer security. A crawling baby may attempt an exploration of the space behind a low partition. However, if he gets there and can't see his caregiver, he may become anxious. He will scurry back out so that the caregiver can be kept in sight. Eventually, he will get up enough courage to further explore the space.

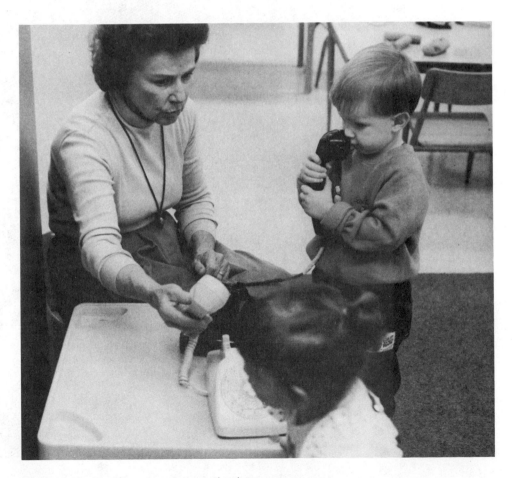

Figure 6–4   Toddlers love to practice language.

Within this environment, there must be constant vigilance to maintain the health and safety of the children. Further details about the special requirements for safety in an infant/toddler environment will be outlined in Chapters 12 and 15.

Play

A good infant/toddler program should allow for many kinds of play. Children should have choices of things to do that are appropriate for their age level and interests. Caregivers should observe the children to determine what they are capable of doing or what they currently want to be doing. They should then provide toys or materials to foster those interests. You may need to consult books or talk to other caregivers to get ideas for play materials. Remember, though, that constant variety is not necessary. Children enjoy familiar toys and will often find many new ways to use them.

Figure 6–5 Toddlers often play on the floor.

Encourage play interactions between children. Put babies on the floor near each other so they can look at, or maybe even touch, each other. Don't always provide two of the same toy, but let two toddlers play together with the same toy. Obviously, this must be the kind of toy that lends itself to use by two children. A pegboard and large pegs or a shape box are examples.

Provide a variety of play materials so children can find those that meet their own particular interests. Include the current favorites of children in the group, but also add new things. Some will use the familiar toys to perfect new skills. Others will find new materials that provide an opportunity to develop additional skills. There should be a balance between new situations and familiar things. Too much novelty, and some children become frightened and will withdraw. Not enough novelty, and they won't be interested and won't learn.

Language

A good infant/toddler program should encourage children to use language skills. Start by choosing caregivers who have good language skills themselves. They should be people who will talk to babies and not feel silly doing so. Toddlers need caregivers who will allow them to exercise the power of words without feeling threatened. Both infants and toddlers need caregivers who will listen when they try out their newly acquired skills. Caregivers should model a balance between talking and listening so that children learn they need both skills.

Caregivers should be able to adjust their communication styles to suit the children they care for. Short, simple sentences are best to use with toddlers. Quiet children need caregivers who listen more than talk. Talkative children must learn to listen to others.

Activities during the day should allow children many opportunities to hear language and to try out their own. Caregivers talk or sing to babies as they carry out routines. Back and forth "conversations" in which the baby makes a sound and the caregiver responds encourage the development of language. Toddlers love to hear words in simple stories or finger plays.

Caregivers should foster children's language use to solidify what they are learning. Adults should use appropriate words to describe daily events and activities, serving as a model for the children. Children should be encouraged to put ideas into words or to describe objects. Whenever possible, children should be motivated to relate past experiences or explain concepts.

Staff

The core of a good infant/toddler program is an educated, stable staff. It takes special people to withstand the tremendous demands on infant/toddler caregivers. Start by choosing personnel carefully. Look for people who are:

- Physically healthy, with lots of energy.
- Able to be nurturing, providing comfort when needed.
- Flexible and able to change routines to meet the children's needs.
- Patient and willing to wait while inept toddlers struggle to be competent.

- Able to anticipate and plan for times a child may need extra attention or help.
- Able to provide an interesting and varied environment.
- Good listeners who also will encourage language development.
- Willing to continue learning about children's development.

And who can:

- Help children learn to get along with others.
- Include parents in decisions affecting their children.

Consistency of caregivers is especially important to infants and toddlers. Therefore, you must do everything possible to retain staff. Become a strong advocate for adequate salaries. Plan training sessions that help them improve their skills. Allow them opportunities to discuss problems and voice frustrations. Encourage them to see themselves as professionals who make an important contribution to the center. Include them in decisions that affect them.

Encourage good relationships between the adults who work together in the infant/toddler room. Start by choosing the caregivers carefully. Try to find those who share common goals and will not have too many conflicting ideas. Encourage them to develop a mutually dependent relationship. There will be times when each will have to rely on another. While one diapers a baby, the other has to assume responsibility for all the other children. They will have to plan activities together so that the needs of all the children are met.

SUGGESTED ACTIVITIES FOR AN INFANT/TODDLER PROGRAM

The following are some suggested activities to help you get started in planning a program for infants and toddlers. They are roughly arranged in developmental order. The first activities are appropriate for young infants; the later ones, for toddlers.

SENSORY ACTIVITIES

Touch
Caregivers wear different textured clothing
Stroking, touching, holding
Warm baths
Tub filled with different textured materials: rice, sand, spaghetti, small beans, plastic balls, cotton balls
Assorted rattles, soft toys
Nylon net balls, soft rubber balls, bean bags
Textile books, textile cards
Squish bags: fill zip-lock bag with Jello™, whipped cream, shaving cream, small beans
Finger paints: starch and tempera paint, applesauce, shaving cream, chocolate pudding
Sand and water play

Hearing
Listening to music, singing
Clapping patterns

Sensory Activities *(continued)*

Make pretend sounds, imitate baby's sounds
Record baby's sounds, play back
Hide and seek with a squeaky toy
Toys that make a sound: bells, rattles, ball with bell inside
Metal pans, objects to pound or drop into to make a sound
Stories and finger games
Experiment with sounds shoes make on different surfaces

Seeing

Caregivers wear different colored clothing
Pictures at child's eye level
Hang a beach ball from the ceiling
Open and close curtains
Bright scarves
Add a fish tank and pets to room environment
Change objects in the room to add new colors: rug, vase and flowers, pillows on floor
Add toys with a variety of colors
Unbreakable mirror at floor level
Cloth or cardboard books

MOTOR ACTIVITIES

Soft, low crawling ramp
Place a toy just outside the reach of baby on the floor
Put baby on a large towel, pull across the room
Hold baby under stomach to encourage arm and leg movements
Pull toys
Large ball to encourage rolling and following
Wagon, simple riding toys
Hang a mobile over baby's crib; lower it so baby can reach it
Provide containers into which balls, large pegs, spoons, or other objects can be dropped
Stacking and nesting toys
Simple puzzles, large pop beads, sorting box
Cups, spoons, plastic glass, bowl
Blocks, large and small
Shape boxes

SOCIAL ACTIVITIES

Imitating sounds baby makes
Mirror
Toy telephone
Dressup clothes, housekeeping equipment
Dolls, small dishes, spoons
Water play

SUMMARY

As the number of working mothers and single parents has increased, the *need for quality infant/toddler care* has become acute. In order to provide the best setting, directors must have a thorough understanding of the stages of development during the first two years.

There are *universal patterns of development* most children go through, although not at the same pace. The period between birth and age two is a time of rapid change during which children move from helplessness to being fairly independent.

Children under the age of two learn by experiencing their environment with all their senses. Piaget called this the *sensorimotor period*. Motor skills develop rapidly, allowing children to find new ways to explore and learn.

During the stage that Erik Erikson called *trust versus mistrust*, most children learn that adults will be there when needed to provide food, warmth, or comfort. When adults are not available or are unresponsive, children develop a sense of mistrust. Either of these has a profound impact upon children's sense of self.

Attachment to others develops during the first two years, but also results in *anxiety over separation* from parents or caregivers. Once separation distress begins to abate, however, children begin to learn they can do things on their own. Newly acquired motor skills increase their feelings of competence and independence.

Language begins to appear during the second year and develops rapidly. Toddlers learn the power of words to tell people what they mean or what they want.

During the first two years, infants and toddlers begin to learn how to *get along with others*. They learn to play together for brief periods, but have limited ability to share and play cooperatively.

Developmentally appropriate infant/toddler programs are based on a set of goals. There should be allowance for maximum interactions between children and caregivers.

A large portion of caregivers' time will be spent on routines. Therefore, that time should be conducted as an important part of the curriculum.

Another important element in a developmentally appropriate program is a close relationship between caregivers and parents. In addition, interactions between children and adults should encourage the development of attachment and the resolution of separation problems.

Good record keeping is also essential so that each new stage of children's development can be anticipated and planned. The environment should be safe, while allowing the maximum possibility of exploration.

A developmentally appropriate program encourages many kinds of play by providing a variety of materials. Children are encouraged to use language.

Lastly, the core of a good infant/toddler program is an educated, stable staff. Characteristics of caregivers include the ability to be nurturing, flexible, patient, and to anticipate and plan for times children will need extra attention.

A variety of program activities are suggested to foster development of all the senses, motor abilities, and social development.

SUGGESTED FURTHER READING

Balaban, N. 1982. "The Role of the Child Care Professional in Caring for Infants, Toddlers, and Their Families." *Young Children*, 47 (5) 66–71.

Bredenkamp, S., ed. 1987. *Developmentally Appropriate Practice in Early Childhood Programs Serving Children from Birth Through Age 8*. Washington, DC: National Association for the Education of Young Children.

Dittman, L. 1984. *The Infants We Care For*, Revised edition. Washington, DC: National Association for the Education of Young Children.

Godwin, A., and Schrag, L., eds. 1988. *Setting Up for Infant Care: Guidelines for Centers and Family Day Care Homes*. Washington, DC: National Association for the Education of Young Children.

Gonzalez-Mena, J., and Eyer, D. 1993. *Infants, Toddlers, and Caregivers*, 3rd ed. Mountain View, CA: Mayfield Publishing Company.

Greenberg, P. 1991. *Character Development: Encouraging Self-Esteem and Self-Discipline in Infants, Toddlers, and Two-Year-Olds*. Washington, DC: National Association for the Education of Young Children.

Honig, A. 1993. "Mental Health for Babies: What Do Theory and Research Teach Us?" *Young Children*, 48 (3) 69–76.

STUDENT ACTIVITIES

1. Make an appointment to visit a child development center that serves children from birth to school age. Spend some time in a preschool classroom and then visit the infant/toddler room. Compare the kinds of toys and materials that are available in each. Are the materials in the infant room appropriate for the age level? If not, why?

2. Interview a caregiver in an infant/toddler program. Find out what is most difficult about the work. What is most enjoyable? What are the most important characteristics for an effective infant/toddler caregiver?

3. Plan a day for a group of four toddlers ranging in age from eighteen months to twenty-three months. Indicate the time allotted for each activity and the materials or equipment you would need.

REVIEW

1. Piaget called the period between birth and two years the sensorimotor period. What is meant by the term?

2. Which comes first in an infant's development, the use of his hands or his arms?

3. What did Erikson call the first stage in a child's development?

4. Some parents believe that babies should develop attachment only to their mothers. Is that belief substantiated by current research?

5. Is the following statement true? Most children completely resolve problems

of separation from their parents at about one year of age.

6. What is meant by the word "synchrony" in reference to infants and their caregivers?

7. This chapter suggested procedures for facilitating parent and child adjustment to separation. List the procedures.

8. It takes special adults to withstand the tremendous demands made on infant/toddler caregivers. List the characteristics a director should look for when choosing these personnel.

9. List five materials that will help infants or toddlers learn by using their sense of touch.

10. Describe three activities that will encourage babies to use their motor abilities.

GLOSSARY

Attachment   strong bond between infant and caregiver.

Caregiver   adult who cares for infants.

Developmentally appropriate program   curriculum based on knowledge of the physical, emotional, social, and cognitive abilities of the children served.

Sensorimotor period   Piaget's first stage of an infant's development, taking place from birth to one year.

Trust vs. mistrust   Erikson's first stage of an infant's development.

7

Planning: School-Age Children

OBJECTIVES

After studying this chapter, the student should be able to:
- Describe children's development between the ages of six and twelve.
- List the components of a developmentally appropriate program for older children.
- Describe the characteristics of a caregiver for school-age children.

Parents and professionals sometimes refer to the middle childhood years as a period of relative quiet between the difficulties of the early years and the storms of adolescence. Changes take place, but they seem to proceed more smoothly than during earlier or later times. Physical growth slows down, cognitive development helps children to learn quickly, and social development allows them to relate easily to their peers and teachers. However, not all children pass through this stage without problems. Those who lack physical skills are not successful in school, or those who have difficulty making friends may pass into adolescence with feelings of inferiority or rejection that will affect them the rest of their lives. Before- and after-school programs can contribute a great deal to help children meet the challenges they face during middle childhood, but to do so, requires a knowledge of the developmental stages during that time span. This chapter will give you an overview of development during the years between six and twelve that you can use as a guide for planning a program for school-age children.

DEVELOPMENTAL CHARACTERISTICS

Physical

In contrast to the rapid-growth spurts of the preschool period, during middle childhood children grow much more slowly. The next rapid change does not take place until the approach of adolescence. However, if you observe children on any elementary school playground, you can see wide variations in height and weight. Some of their differences can be attributed to heredity, but nutrition also plays a part. Another cause of variation is the different growth rate of boys compared to girls. Girls grow faster and are often noticeably taller than boys during part of this stage. However, girls stop growing earlier than boys, and by adolescence the boys catch up, and soon surpass the girls.

Motor abilities develop rapidly during middle childhood and both boys and girls are usually equal at most tasks. However, there are some differences. Girls develop small muscle control earlier than boys and thus, are more adept at writing tasks. Boys have greater forearm strength and may do better at games like baseball. Girls seem to excel at gymnastics. However, neither sex nor body size is as important as experience. These children need to be active, and both boys and girls benefit from practice. When they have ample opportunities to perfect their skills, differences lessen.

During middle childhood, children's cognitive development allows them to be much more aware of others than during the previous years. Therefore, any differences in appearance are noted as they judge themselves and others. Children who are obese often are teased or rejected. Early- or late-maturing youngsters may feel they do not belong. Many sixth-grade girls already have maturing breasts, and some even begin their menstrual cycles. These girls may suffer because they contrast themselves to their peers and are embarrassed by menstruation. Late-maturing boys also have difficulty. They compare themselves with boys who are beginning to show signs of puberty, such as facial or pubic hair and greater height. They worry that they will never catch up to their peers in appearance.

Language

During the preschool years, children's vocabulary, grammar, and pragmatic language skills develop rapidly. By the time they reach middle childhood, they are ready to use language in new ways. They enjoy experimenting with words and use them as the subject of jokes, changing words around, or playing with the ambiguity of words. They test the power that certain words have to evoke reactions in others by using slang or profanity. Groups of children coin their own words. Those who use the words are accepted as part of the group, and those who do not are excluded. During this period, children also learn to use words to achieve more positive ends. They learn to express feelings and to resolve conflicts through discussions.

Middle childhood youngsters are adept at changing from one form of speech to another, a process called code-switching. When they talk to their parents, for instance, they omit profanity or the words used by their peer group. The most obvious example of code-switching occur when children use one form of speech in the classroom and another when they are on the playground with their friends. When addressing the teacher, they use complete sentences, attempt to speak grammatically, and eliminate slang. On the playground they lapse into "street" talk, "Black English," or include words specific to their own native languages.

FYI

Approximately 35 million children between the ages of six to seventeen have mothers who work outside the home.* A large proportion (44 percent) of these children care for themselves before and/or after school.**
   Mounting evidence from reseach studies suggests that self-care often results in added pressures from peers to engage in troublesome activities, increased fearfulness and loneliness, and the greater likelihood of substance abuse.

SOURCES: * *U.S. Bureau of the Census.* ** The National Child Care Survey, 1990. *National Association for the Education of Young Children.*

Thinking

Children's thinking abilities change dramatically during the period between five and seven. They have a good memory for concrete ideas and can remember facts and events. They are able to sustain interest in an activity over a long period of time, enabling them to plan ahead and postpone the achievement of a goal until a future time. They are sometimes able to apply logic to practical situations and can give thought and judgment to decisions or problems. They weigh cause and effect, consider alternatives, and choose appropriate actions or solutions.

One change that is particularly important in a child care setting is children's increasing ability to understand and abide by rules. At age five or six, they begin to accept that rules are for everyone, that rules are guidelines for play, and that rules must be followed. This comprehension allows them to engage in organized sports and games, activities that were difficult or impossible a year or so earlier. It is well to remember, however, that not all five- or six-year-olds will be ready to play by the rules. Some will still need flexibility when they engage in organized activities.

Independence

Middle childhood brings about children's greater independence from their families. They spend a large portion of their days outside the home, either at school, in child care, playing in neighborhood parks, or on the streets. In doing so, they broaden their horizons, meeting new people and new ways of life. They form clubs, "cliques," or "gangs" to strengthen bonds with their peers and to free themselves from adult supervision. They feel more secure as part of a group while they learn how to find their own way in the world outside their families.

However, the groups often impose their own rigid standards on their members. Each group has its own social codes, its own games, its distinct manner of dress. To be a member of the "in" group, members must adhere strictly to the rules. Those who do follow the group rules have a sense of belonging, while others who are left out suffer. The group influence is powerful and can induce children to engage in behaviors they would not attempt by themselves. This can be a positive influence, encouraging children to develop new skills and gain new experiences. However, sometimes the behaviors encouraged by the group are socially unacceptable ones such as shoplifting, smoking, or drinking. In the case of gangs, behaviors may include some that are destructive or even illegal.

Peers

Friends are extremely important to school-age children. Although they still depend on parents for some kinds of support, they begin to rely more heavily on their peers. Their self-esteem is closely related to how their peers perceive them. If other children like them and seek them out, they feel good about themselves. Friends also provide a sounding board for weighing parental values, deciding which to keep and which to discard. A good friend can help with the emotional "ups and downs" of development. There is comfort in being able to talk to a friend about one's worries and fears, and to find that others have similar feelings.

Children tend to seek out friends who are like themselves in regard to age, sex, race, socioeconomic status, and interests. Friendships are intense and usually last for many years. Many children, especially girls, acquire one "best friend" on whom they depend a great deal while they negotiate new experiences and environments. Temporary setbacks in the friendship, or its dissolution, may cause severe suffering in some children.

Skills

Erik Erikson calls middle childhood the stage of *industry vs. inferiority*. During this period, children acquire the skills they will need as adults in their particular environment or culture. Children acquire many of these skills in school, so curriculum planners try to predict what children will need as future workers. Consequently, today's children not only learn to read, write, and compute; they also learn about complex technology. In addition to work-related skills, children need to learn practical, everyday skills: how to use tools, how to build and repair objects, how to cook, and how to care for babies or animals. In the past, it was parents who taught children to perform those tasks. At present, as more and more children spend their out-of-school hours in child care, those kinds of experiences need to be included in group programs.

Children also need to develop social skills such as helping, cooperating, negotiating, and talking to others to resolve problems. Group settings are ideal situations to learn new ways of interacting with others. Caregivers can help children through difficult encounters with individuals or can plan specific activities to enhance social skills.

Self-Esteem

The most important key to success and happiness is a positive self-concept. As children pass the preschool period, they begin to develop theories about who they are. These ideas change based on a combination of past experiences, the opinion of

Figure 7–1 Children need time and a place to do homework.

others, and, as yet, untested assumptions about themselves. Past experiences with *success* contribute to a *positive self-image*, while *failures* can add to a *lack of self-worth*. Children who perform well in school or are competent at other activities such as sports, music, or art, feel good about themselves. When peers, parents, or teachers praise or reward them for their achievements, their esteem is boosted. In addition, children test their assumptions about themselves. They look at themselves with greater cognitive awareness and become more accurate in assessing which are true, and which are false. As an example, some children will say, "I know I am not very good at math, but I'm getting pretty good at music."

Children look to role models to help them shape their own identity. During the preschool period, children modeled their behavior after the people closest to them, their immediate family members. In middle childhood, they have a broader circle of role models from which to choose. Although they continue to imitate some of the behaviors they see at home, they can now take on the characteristics of friends, teachers, or caregivers. They may also admire and try to emulate the people they see on television or in films. Sometimes family cultural values conflict with the other role models in children's environments.

CHARACTERISTICS OF A DEVELOPMENTALLY APPROPRIATE PROGRAM

Goals

The National Association for the Education of Young Children has developed guidelines for *appropriate practices in the primary grades*. Although those guidelines are written as curriculum goals for academic programs, they are still pertinent to before- and after-school programs. They state that appropriate practices should be:

- Designed to develop children's knowledge and skills in all developmental areas—physical, social, emotional, and cognitive.

Figure 7–2 Best friends are important during school ages.

- Designed to develop children's self-esteem, sense of competence, and positive feelings toward learning.
- Responsive to individual differences in ability and interests.

Use these guidelines to develop goals for your school-age program. Remember that the ways in which they will implemented will differ from implementation in an elementary school classroom. The emphasis should be on allowing children a great deal of freedom to choose their own activities, or to follow their own interests.

Pace

A child care program for older children must offer a *change of pace from the day at school*. Remember that children have been sitting down for long periods of the day before they come to you. They need an opportunity to work off some of their pent-up energies. Allow them time to actively participate in games or sports or to use outdoor equipment.

Some children may want a quiet time, away from the pressure of group activities. They should have places where they can work on an individual project, read, or "just do nothing" for a while. Some children need a short rest period, occasionally falling asleep. Other children look for an adult to help them make the shift from school to day care. A brief period of time talking with a caregiver allows these children to move into more active participation.

Independence

Child care should offer children *many different ways to develop their need for independence*. A wide variety of materials should always be available so they can initiate their own activities. Materials for creative activities should be easily accessible. Have different kinds of paint, paper, collage materials, fabric, and the like available so they can devise interesting art projects. Materials for dressing up can encourage impromptu dramatic play or more planned and structured productions. A record or tape player, and a variety of instruments can lead to experimentation with music. Some adults are successful in getting children to do some creative writing.

Children can develop independence by planning and preparing their own snacks. Allow them to decide on snacks for a week, let them make a shopping list, then send them with a caregiver to purchase the supplies. Simple cooking activities can be part of each day's program.

Participation in planning and decision-making also increases children's feelings of independence. They should have opportunities to plan their own program, including special events. They should be able to decide what kinds of activities will be scheduled next week or next month. Children really get involved when they set out to plan a special day for parents or a trip to the zoo or park.

You foster independence when you allow children to resolve their own problems. This means that caregivers should not be quick to step in when two children are involved in an altercation unless there is danger that one will get hurt. Encourage children to work out their differences in ways that are satisfying to each of them. When a group has a common problem, caregivers can encourage independence by leading a discussion. The children should clarify the problem, offer solutions, and institute a plan of action.

Figure 7–3   Activities should fit the age level.

Skills

A good program for older children will *allow many opportunities for the development of skills*. Set aside time for children to complete their homework. Additional time and tutors should be available as needed. Devise games that teach math concepts or necessitate reading so they can learn those skills in ways that are fun.

Both individual physical activities and organized sports offer additional ways to develop skills. Some children just want to practice "shooting baskets," for instance, while others need the competition of a game. Some children want to increase their skills by using gymnastics equipment, while others want organized competitions. Provide opportunities and equipment for both individual and group activities.

Children can develop needed skills when they are involved in planning and maintenance of their play areas. They can learn how to do simple repairs using real tools. They can learn that materials must be put away after use so they will be available when needed at another time. At times, they will also have to use their problem-solving skills as they perform these tasks. Make sure the children see these as real jobs that they take responsibility for, not just something to occupy their time. In that way, not only will they learn the skills involved, but also increase their sense of independence.

Friends

A good child care setting will provide *opportunities for children to make friends*. Set aside times when children can choose to participate in an activity with one or two "best friends." These should not be used by the children as times to exclude others but as a way of solidifying friendships.

Also allow times when children are encouraged to include a larger circle of peers in a play activity. At these times, emphasize accepting differences and learning to compromise. Activities such as producing a newspaper or putting on a play can draw on the talents of many children. These joint efforts can benefit from the diversity. Group sports are another time when a larger number of children can be included. Remember to help those children who feel inadequate at sports to find a place in the game. However, respect the wishes of some children who do not want to be involved in competitive sports.

Children should have opportunities to develop friendships with their caregivers. There should be times when adult and child can sit and talk, or times when they can work together at a needed task. Some children miss the comfort that a parent traditionally provided at the end of a day at school and need to find that same kind of comfort in their child care worker.

Parents

By the time children reach middle childhood, parents do not need to be as closely involved in their child's school and day care center as in earlier years. However, parents should be kept informed about the child's progress. They need to know that the transition from school to the child care setting is going smoothly. They certainly want to know about the kinds of activities in which their child participates. They want to be included in special events. They need to know about any signs of illness the child might show during the day.

FAVORITE ACTIVITIES FOR SCHOOL-AGE CHILDREN

The following are some activities most children between five and twelve seem to enjoy. There are many more to be found in curriculum books. Start with these, but add your own when you can.

CREATIVE ACTIVITIES
Painting with brushes, hands, string, marbles, sponges
Clay, play dough, Papier-Mâché
Collages from leaves, flowers, fabrics, buttons, ribbons
Crayon etchings, chalk drawing, textile painting

Basket-making, sewing, knitting, crocheting
Tie-dying, batik
Puppets, puppet shows
Making and playing musical instruments
Painting to music
Writing a play, making costumes, producing the play
Dancing to popular, classical, or ethnic music

GAMES

Mother May I?, Simon Says, Charades
Tic-Tac-Toe, memory games, card games, dice games
Gossip, twenty questions, guess the Number
Jump rope, hopscotch, leapfrog race, obstacle race

FIELD TRIPS

Beach or zoo
Print shop, computerized office, newspaper
Local radio or television station
Artist's studio
Museum, children's museum

ACTIVITIES

Science and math activities
Care for animals such as fish, bird, gerbil, guinea pig, hamster, kitten, rabbit, snake, lizard, tortoise
Cultivate a garden outdoors, keep potted plants indoors
Collect shells, rocks, fossils
Experiment with magic
Chart the weather, make predictions
Weigh a variety of objects, weigh themselves
Play table games that require counting
Cook a snack using a recipe that requires measuring

CHARACTERISTICS OF TEACHER/CAREGIVER

The adults who care for children in before- and after-school programs have a variety of titles: aides, teachers, assistants, caregivers, leaders, guides, and recreational supervisors. The author prefers the term caregiver because it implies an essential function of these adults: the ability to provide a caring, nurturing environment for children who must spend their out-of-school hours away from home. Whatever you choose to call the staff members you hire for your school-age program, they should have certain characteristics. Look for people who:

- Like being with school-age children.
- Can allow children to be independent.
- Have a knowledge of the developmental stages during middle childhood.
- Are good role models for children to emulate.

- Have a lot of interests they can share with children.
- Can allow children freedom to be independent while also setting limits.
- Have good communication skills, including the ability to listen.
- Enjoy physical activity such as active games or sports.
- Care about families and can accept each family's uniqueness.
- Understand the role of caregiver, a blending of teacher and parent.
- Are able to work as a team with other staff members.

Beyond the personal characteristics listed above, there are two broad areas of education and experience that are usually required in school-age child care. Some directors want adults who have *completed courses in early childhood education*, including human development and curriculum planning. Other directors lean more heavily toward persons who have backgrounds in recreation. Those staff members will have *taken courses in physical education* and may have had experience in supervising playgrounds or working in summer camps. The ideal staff member for a school-age program would have both, but there is an alternative. Balance your staff with some having an *early childhood education* background *and* others with *recreation experience*. Provide further balance by including both men and women so that children have additional role models.

SUMMARY

Middle childhood is often referred to as a period of quiet since changes take place more slowly and smoothly. Children's physical growth slows down. Motor abilities develop rapidly, and boys and girls are about equal at most tasks. Girls have better small muscle control, while boys excel at tasks requiring forearm strength. When given opportunities to practice skills, differences lessen.

School-age children enjoy experimenting with words, using them as the subject of jokes. They test the power of words by using slang or profanity. They are adept at code-switching, changing from one form of language to another as the situation warrants. Between ages five and six, children's thinking changes. Their memory improves, they can sustain interest for long periods of time, and can use logic at times. They are also able to understand and abide by rules.

Middle childhood brings greater independence from their families. In order to accomplish this, children form strong bonds with peer groups. The influence of the group can be positive in that it enables children to try things they would not attempt alone. However, peer groups may induce children to engage in antisocial or illegal activities.

Friends are extremely important to school-age children. They seek out friends who are like themselves in regard to age, sex, race, socioeconomic status, and interests. The school-age period is a time when children acquire many of the skills they will need as adults. As future members of the work force, they will need to be able to read, write, compute, and manage complex technology. They also need practical skills such as how to use tools, build or repair objects, and care for children.

Children's self-concept is based on a combination of past experiences, the opinions of others, and untested assumptions about themselves. They also look to role models to help them shape their own identity.

Characteristics of a developmentally appropriate program for children during middle childhood have been suggested by the National Association for the Education of Young Children. Appropriate practices should include:

- Opportunities for children to develop skills in all developmental areas.
- A program designed to enhance children's self-esteem.
- A responsiveness to individual differences in ability and interests.

The adults who care for children in before- and after-school programs have a variety of titles, but whatever their title, they should have certain characteristics that promote the development of children during middle childhood.

SELECTED FURTHER READING

Berger, K. 1993. *The Developing Person Through the Life Span*, 3rd ed. NY: Worth Publishers, Inc.

Blau, R., et al. 1989. *Activities for School-Age Child Care: Playing and Learning*, Rev. ed. Washington, DC: National Association for the Education of Young Children.

Bredenkamp, S., ed. 1987. *Developmentally Appropriate Practices in Early Childhood Programs Serving Children from Birth Through Age 8*. Washington, DC: National Association for the Education of Young Children.

Click, P. 1994. *Caring for School-Age Children*. Albany, NY: Delmar Publishers, Inc.

Curry, N., and Johnson, C. 1990. *Beyond Self-Esteem: Developing a Genuine Sense of Human Value*. Washington, DC: National Association for the Education of Young Children.

Haas-Foletta, K., and Cogley, M. 1990. *School-Age Ideas and Activities for After School Programs*. Nashville, TN: School-Age Notes.

STUDENT ACTIVITIES

1. Write a few paragraphs describing yourself when you were seven. Then write down what you were like when you were eleven. Did you change a little or a lot during that period? What were the changes?
2. Observe a group of school-age children on a playground or in your child care group. Are there some children who are much taller or much smaller than the others? How do they seem to get along in the group? Are there children who are excluded? Why do you think they have difficulty joining the activities?
3. Compare your own characteristics with those listed in this chapter as being important for a caregiver of school-age children. Do you fit the profile? If not, what can you do to increase your effectiveness as a caregiver?

REVIEW

1. In what ways do the motor skills of boys and girls differ during middle childhood?
2. What is meant by the term code-switching?
3. What changes take place in children's thinking during the period between ages five and seven?
4. During middle childhood, children form clubs, cliques, or gangs. What are the purposes of these alliances?
5. What criteria do children use when choosing their friends?
6. What are the bases for children's self-concept?
7. What kinds of child care activities can help children to develop their need for independence?
8. How can caregivers provide opportunities for children to make friends?
9. List three games with rules, and three impromptu games that school-age children like to play.
10. List three field trips that would be of interest to school-age children.

GLOSSARY

Caregiver   one who provides a caring, nurturing environment for children who spend long hours away from home.

Clique   a group formed by school-age children as a means for strengthening bonds with peers and to be free from adult supervision.

Industry vs. inferiority   Erikson's middle-childhood stage during which children acquire skills needed for adulthood.

Peer   a person of the same age as oneself.

Part III

Staff

8

Staff Selection/ Personnel Policies

OBJECTIVES

After studying this chapter, the student should be able to:
- State the procedures for finding qualified staff.
- Plan the steps in recruiting employees.
- Describe the process of selecting a staff member from qualified applicants.
- List the kinds of information contained in a personnel policy statement.

A beautiful building and excellent equipment cannot make a good school. It takes well-trained teachers to make the environment come alive. So you want the very best teachers *for your school* you can possibly find. The phrase "for your school" is italicized because your staff should fit your requirements. The school "down the street" will probably have different ones. Having found the best teachers, consider their retention. One means of doing this is to have clearly thought out and consistent personnel practices. These should be written and understood by everyone concerned.

STAFF QUALIFICATIONS

Before you begin recruiting qualified staff for your center, assemble a profile of the kind of person you want to hire for each position. Consider the skills or knowledge that person should have in order to fulfill the duties of the position. What kinds of experience will be important? What personal characteristics do you think are essential? When completed, this profile will serve as the basis for evaluating persons who apply to work at your center. It, along with a statement of duties, will also become part of a job description for each staff person.

Education

Check your state's licensing requirements for the academic background of teachers of young children. Specifications are usually minimal. The educational requirement may be as low as twelve postsecondary semester units in early childhood education or child development. A teacher in an infant/toddler room is sometimes required to complete an additional course in infant studies. Teachers in a before- and after-school program for older children might be able to substitute credits in recreation, physical education, and elementary teaching for early childhood education courses. Set standards for your school as much beyond the minimum as you wish and can afford.

Publicly funded programs have different requirements for teachers. In public school early childhood education programs, teachers must have teaching certificates for the primary grades. They must also meet any other requirements set by the local school board. Head Start teachers have four-year degrees in early childhood education or elementary education. Degrees in psychology or child welfare may also prepare someone for Head Start teaching. Head Start teachers who do not have a four-year degree are encouraged to work toward the Child Development Associate credential sponsored by the National Association for the Education of Young Children.

Nonteaching staff in your school also must meet minimum standards stated in licensing requirements. They must be in good physical health and free of diseases that might be transmitted to children. A background check should indicate that they have not been convicted of a crime other than a minor traffic violation.

Experience

Decide how much and what kinds of experience staff members should have. Licensing guidelines for your area will specify a minimum amount, but you can decide to require more. In some states, teachers are required to have as little as a year of classroom experience with children while assistant teachers need none. If yours is a new school, look for experienced teachers who will be able to function without initial training or supervision. Your first year of operation will be smoother, and although it may increase the percentage of your budget allocated to salaries, it may be worth it.

Personal Characteristics

The success of a school depends largely on the adults who work there and the kind of relationships they establish with each other and with children. In order for that to happen, staff members must be chosen carefully based on a clear picture of the kinds of characteristics needed. The following characteristics are those that are cited most often by experienced directors. They say they look for staff members who:

Like being with children. (Remember that some adults prefer being with infants while others prefer preschool or older children.)

Are able to be nurturing. (Especially important for infants and toddlers.)

Are able to be flexible.

Are patient and willing to wait while children accomplish tasks themselves.

Are good role models for children to follow.
Have good communication skills, including the ability to listen.
Can allow children to be independent and resolve their own problems.
Can accept individual differences in both children and adults.
Are able to work as a team with colleagues and with parents.
Are healthy, energetic, and enjoy physical activity.
Have lots of interests that can be shared with children and adults.
Are willing to continue learning.

Required Skills

Now you are ready to make a list of the skills each position requires. According to the dictionary, a skill is an ability that comes from knowledge, practice, or aptitude. It simply means the ability to perform certain tasks as part of a job. A word that is currently used is "competencies." It is applicable to all positions.

Teachers need to be able to do a variety of things as part of their job. The choice of which ones to include in your job requirements depends on the type of school you have. The following list is a compilation of skills that might fit several settings. Use it as a guide to develop your own list.

A teacher should be able to:

- Set up an environment that motivates children to participate.
- Design activities that stimulate children to think, solve problems, and make choices.
- Encourage children to use language by listening, and responding to their communications.
- Promote children's physical development.
- Help children feel successful.
- Create an environment that helps children accept ethnic differences.
- Assess and measure children's achievement.

For further help, the National Association for the Education of Young Children has a useful pamphlet that lists the competencies for several levels of educational personnel. It is pamphlet #530, entitled "NAEYC Position Statement on Nomenclature, Salaries, Benefits, and the Status of the Early Childhood Profession." You can obtain a copy by writing to the Association's Washington, DC office.

Knowledge

Knowledge is a familiarity with a particular subject or branch of learning. It can also mean an acquaintance with facts, truths, or principles. Knowledge provides the information that allows workers to do their jobs. Should the teacher have a knowledge of child development? Do you want your cook to know something about nutrition in order to plan meals? Will your secretary need to know public relations techniques? To make these decisions, you must have an understanding of the functions and needs of each job. Then consider the knowledge necessary to perform those functions.

Some examples of what teachers need to know are:
- Stages of development, with special emphasis on cognitive, language, physical, social, and emotional development.
- Atypical development.
- How young children learn.
- Ways to present materials and activities so children will want to get involved.
- How the family influences the child's development.
- Ways to form a partnership with parents for the education and care of the child.
- Communication and conference techniques.

Some examples of what a secretary needs to know are:
- How to type or use a computer.
- How to set up and maintain a filing system or computer database.
- How to perform bookkeeping tasks either manually or on a computer.
- How to set up and maintain a schedule.

A food-preparation person may need to know:
- The food group pyramid.
- Recommended serving sizes for children.
- How to prepare and store food for maximum health and safety.
- The kinds of food most children enjoy.
- How to present food in appealing ways.

STAFF RECRUITMENT

Now that you have a clear picture of the kind of people you are looking for, you are ready to begin the search to find them. Prepare a concise statement for each position. As shown in Figure 8–1, include the following in the statement:
- Name of your school.
- Address of your school.
- Job title and brief description.
- Contract period (September to June or the calendar year).
- Salary range.
- Brief statement of qualifications.
- Name and phone number of person to contact.
- Application process.
- Deadline for applying.
- Starting date of position.

This notice does not have to be fancy or costly. If you have a computer, you can easily put together an attractive notice. Vary the type font, use bold letters, or add a border. With a typewriter you can use capital letters or underline for emphasis. Brevity is the key. Most people will not read a lengthy notice with "wordy" sentences.

RECRUITING NOTICE

The Village Child Care Center at 8126 West 8th Street is seeking a Head Teacher for a group of 18 four-year-olds. Responsibilities include planning and conducting the program for the group, working with parents, and participating in staff planning and decision making.

The applicant selected will be given a one-year contract with a salary ranging from $12,500 to $15,000. The school is in session all year, with each staff member entitled to 15 days paid leave each year. Starting date for this position is August 1. Deadline for applying is July 1.

Applicants should have a B.A. degree in child development or related fields and have had at least two years' experience in a preschool program.

An application, resume, and three letters of reference are required. The application form may be requested by calling:

Mary Anton
924-8659

Figure 8–1   Sample recruiting notice.

Distribute this information as widely as possible. The more people who see it, the better your chances of finding the right person. If you are trying to fill several positions, you may expect many applicants. In that case, you might want to omit the telephone number from this information. Request that applicants write for application materials.

If your school is already in operation and you need to fill one position, notify those already on staff. An assistant teacher may feel ready to apply for a position as teacher. A secretary who has taken some early childhood courses may be ready to move to an assistant's job.

Further distribution sources are:
- Public and private schools.
- Unemployment service offices.
- College and university placement offices.
- Civic groups, clubs, special-interest groups.
- Professional organizations.
- Churches.

You can also place an ad in local newspapers. The ad needs to be much shorter than the recruitment notice. It should be only a few lines long and contain the following information:
- Name of school.
- Position being filled.
- Required background and experience.
- Contact–address or telephone.

Many directors find the search for qualified staff a difficult and frustrating part of their job and the high turnover in early childhood centers causes the search to be a constant one. Although turnover of employees cannot be entirely eliminated, it may be significantly decreased by creating a climate in which staff members feel valued. This will go a long way toward retaining staff. A good personnel policy statement is also important, as you will read later in this chapter.

APPLICATION INFORMATION

Develop an application form you can use each time a position needs to be filled. You may be able to use one basic form for all jobs or have one for teachers and one for other categories. Forms should be simple and short. Questions should be clear and related to the job.

The application form might include:
- Date the application is made.
- Name of applicant.
- Address of applicant.
- Telephone number of applicant.
- Position applied for.
- Job or volunteer experience (include dates and type of work).
- Social Security number.
- Educational background.
- Hobbies or special interests.
- References (include name, address, telephone).

In addition, the application for a teaching position may include:
- Credentials and/or academic degrees.
- Professional affiliations.
- Published works.

Do be sensitive to the fact that some applicants may need help in filling out an application form. Language differences, inexperience with forms, or limited education should not deter a potentially qualified person from applying. You, your secretary, or another staff member should be available to help.

SELECTION PROCESS

Screening

After the application deadline has passed, you can begin the screening process. Consider asking an advisory committee member or a teacher to help. Although you or your board of trustees will make the final choice, others can make recommendations. When staff members participate in this process, they have a chance to learn some new skills. Having some "say" in choosing their colleagues can promote staff solidarity as well.

Look through each of the applications for those who meet the minimum requirements. This usually includes academic background, experience, and credentials or licenses. Make three groups of applications. One will be for those who meet all the minimum requirements. The second will be for those who meet some. The last will be for those who meet none. You usually can immediately disregard the last group.

Check the references. A reference can be in the form of a letter submitted along with the application, or it can be the name of a person to contact. If written references are required, but not received, you may want to contact the applicants. It is their responsibility to see that you have all relevant information.

Look for any special characteristics or skills that are important to you. You may be looking for someone who has a special interest in art. Look to see what hobbies the applicants list or other jobs they have held.

When you have narrowed the field of applicants to a few likely candidates, you are ready to schedule interviews. Usually three to five applicants who meet all your requirements will yield someone you want to hire.

Interviewing

The interview portion of the application process is the most difficult, but it can be the most valuable. When you meet with a prospective staff member, you have an opportunity to explore the "fit" of the person to the school. This is a two-way process. The applicant needs to find out if your school is "right," and you need to find out if the applicant will suit your philosophy and goals.

Allow plenty of time. Allot at least a half-hour to the actual interview. Leave ten or fifteen minutes between candidates for jotting notes about each person. Do not rely on your memory. When you have completed several interviews in a row, the applicants will begin to "blur" together. Notes will refresh your memory when you are trying to make a final decision.

Precede an interview with a tour of your school if time permits. This will allow the applicant to get some information about your school. It will also give you a chance to see how the person responds to children. Comments or questions during the tour can provide you with important insights about the applicant.

In some settings, several people will compose an interview committee. The director, a board member, a parent, a supervisor, or a teacher may be included, depending on the organization of the school. If several people are to be involved, you may want to schedule separate interviews for each, or it can be done as a group. Remember, though, that too large a committee may overwhelm some candidates.

For purposes of later evaluation, the interview should have some structure. This applies whether you alone interview candidates or a committee is involved. Ask each applicant similar questions. This is not to say that you write out questions and read them off during the interview. It does mean, however, that you have a list of areas to cover. You can state the questions in different ways, but if the content is the same from one applicant to another, it is easier to evaluate. In a committee, one person should be designated to lead. To avoid repetition of information, each member should choose an area to question. For example, one might ask about curriculum skills, while another asks about previous experience.

The procedure is still the same if committee members conduct separate interviews. You should agree ahead of time about the questions that will be asked. Each may pursue particular areas, or they may all ask similar questions.

Avoid questions that require only a one-word answer. You get very little information that way. "Did you decide to become a preschool teacher because you like children?" is an example. Avoid also, questions that already imply the kind of answer you expect. "What kind of punishment would you use for a child who hits others?" Here the implication is that punishment is the only way to handle that kind of behavior.

Provide a quiet place for the interview, free from interruptions. Make sure the applicant will be comfortable by providing a suitable chair. If you are a member of a committee, ensure each will be included in the discussion. Do not ask the applicant to sit facing a row of committee members, or barricade yourself behind your desk.

Allow time for each committee member to review the application material. This way they can familiarize themselves with the applicant's academic background and previous experience. You will save time by eliminating direct questions about that kind of information in the interview.

Begin the interview by introducing yourself, and others, if more than one person is participating. If the applicant has not had a tour of the school, you can describe the school briefly. You might talk a little about the specific class in which there is an opening.

Ask an easily answered question first, mainly to help the applicant start talking. Choose a nonthreatening area such as the person's past experience. "I see by your application that you have worked at . . . Tell us what you liked best about the job." Or "Describe any aspects of that job that might be applicable to the position here." Use words like:

- Tell me . . .
- Describe . . .
- List . . .
- Outline . . .

To find out about personal qualifications, pose a question that might show the person's feelings or attitudes:

- *Enthusiasm for teaching:* "What do you like best about working with young children?"
- *Attitudes toward differences in people:* "Suppose you had a child in your class who was blind. What are some things you would do to integrate that child into the classroom activities?"
- *Ability to manage problem situations with children:* "You have a child in your class who refuses to participate in any of the group activities you plan. She either won't come to the group area, or if she does, she never says anything. What would you do?"

To get information about specific skills, ask the applicant to plan a specific learning activity for a particular age group. Do not ask for a week's curriculum plan. That is too much. You might ask the applicant to:

- "Describe one science activity that would be appropriate for a group of four-year-olds."

- "List three things you might do to encourage parents to get involved in the education of their children."
- Plan a cooking activity that would be appropriate for a group of children in an after-school program.

To find out the applicant's knowledge of child development:
- "Briefly describe how you would design an indoor environment for a group of four infants and six toddlers."
- "Name three art activities that most two-year-olds should be able to do successfully. Name three that might be a little difficult."

To elicit unstructured information, encourage them to talk freely about themselves:
- "What else would you like to tell us about yourself that might be important as we consider you for this position?"
- "Tell us what you feel your strengths are. What are the kinds of things you would like to do?"
- "What kind of job do you expect to be doing ten years from now?"

There are some areas of inquiry that should be avoided, information that should not be requested either in an interview or on an application. Familiarize yourself with what you can ask and what is illegal. The following are some guidelines:
- You can ask for place of residence, but not whether the person owns or rents.
- You can require an applicant to provide proof that he or she meets a minimum age requirement, but not seek any information that identifies someone over age 40.
- You can ask the name and address of a parent or guardian of a minor. You cannot ask questions that indicate applicant's marital status, number and ages of children, or provisions for child care.
- You cannot ask any questions regarding the applicant's race or complexion, color of skin, eyes, or hair.
- You can state that employment is contingent on passing a physical exam and ask if there is any physical condition that would limit his or her ability to perform the job. It is unacceptable to inquire about the applicant's general physical and mental health.
- You can require references, but may not directly ask those persons questions about the applicant's race, religion, national origin, medical condition, marital status, or sex.

During the interview you will have an opportunity to observe many things about the applicant. Depending on what is important to you, you might look for:
- Ability to communicate: how clear are the answers?
- Organizational ability: does the applicant organize answers logically and in a way that is easy to understand?
- Sense of humor: does the applicant see some difficult situations from a humorous viewpoint?
- Tense or relaxed: look at body language to see if extreme tenseness or relaxation is being communicated.

Allow time at the end of the interview for the applicant to ask questions. The kind of questions asked will give valuable clues to the person's ability to understand the job being filled. You might also get an insight into the person's particular interests or even biases.

You can use this format for an interview for employees other than teaching staff. You can ask the same kinds of questions; however, modify the content of the questions so that they are specific to the job. The following examples will help you to develop your own questions:

- *To find out how the maintenance person will react to children*—"The children have been playing in the sandbox with water from the drinking fountain. You arrive just in time to see a child using a very sandy bucket to get some more water. What would you say?"
- *To find out whether the cook can plan nutritious meals that children will like*— "What would a typical lunch for a group of four-year-olds consist of?"
- *To find out whether the secretary has good public relations skills*— "Some irate parents tell you there is a mistake on their bill and that you have overcharged them. You know the bill was correct and that a payment was missed. What would you say?"

Record your information and impressions as soon as the interview is concluded. Do not talk to your co-interviewers first. (Caution: *Do not write notes during the interview.* The applicant may spend so much time worrying about what you have chosen to write down that you may not get an accurate picture of the person's abilities.) Some situations may require rating each candidate on a numerical scale. Do so at this time. Finally, in your notes include a recommendation for hiring or not hiring.

Evaluating

Evaluation of applicants is the final step of the selection process and is sometimes the hardest. Remember that your evaluation will be based on several sources of information: the applicant's background and experience, responses to your questions, and image. Try to be as objective as possible.

It is not too difficult to evaluate background and experience. If a specific degree or credential is required, you can see that on the application. You can also determine experience by the application. However, you can determine the quality of the background or experience only in the interview. A person can take a course in human development, but still have little understanding of the stages of development. Someone may have taught in a preschool, but it may have been one vastly different from yours.

Evaluating answers to questions posed in the interview seems an almost impossible task. It does help if you know what you are looking for. Listen for key words or ideas that coincide with your own beliefs.

Remember, too, that some very well-qualified applicants may not perform well in an interview. The opposite is also true. Someone who comes across well in an interview may turn out to be a poor choice for your school. There is a way to give an applicant a further chance. Ask the finalists to spend a day working in one of your classrooms. Pay the going salary rate for their time. Even though this procedure has some drawbacks, it will certainly give you additional information for making your final choice.

Finally, there is no foolproof way to find the exact person who will do well in your school. Trust your own ability to listen, watch, and judge each candidate. The more often you go through this process, the more accurate you become in choosing staff who are right for you.

NOTIFICATION OF EMPLOYMENT OR NONSELECTION

When you have finally chosen a new staff member, you will be eager to settle the matter. If you telephone the person, follow the call with a letter. The letter should give the starting date of employment and the salary offered. If your school has a contract, enclose it with the letter.

The successful candidate should be given a time to return the contract or to come to the school to complete the process. This may include submitting the required credentials or transcripts and completing payroll and personnel forms.

When the hiring process is completed, send information about your new employee to any interested persons. This may include board members, advisory committee members, or existing staff. You will also want to tell parents about the new staff member. Don't forget that children, too, need to know who their new teacher is going to be.

Those who were interviewed and not hired should also be informed. This is never a pleasant task, but they should not be left wondering. If you can, telephone the several people you interviewed. Thank them for their time and tell them the position has been filled. You may wish to ask whether you can call them for substitute jobs, or if future openings become available. If a telephone call is too difficult, then send a letter like that in Figure 8–2 to these people. In addition, a simple note to each person who sent in an application would be both courteous and professional (see Figure 8–3).

FYI

The average annual teacher turnover in early childhood centers is 50 percent. (That figure does not include assistant teachers or aides.) Public school programs and Head Start have the lowest turnover while for-profit chains have the highest.

SOURCE: The Demand and Supply of Child Care in 1990, *joint findings from* The National Child Care Survey 1990 *and* A Profile of Child Care Settings. *Published by The National Association for the Education of Young Children.*

VILLAGE CHILD CARE CENTER

(Date)

Dear _____ ;

Thank you for your interest in Village Child Care Center and your desire to become a member of our staff. We wish to inform you that we have made a selection from the applicants for the recent opening.

Your application will be kept on file, and should an additional opening become available, you will be notified. If you are still interested in working with us, we would hope that you would reapply.

Sincerely,

Mary Anton, Director

Figure 8–2   Notification of nonselection.

VILLAGE CHILD CARE CENTER

(Date)

Dear _____ ;

Because of the large number of requests to our recent recruiting efforts, we were unable to interview all applicants. However, we wanted to notify you that the position has been filled. Your application will be kept on file, and you will be notified when we have other openings.

Sincerely,

Mary Anton, Director

Figure 8–3   Notification of applicants who were not interviewed.

Finding, hiring, and then keeping qualified staff is not an easy task. It will test your skills in human relations and sometimes give you sleepless nights. But when you do find that "gem of a teacher," it is worth the hard work entailed.

PERSONNEL PRACTICES

In some preschools and day care centers, staff members stay for years. In others, turnover occurs frequently. What accounts for the difference? Sometimes people leave a job looking for higher pay. Others stay in a job in spite of low salaries. Teachers who stay in a school when they could get more money elsewhere say they stay because "It's a good place to work." One way to make yours that kind of school is to treat your staff as professionals. Provide job security and develop fair personnel practices. Pay the best salary you can for the job each person does. Support fringe benefits and retirement plans for your employees. Offer employees a contract.

Contract

A *contract* is a written commitment between you and your employee that promotes job security. A contract states that during a specified period of time, each has an obligation to the other. You agree to employ the person for that period at a designated pay level. The staff member agrees to carry out the functions of the job (see Figure 8–4).

VILLAGE CHILD CARE CENTER

This agreement is made the ___ day of _____ , 19___, between Village Child Care Center and _____ (employee).

It is mutually understood that you will be employed as _____ (position) for a period of one year, beginning _____ , 19___ and ending _____ , 19___. During that time, you will perform the duties of the position as prescribed by the board of trustees of Village Child Care Center and any state laws or ordinances governing your position.

You will serve for twelve calendar months and shall be entitled to twenty-two (22) vacation days. One (1) day sick leave will be allowed for each month of service to a maximum of twelve (12) days. You will also be entitled to the other benefits provided by the board of trustees of Village Child Care Center. It shall be understood that should this agreement be terminated, you will be entitled to compensation for such accumulated vacation time that you have accrued at the time of termination but not used as of that date.

As a new employee, you will serve a three (3) month probationary period after which the full contract will be in effect. This agreement may be terminated after due process if it is determined that you have not fulfilled the responsibilities of the position as prescribed. Termination by either party to this agreement must be preceded by a notification period of thirty (30) days.

Village Child Care Center agrees to pay you the sum of _____. This will be paid at the rate of _____ per calendar month, beginning _____, 19___.

Date_____   For the School _____
                                                         Director or Board Member

I have read the above statement and agree to abide by the provisions of the contract.

_____   _____
      Signature of Employee   Date

_____   _____
      Signature of Director   Date

Figure 8–4   Sample contract.

A contract is essential for good morale in your teaching staff. Young children need to have the security of teachers or caregivers who are predictable and who are there for a long period of time. It is hard for a child to learn to trust that school is a good place if adults disappear frequently, never to be seen again. Working parents, too, feel better if they know the adult who cares for their child will stay for a while. Learning to trust their child's caregiver takes time. Teachers need time, too, to find ways to work together. Teachers sometimes say that working together in a classroom is a bit like a marriage. It takes "working at" and does not happen overnight.

The contract should be a statement of all the conditions of employment. The following points should be included:

- *Time period of the contract*—the date when the contract goes into effect and the termination date.
- *Probationary period*—the time before the full contract goes into effect, usually from one to three months.
- *Salary*—pay for the period covered by the contract.
- *Fringe benefits*—the number of days of vacation and sick leave, and the medical and retirement benefits.
- *Termination*—conditions for termination of the contract. (This would include termination by either the employer or employee.)

Statement of Personnel Policies

A *statement of personnel policies* is a written document covering employer-employee relations. It spells out the conditions of employment. Given to new employees, this kind of document will convey information about the job in a concise manner. Even though all employees may not read it from cover to cover, the information is there for reference as needed. It will not eliminate problems, but when they do arise, the statement may provide a solution or prevent misunderstandings. If you want your employees to read the entire document, then ask them to sign a statement indicating they have done so.

A written statement of personnel policies should be:

- Short and to the point.
- Clear.
- Organized into logical sections.

Many directors say they do not have a written policy statement because conditions change each year. Some do change, but many stay the same. It is fairly easy to redo a few pages to meet any changing circumstances in your school. This is another time-saving use for a computer. When you must add information, this can easily be done with a computer. Photocopy the pages, then put them together into a looseleaf booklet.

You must decide what is appropriate to put into your school's statement of personnel policies. An overview of the sections you might include is presented in the following paragraphs. Choose those that fit your school.

DETAILS OF EMPLOYMENT

Devote a section to the details of employment: the number of hours per day, holidays, and vacations. A calendar showing holidays and starting dates of the school year is helpful. The length of the probationary period and what is to take place during that period could be outlined. An example is the following:

EXAMPLE

The probationary period is three months. During that time you will be observed by the director at least once a month. A conference will be scheduled at the end of that time to evaluate your performance. If performance has been satisfactory, the full contract will go into effect.

New employees should know the lines of responsibility in a school. When problems arise, they should know whom to go to first. They should also know who will be directly responsible for supervising them. Include an organizational chart in your personnel policies manual to show these personnel relationships.

If your school provides payment for—or requires—continuing professional training, include that information. Some schools pay for conferences and professional dues. Some offer full or part tuition payments for staff to attend classes.

PHYSICAL ENVIRONMENT

Your personnel policies might contain a section on managing the physical environment. In some situations you may have to tell staff how to get the keys to the classroom and where to park. You will probably want to include a statement about the teachers' responsibility for maintaining their classrooms and equipment.

HEALTH AND SAFETY MATTERS

Your employees should be told if *health examinations* are required and how often they are needed. Do they pay for the examinations? Does the school contribute toward the cost or provide free examinations? Consider requiring that staff members be immunized for hepatitis B or receive booster measles immunization (if this was done when they first entered school).

How many "sick leave" days does each employee have? Can the days be carried over from one year to another? What are the conditions under which employees will be excused from work due to illness?

Outline procedures for *reporting employee accidents*. If a form is required, include an example and indicate where it can be obtained. Explain procedures for dealing with disasters such as fires, earthquakes, or tornadoes.

Detail the *fringe benefits* the school provides to employees. If you offer a medical and hospital plan, spell out the procedure for enrolling. If you have a retirement plan or pay into Social Security, include that information. Any other types of benefits such as group life insurance, unemployment insurance, and workers' compensation should be covered.

It is appropriate to include in this section information about employee relief periods. Each staff member should have at least ten minutes of relief during every four-hour period. If a staff member works more than four hours, a thirty-minute break should be scheduled for rest and lunch away from the children. Some schools allow staff members an hour while children are napping as long as they stay on the premises. In that way, they are available if needed in an emergency.

TERMINATION OF EMPLOYMENT

Your personnel policies statement should include procedures for *terminating employment*. How much notice is required when you or the staff member ends employment? It is customary to have a two-week notification. State the causes for termination.

Set up a grievance process that can be followed when problems arise. Such a procedure might prevent termination of employment, increase staff morale, and decrease turnover. One church school has the following statement:

> In the event of disagreements between members of the teaching staff, the Director will make the final decision. When there is a disagreement on procedure between members of the teaching staff and the Director, the Director may ask the Vice-President, Education, to arbitrate. Both parties, Director and staff member, will abide by the decision.

This statement provides for most disputes to be settled by working through the chain of command from staff member to director to church board. In some cases, staff members might have such serious disagreements with a director that some other method needs to be in place. You may want to designate some person within your school organization that staff members can contact when problems cannot be resolved by going through the usual channels.

THE JOB DESCRIPTION

Include a *job description* for each position. This is a list of duties and responsibilities. A teacher's job description should include all activities related to teaching, communicating with parents, and attending staff meetings. You might want to include minimum legal and local qualifications for the position as well (see Figure 8–5).

Job Descriptions for personnel other than teachers will have information related to the particular position. As an example, a cook's job description may include statements about planning menus, preparing food, purchasing food items, storing food, and maintaining kitchen cleanliness (see Figure 8–6).

ADVANCEMENT OPPORTUNITIES

Your school may offer opportunities for staff to *advance to higher pay levels or to other positions*. If so, include that information in your personnel policies manual. State the conditions for advancement, either further education or time of service. A salary scale showing the steps, the requirements for each step, and the salary at each level is an easy way to furnish this information.

JOB DESCRIPTION: CLASSROOM TEACHER

The person in this position is responsible for the general management of a group of fifteen children between the ages of two and five.

QUALIFICATIONS

The person selected for this position must have successfully completed at least twelve postsecondary units in early childhood courses. In addition, this person must have had two years' experience as a teacher in a preschool classroom. Personal qualifications for this position include the ability to interact effectively with both children and parents, the ability to work cooperatively with other staff members, and the ability to be flexible. Good health would be beneficial.

RESPONSIBILITIES

The teacher will be responsible for planning and conducting a program for a group of children and all activities relating to that program. Duties will include, but are not limited to:
- Planning and conducting daily experiences for the children based on the goals of the school.
- Preparing all materials required to implement the program.
- Planning and maintaining a physical environment that meets the goals of the school, is safe and free of health hazards, and is attractive.
- Planning for the needs of individual children in regard to their interests, handicaps, pace, and style of learning.
- Including materials and experiences in the classroom that foster children's cultural or ethnic identity.
- Attending and participating in staff meetings, training sessions, and planning activities.
- Participating in recommended courses, conferences, or other activities for professional growth.
- Participating in ongoing assessments of children's development and progress.
- Planning and participating in activities designed to include parents in the education of their children.
- Conducting ongoing parent contacts and conferences to notify parents of their children's progress.
- Assisting in public relations events sponsored by the school.

Figure 8–5   Sample job description for teacher.

PERSONNEL RECORDS

Licensing guidelines usually require each school to maintain up-to-date records on each employee. So it is important to complete each file as soon as possible after hiring and to update it as necessary. The contents of the file may vary from school to school but generally will contain similar kinds of information. The following paragraphs describe the categories of records in a personnel file.

Application Materials

Each file should contain an application form that is usually completed even before the person is hired. The form should have a place to record the employee's name, address, Social Security number, and a person to contact in case of emergency. Application records may also contain:

- Records of education and relevant experience.
- Transcripts and/or credentials.
- Reference letters or forms.

Health

Maintain health records on each employee. If your school requires a preemployment physical examination, place a summary of that exam in the file. Many states require periodic tuberculosis testing for preschool and day care personnel. The test results should be in the file. Immunization against hepatitis B is recommended. Include the record in each personnel file.

Any on-the-job injuries should certainly be recorded in the employee's file. Include the treatment given and the outcome. You might also want to keep a record of each person's absences due to illness. Frequent illness may indicate that some measure needs to be taken to ensure better health in that employee.

JOB DESCRIPTION: COOK

The person in this position will be responsible for the general planning and implementation of all food services of the school.

QUALIFICATIONS

This person must have had experience in quantity cooking and have shown an ability to plan for economical purchases of foods. This person should be able to plan, prepare, and serve nutritious and appetizing meals under the supervision of the school's nutritionist. This person should have good personal cleanliness habits and should be able to maintain an orderly and hygienic kitchen. Lastly, this person should like being in an environment with young children and be able to work well with other adults.

RESPONSIBILITIES

- Using menus planned by the nutritionist, purchase, prepare, and serve two meals and two snacks each day to all the children.
- Reviewing the food service periodically with the nutritionist and the director.
- Coordinating food services with other activities of the school.
- Incorporating foods for special celebrations into the regular menus.
- Maintaining a clean and orderly kitchen and storage area.
- Storing foods in such a way as to minimize waste.
- Participating in periodic training sessions with other staff members to increase knowledge of child development.
- Attending training sessions as required to upgrade knowledge of nutrition and food preparation.

Figure 8–6 Sample job description for cook.

Employment Record

Include an employment record form in each file. This should show the starting date, any leaves that might have been granted, and the final day of employment. Allow space for salary levels during the time of employment. When pertinent, include any promotions or transfers to another school within your organization.

Allow staff to add to their own files if they wish. Special awards or commendations are examples of additional information to add to an employment record.

Evaluation

If your school has a system of evaluation, place the record of each rating in the employee's file. A series of assessments over a period of time will provide you with a good record of each individual's job performance. A periodic review of evaluations may point to the need to provide more, or different kinds of, in-service training.

Conferences

Record any conferences you schedule with your staff members and place them in each employee's file. This will include routine conferences that follow each evaluation. But it should also include conferences that you or the employee request to discuss a problem. Keep the record brief and to the point. State the problem that was discussed and briefly describe any resolution.

Termination of Employment

When employees leave a job or are fired, place a record in their file. A brief note stating the reason should be enough. Be objective and factual.

Recommendations

Employees who have left your school may ask you for a reference letter for a new job. When you do write a letter, put a copy in the employee's file. You can fill future requests, unless asking for specific information, by copying the first letter of recommendation. Note in the file the dates and to whom copies have been sent.

The creation of a professionally oriented atmosphere in your school is a challenge. It often means a delicate balance between economic pressures and personnel requirements. Offer the best possible salary you can afford and some fringe benefits. Beyond that, personnel policies that convey to your staff members they are important will go a long way toward making your school "a good place to work." These efforts should result in less employee turnover and greater harmony among staff.

SUMMARY

Develop and follow systematic procedures when seeking new staff members. Important factors to look for are education, experience, personal characteristics, skills, and knowledge.

Prepare a statement listing full requirements for each specific position. Repeat these in advertising for positions both inside and outside the school.

Standardize the selection process. Screen applications for minimum requirements, check references, and note special talents.

Prepare an interview schedule. Set up the interviews and interviewing committee. A chairperson designates uniform question areas to be covered. Everyone on the committee should record impressions of each candidate immediately after the interview.

Notify the person selected as soon as possible, and also inform those not selected. Personnel selection is not an easy process, but careful procedures pay big dividends.

Once the personnel are hired, induct them into fair and consistent employee practices. A written contract is one of the best ways to do this. Spell out other procedures in a policies statement. These should include their physical environment, health and safety conditions, terms of employment, job description, and advancement opportunities.

Personnel records are vital and often required by law. A permanent file should include the original application, health records, dates of employment and duties involved, evaluations and conferences, and date and reason for termination (if needed).

Everything considered, open, frank, and reasonable personnel practices lead to happier employees and reduced turnover.

SELECTED FURTHER READING

Blood, P.J. 1993. "But I'm Worth More Than That!" *Young Children*, 48 (3) 65–68.

Bredekamp, S., and Willer, B. 1993. "Professionalizing the Field of Early Childhood Education: Pros and Cons." *Young Children*, 48 (3) 82–84.

Goffin, S., and Lombardi, J. 1988. *Speaking Out: Early Childhood Advocacy*. Washington, DC: National Association for the Education of Young Children.

Manfred/Petitt, L. 1993. "Child Care: It's More Than the Sum of Its Tasks." *Young Children*, 49 (1) 40–42.

Phillips, C. 1990. "The Child Development Associate Program: Entering a New Era." *Young Children*, 45 (2) 24–27.

National Association for the Education of Young Children. 1990. "NAEYC Position Statement on Guidelines for Compensation of Early Childhood Professionals." *Young Children*, 46 (1) 30–32.

Whitebrook, M., Howes, C., and Phillips, D. 1989. "Who Cares: Child Care Teachers and the Quality of Care in America. Executive Summary of the National Child Care Staffing Study." Oakland, CA: Child Care Employee Project.

STUDENT ACTIVITIES

1. Write a statement for recruiting an applicant for your job.
2. Get application forms from three different schools. Note the different kinds of information each asks. What does this tell about the school?
3. Role-play an interview with a prospective teacher. Alternate the roles of teacher and director. Ask for subjective feelings involved in each role. What insights does this give in this process?
4. Write a job description for child care assistant.
5. Invite several teachers and directors to discuss salaries and fringe benefits with your class.

REVIEW

1. List five sources for recruiting teacher applicants.
2. This chapter listed characteristics most directors look for when recruiting staff members. How many can you recall?
3. List the skills teachers need in order to fulfill their job responsibilities.
4. What information should be included in a recruitment statement?
5. Describe the process for screening applicants for a staff position.
6. Who should be included in the screening process for new staff members?
7. Formulate questions to be used in an interview to obtain the following kinds of information:
   a. attitudes toward differences in people
   b. specific skills
   c. knowledge of child development
8. What points should be covered in a contract?
9. List the kinds of information that are contained in a statement of personnel policies.
10. What kinds of information should be included in a personnel file?

GLOSSARY

Contract   written agreement between a child development facility and the employee that promotes job security.

Knowledge   a familiarity with a particular subject or branch of learning.

Probationary period   the time before the full contract goes into effect, usually from one to three months.

Skill   an ability that comes from knowledge, practice, or aptitude (sometimes called competency).

Statement of personnel policy   written document covering employer-employee relations.

9

Staff Supervision and Training

OBJECTIVES

After studying this chapter, the student should be able to:

- Discuss the components of effective supervision.
- List the steps in an evaluation process.
- Cite methods and sources for staff training.
- Discuss strategies for preventing burnout among employees.

Staff members in early childhood programs come from a variety of backgrounds. Typically, there are *three different paths* taken by those who become teachers or caregivers: the traditional path of *academic preparation*, the parent path of *first-hand experience*, and the accidental path beginning with *an unrelated job*. In the first group are persons who set out to prepare for an already chosen profession in early childhood education. They attend college and do supervised teaching. In the second group are persons who learn from first-hand experience of caring for their own children. They may gain additional experience through becoming home-based child care providers or participating in Head Start. In the third group are persons who prepare for a career unrelated to teaching but by luck or chance find themselves in a setting where there are children. The work is rewarding and they decide to change careers.

Almost every child development center or child care center will have on the staff individuals who fit the above three categories. The reality is that directors cannot afford to recruit only persons with *extensive academic preparation* in early childhood education to fill the positions in their school or center. One reason is that the supply is so limited that *untrained persons are desperately needed to care for all the children* who are in group settings. Another reason is that there is a great need to staff early childhood centers with persons who *reflect the backgrounds of the children* who are enrolled. The children need teachers who come from their own communities, who understand their culture, and who speak their language. Some of these adults will not have extensive academic backgrounds.

FYI

Over half of teachers in 265 high-quality early childhood centers surveyed by the National Association for the Education of Young Children had at least bachelor's degrees. An additional eighteen percent had associate degrees, and another twenty percent had taken some college courses.

SOURCE: Early Childhood Education: What Are the Costs of High-Quality Programs? *Briefing Report to the Chairman, Committee on Labor and Human Resources, U.S. Senate, 1990.*

Directors who *view individual differences of staff members as an asset* will value every staff member regardless of their training or credentials. These directors will also help each to continue to grow as professionals. This can be accomplished through effective and fair methods of *supervision and evaluation, followed by training activities* that motivate staff members to increase their skills. The Council for Early Childhood Professional Recognition is addressing differences in staff education and training on a national level through its Child Development Associate program. The program is administered by the CDA National Credentialing Program in Washington, DC. Teachers in Head Start, early childhood centers, and child care programs can participate. To qualify for a Child Development Associate credential, teachers must show evidence that they are competent to do the following:

- Plan and set up a safe and healthy learning environment.
- Cultivate physical and intellectual competence.
- Support social and emotional development.
- Ensure positive participation of children and adults in the learning environment.
- Establish and maintain close coordination between school and families.
- Sustain a commitment to professionalism.

Participants in the CDA program go through *three steps* before the credential is awarded. They do *field work*, *take courses*, and are *evaluated* by a person appointed by the Council. There are approximately 41,000 CDAs in the United States, with the largest percentage in Head Start. About fifteen percent are in private sector early childhood centers. To receive a copy of *CDA Competency Standards,* write to: Council for Early Childhood Professional Recognition, 1341 G. Street, N.W., Suite 400, Washington, DC 20005, or telephone 800-424-4310.

SUPERVISION OF STAFF

As the director of an early childhood center, you will probably be responsible for supervising all employees, although in Head Start or in large corporate organizations, another employee may fulfill this function. In its narrowest sense, supervision means overseeing staff members during the performance of their jobs. But from a broader perspective, *supervision is a constantly changing relationship between you and your employees that is based on mutual respect.* Your daily contact with employees and the many hours spent talking together facilitate that kind of relationship. This is the basis of an essential support system in which employees can try out new ways of fulfilling job responsibilities.

You can establish a rapport with each staff member by *being available as often as possible.* Start by greeting staff members when they arrive and plan to be free for a short chat. Do relief teaching for short periods while a teacher takes a break, prepares materials, or meets with a parent. Help out in classrooms when there is an emergency such as a sick or injured child. Staff members may need you to be available at the end of the day as well. This is a time when teachers are often tired or discouraged and your willingness to listen may relieve some of the negative feelings. Remember that the above strategies will be effective in developing a relationship of mutual trust only if your attitude expresses genuine caring and willingness to help.

An important part of supervision involves *seeing that policies and procedures are carried out.* In some instances, you issue directives and expect your staff to comply. Safety rules, health procedures, schedules, and methods for ordering materials are all examples. It is important to communicate your expectations clearly to every employee and then do a follow-up to see that they are being carried out. Are the teachers in the infant room following the health procedures when they change diapers? Is the cook following guidelines for ensuring the safety of food during cooking and while serving? In other instances, there is room for differences in interpretation of guidelines. Curriculum goals are a prime example. Each teacher will implement your school's goals somewhat differently. Here, supervision involves assessing whether each teacher's method of implementation follows the guidelines closely enough, or if there is a need for change. You will need to spend time observing in each job setting and then discussing your observations.

When changes are indicated, your job becomes one of *helping employees change.* This is one of the most difficult aspects of being a director/supervisor because it demands a great deal of time and extensive expertise in communication. You become a one-on-one coach, providing ideas, encouragement, and feedback. Sometimes you will observe while at other times you might model behaviors. Inexperienced teachers will need more of your time and coaching, but there will come a time when you can step back and let them be more autonomous. Teachers who have a lot of experience need less time, but still benefit from your support. They need constructive criticism at times, and positive reinforcement at others. As staff members become more accomplished and learn to work within the framework of your school, there is another way in which you will provide supervisory support. These staff members can be helped to *develop ways to evaluate their own performance,* and to discover ways to perform their jobs more effectively. Finally, you may begin to *help these persons develop the skills* needed to take on the responsibility of supervising aides, assistants, student teachers, or volunteers.

EVALUATION OF STAFF PERFORMANCE

Evaluation is a process that determines if the goals of an early childhood center are being met. Teachers are evaluated on their ability to implement the educational goals of the center. Support staff are assessed on their ability to perform their jobs in ways that supplement the educational function. In most education settings, all staff members are evaluated at least once a year. Teachers will often welcome and benefit from more frequent reviews.

Although most teachers and directors see evaluation as a means of professional growth and the basis for improving performance, evaluation has some inherent problems. First, the process creates anxiety in both the person to be evaluated and the one who will do the evaluating. As a rule, few teachers are completely comfortable having someone judge their performance. And many directors are uneasy about judging their staff members.

The second problem is that two different levels of performance are evaluated. On one level are things that are obvious. Performance can be seen and sometimes measured or counted. The secretary types ten letters a day with great accuracy or only eight with quite a few errors. The teacher keeps the room in order or leaves it an absolute mess. On the other level are factors that cannot be seen, touched, or heard. How do you evaluate the ability of a teacher to encourage decision making in children? How do you evaluate the secretary's ability to create an accepting atmosphere for visitors? If only one performance level is used, you may get an incomplete or skewed picture of the staff member's ability.

Third, you must decide who is to be responsible for evaluation. The final responsibility is yours. The actual rating may be done by any of a number of people in a school. Also, you may want to involve more than one person, each one having a specific part in the procedure.

In a small school, you will probably evaluate all the employees. You may work cooperatively with the staff in developing procedures, but you will personally carry them out. This is a director's major responsibility.

In a larger school, you may work within a more complex organization for evaluating performance. Staff members at different levels may be responsible for those under their immediate authority. The head teacher evaluates the assistant teacher(s), and the head cook evaluates the assistant cook, for example.

In a very large system or organization, one person may evaluate all employees. This evaluator works with you and possibly a few other staff members to design and facilitate the process. In some situations, people on a specific job level might evaluate others on the same level. As an example, one teacher might evaluate another teacher. This is called evaluation by one's peers.

Some evaluation systems may include self-evaluation by the employee. This would not replace other evaluations but would supplement them.

You must decide if all employees should be evaluated, or if only those in certain job categories should be rated. Should only teachers and aides be evaluated, or should the performance of all employees in the school be examined? If a school is to create an atmosphere in which children can grow and change, no staff member can remain static. All employees must be aware of their own strengths and weaknesses and be helped to find ways to improve. If the atmosphere is one in which real learning is encouraged, the dynamics must apply to every staff member.

THE EVALUATION PROCESS

Obviously, evaluation cannot focus in great detail on all areas. An overall evaluation in some specific areas may be enough at certain times. Whatever the focal point, the decision of when and what to evaluate should be a cooperative one between the evaluator and the person to be evaluated. No employee should be formally rated without knowing about it in advance.

Objectives

Begin the procedure for evaluation with an agreement between you and the staff member concerning what is to be accomplished during a stated period of time.

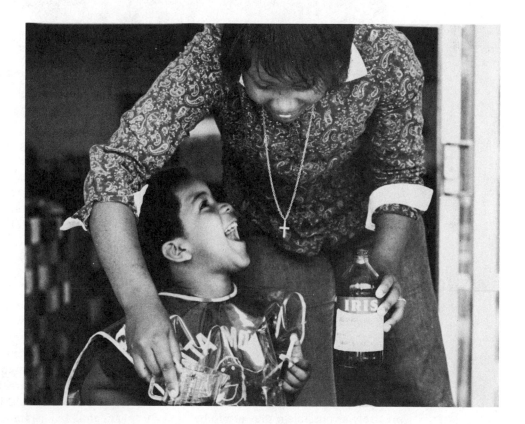

Figure 9–1 Teachers have their own styles.

Figure 9–1 (*continued*)   Teachers have their own styles.

These expectations should flow from the statement of goals for the entire school or
the job description for that position. For example, on of your school's goals might
be the development of decision-making skills in children. You and the teacher may
list as many ways as possible this can be done. The evaluation will determine how
effectively these were actually carried out.

Standards

You and the staff member should also agree on the standards to be used in judging
achievement or nonachievement. The staff member should know what will be considered a satisfactory level. In the example just given, the teacher should know
whether all possible ways of developing decision-making skills must be implemented or whether a certain percentage will be acceptable. A refinement of this is
the establishment of various levels of achievement: outstanding, superior, average,
below average, and inferior . . . or like terms. Each of these should be defined as
precisely as possible if they are to be used. A "pass" and "fail" standard is easier to
understand, but it is sometimes more difficult to use.

You and the staff member should decide when the rating will take place. There should probably be a written understanding that the evaluation will be done at a certain time and will cover a specified period. For instance, the rating will be done on March 8, and will cover the period from September 1 to March 8.

You and the person to be rated should agree on the form of the evaluation. Each one should understand that a checklist will be used, or that there will be two observations on certain dates (October 11 and March 8), followed by a conference. If you are going to observe, let the staff member know what your objectives are. If a checklist is to be used, give a copy to the teacher well in advance of the first visit.

METHODS OF EVALUATION

In an earlier unit, methods of evaluating curriculum were listed and examined. Similar procedures are used for evaluating staff members.

Tests

Tests are primarily an entry-level screening device. However, you can use them to gauge staff development, especially in subject-matter areas. In rare instances, you may want to use personality inventories. Colleges and universities offering teacher-training programs are a good source for locating appropriate test materials. Educational testing services are another source for prepared tests. You may especially want to measure knowledge of child development, curriculum construction, main points of nutrition, and first aid. Teacher competency tests are being developed but, in general, are no substitute for direct observation.

Performance Elements

A newer approach to evaluation begins with the listing of the most important elements in the total job of teaching. This is a joint effort initiated by you and executed by the teacher. From this list, you both choose a number (usually three to five) of critical job elements: things that, if they were not done, would seriously impede the total teaching practice. Or you can both agree to elements that this particular teacher wishes (or needs) to focus on for the next period. These elements would form the basis of evaluation for the next rating cycle. These elements will very likely be unique to each teacher. When these are agreed upon and written down, you may try to agree on a rating scale of, again, three to five points (outstanding through unsatisfactory). The scale is far less important than is agreement on the major critical elements.

The performance elements methodology is an ongoing process. It probably should be for rather limited time periods and a restricted number of elements. One benefit of this method is that you get to know each teacher much more intimately than you would using almost any other rating method.

Observations

When you and your staff members have agreed on objectives to be met, it is time to schedule observation visits to each classroom or work site. Let the staff member know when you will visit, and plan to spend an adequate amount of time. Record as accurately as possible everything you see and hear. (If you use abbreviated words, you will be able to record more information.) Some staff members may be open to having you use videotape or a tape recording, but many will feel intimi-

---

RATING SHEET

Date _____

Name _____   Rated by _____

PERFORMANCE CHARACTERISTICS	Often Sometimes Never
Personal Qualities	
Has a sense of humor	_____
Is friendly, cheerful	_____
Assuming Responsibilities	
Is independent in assuming responsibilities	_____
Initiates solutions to problems	_____
Working with Children	
Determines and plans for each child's needs	_____
Creates a stimulating learning environment	_____
Working with Adults	
Cooperates with other staff members	_____
Includes parents in plans for their children	_____

Specific Strengths _____

_____

Areas for improvements_____

_____

I have read this evaluation.

Signed: _____

(Employee and Title)

Further comments by either employee or supervisor _____

_____

Figure 9–2   Sample rating form.

dated. It is best not to do so unless the person is comfortable with it since you probably will not get an accurate record of performance anyway. Plan more than one observation at different times of the day or several over a period of a month. You and your employees will benefit immeasureably as you get to know each other better through these contacts.

Sampling of Behaviors

Another method you can use to evaluate teacher performance is to record samples of specific kinds of behavior. For example, a teacher might decide that one objective or critical element would be to encourage language development. One way to measure success in meeting this would be to count the number of words spoken by the teacher and by the children at a particular time. This count would be repeated at intervals. Analysis of the results would show whether the children were encouraged to talk. You can also make samplings of other behavior at specified intervals.

You can evaluate performance by collecting products made by the children. An increase in the number or changes in the quality would determine whether an objective or critical element had been achieved. As an example, if a teacher's objective was to develop more extensive use of art materials, a comparison of the number and quality of paintings at the beginning and the end of the semester would yield some information.

Questionnaire or Checklist

The evaluator may complete questionnaires or checklists privately or in the presence of the teacher in a colleague-like way. Self-designed lists may be constructed to be answered by a simple "yes" or "no," but these are often overly simplistic. Lists requiring longer answers or multiple responses are usually preferred. An example might be, "Does this teacher encourage the children to take care of their own physical needs?" The question may be answered *yes* or *no*, but it may also be answered on a scale such as *often*, *sometimes*, or *never*.

USE OF EVALUATIONS

Every evaluation should be followed by a conference between you and the staff member. Focus first on the strengths that person exhibited during the assessment process. Be specific, pointing out the ways in which teacher behaviors support the goals of your school. Then, if there are areas that need improvement, remember that few persons take criticism easily. Be objective, relate your observations in a nonjudgmental manner, then ask the staff member whether his or her perception is the same. If not, how is it different? Ask also "Why did you do it that way?" or "What was your reason for doing it that way?" Listen carefully to responses. Keep in mind that there is seldom a "right way" in any teaching environment. What a teacher does should reflect sound educational practices, and there are many ways to do that.

Whatever the method or combination of methods of evaluation, keep a permanent record of the results. The personnel file of each staff member should contain the periodic evaluations. Each staff member may then see the total picture of development, and the evaluator has a record of past performance.

Give a written copy of the evaluation to each person evaluated. This can be a written copy of the rating or a summation of notes of the conference. There should be no doubt as to the outcome of the evaluation or the areas in which improvement is recommended. On the other hand, reward excellent performance with due praise.

When a staff member gets an unsatisfactory or borderline rating, make a great effort to bring about improvement. Agree as to the specific steps to be undertaken. There are few things so discouraging as to be rated unsatisfactory without being told how to improve. Lists of things to do with milestone dates are sometimes helpful. Simple encouragement often works. Above all else, try to end on an optimistic note.

As will be seen later in this chapter, the evaluation process can reveal strengths and weaknesses in the teaching staff. A good many of these weaknesses, insofar as they involve lack of knowledge, may be remedied by various means of staff training.

Evaluation is an effective and powerful tool to be used with great care and sensitivity. It can be an instrument for change and self-growth. It can also produce profound discouragement if not done well. The following suggestions may help you:

- *Be objective*—Describe specific incidents to illustrate behavior being discussed. (Count them, if possible.)
- *Be gentle*—Discuss the positive things you have observed before going on to the negative.
- *Establish a climate for discussion*—Let staff members know what you are criticizing, but allow time to listen to their points of view. Try to look at the behavior from the teacher's view.
- *Be constructive*—Help teachers or other staff to find alternatives. Provide resources for further information where applicable. Offer help and continued support.
- *Be professional*—Do not discuss evaluations with other staff members unless they share evaluation responsibilities.

STAFF DEVELOPMENT

Staff development is a broad term that refers to all the processes that *encourage personal growth* in employees in any work environment. In an early childhood setting it usually refers to procedures that help the teaching staff achieve greater professionalism. Earlier in this chapter, you read about the supportive relationship between a director and staff members that enables staff to try new ways of carrying out the various functions of their jobs. In addition, changes in teacher behaviors can be brought about through *specific training activities*.

PURPOSE OF TRAINING

All personnel in an early childhood facility come to the job with a certain level of skills and knowledge. Training activities should help them *move to new levels of effectiveness* in carrying out their jobs. Some beginning teachers, for instance, are at a "survival level." They just try to get through the difficulties of each day. In-service instruction can help them interact with children in ways that not only minimize their frustration, but also increase their enjoyment. Experienced teachers sometimes feel "stale" and in need of new ideas or challenges. Training can give these people curriculum ideas that will spark a new enthusiasm for teaching.

Another purpose of staff training is to help those who want to *move to new job categories*. Assistant teachers may dream of having their own class. A teacher may feel ready to assume some administrative tasks. A secretary may want to assist in the classroom. Training activities can give these employees opportunities to gain the skills necessary to move to those new positions.

Another important purpose of staff training is to develop *professional identity*. Teachers sometimes have difficulty defining who they are and relating the importance of what they do. Consequently, others also regard early childhood education as less important than other levels of schooling. As teachers gain knowledge and add to their skills, they will be able to take pride in their work and project a more professional image.

An additional reason for promoting staff development is that *parents are much more demanding of their child's caregivers than they were in the past*. Parents know more about child development and what their children should be learning. They ask teachers questions about their child's stage of growth. They want to know about the school's curriculum and to discuss issues of child rearing. Teachers must have the background to respond knowledgeably.

Stress and burnout are often a fact of life for those who staff all-day, year-round centers. Working with children is exhausting at best. It is even more difficult for the person who has minimal skills to deal with the problems that arise. Staff training can furnish some new strategies that minimize stress and decrease burnout.

PLANNING STAFF DEVELOPMENT

You may want to offer staff training but do not know how to get started. If so, you are not alone, as many directors feel much the same. There is always so much new information available. Research studies and pilot programs reveal more and more information about children's development, curriculum, and family influences. Each time you attend a conference or meet with other professionals, you gain new insights. It is difficult to choose from such a wide variety of training topics. So you have to identify the areas your staff needs at a particular time. There are several ways you can do this.

Staff Needs Assessment

One of the simplest ways to find out where your staff needs additional training is to establish an *open-door policy*. Be available to listen to both staff members and parents. Encourage suggestions and discussion of issues. Be open to questions and welcome ideas for change. You will hear about the areas that staff feel they are weak in or that parents want stressed.

Use either *staff self-evaluation or your own evaluation* as a basis for selecting training activities. As discussed earlier, evaluation should be seen as an instrument for growth. The process should pinpoint areas where training is needed.

Your *own observations* of staff members as they perform their jobs will also give you some ideas about training needs. Obviously, you must have a good knowledge of each job to do this. You should know the basic tasks a person in this job must be able to do. In addition, you should know what will make an "acceptable" performance an "outstanding" one.

Information from professional sources will also give you data to use as you plan staff training. Organizations such as the National Association for the Education of Young Children have lists of competencies that teachers should acquire. College and university child development programs may also have compiled information about teaching skills.

Get regular feedback from your employees about their own progress. Find out if they feel they are using information from previous training sessions. If not, what is standing in their way? You may find that they were not ready to use that information but needed to "fill in some gaps" before doing so. And don't forget to give them positive feedback when you see them striving to be more capable.

Make a list of the topics your staff individually have indicated as training needs. Circulate the list among all staff members. Don't forget the nonteaching staff. They, too, may want to know more about child development or how to manage child behaviors. Ask your employees to rank the topics in the order that is most important to them. In this way, you reassure your staff that you will weigh their concerns.

Once you develop a prioritized list, you will probably see that there are several levels of needs. Some people must "fill in the gaps" of very basic information that all persons who interact with children need to know. Others want practical information such as planning a more exciting and challenging curriculum. Still others may be ready to explore theoretical issues such as learning theory or the influence of environment on children's development.

Size of Groups

Decide next if you will do staff training for all personnel or for small groups at a time. If your staff members are extremely diversified in their levels of knowledge, you may want to divide them or even provide individualized training for some. On the other hand, people learn from others. So sometimes a group with mixed abilities allows for learning from peers.

If you have a large number of employees, you might find that the entire staff makes an unwieldy group for certain kinds of training activities. A discussion is difficult if there are more than ten people. A workshop can often accommodate as many as your space allows. Conversely, a small group sometimes needs outside stimulation and ideas. If you have only a few employees, consider using films, lectures, or field trips.

STAFF INTERESTS SURVEY

I need information concerning topics for upcoming staff training sessions. The following is a list of some suggestions that have been made in discussions with staff members. Choose six and rank them in importance to you with "1" being the highest priority.

_____ Ways to enhance children's language development

_____ Using computers in our classrooms

_____ Stimulating more creative outdoor play

_____ Involving children in snack preparations

_____ Individualized music activities

_____ Rearranging our environments to achieve our goals

_____ Carpentry skills for teachers

_____ Easy to plan and implement science activities

_____ Kits for stimulating dramatic play

_____ What are babies really learning?

_____ Conducting more effective parent conferences

_____ Avoiding burnout

Suggestions or comments: _____

_____

_____

_____

Please return your form to me by the end of the month so I can begin to plan upcoming sessions.

Thanks,
Betty Beaumont
Director of Country Day School

Figure 9–3 Staff interests survey.

Time

Finding the time for staff training is very difficult in an all-day school. Many schools resolve this problem by scheduling meetings while the children are napping. Teachers can rotate nap room duty, allowing the others to attend. Do not make the mistake of always assigning one person to nap room duty, thus excluding that person from training sessions.

Consider scheduling *training meetings before or after school hours.* Hold small group meetings early in the morning before the children arrive. Serve a light breakfast. You can also hold meetings right after the last child leaves in the evening. Arrange a "pot luck" dinner and have your meeting while you eat. This serves two purposes. It *provides staff social time* and *avoids the fatigue* that comes when you expect staff to return later in the evening. Also, remember that when people are actively involved in discussion or an interesting workshop, they tend to overcome any fatigue they may have felt at the beginning. So if your activities are exciting, staff will be "recharged" rather than tired out at the end.

Place

Choose an appropriate setting for the kind of training activity you choose. If you are planning a workshop, be sure there is enough space for everyone to work. Provide comfortable tables and chairs. Teachers who sit on child-size chairs all day will appreciate your thoughtfulness in providing adult chairs. If you plan a discussion, make sure that everyone can be included. Don't have any "back row sitters," for they will not really feel a part of the proceedings.

Attendance

A question many directors ask is whether attendance at training sessions should be required or voluntary. Staff will be there "in body" if you require it as a condition of employment, but you cannot make them learn. On the other hand, a purely voluntary training policy may result in avoidance by the people who need it most. It is probably best to require staff to attend, and then do your best to make the training provocative and practical.

Skills Application

When a training session has been completed, encourage your staff to practice their new skills as soon as possible. Provide them with the materials they will need. Allow them time to plan and prepare lessons. Following a science workshop, for instance, see that teachers have the kinds of equipment they need to put their new ideas into effect. Many teachers feel really anxious about offering science lessons and need a lot of encouragement. If they have the right equipment, they may feel a bit more secure.

Learning Styles

Just as children learn in very different ways, so do adults. Some people can learn by *seeing or hearing information*. Others need to be actively involved in *doing* before they learn. Ask your staff members to tell you how they learn best. Then choose training activities to meet those needs. For some, a workshop will be the best way to help them learn. For others, films, discussions, or even reading will turn out to be the most effective.

POPULAR TRAINING METHODS

You may choose from a wide variety of available training methods. You will probably use several during any one year, depending on the topics being covered.

Orientation

Begin training as soon as a new employee is hired. Start by giving the new worker your employee handbook. Then sit down with that person to answer any questions. Take the person to the work site (the classroom or the kitchen, for instance). Show where materials are and how to operate the equipment. Introduce other staff members.

Orientation for teachers has some added dimensions from those of other employees. Teachers can read your philosophy and goals in the handbook, but they may need to understand how to implement them in the classroom. So, spend extra time with all new teachers during the early weeks of employment. Visit their classrooms briefly and get to know their teaching styles. (Visits too frequent or too lengthy may overwhelm or frighten some new teachers.) Meet more frequently with new teachers than with your experienced staff. These can be brief meetings before or after school to answer questions or clarify problems. Additional effort in the beginning will often prevent difficulties down the line.

Mentor

Consider using a mentor relationship to help some new teachers. *A mentor is someone who can serve as a role model* to help an inexperienced teacher gain new skills and knowledge. Other words that are sometimes used to describe a mentor are "master teacher," "critic," "supporter," "collaborator," and even a "shoulder to cry on." Choose an experienced teacher to be a mentor. Look for a person who is able to be patient, can accept differences in others, can be an uncritical evaluator, and can search out sources of information as needed. The mentor first establishes a relationship of trust with the beginner, then begins to coach the neophyte in areas of difficulty. The ultimate goal is to reach a stage where the teacher can function independently of the mentor; at this point they become colleagues. Professionals who advocate this kind of training use a variety of methods that seem to have positive results. They:

- Model behavior, or start an activity and ask the trainee to finish.
- Set up activities that the trainee can try later.
- Observe for a whole day, then consider what changes are doable and which are not.
- Give frequent and immediate feedback.
- Encourage experimentation.
- Ask questions that lead to thoughtful discussions. "What gave you the most difficulty today?" "What would have made it easier?" Discuss the responses.

Team Teaching

Another way you can provide informal and ongoing training is to set up a partnership style of training. In this method, two teachers work closely together as equal
partners. Expect them to function as a team, with common aims. Each learns from
the other, as they come to recognize their own strengths and weaknesses. To make
this kind of relationship work, they must be able to overcome the competitiveness many teachers feel. They also have to spend time talking with each other,
planning, learning, and resolving problems. Your participation should be to meet
with them periodically to assess their progress and perhaps suggest resources for
learning.

College and University Classes

Colleges and universities offer another source for training staff. The advantage of
using this resource is that the courses are often taught by well-qualified persons
with wide experience. In addition, other students from varied backgrounds offer
stimulus for learning. The campus setting often offers facilities such as a laboratory school, a library, and even remedial help for those with learning or language
difficulties.

Weigh the disadvantages of college courses for staff training before choosing
this method. You have little control over what is being taught, and the philosophy
of the instructor may differ markedly from your own. It is disruptive when staff
come back to school and want to carry out ideas that differ from yours. The cost of
tuition may be prohibitive for the student and more than your school can support.
An added difficulty is that many college courses are scheduled during the day.
Teachers who work all day cannot attend.

Staff Meetings

The most frequently used method of staff training is the staff meeting. In fact, in
many schools, this is the only time set aside for training. Often, though, these
meetings are not planned and tend to dissipate into unimportant discussion of the
same old topics. They may also become dull vehicles for conveying information
that could be done more efficiently in written form. Neither of these outcomes is
appropriately called "training."

If a staff meeting is the only method you have, then make the most of it. Plan
each meeting and write out an agenda. Distribute the agenda to staff ahead of
time so they can come to the meeting prepared. Set limited objectives for each
meeting to allow for more thorough coverage. Suppose you want to give your staff
a greater understanding of child development. Choose one age level and discuss
physical, cognitive, or emotional growth. Do not try to cover several ages or several
areas of development. Cover one thoroughly and leave time for discussing how the
teachers can use that information in the classroom.

Portfolio

Writing a portfolio can be a meaningful way to encourage teachers to evaluate their own abilities and to upgrade their skills. It is a written documentation of what teachers do, why they do it, and how it relates to competency as a professional. *Portfolios are used as a self-study vehicle and as the basis of discussions* between teachers and supervisors. They are the primary means for assessing competency of Head Start teachers who are candidates for the Child Development Associate credential. However, portfolio writing is an effective instrument for staff development in any early childhood setting. An important benefit your teachers will gain from portfolio writing is practice describing the teaching processes in their own words. As they learn to refine and clarify their writing, they will be able to view differently what they do. They will gain insight into their own strengths and weaknesses plus an awareness of where changes need to be made.

Schedule time to discuss portfolio entries with teachers. This can be a time when you can focus on teachers' strengths and show genuine interest in their progress. A dialogue about recorded incidents will also give you a greater understanding of how each teacher functions in the classroom. At times, you will need to answer questions or to be a resource for finding information.

Workshops

A workshop is sometimes called a "hands-on experience." Participants get actively involved in doing or in making something to broaden their practical skills. In a workshop, teachers can learn songs, make curriculum materials, and practice reading or telling stories. A workshop could just as easily be planned for other job categories as well. Imagine a workshop in which the cooks from several schools get together to try out new recipes that children might like.

Again, planning is the key to the success of a workshop. Provide a comfortable setting with places for everyone to work. Make sure that the task to be accomplished can be done in the time allotted. Have enough materials for everyone to use. Distribute copies of directions or any information needed to complete the task. Be available to offer help or give encouragement as participants work.

Group Discussions

The format of a group discussion can range from open discussion during the entire meeting, to a short interchange following a presentation. Group discussion is one of the most effective ways to help adults learn. One of the tremendous advantages of this format is that often your whole staff can be included, not just teachers. Some of the same problems are encountered whether a staff member works in the kitchen, drives the bus, or manages a classroom. Each frequently has the same kinds of reactions to children's behaviors and needs to have an outlet for expressing those feelings.

Use group discussions to pursue a specific topic. As an example, discipline is a commonly requested topic for discussion. Ask any group of adults who are around children all day, and they will tell you that discipline is their biggest problem. You could just give them a list of techniques to manage difficult children. But a more effective way of helping them is to encourage a discussion of their own feelings about children's behavior. They may find that their own reactions contribute to the trouble. Once they have gained that kind of insight, they will be more open to trying new techniques for managing children's behavior.

Role Playing

Role playing is a drama in which the participants put themselves into a designated situation. It is an informal type of meeting that can be adapted to many kinds of problems.

Role playing is an excellent tool for resolving interaction problems between adults. Several participants act out the problem or situation. The audience watches, listens, and then discusses what happened. The "actors" can contribute how they felt as the play progressed. The final result may be a discovery of alternate ways of behaving, or just the insight gained from understanding the feelings involved. When two staff members are having a problem, ask them to role play, reversing their parts. When each is asked to "assume the role" of the other, the situation may look quite different.

Exchange Observations

Exchanging observations between teachers within your school is another way of encouraging new ideas. By mutual agreement, two teachers observe each other in the classroom. After the visits, they meet to discuss their observations.

Obviously, this kind of staff training can work only when teachers trust and respect each other. Do not try this at the beginning of a school year, or with new or insecure teachers.

Films, Slides, and Tapes

Use audio-visual materials to add other dimensions to your training sessions. Public libraries have many materials that are free. Also, allow some money in your yearly budget for renting or purchasing materials. Watch the local television schedule for programs that can be used. (Remember that copyright laws forbid you to keep taped materials longer than 45 days.) If you or a staff member owns a video camera, make your own tapes. Look for slides or tapes at professional conferences. Write to the National Association for the Education of Young Children for a listing of their offerings. Some of their videos that can be used for staff training are the following:

- #832 "Music Across the Curriculum."
- #887 "NAEYC's Position on Developmentally Appropriate Practice: A Panel Discussion and Critique."
- #807 "Play and Learning."
- #808 "Reading and Young Children."
- #889 "Testing and Tracking."
- #810 "The Uniqueness of the Early Childhood Professions."
- #831 "Whole Language Learning."

Field Trips

You can help broaden your staff's learning by arranging field trips. Some visits can be made as a group in the evening or on weekends. Others will have to be made by individuals when they can be relieved from duties at school. Visits to other schools always give teachers new ideas for curriculum or arranging their environment. Often, just the opportunity to talk to other teachers in different settings renews enthusiasm for teaching. On a weekend, go as a group to a supplier of learning materials. Many of these places have employees who are knowledgeable about children and can offer new ideas for learning activities.

Professional Meetings

Encourage your staff to attend meetings and conferences of professional organizations. Chapters of the National Association for the Education of Young Children are found in many areas of the country. Both you and your staff will benefit from membership. Meetings and conferences offer a wide variety of speakers, workshops, and displays from which teachers can learn. Publications are also available through the organization.

Reading

Provide your employees with books, pamphlets, and magazines that will help them develop their skills. Encourage them to use the materials by bringing some to a staff meeting. Point out some of the interesting articles or parts of a book that they might want to read. Add to your collection as often as you can afford to do so. If your budget is limited and does not allow for the purchase of books, search out what is available in your public library. Make book lists and distribute them to your staff.

FORMAT FOR TRAINING SESSIONS

It may be helpful to have in mind some principles for effective training sessions that can be used for several different methods. Vary them to fit each method of training you choose.

- Arrange the setting for the purpose of the session.
- Provide participants with an agenda, including objective.
- Prepare the setting ahead of time.
-    a.   Put out materials, arrange chairs, provide coffee.
-    b.   Check audio-visual equipment if to be used.
- Carry out the procedure as planned.
-    a.   Begin and end at the time planned.
-    b.   Stay as close as possible to the objective.
- Ask participants to evaluate the meeting.
- Follow through.
-    a.   Provide materials so participants can practice new skills.
-    b.   Get feedback after staff put new ideas into practice.

STAFF RELATIONSHIPS

A discussion of staff development would not be complete without considering how the people in a school get along with each other. They spend long hours together each day. Nerves become frayed with the constant demand that young children make on their patience and energy. Bickering, competitiveness, or burnout may result. As the director, you are the key person in changing destructive patterns of interacting to ones that are positive and cooperative.

Communication

Start by helping your staff to develop good communication skills. Plan a workshop on effective communication using Thomas Gordon's "I" messages. Ask staff to practice stating problems or concerns by starting a sentence with phrases such as "I feel sad," "I get upset," or "I am discouraged." Discuss the reactions on listeners when this approach is used. Focus their attention on nonverbal communication as well. Discuss the messages that might be conveyed by a clenched jaw, tightly folded arms, lack of eye contact, or raised eyebrows. Follow the discussion with a role play and ask the participants to note whether "I" messages were used and whether what was said was congruent with the body language used.

After this kind of workshop, encourage your staff members to resolve some of their own problems. Rather than having them "run to you" each time a difference arises, send them back to talk to each other. They will probably find they like the feeling of competence that comes from dealing with difficulties themselves. You will also see that a closer rapport develops among staff members.

At staff meetings, encourage each member to participate. In any group of people, some speak out whether they have something important to say or not. Others seldom say anything. Limit the participation of the "big talkers" and encourage the nonparticipants to contribute.

Decision Making

If you have established a democratic atmosphere in your school, you will want your staff to develop good decision-making skills. Rather than making all decisions yourself, allow your staff to make some. The purchase of expensive pieces of playground equipment is an example. You will probably find that some want one type and others want another. If you choose, part of the staff will be happy and the other part disgruntled. So ask them to go through a decision-making process and make the choice themselves. They will learn from the process and will probably be more satisfied with the result.

To decide which playground equipment to purchase, ask staff to go through the following steps.

1. *Gather information.* In this case, they will want to find out as much as they can about the possible choices. What do the pieces look like and how long are they expected to last? What is the cost of each piece? What possible uses can children make of each? Is there a good place on the playground to put all the pieces?

2. *Set priorities.* The next step is to list their priorities based on the goals of the school. One piece may lend itself to imaginative play, while the other will develop children's physical abilities. Which will more closely fit the school's goals?

3. *Make a choice.* A consensus should be reached among staff about which one to choose.

4. *Decide how to implement the choice.* Is the equipment to be purchased immediately? Will it be installed during school hours so the children can watch, or on weekends so the children can be surprised?

5. *Evaluate the choice.* For future learning, ask staff to evaluate the decision after a period of time to determine whether the choice was a good one. In this example, are the children using the equipment as expected? Are there other ways it is used that weren't expected? Should a different choice have been made?

This process of decision making has been described in terms of a concrete object, the piece of equipment. The same steps can be adapted to other kinds of decisions.

BURNOUT

Stress and burnout are problems that plague many people who work in jobs that require a lot of emotional energy. The very character of early childhood programs contributes to the likelihood of staff burnout. Several causes of burnout can be identified.

Causes

Lack of recognition as a professional is one cause that is often listed by teachers. Their low status is reflected in the minimum salaries that many schools pay their staff. Along with low pay, few have fringe benefits such as a medical or retirement plan. Low status is also seen in the reaction of some parents to early childhood teachers and caregivers. They may comment "You only play with the children all day," or they refer to the day care center teacher as their child's "babysitter." Few parents have a real idea of the curriculum of their child's school and, thus, little appreciation of what is being taught. All these things contribute to feelings by teachers that they are not worth very much.

Time pressures also lead to fatigue and burnout. Day care teachers spend six to eight hours a day with children. During that time, children's demands leave little opportunity for any planning or preparation. Few schools pay teachers for time away from the children. Any work they might do to enhance classroom activities must be done at the end of a long day. Consequently, planning may be haphazard, further contributing to dissatisfaction with their job.

An unrealistic view of their role may be another cause of burnout in teachers. In their book *Planning and Administering Early Childhood Programs*, Decker and Decker write that teachers are "unable to maintain a detached concern" because they see themselves as surrogate parents. These authors also feel that teachers are so indoctrinated with the importance of the early years that they are let down if they don't achieve what they expect. Preschool teachers do often feel personally responsible for the development of the children in their care. Any achievements the children make confirm their own value as teachers. Any failures to move forward are considered evidence of the teachers' failures.

Classroom management problems sometimes cause extreme stress, and then teacher burnout. One difficult child in a group can create chaos for all the others if the behavior is not curbed. Inexperienced teachers who have not developed ways of managing these children have an especially difficult time. More experienced teachers, who still have difficulty being firm, may also find this kind of child "trying."

Administrative incompetence and insensitivity should certainly be mentioned in a discussion of burnout. This refers to directors who fail to take into account the needs or feelings of employees. Sometimes this happens when directors make decisions that affect staff without consulting them. Other times, directors are unaware of how teachers feel. When asked, teachers will describe a variety of behaviors that fall into this category. "I came in one morning to find that I had two new children in my group." "I was told that I couldn't take the time off to go to my daughter's school play because they couldn't pay a substitute." "My director does not really understand how much that one child disrupts my group. She says I should be able to control him." All these examples are indications that the directors did not take the time to consider their employees' feelings. The result could be built-up resentment and then burnout.

Prevention

A variety of sources offer suggestions for alleviating stress and preventing burnout. The following have been culled from several of these sources. For more in-depth reading, look to the Selected Further Reading at the end of this chapter. Among the items on the following list, you will find some that you as director can facilitate. Pass the others on to your employees as suggestions to help themselves.

1. Deal with problems as they occur. Don't let them build up.
2. Find an outlet for tension that works for you. Try walking, gardening, games, crossword puzzles, etc. Stay away from the things that work for only a short time, such as eating or drinking too much.
3. Learn more about child development. When you know what to expect of children at different age levels, you will be neither surprised when some behaviors appear, nor disappointed when others don't.
4. Be prepared each day with lesson plans, but be flexible and willing to adapt or change those plans as needed.
5. Keep records on children so that you can really see they have made some progress.
6. Try to detach yourself from situations that can't be changed. There will always be some children you cannot change, or some families you cannot help. Learn to accept this.
7. Keep in good physical health. Get enough sleep; eat a balanced diet.
8. Get away from the children for brief periods during the day. A ten-minute break can definitely help.
9. Try to avoid getting caught up in the daily "gripe sessions" with fellow employees. It does little good and only makes you feel worse.
10. Become an advocate for recognition of early childhood education as a profession with adequate and competitive compensation.

Your challenge as a director of a school for young children is to help your staff become the very best they possibly can be. This is admittedly more formidable than trying to help children change. Adults are less malleable and are more set in their ways. They resist any change with reactions of anger or anxiety. But when you begin to see the results of a good staff training program, you will feel that all your efforts have been worth it.

SUMMARY

Staff members in early childhood programs take different paths to become teachers: the traditional path of academic preparation, the parent path of experience, and the accidental path beginning with an unrelated job. All are needed to care for all the children who are in group settings.

Directors who value individual differences will be faced with the task of helping each to grow as professionals. This can be accomplished through fair and effective methods of supervision and evaluation, followed by training activities. Another way that teachers can become more professional is to participate in the Child Development Associate credential program.

Supervision means overseeing staff members during the performance of their jobs. It is also a constantly changing relationship between director and employees.

Evaluation is a process to determine if the goals of an early childhood center are being met. The evaluation process should begin with an agreement on goals to be reached during the time period being assessed and include standards of measurement. Methods of evaluation may be a combination of tests, observations, samplings of behavior, questionnaires, and checklists. A record of evaluation results should be placed in personnel files and a written copy given to the teacher. Every evaluation should be followed by a conference between the director and the staff member.

Staff development is a broad term that refers to all the processes that encourage personal growth in employees in any work environment. In an early childhood setting, it refers to procedures that help teaching staff achieve greater professionalism. Staff training needs are revealed during supervision and evaluation activities. Other sources of information include staff self-evaluation and information from professional sources.

Plan training activities: group staff appropriately, find a time that fits staff schedules, choose a place that fits the activity, and decide whether attendance is voluntary or mandatory. When a training session is completed, encourage staff to practice their new skills.

Popular training methods are: orientations, mentor relationships, team teaching, college classes, staff meetings, portfolio writing, workshops, group discussions, role playing, exchange observations, audio-visual materials, field trips, professional meetings, and reading.

Staff development must include helping staff get along with one another. They will benefit from practice in communication and decision making.

Burnout may occur among persons who work in early childhood settings. It is important to identify the cause and to provide staff with suggestions for preventing or alleviating stress.

SELECTED FURTHER READING

Abbot-Shim, M. 1990. "In-Service Training: A Means to Quality Care." *Young Children,* 45 (2) 14–18.

Bloom, P.J. 1988. *A Great Place to Work: Improving Conditions for Staff in Young Children's Programs.* Washington, DC: National Association for the Education of Young Children.

Bredecamp, S. 1992. "Composing a Profession." *Young Children.* 47 (2) 52–54.

Caruso, J.J. 1991. "Supervisors in Early Childhood Programs: An Emerging Profile." *Young Children,* 46 (6) 20–24.

Decker, C.A., and Decker, J.R. 1992. *Planning and Administering Early Childhood Programs.* New York, NY: Macmillan Publishing Company.

Eiselen, S. 1992. *The Human Side of Child Care Administration.* Washington, DC: National Association for the Education of Young Children.

Goffin, S., and Lombardi, J. 1988. *Speaking Out: Early Childhood Advocacy.* Washington, DC: National Association for the Education of Young Children.

of growth. In curriculum courses, they have been taught how to plan learning activities. They may have some understanding of children's behavior from formalized opportunities to observe children.

Student teachers receive college credit for their field experience so they are likely to have a commitment to completing the required number of hours. As part of their teaching assignment, they must plan lessons and then present them. They usually are eager to use the skills they have learned in their course work.

Student teachers know they will be evaluated on their work in the classroom. This brings about a certain amount of anxiety in some, but it also causes them to work harder to do well. They are aware that future jobs may depend on their success in student teaching.

Many student teachers are quite young, in their early twenties or younger. They may have chosen this field because they enjoyed caring for younger siblings at home. Their age and experience place these young people somewhere between adolescence and adulthood in their own development. Sometimes their interactions with children are more like that of siblings than teacher to child. On the other hand, their youth and energy enable them to interact with children enthusiastically. They often bring a sparkle to the classroom that is missing when teachers are becoming "burned out."

Today, more and more older women are returning to college. They, too, liked being with their children, so they turn to early childhood education as a career. But their performance in student teaching is different from that of the young students. Because of their maturity and experience, they play more of a parental role in their interactions with children. They tend to accept children's behavior more easily since they have been through it all at home.

Some student teachers may be young men. Although the low salary level keeps many from entering this field, a few choose to do so in spite of the low income. Their presence is particularly valuable in today's schools where many of the children do not have fathers living with them. "Psychological fathers" is the term David Giveans, producer and narrator of the film *Men in Early Childhood Education*, uses to describe these teachers. He views the male teacher of young children as a balancing role model in the traditionally female world of the preschool.

ROLE OF THE DIRECTOR

As director of the school, your participation with student teachers will probably be limited. Your primary responsibility is to see that the partnership with the college or university is a positive one for all involved.

Each student teacher is assigned to a classroom under the direction of a staff member, who is often called a "master teacher." Students may spend one or several days a week in this placement. The master teacher and student should meet after each day of practice teaching, so allow your teachers extra time for this purpose. Recognize the extra time and energy needed, and relieve them of some other responsibilities. Acknowledge their efforts by praise or a salary differential if pos-

Hildebrand, V. 1993. *Management of Child Development Centers*, 3rd ed. New York, NY: Macmillan Publishing Company.

Levine, M. 1992. "Observations on the Early Childhood Profession." *Young Children*, 47 (2) 50–51.

STUDENT ACTIVITIES

1. With permission of the director, survey the staff members of a child care center. Ask the following questions:
    a. How long have you been a teacher/caregiver?
    b. Where did you work before your present position?
    c. What kinds of academic preparation or experience qualified you for this job?

    Summarize your findings. Compare the profiles of staff members at this center with the three paths leading to a teaching profession that are described in this chapter.
2. Interview a director of a child care center. Ask about the methods used to evaluate teachers. Are support staff evaluated as well? If so, what methods are used?
3. Plan a staff training workshop. State specifically what will be accomplished, materials needed, and room arrangement. If possible, implement your plan at the school where you work. How successful was the session? Are there things you should have done differently?

REVIEW

1. There are three different paths that lead to becoming teachers or caregivers. What are they?
2. Teachers must show evidence that they are competent in six areas in order to qualify for a Child Development Associate credential. List the six competencies.
3. Define the words *supervision* and *evaluation*.
4. Briefly describe the following methods of evaluation and the ways they are used:
    a. tests
    b. performance elements
    c. sampling of behaviors
    d. observations
    e. questionnaire or checklist
5. State two purposes of staff training.
6. Finding time for staff training is often difficult in an all-day school. What suggestions were made in this chapter?
7. List seven popular training methods.
8. Discuss the use of portfolio writing as a staff training method.

9. Describe the steps in setting up a training session.
10. List the steps in a democratic decision-making process.
11. What are the causes of professional burnout?
12. List the suggestions for preventing burnout.

GLOSSARY

Critical job elements   things which, if not done, would seriously impede the total teaching practice.

Evaluation   process to determine whether the goals of an early childhood center are being met.

Mentor   someone who can serve as a role model to help an inexperienced teacher gain new skills and knowledge.

Supervision   overseeing staff members during the performance of their jobs.

10

Student Teachers/Volunteers

> **OBJECTIVES**
> After studying this chapter, the student should be able to:
> - Describe the role of director regarding student teachers.
> - List the criteria for choosing a master teacher.
> - Discuss how children may react to student teachers.
> - Explain how volunteers may most effectively be used.
> - List several sources of volunteers.
> - Define what qualities make volunteers most valuable.
> - Describe how volunteers may be trained.

Many postsecondary institutions offer a course in early childhood education or related fields. Often, degree requirements for these fields include some time spent in practical experience with children. Practice teaching, sometimes called field experience, provides that exposure.

Although some of these institutions have their own laboratory schools where students get their practical experience, many do not. To fill the need for field experience, they use schools and day care centers in their communities. Even when there is a lab school, many use outside placements to provide additional experience for students. Community schools are seen as a step into "the real world." Thus, your school may be asked to provide placements for student teachers. Before you and your staff agree, you should know as much as possible about the students themselves and what will be expected of you.

CHARACTERISTICS OF STUDENT TEACHERS

Student teachers, like volunteers, are unpaid. However, they differ from volunteers in some significant ways.

Before they come to your school, student teachers will have taken some courses in early childhood development. They usually have a basic knowledge of the stages

sible. When necessary, be prepared to give support or help to resolve any problems that arise.

Notify all master teachers well in advance of the time a student will be starting an assignment. Teachers should have plenty of time to prepare for the arrival of a new person in the classroom. They will want to let parents know about the student. Children should certainly be told. Teachers can tell children, "Melissa will be coming to our room tomorrow and will be here every Tuesday. She is learning how to be a teacher at her own school. She will be one of your teachers on that day and will read stories, help with art, and do a lot of other things with us."

Figure 10–1   Male teachers make good role models.

An adviser or supervisor is usually appointed by the students' institution to work with their off-campus placements. You and your master teachers should meet with the adviser before the placement starts. Clarify goals and discuss expectations for the students. Be clear about when and how often the college supervisor will visit.

CHOICE OF A MASTER TEACHER

Several teachers in your school may indicate their willingness to accept student teachers into their classrooms. It is up to you to decide whether each of these staff members will be able to offer a good learning atmosphere for the students. Some criteria to help you judge may be helpful.

The first determinant should be *willingness* to accept a student teacher. Some teachers may not feel ready to work with student teachers. Respect their judgment and do not try to change their minds. Discuss their reasons with them but allow them to decline. They may feel more capable later.

Teachers must be amenable to *sharing* children and teaching tasks with student teachers. Most teachers are accustomed to being in charge of all the day-to-day planning and execution of activities. They cherish and jealously guard their close relationships with children. When they decide to accept a student teacher, they must be able to give up some of this autonomy. They will need to step back while student teachers learn how to manage children, watch while student teachers carry out lessons. At first many find it painful, but later they take pride in the increasing competence of their student teachers.

Master teachers must have enough *self-confidence* to withstand the kinds of questions student teachers are likely to ask. From their curriculum courses, student teachers often have formed their own ideas about how lessons should be planned or presented. They may have learned methods of teaching or ways of interacting with children that are different from the master teacher's. They often ask "Why?" when they see things that are unlike what they have been taught. Their questions give them the opportunity to test out their knowledge, but it takes a strong teacher not to feel intimidated.

Master teachers must be able to *allow others to make mistakes*. Many can excuse children but are intolerant when adults make mistakes. When student teachers plan a lesson that turns out to be a fiasco, they get terribly upset. A good master teacher will help the student teacher see what went wrong and make suggestions for changes the next time.

Just as with children, *positive feedback* works with student teachers. The master teacher who can be liberal with praise and positive feedback will give the shaky student teacher more confidence. A good laugh about the disaster of the day helps to put things in proper perspective. Reassurance that the ability to be a good teacher takes time will do wonders.

The most obvious characteristic needed by master teachers is to be good *role models* themselves. Student teachers will observe and often copy what their master teacher does. Choose only your best teachers to help student teachers.

ORIENTATION OF STUDENT TEACHERS

Orientation for student teachers is similar to the introduction given to paid staff members or volunteers. In this case, though, some will take place on the student's campus and some in your school. Often the campus coordinator prepares a handbook for student teachers in addition to presenting information in a pre-placement seminar. You and your staff should have a copy of the handbook and other information presented to the student teachers by the coordinator. Orientation at your school should then supplement campus orientation.

A student teacher should know the following:

- *Details of the placement*—hours, number of weeks, holidays. A calendar will clarify dates.
- *Evaluation procedures*—who will evaluate, when it will be done, how a grade will be given.
- *Supervision*—when college adviser will visit, what will be observed.
- *Requirements*—written lesson plans, daily log, additional papers.

Figure 10–2 Student teaching is hard work.

- *Extra activities*—attendance at staff meetings, parent meetings, parent conferences.
- *Absences*—procedures for reporting to school and making up the time.
- *Organization of school*—lines of responsibility.
- *School characteristics*—goals, grouping of children.
- *Curriculum*—overall curriculum of class where student teacher is assigned.

Figure 10–3   A student teacher begins by observing.

- *Discipline*–school policies for disciplining children.
- *Children*—general information about children in student teacher's class. (Further information about children should be left to your discretion).
- *Problems*—procedures for reporting and resolving any problems student teacher might have.
- *Professionalism*—professional conduct and attitude.

RESPONSIBILITIES OF THE MASTER TEACHER

The master teachers are key persons when student teachers are placed in community schools. It is they who have daily contacts with the student teachers and who make it either a positive or negative experience. Therefore, you can pass some of the following practical suggestions on to your teachers.

- Learn as much about the student teacher's background as possible. Often the college will supply information concerning the courses the student teacher has taken and kinds of experience completed.
- Introduce the student teacher to children, parents, and other staff members. Treat the student teacher like a colleague.
- Allow time for the student teacher to become familiar with the total school environment, the assigned room, and the storage areas.
- Allow the student teacher time to observe before taking over any part of the program.
- Discuss school goals with the student teacher, indicating how these are implemented on a day-to-day basis.
- Plan a calendar for the student teacher to gradually assume teaching responsibilities.
- Pace the student teacher's teaching responsibilities according to readiness to do so. Some student teachers are ready to "plunge in" immediately, but others need time to get acquainted with the setting and the children.
- Let the student teacher know that failure can be a way of learning. Suggest changes and encourage the student teacher to try again.
- Allow the student teacher to try out new ideas. Student teachers often bring a fresh approach to teaching. However, discuss lesson plans before they are presented. Slight changes may forestall problems.
- Schedule time for regular conferences. After each teaching day is the best time. Discuss lessons the student teacher presented as well as interactions with children. Make suggestions for changes if needed.
- Be generous in providing materials and resources to the student teacher.
- Evaluate the student teacher's performance midway in the assignment. This allows time for improvement in any areas that need it.
- Maintain continual communication with the college adviser concerning the student teacher's progress. Immediately discuss any problems. Don't let difficulties build up until they cannot be resolved.
- Be objective when writing the final evaluation. Remember the evaluation may affect the student teacher's future job opportunities.

REACTIONS OF STUDENT TEACHERS

Student teachers will come to your school with mixed feelings. You may have forgotten how you felt when you first faced a group of children. So it will be helpful to review some of the concerns student teachers express. Understanding these feelings may allow you to deflect problems.

The most frequently mentioned fear is that *they will not be able to control children's behavior*. When faced with a child who is saying "You can't make me," many student teachers are at a loss. This is especially true of the young student teachers who seem to forget they are bigger and stronger than the child. Male teachers seem to carry more authority and thus, feel more confident. In addition, children see men as more powerful and tend to be more compliant with them.

Student teachers often say they are *unsure of their role in the classroom*. During their practice teaching period, they take on many of the teaching tasks. But they often do not know how far they can go to make changes in the classroom environment or activities. Children sometimes say, "You're not my real teacher," making it even more difficult for the student teacher.

Student teachers may be *afraid that the children will not like them*. When the children do not respond immediately to student teachers, they often interpret it as dislike. Student teachers get the same feelings if the children refuse an activity they have prepared.

Gaps in their knowledge may make some student teachers uneasy. They may have learned that two-year-olds often bite other children, but they do not know what to do when confronted with this behavior. They may be afraid that if they ask for help they will be considered inadequate.

Some master teachers push student teachers into assuming too many responsibilities too soon. As a result, the student teachers *feel exploited*. They work while the master teacher takes it easy.

"Tell me what to say when . . ." is a frequently heard plea from student teachers. When the answer isn't readily available, they *feel frustrated*. They sometimes think experienced teachers have found the magic formula but are withholding the information from them.

Young student teachers sometimes *identify more closely with the feelings of the children than with adults*. They may become upset when the master teacher disciplines a child, or at the way a parent reacts. It is hard for them to see the situation from the viewpoint of the adult.

When first confronted with the intensity of their own feelings, they may become *afraid of their reactions to children*. The first time they get really angry at a child, they worry they will never become good teachers. Or conversely, they often fear becoming too attached to children because they know that parting from them will be painful.

Student teachers are being graded, so there is a tremendous pressure to perform well. They often feel that their *every word and action are being judged*. They are certain that every mistake or lapse is noted and will be criticized.

Welcoming student teachers into your school can be a rewarding adventure for you and your staff. It can bring new life to your program and give your teachers an added dimension of experience. You can feel proud to be able to foster the professional growth of a neophyte teacher. But it can also be difficult and time consuming. If you follow these logical and progressive steps, the chances for success are good. Time and patience are rewarded.

> **FYI**
>
> *The large numbers of elderly persons in the United States is an almost untapped resource for volunteer help in child care programs. Many of these persons remain healthy and have much to offer children who spend long hours away from their homes. Children can learn a great deal about the aging process through contact with older individuals. They may learn:*
> - *Each stage of life is full of unique potential.*
> - *To question stereotypes of the elderly.*
> - *That older people are part of a diverse group, made up of individuals with a variety of characteristics.*
> - *How to care for, and cooperate with, persons of different ages.*

VOLUNTEERS

Volunteers share some of the characteristics of student teachers. Generally, however, volunteers have less theoretical background in child development. Both groups are normally enthusiastic and eager, but the basic motivations differ. Student teachers have made a commitment to early childhood education as a career. Volunteers may be equally sincere, but they generally have different goals and experiences.

All that considered, volunteers may add a whole new dimension to your school. They are almost always filled with vigor and energy. Used with perception and care, they may supplement areas of your school that may badly need bolstering. Two criteria are foremost: *selection* and *training*.

A PLAN FOR VOLUNTEER SERVICES

Once your total schedule of activities is almost completed, you may notice "holes" that are not filled. These may be as disparate as "short breaks" for teachers, trips to the market, or helping at a parent event. This is when you may decide that volunteers could help.

A logical next step is to consult with permanent school personnel as to whether volunteers are a valid solution. Board members (in policy determination), teachers, nonteaching people, and parents should all be involved. All should agree that volunteers will be welcome and useful.

If you make a positive decision, reexamine the total program noting where to place volunteers. Because of the attractiveness of working with children directly, many other opportunities for placement are often overlooked. Most volunteers on first call want to work directly with children, and some may help teachers. Pay close attention to the experience of each volunteer and how it will fit with the school needs.

When present staffing needs are adequately met, explore how volunteers may expand or extend your program. Try to find the unique background that each volunteer offers. You may find that some have business, secretarial, educational, medical, or other training that may help immensely. They may enrich curriculum, suggest field trips, or help in building redecoration. The list is almost endless.

The Volunteer Coordinator

Appoint someone on the full-time staff as the coordinator of volunteers. Unless you are in a very large school, this will not be a full-time position. In a small school, you, the director, will probably be chosen. But one person must have the responsibility of selecting, training, assigning, and evaluating each volunteer. The stakes are too high to have unsupervised volunteers at large in a school. After the program has been successful for a period of time, it may be possible to use a volunteer as a coordinator.

The coordinator should know each person in the program as intimately as possible. The school should be able to use the volunteer's strengths wisely and avoid their weaknesses. The coordinator should know training methods and which ones to apply to each volunteer. But mostly, the coordinator must be "inspirational" and be able to praise sincerely. Praise is the only pay that most volunteers will get. Everyone should feel that their work is necessary and their efforts are genuinely appreciated.

RECRUITMENT OF VOLUNTEERS

Very likely, the best volunteers are recruited from people already known to the staff. These are parents, grandparents, and other relatives, primarily. In general, it is far better to seek a volunteer than to accept one casually.

Senior citizens' groups are an often-overlooked source. The American Association of Retired Persons has a special section of members who have volunteered to work in the community. You may have a local chapter of the AARP in your neighborhood. If not, they may be reached at 3200 E. Carson St., Lakewood, CA 90712. A special section of retired executives are eager to give help in business problems and budgeting. Counselors and other retired professionals are often available. If your school has an infant program, older persons are often helpful in nurturing situations.

Senior citizens' centers can sometimes provide shelter for children whose parents have been delayed in picking them up. Some older people enjoy reading stories to children. Art specialists, who have retired, are useful. Seniors have been known to staff telephone hotlines for "latchkey" children. The benefits are not entirely one way. Seniors seem to benefit greatly by their contacts with young children. However, screening of individuals is important here. You must be aware of health considerations, including a chest X-ray for participants.

Figure 10–4 Senior volunteers do many jobs.

An increasing number of high schools are offering child development courses. Students from these courses, screened by both you and the high school teacher, may be used productively. Exemplary high school students are known for their high energy level (and sometimes limited perseverance). However, their vitality and interest can bring renewed vigor to teachers.

Some cities or localities may sponsor volunteer bureaus. These may be the source of miscellaneous personnel. Usually very little screening is done, and the job of evaluating the volunteer's personality and health requirements becomes that of the school.

If the need for volunteers is really acute, and all other sources fail, the local newspaper may carry a feature article on the school and its requirements. Or, of course, you can place an advertisement.

Some schools have prepared a simple brochure focusing on volunteers: standards, jobs needed, rewards, school policy, etc. This can be a simple $8^1/_2 \times 11$ folded colored paper, with one basic art caption. It can be handed out or mailed to those seeking volunteer positions.

SELECTION OF VOLUNTEERS

The rigorous screening of volunteers is vital to the success of the program. Selection should have two major objectives: fitting the right person to the job and eliminating the obviously unfit. It is important to the success of the school that those who volunteer but are not accepted be helped to find other outlets for their enthusiasm.

Volunteers should first file a written application. Suggested information to request follows:

- Name, address, phone number.
- Educational background.
- Interests and hobbies.
- Car, license, insurance coverage.
- Special skills (dance, art, music, etc.).
- Work experience.
- Health record.
- Kinds of volunteer work preferred.

In a few cases, you may want to include arrest record, but if you do not have the cooperation of your local police department for checking, this may produce more ill will than not.

The coordinator of volunteers should interview each volunteer. Keep in mind good relations with children. The main thrust of the interview should be to determine the applicant's special skills in the interests of the school. The applicant may meet with children in the classroom so that you can observe the results.

Many volunteers want to work directly with the children. You must ascertain their motivation, as well as their ability to relate to young people. Health and physical stamina of older persons is always a question. The advisability of having a physical examination more rigorous than that required by state standards must be settled at each school.

Sometimes, the requests of the volunteer and the needs of the school are not congruent. Then, the best skills of the coordinator are required to channel the volunteer either into school needs or outward into other activities.

Once the volunteer has been tentatively chosen, agree upon a schedule. Impress upon the volunteer the need for promptness and attendance. This is particularly true if the projected work involves the children. Children adjust more easily to the presence of "outsiders" if they know that they will appear at specific times.

Volunteers who are to work with children should also be assigned to one group and one teacher. It is too difficult for an untrained person to learn to work with several teachers and large numbers of children.

ORIENTATION OF VOLUNTEERS

Give all new volunteers a thorough introduction to the school and its policies. This should be systematic and may involve a checklist. It is both unkind and unwise to throw a new volunteer into service without an orientation. The overview may be one intensive day or extended over a week or more with shorter periods of training.

Include in this activity as many of the permanent staff as possible. Introduce them by name and repeat their names as often as possible. Sometimes, wearing name tags is advisable. Encourage the volunteer to feel part of the school; each volunteer should be introduced to everyone possible.

A volunteer assigned to office work should become familiar with the teaching routines. Parents doing physical labor should know each other and the teachers. Most importantly, the children should learn to accept the volunteer. Basic, also, is an understanding of the goals of the school and what each teacher is attempting to accomplish.

Because there is seldom time for extensive training of most volunteers, on-the-job learning is vital. This can most easily be accomplished by assigning the volunteer to one particular person. The volunteer should have the opportunity to have any questions answered as soon as possible. Do not allow misunderstandings to develop. Informal breaks are important in learning, too. There should be times available to socialize with the staff.

In summary, cover the following general areas during the orientation period:
- *School organization*—structure of the school, names and functions of each staff member, different children's groups.
- *Educational beliefs*—program goals and objectives, and how they are being implemented.
- *Developmental information*—ages and age-groups of the children, general information regarding children, and what to expect (or not expect) from them.
- *Volunteer responsibilities*—general expectations, overall schedules, and written assignments.
- *Volunteer supervision*—to whom they will be responsible, to whom they can direct questions, who will evaluate them, and to whom they can go for help.

HANDBOOK FOR VOLUNTEERS

Make a short, concise handbook available to all volunteers. In addition to the information already listed, it might contain:
- Rules and regulations of the school.
- A sample time sheet with instructions for signing in and out.
- A sample evaluation sheet (if used).
- Suggestions for dealing with children in problem situations.
- Safety rules for staff and children.
- Procedures for field trips or excursions.
- Simple "dos" and "don'ts" in working with children.

The more condensed and simple this information, the better. You cannot expect volunteers to spend great amounts of time with this material.

Plan for continued on-the-job training for all volunteers. They should be given ample opportunity to attend workshops, films, discussions, or visits to other schools. Include volunteers with regular teachers for in-service training activities. If they are working with children, workshops in art, science, or other specialized fields will help. Persons involved with fund-raising will profit from discussions with professional fund raisers. Anything at all that will add to the effectiveness of the volunteer may be used, especially intermingling with regular staff.

SUPERVISION OF VOLUNTEERS

The activities involved in training and supervising volunteers are really inseparable. In the beginning, assume nothing about any volunteer, no matter how extensive the background. This, of course, must be done without "talking down" to the person. But it takes time for even the most adept person to fit into a school. Gentle guidance and suggestions will accomplish a great deal.

The same principles of supervision that apply to the regular staff are just as valid for the volunteer. Insofar as possible, get to know the individual. Be sure that the volunteer knows what is expected in the particular job assigned. The limits of each job should also be made very clear. Written schedules are imperative.

When new tasks are assigned, run through each routine once with the volunteer. As with everyone, volunteers learn at different rates. Know when something has been mastered and when to "turn the person loose." Supervision can then become minimal.

Positive reinforcement is a rewarding technique for training and supervising. Immediately recognize and praise achievements. Give some small "reward." Do not dwell on failures, but steer away from them discreetly. Emphasize the positive in all actions. All volunteers should feel that they have made a contribution each day. Volunteers should also assume the status of co-worker and equal. On the other hand, do not grant elaborate privileges in lieu of pay.

You may want to use written evaluations similar in form to those used with regular staff members. Special abbreviated procedures may fit the situation better. Follow each observation or evaluation with a conference. Draw plans to improve skills, techniques, or knowledge. Volunteers should feel that the evaluation is a real learning experience.

If you are using a number of volunteers in the school, hold periodic meetings with the entire group. Discuss problems and introduce items of general interest to everyone. Make an attempt to implement a group feeling of sharing and contribution. Identification with the school is important, as is sharing common goals.

RECOGNITION OF VOLUNTEERS

For many volunteers, some tangible evidence of service is important. This can take the form of a "Certificate of Service." A one-time contribution may be acknowledged by a personal letter. For long-time service, a small token emblem in the form of a plaque or statuette may be given at an appropriate ceremony. Ask members of the board of trustees to make the presentation. Send ample publicity to local media sources. Some schools have an annual party for volunteers, coupled with a fund raiser.

Sometimes you may want to acknowledge everyone at a party, with or without the children. An evening affair along more formal lines is sometimes indicated. In other situations, an informal picnic is more fun. Following the trends of industry, some schools even award a pin for so many years or hours of service.

Newspaper or media coverage of volunteer service is another way to show your appreciation. Call the newspaper or radio office and explain your program and the important work that volunteers do. If possible, arrange a photo session or radio interview. Let the children plan a form of thanks to their volunteers. They can:

- Write individual notes.
- Draw pictures of favorite activities they do with the volunteer.
- Prepare a plaque honoring the volunteer.
- Put together a booklet describing all the things the volunteer does with the children.
- Give a framed photograph of all the children.
- Prepare a special lunch.

RECORDS OF VOLUNTEER SERVICE

Keep a permanent record of all volunteer service to ensure continuity in the program. After a period of recordkeeping, it is also easier for you to view the program in perspective and reevaluate it. Volunteers, themselves, on entering the program may find the record invaluable. Also, any extra time and effort expended in the volunteer program may be justified by such a record.

Although they may vary somewhat from school to school, some major points you may want to include in your volunteer records follow:

- Overall plan and objectives.
- Kinds of work open to volunteers.
- Sources for recruiting volunteers.
- Applications for volunteer work.
- Beginning and ending dates for each volunteer.
- Jobs successfully filled by volunteers.
- Major points of orientation sessions.
- Evaluations of volunteers.
- Evaluations of the total program.
- Minutes of meetings concerning volunteers.
- Records of awards given for service.
- Correspondence file.

Finally, you will find that although the use of volunteers requires considerable start-up time, it is generally repaid fully in extensive and beneficial returns to your school. Be sure you are getting full return from the services of your volunteers by careful planning and thoughtful administration.

Several organizations can provide information. Those listed below have publications with information on aging and guides for intergenerational programs.

> American Association of Retired Persons
> 1909 K Street, N.W.
> Washington, DC 20049
> 202-872-4700

> The Gray Panthers
> 311 S. Juniper Street, Suite 601
> Philadelphia, PA 19107
> 215-545-6555

> National Council on the Aging
> 600 Maryland Avenue, SW, West Wing 100
> Washington, DC 20024
> 800-424-9046

Teachers who work with senior volunteers will need to understand the aging process and to recognize the benefits of intergenerational programs. There are some films or videos that can help:

"Across the Ages: A New Approach to Intergenerational Learning" (video), 1980.
> Temple University Institute on Aging
> 1601 N. Broad Street, Philadelphia, PA 19122
> 28 min., color, $3/4$"

"Generations Together—SCARP" (slide/tape), undated.
> University Center for Social and Urban Research
> University of Pittsburgh
> 600 A Thackery Hall, Pittsburgh, PA 15260
> 7 min.

"Old Mother Goose Ain't What She Used to Be" (video), 1983.
> College Avenue Players
> 546 Crofton Avenue, Oakland, CA 94610
> 30 min., color, $3/4$" and $1/2$"

"One to One: The Generation Connection" (film or video), 1989.
> Terra Nova Films
> 9848 S. Winchester Avenue, Chicago, IL 60643
> 24 min., 16 mm., $3/4$" and $1/2$"

"Partners in Education: Teachers and Volunteers" (slide/tape), undated.
> National Association of Partners in Education, Inc.
> 601 Wythe Street, Alexandria, VA 22314
> 10 min.

SUMMARY

Student teachers have a good deal of theoretical knowledge of child development but limited practical experience. Also, their characteristics are becoming more varied.

The director's role is one of a stage manager.

The appropriate choice of a master or supervising teacher is vital.

If your school accepts student teachers, you should have a well-organized orientation schedule.

Support of student teachers will ensure a flow of quality persons into the profession.

A majority of schools find some way to use unpaid persons to perform staff functions, often part time. Consult everyone in the school when volunteers are used; everyone on staff should agree.

Name one person volunteer coordinator, with the responsibility for their recruitment, use, and evaluation. Very likely the best source of volunteers is a recommendation from someone already associated with the school. However, senior citizens, high school and college students, people within the local neighborhood, and advertising are other sources if careful screening is done.

A carefully planned program of orientation for volunteers is necessary. It is closely related to later supervision.

Consider a concise manual for volunteers. Much of the training will be on the job.

Use techniques of positive reinforcement. Give praise promptly when due.

Supervision and evaluation of volunteers are important. Public recognition for service rendered is vital. A certificate, a party, or a long-service pin are ways a school may show appreciation.

A permanent record of volunteer activities is necessary for continuity and total evaluation of the program. The use of volunteers should yield very positive results over a span of time.

SELECTED FURTHER READING

Abbot-Shim, M. 1990. "In-Service Training: A Means to Quality Care." *Young Children*, 45 (2) 14–18.

Brand, S. 1990. "Undergraduates and Beginning Preschool Teachers Working with Young Children: Educational and Developmental Issues." *Young Children*, 45 (2) 19–24.

Harris, R. 1985. *How to Select, Train, and Use Volunteers in the School.* Lanham, MD: University Press of America.

Peterson, K., and Raven, J. 1982. "Guidelines for Supervising Student Teachers." *Child Care Information Exchange* (September/October), 27–29.

Seefeldt, C., and Warman, B. 1990. *Young and Old Together.* Washington, DC: National Association for the Education of Young Children.

Shirah, S., Hewitt, T., and McNair, R. 1993. "Preservice Training Fosters Retention: The Case for Vocational Training." *Young Children*, 48 (4) 27–31.

Watkins, K., and Durant, L. 1987. *Preschool Director's Staff Development Handbook*. West Nyack, NY: The Center for Applied Research in Education.

STUDENT ACTIVITIES

1. Discuss your experience as a student teacher. How did your reactions compare with those discussed in the text?
2. Observe a master teacher. List several reasons this person was chosen for the job.
3. Interview several directors, each from a different type of school. How does each see the school's relation to training teachers?
4. Visit a school that uses volunteers. Observe what volunteers do that benefits the school.
5. Discuss the role of the director as coordinator of volunteers.
6. Use role playing to interview a prospective volunteer.

REVIEW

1. Why is it important to have the director take an active interest in the "utilization" of student teachers?
2. List a few major characteristics of an ideal master teacher.
3. What are the chief responsibilities of the master teacher regarding the student teacher?
4. Do student teachers have fears in common? What are they?
5. How can the concerns of student teachers be most easily handled?
6. What are some safeguards to observe when recruiting volunteers?
7. What are some acceptable sources of volunteers?
8. Why are selection and training vital when using volunteers?
9. Who should supervise volunteers?
10. How can volunteer service be compensated?

GLOSSARY

Student teacher   college or university student who is enrolled in a practice teaching or field study course requiring placement in a school or child care center.

Master teacher   experienced, model teacher who can provide a positive learning environment for student teachers.

Volunteer   unpaid person who offers his or her services freely.

Part IV
Management

11

Budget

OBJECTIVES

After studying this chapter, the student should be able to:
- Define a budget.
- List the major categories of expenses.
- List the sources of income.
- Describe a budget process.

Your budget is very likely the most important written document you will have. A budget, in the simplest terms, is a statement of goals for one year expressed in financial terms. It is not mysterious or difficult. It involves nothing more than elementary arithmetic, logic, and some experience. The first budget you assemble will be the most difficult one by far.

Although at the time it may seem more demanding, the more people you involve in the budget-making process, the easier and more satisfactory will be the final result. The trustees, assistant director, teachers, secretaries, cooks, and even handymen can contribute to the budget. By doing so, each will have a stake in its success and fulfillment.

The budget must be viewed realistically. A child care center, of almost any type, is a small business. It has all the strengths and weaknesses of this kind of enterprise. It cannot lose money and continue to function. Laudatory and high-sounding aims should not obscure this fact.

DEVELOPMENT OF THE BUDGET

Since the budget reflects previously formulated goals, you should state them as succinctly and briefly as possible at the beginning. If you have any special objectives for the current year, list them in rank order. Sometimes it is necessary to "lop off" lower-ranking priorities, and as many people as possible should agree on what these will be. Most "budget crises" arise from failing to foresee this type of shrinkage.

If you feel totally defeated in preparing a first budget, you may want to seek the help of an accountant. Although accounting and legal fees may seem high, they are well worth the price if they help you navigate through an especially troublesome year. If you have the luxury of appointing an accountant or attorney to your board of trustees, you may have a ready-made consultant.

Time is an important consideration in planning any budget. Most organizations have a budget cycle that is really endless. When one budget is finished, planning for the next year begins. A standing committee of the board, or of the staff, may concern itself primarily with the budget. The process consists of gathering reasonable requests from all concerned. Considerable guidance is sometimes needed for the staff to define "reasonable" in achievable terms. Experience does help. It is the director's responsibility to keep the budget process moving forward.

So, after (re)stating goals and objectives, the most common activity is to prepare a budget calendar. This will consist of dates that are essentially deadlines that must be met. Circulate this document to all concerned. It is important to establish a "tickler"file of your own that will remind you of important budget milestones. You must hold meetings and make decisions as the process unfolds.

A justification must accompany budget requests from various areas of the school. This is a reason for being, not just a statement like "this would be nice" or "I've always wanted one." The justification must be goal and objective linked as nearly as possible. It should withstand independent scrutiny, or it should not be included. Make this clear to everyone who has a hand in making the budget.

Once all budget requests have been assembled, you are ready to put together a working budget. If you have a computer and a data management software program, the budget process will be much simpler. (Appendix A lists several that are designed specifically for early childhood centers.) If you do not have access to a computer, you must decide on a form for the budget at this point. Corporate or government-sponsored schools often have a predetermined budget form. If yours is a for-profit entity and this is your first budget, you will have to develop your own form. Figure 11–1 shows a sample. There are two major sections in a budget: *income* and *expenses*. Expenses are divided into two subcategories: *controllable* and *fixed*.

EXPENSES—PERSONNEL

Staff Salaries

Recall in Chapter 3 that salaries comprise the largest proportion of your budget, on average 65 percent, but in some schools as high as 75 to 80 percent. This budget category includes administrative personnel (director and assistant director), teaching staff (teachers, assistants, substitutes), and nonteaching staff (secretary, cook, janitor, bus driver, maintenance person). Your decisions concerning salary levels for all employees will be influenced by several factors. The first is the education and experience of the teaching staff. Teachers with bachelor's or master's degrees and previous experience will expect higher pay than those without degrees. Second, you must take into account the going rate of pay in your particular community or area of the country. Salaries tend to be the highest in the Northeastern states and lowest in Southern states. Third, you must comply with minimum wage laws and tax laws. One last factor may affect the pay level of your employees. Some may be members of a union that has a mandated pay scale. You may also be part of another entity, a public school or community agency. Each of these will have a predetermined pay scale.

Personnel costs include taxes you are required to pay to various governmental agencies, and fringe benefits you offer your employees. Required payments include the percentage of an employee's salary for Social Security, Worker's Compensation, and unemployment insurance. A growing trend in early childhood centers is to offer fringe benefits as a means of keeping qualified staff. Although benefits may seem expendable, they will reduce turnover and the resulting cost of finding and training new staff members. Fringe benefits may include health insurance, sick leave and vacation pay, reduced cost child care, or retirement plans. Fringe benefits can comprise 10 to 15 percent of the total salary amount. If you are doing a first budget estimate, use that figure as a guideline. A computerized budget form will facilitate determining actual fringe benefit costs for employees at each pay level.

EXPENSES—CONTROLLABLE

Controllable expenses are those over which you have some measure of control. They will vary depending on how much you spend for supplies and equipment, which services you decide to use or eliminate, and how much you spend for food or transportation.

Consultant or Contract Services

Not all schools will require the services of a consultant or someone who contracts for a service. In this category are persons who perform specific services, sometimes on a one-time-only basis. Included are educational consultants, accountants, lawyers, dentists, doctors, nurses, social workers, psychologists, and nutritionists. In public school systems or in large organizations, these persons may be considered regular employees rather than consultants. In other situations, they work for a fee, agreeing to provide specific services to the school.

Fees for consultants are usually on a per diem basis, including any expenses they incur while working under their contracts. The rate will include food, transportation, and lodging if the consultant is not local.

Equipment

Equipment is usually defined as nonexpendable items, ones that are not consumed in a short period of time. Three to five years is the usual time allocation. Tricycles, typewriters, garbage cans, and desks are all examples. Traditionally, it is easier to subdivide equipment into several types: educational, office, maintenance, and kitchen. Keep a chart of the state of repair of each major item and schedule replacement at regular intervals. Each item usually has a "period of obsolescence." If this can be ascertained, the piece should be replaced well ahead of complete breakdown.

Supplies and Other Materials

Place readily expended items in this group. They are naturally consumed and used up. Art materials, floor wax, office supplies, tissues, etc., are supplies. Use the same categories as with equipment: educational, office, maintenance, and kitchen. Consider food separately.

Transportation

This item varies with the services your school furnishes. Bus service is expensive. But be sure to include field trips, journeys to other schools, conferences, and workshops.

Food

This item includes all meals served at the school. Compute all lunches and snacks. If you have some experience in food service, or can tap the resources of another school, calculate the average cost per child per day. Add a small margin each year for inflation. If this is your first budget, you must estimate, but be sure to err on the high side, if at all.

EXPENSES—FIXED

Fixed expenses are those that either do not vary or change very little over long periods of time. You have limited or no control over them.

Space Costs

This cost will most probably be present as either rent or payments on a building you are buying. In either case, analyze this cost most carefully. Rental costs are on an upward spiral, and the purchase of some property is almost prohibitive. Since this cost will be with you "forever" in one form or another, give it the greatest possible consideration. Some states or localities may specify a minimum number of square feet per child. In any case, a current practice is to define space as cost per square foot per child. This figure should include both interiors and exteriors. If you are renting, computation is easy. If you are buying, be sure to amortize on some fixed, long-term period. This factor will vary greatly according to the location of your school. But remember, this single item—relatively constant or increasing—may limit growth of your school in other ways.

Utilities

Include water, gas, electricity, telephones, and trash removal. You may also have to include sewer charges. If you are renting and some of these are included in the rent, do not duplicate here.

Insurance

In recent years, liability insurance has become an increasingly high-expense item. The only advice that is sound is to shop around for insurance before starting your budget and try to get the best coverage for the least money. You may purchase fire insurance and some incidental coverages at the same time. A reduction in rate is sometimes given if all insurance is purchased as a "package." More details on insurance may be found in Chapter 3.

Taxes

Tax implications vary according to the type of school you operate. Not-for-profit schools may have significant tax advantages over profit-making ones in some states. Be sure to make adequate inquiries of your CPA or local tax authorities: local, state, and federal.

Other Costs

This miscellaneous area covers fees, licenses, advertising, petty cash, and other one-time expenditures. There is a growing trend to include some kind of reserve or contingency here, too.

INCOME

Tuition

The first operating budget must estimate income from all sources. Tuition will be a major source. If this is your first year of operation, you must do some research on current practice. Call a number of neighboring schools and ascertain what their level of tuition is. You cannot go too much higher than is presently charged and expect to compete successfully. On the other hand, you cannot become a "bargain" and expect to stay in business. Since tuition will form a major source of income, the setting of reasonable charges is vital.

Once you have decided on a tuition fee, you are ready to calculate the total income. Multiply the fee by the number of children your school is licensed to enroll. In practice, it is not that simple. First, many schools either do not want to enroll the maximum number of children they are allowed, or cannot attain full enrollment. To fill enrollment and to accommodate parents, many schools accept children two or three days a week. In addition, some schools have children who attend only before they leave for elementary school, and then again after school.

All these schedule changes can make it extremely difficult to estimate income, especially the first year. So the best you probably can do is estimate.

Some Other Sources

In general, any fees charged beyond tuition are meant only to cover expenses. It is traditional for private, church, and corporate schools to require a *registration fee*. This may range from $25 to $75 and is payable each year before school begins. Fee payment is included in the process of enrolling a new child or reenrolling a child. Since traditionally this fee is nonrefundable, it is a method of partially ensuring enrollment for a future period.

A *materials fee* is levied when special curriculum materials or books are required. It should include the cost of the articles plus handling and storage charges.

A *transportation fee* may, or may not, be charged. Some (usually more expensive) schools include this in the tuition. Some parents prefer to deliver the children personally. Be sure not to omit this factor if you are providing bus or other transportation, since this item can become very expensive.

Although it is not too general, some schools do charge a *food fee*. Many schools today find it too costly to serve school-prepared meals, preferring to confine their food service to snacks, and perhaps milk at lunch. Children bring their own lunches from home. A few schools, though, still serve a meal as a convenience to parents. It then may be necessary to charge an extra fee for this service. Generally, it is probably better to include food under tuition charges if at all feasible. Some parents may object to a number of isolated fees.

Special activities such as dance, swimming, etc., are expensive; charge for these activities separately. In fact, examine any activity that only a few children require for its fiscal impications, and charge appropriately for it.

Fund raising and contributions vary tremendously as sources of income. Very few schools start with an "endowment", or a free gift of investment capital. However, as time goes on and the school prospers and gains in reputation, do not omit a fund raiser of any type, or a request for contributions in your planning. Annual dinners, picnics, parents' days, award banquets, or any festive occasion may be converted into a fund raiser. And if your school is certified as nonprofit by the IRS, contributions may be tax deductible.

Federal, State, and Local Items

There are other sources of income, occasionally of great value, that are not covered in detail in this text. One of these is federal grants, both direct and given through states. Generally, your school must be IRS-certified nonprofit to qualify, although there are exceptions. You should have a copy of the *Catalog of Federal Domestic Assistance* issued yearly by the Government Printing Office in Washington, DC. However, the bulk of government aid is allocated through the State Departments of Education, located in the various state capitals. Write to your SDE for pertinent information.

The techniques and procedures of application, and of being eligible, for all types of grants are quite complex. The whole field is often referred to as "grantsmanship" and is one that requires special study. See the Kiritz reference in the bibliography at the end of this chapter.

Often as fruitful in a search for funds, especially when launching special projects, is the local service club or area philanthropy. Rotary Clubs and other service groups, the United Way, private donors, and even the department of social services are sometimes interested in things that benefit the community. You may find that a trip to your local library and a consultation with the librarian may unearth unexpected resources.

Some Intangibles

When computing income for your first operating budget, one of the most uncertain areas of income is estimation of the "shrinkage," or vacancy and drop-out factors. These may vary widely according to school location, economic factors, tuition cost, and many others. Only experience can be a reliable guide here. The one certain thing is that you will not end the school year with exactly the same number of children with which you started. Therefore, estimate tuition sparingly, allow for continuous enrollment, and recognize a need to recruit pupils.

A final caution is to provide for uncollected or uncollectible tuition. You cannot act as a director and a collection agency. An efficient secretary is indispensable here. You know only that some tuition will go by default. The hiring of a collection agency is expensive and may harm the image of the school. Make tuition payable before most services are performed, or prorate at frequent intervals so that defaulting parents are not too much in arrears.

TRIAL BUDGET

When you have assembled all *Income* and *Expenditure* items, the hardest part of budget making begins. Tell the trustees, corporate headquarters, or other higher authority of the results. A special meeting of the trustees may be solely devoted to budget, or the budget committee of the trustees may meet, or the data may go in to corporate headquarters according to schedule.

Needless to say, there must be no deficit apparent in the budget balance. At this time, it is necessary to ensure a small surplus balance, either for reserve funding or for unexpected additions before the budget is finalized. And if you are in business to make a profit, now is the time to calculate the amount of that profit.

Hold a staff meeting where everyone concerned may make comments on items submitted. Almost without fail, some entries must be curtailed or eliminated. This is painful. But throughout the budget process, try to keep everyone involved with it informed. The watchword is "no secrets!" Try for tradeoffs, substitutions, and the establishment of priorities that extend from year to year.

SAMPLE BUDGET FORM

INCOME

Registration fees   _____

Tuition   _____

Gifts and contributions   _____

Fund-raising   _____

Investment income   _____

Grants   _____

                Total Income   _____

EXPENSES – Personnel

Staff Salaries   _____

_____

_____

_____

_____

           Total   _____

Fringe Benefits   _____
(10-15% of Total)

Total Salaries & Fringe Benefits   _____

EXPENSES - Controllable

Consultant Services   _____

Equipment

    Educational   _____

    Housekeeping   _____

    Office   _____

Supplies & materials   _____

    Educational   _____

    Housekeeping   _____

    Office   _____

Food   _____

Transportation   _____

Advertising   _____

Uncollected tuitions   _____

Figure 11–1 Sample budget form.

EXPENSES – Fixed

Space costs   _____

Utilities   _____

Insurance   _____

Taxes   _____

Other costs   _____

TOTAL EXPENSES   _____

Cost per child   _____

NET – (income minus expenses)   _____

Figure 11–1 *(continued)*   Sample budget form .

Set a date for the accomplishment of the publication or summary budget. This should be the next to the last step. Solicit final input. Then again send the budget for final approval to the next level of administration (if any).

Finally, by the last day of your fiscal year on your budget calendar (or considerably before), you should have the final budget completed. This is your working financial outline for the coming year. Beyond this date, you cannot alter the budget. Some changing among categories of expenditure may be made, but we do not recommend this practice. Figure 11–2 shows a budget for a single for-profit school.

After a year or so in operation, enough data should have been collected to ascertain at what particular month of the year specific expenditures should most advantageously be made. Note that where *Equipment Rental* and *Parent Communications* do not vary during the year, spending for *Educational Supplies* and *Maintenance* change to fit the calendar. For example, maintenance projects are done before the heavy enrollment in September, during Christmas (billed in January), and at the close of the fiscal year in September. It was also found when *Supplies* ran low, this was compensated for, too, on a month-by-month basis. For this data to be useful, it is almost vital to have a computer. Then you can compare current expenditures in a timely manner on a month-by-month basis by computer output. The computer compares actual versus allocated values and imposes tighter budget controls in a timely way.

SUMMARY OF BUDGET CYCLE

1.   The budget is a cyclical process. Begin a new one when the current one is completed.
2.   Start with your goals for the year. List them.

BUDGET FOR A SINGLE FOR-PROFIT SCHOOL

INCOME
Tuitions

Infants : 6 @ 560/mo.	40,320	
Toddlers: 8 @ 500/mo	48,000	
Preschool: 60 @ 400/mo.	240,000	
School-age: 25 @ 150/mo.	45,000	
		373,320
Vacancy: 5%	<25,000>	
		348,320
Registration Fees	4,450	
Total Income		**352,770**

EXPENSES: PERSONNEL
Personnel

Director	22,000	
Teachers: 4 @ 15,500	62,000	
Teachers: 4 @ 14,000	56,000	
Teachers: 4 PT @ 8,000	32,000	
Assistants: 5 @ 8,000	40,000	
Substitutes	2,000	
Secretary	10,500	
Cook: PT	4,000	
		232,500
Benefits (FICA, Worker's Comp., Unemployment, Medical): 13%	22,800	
Total Personnel		**255,300**

EXPENSES: CONTROLLABLE
Equipment

Educational	1,500	
Supplies & materials		
Educational	4,800	
Office	700	
Housekeeping	500	
Food	22,500	
Staff development	1,000	
Advertising	3,000	
Total Controllable		**33,000**

EXPENSES: FIXED

Lease of building	36,000	
Utilities	12,000	
Insurance	9,000	
Taxes	600	
Other	500	
Total Fixed		**58,100**

TOTAL EXPENSES	**346,400**
Cost per child (99 children)	3,498
NET (Income minus expenses)	**6,370**

Figure 11–2 Budget for a single for-profit school.

3. Seek outside help if necessary on a first budget.
4. Assign one person central authority for budget.
5. Publish budget deadlines and what is expected of each staff member.
6. Try to include as many people as possible in planning.
7. Ask for written budget requests on a standard form.

MONTHLY FINANCIAL REPORT FOR BUDGET TRACKING

Period covered: From _____ To _____

INCOME	This month	Year to Date
Tuition	_____	_____
Fees	_____	_____
Donations	_____	_____
Total Income	_____	_____
EXPENSES		
Salaries and wages	_____	_____
Taxes and benefits	_____	_____
Staff training	_____	_____
Lease payment	_____	_____
Food purchases	_____	_____
Utilities	_____	_____
Supplies	_____	_____
Equipment	_____	_____
Insurance	_____	_____
Advertising	_____	_____
Total Expenses	_____	_____
Previous Balance	_____	
Income for (month)	_____	
Expenses for (month)	_____	
CURRENT BALANCE	_____	

Figure 11–3   Monthly financial report for budget tracking.

8. Ask for a justification for each major request.
9. Assemble a trial budget and establish priorities.
10. Be sure positive budget balances or profit is calculated.
11. Consider using computerized methods.
12. Publish the trial (preliminary) budget and circulate it for written comments.
13. Keep major divisions of Income and Expenditures.

14. Get committee approval at board, staff, or other level.
15. Submit final budget for approval by higher authority after incorporating last comments and discussion.
16. Publish final budget.
17. Begin new budget.

Of course, this list is an idealized schedule. It does not include the traumas and drama of any real budget. Yet, you must have an agenda and stick with it.

BUDGET ANALYSIS

Before you finalize your budget, do a last analysis. Make sure every item is included and that this document will achieve the goals you set for the year. You will find that keeping notes in your budget folder is a valuable practice as the year progresses. It is a rather frightening (and sometimes "fatal") experience to "run out of budget" before the close of your fiscal year. Good planning and analysis will eliminate this.

Listed below are a few hints to use in scrutinizing your budget:

- Is every item necessary to meeting the goals of the school included? Have obsolete goals been abolished and new ones provided for?
- Has every cost been included? Part of the review process is to ensure inclusion of every vital factor. Be sure to alert reviewers to this necessity.
- Are there marked differences between this budget and last year's? Between this one for your school and a similar group? If so, what has changed? Are the changes necessary? Have changes been fully justified?
- Has any single item shown a marked increase or decrease? If so, have objectives changed? Marked increases may signal need for cost-control measures.
- Was there great difficulty in reconciling differences between Income and Expenditure? If so, major equipment, maintenance, or other items may have to be postponed.

It is a major test of administrative skill to have everyone reasonably satisfied with the final budget. No one gets everything; everyone should get a little bit.

FYI

In full-day, full-year accredited early childhood centers surveyed by NAEYC, the average yearly cost throughout the United States was $4,200 per child. They also found that another $600 was added through in-kind donations, bringing the total cost per child to $4,800.

SOURCE: U.S. General Accounting Office Report. "Early Childhood Education: What Are the Costs of High-Quality Programs?"

CONTROLLABLE EXPENSE	OCT	NOV	DEC	JAN	FEB	MAR	APR	MAY	JUN	JUL	AUG	SEP	TOTAL
* * *													
Educational Supplies	484	484	1,166	497	506	870	524	510	1,155	494	494	1,176	8,360
Equipment Rental	123	123	123	123	123	123	123	123	123	123	123	123	1,476
Maintenance	2,500	800	875	1,350	875	1,125	800	850	875	900	875	1,250	13,075
Parent Communications	150	150	150	150	150	150	150	150	150	150	150	150	1,800

Figure 11–3 Sample budget detail, month by month.

IMPLEMENTING THE FINAL BUDGET

The approved paper budget is only the road map; a skilled driver is necessary to arrive safely at the destination. That person is the director. The director implements the budget during the year by using skillful management techniques.

- Only one person should have purchasing authority. Requests for budget expenditures must be submitted in writing.
- One person has the responsibility for disbursing money. The bank should honor the signature of only one (or at most two) authorized people.
- Each person involved with the budget should have an overview copy as well as a detailed subsection for particular expenditures.
- Issue monthly progress reports of budget income/outgo to all vitally concerned. This is especially easy to do if a computer is involved.
- Curtail overspending early. Investigate underspending at the end of the year. Allow some "corrective" factors if this is a first budget.

KEEPING BUDGET RECORDS

You can ease future budget preparation by maintaining accurate records as the budget yet progresses. Budget tracking information for each month is shown in Figure 11–3. As a minimum, include the following as permanent file entries:

- Current cost of all budget items.
- Budget forms used by school or other agencies.
- Copies of taxes, insurance, licenses, and assessments.
- Copies of budgets for last three years.
- Copies of cost control practices used.

- Budget correspondence.
- Minutes of budget review meetings.
- Copies of the annual report for three previous years.

SUMMARY

A budget is the statement of goals for one year given in financial terms. Begin to compile it with lists of services to be provided, programs to be included, and goals to be reached.

Include the following items as major headings of budget expenditures:
- Staff salaries.
- Fringe benefits.
- Consultant services.
- Equipment.
- Supplies and materials.
- Transportation.
- Insurance.
- Cost of space.
- Utilities.
- Food.
- Taxes (if any).
- Other costs.

List the following as major income items:
- Tuition.
- Materials fee.
- Transportation fee.
- Food fee.
- Special activities fee.
- Fund raising and contributions.
- Possible federal, state, or private sources.

Take care to allow for "shrinkage" factors and for uncollected tuitions.

Establish a budget calendar with deadlines for meeting each milestone in budget development. *Estimate Income and reconcile Expenditures.* Keep everyone involved in the budget process informed.

After you make a trial budget, request further input. Analyze the budget for omissions and unneeded items. Make compromises. Reconcile budget income with outgo and establish profit, if any. Achieve final approval and publish the final budget.

Authority for budget administration is centralized. Examine the budget continually. Make every attempt to stay within budget bounds. Good recordkeeping will ease future budget preparation.

SELECTED FURTHER READING

"Determining Your Total Costs Per Child," 1993. *Child Care Review*, 7 (2) 5.

Kiritz, N. J. 1979. Program Planning and Proposal Writing, expanded version. Los Angeles: Grantmanship Center Reprint Series.

Richard, M. 1991. *Before & After School Programs: A Start-Up and Administration Manual*. Nashville, TN: School Age Notes.

Stephens, K. 1991. *Confronting Your Bottom Lines: Financial Guide for Child Care Centers*. Redmond, WA: Exchange Press, Inc.

United States General Accounting Office. January 1990. "Early Childhood Education: What Are the Costs of High-Quality Programs?" Briefing Report to the Chairman, Committee on Labor and Human Resources, U.S. Senate.

Willer, B., ed. 1990. *Reaching the Full Cost of Quality in Early Childhood Programs*. Washington, DC: National Association for the Education of Young Children.

STUDENT ACTIVITIES

1. Contact several child care directors. Ask for an estimate of their cost per child per year. How does it compare with the amount shown in Figure 11–2? What accounts for the difference?

2. Prepare a questionnaire to distribute to your fellow students. Tell them their answers will be anonymous. Ask the following:
   a. Are you currently teaching in an early childhood center?
   b. How many hours a week do you work?
   c. What is your weekly pay?
   d. Do you receive any benefits other than those required by law? If so, please list them.

   Summarize your findings and report to the class regarding working conditions for early childhood teachers.

REVIEW

1. Define a budget.
2. List at least six items of expenditure in a budget.
3. What should one of your first actions be in beginning a budget?
4. Who has responsibility for budget preparation?
5. What single item constitutes the largest budget expenditure?
6. What are some of the major steps in the budget cycle?
7. What is a reasonable percent of profit for a preschool? Defend your statement.
8. Specify some methods of budget review.
9. Tell how a budget can be controlled. Why is this important?
10. What items should be included in budget records as an aid to planning?

GLOSSARY

Budget   a statement of goals for one year stated in financial terms.

Budget calendar   a schedule for compiling budget data.

Controllable expenses   expenses that vary and over which the director has some control.

Fixed expenses   expenses that do not vary, or change very little, over periods of time.

Fringe benefits   mandated or voluntary benefits that are added to personnel expenses.

12

Maintenance, Health, and Safety

OBJECTIVES

After studying this chapter, the student should be able to:

- Differentiate between maintenance and operations activities.
- Tell how maintenance, cleanliness, and safety are related.
- Discuss the components of a safe environment.
- Describe how to deal with an emergency.
- State goals for a health plan in a childhood center.
- Discuss ways to implement health goals.

When so much emphasis is put on other aspects of an early chilhood program, you can easily overlook the physical environment. This can be a costly error both psychologically and financially. Teachers and children spend their day either in pleasant and safe surroundings or in a mess. Order and safety have logical connections, and a regard for healthful conditions is both a legal and parental concern.It is your responsibility as the director to ensure orderliness and security in your school. These are not the least of your duties.

MAINTENANCE OR OPERATIONS?

Many schools distinguish between maintenance and operations. *Maintenance* consists of major repairs and projects such as repainting exteriors and interiors, repaving, and reroofing. *Operations*, however, is concerned with day-by-day housekeeping such as sweeping, dusting, cleaning, emptying, and other seemingly endless tasks that go into making up a tidy and attractive school. The difference may be especially important at budget time. Most maintenance efforts are scheduled at yearly (sometimes longer) intervals. Maintenance tasks are often costly, and you must set aside money each year to cover the expense when it finally occurs. Operations take place each day and are essentially short range. This kind of expense must be part of each month's expenditures.

Maintenance

Aside from high cost, a major problem with maintenance projects is scheduling. Repainting is very difficult to do when school is in session. You might try weekends, but a better solution is to group all major maintenance for times when children are not present for at least a few days. Although there are increasingly more year-round schools, you can probably find time for a few days or a week during the year when rooms are vacant. If you can, plan a year or so ahead for this. It helps to keep a log of when major maintenance tasks are due.

In addition to charting due dates of all projects, keep a list of local maintenance services. Once used, note their cost and reliability. Such services as plumbing and electrical are sometimes needed in an emergency. Keep the phone numbers handy and retain comparative prices. Figure 12–1 gives a suggested format.

Proper maintenance may also include periodic replacement of some furniture or equipment. A day care center, open ten or twelve hours daily, will need a larger budget for maintenance and operations than one that is in session only a few hours. Active, young children are physically demanding on their environment. "Things" wear out rapidly. Figure 12–2 is a sample equipment maintenance card, and Figure 12–3 is a repair and replacement record form that will also aid you.

Operations

Seldom can a child care center afford an in-house custodial staff. Some corporate schools do have crews that clean and repair, but this is not the norm at most preschools. So you must provide some other means of routine cleaning. Your aim

REPAIR AND MAINTENANCE SERVICES				
Name	Address	Telephone	Rate	Comments
Plumbing				
Carpentry				
Painting				
Paving				
Roofing				
Electrical				
Gardening				
General Repairs				
Other				

Figure 12–1 Sample repair and maintenance service form.

EQUIPMENT MAINTENANCE RECORD			
Item _____		Date Purchased _____ Price _____	
Purchased from _____			
Warranty No. _____		Manufacturer _____	
Warranty Expiration Date _____			
Maintenance Record			
Service Date	Description	By whom	Charge

Figure 12–2 Sample equipment maintenance record.

should be the maximum health and safety of the children. Of course, you must observe reasonable fiscal restraints. There is a balance and trade-off operating here. To give optimum results, an outside cleaning service, hired on a part-time basis, is about the only solution economically possible.

There are many such cleaning services, and they perform at all levels of efficiency. Therefore, you should prepare a list of essential tasks that must be done before you begin negotiations with any of them. One way is to list your specifications and ask for bids. Examine the two or three lowest bidders, and interview the owners or managers. Ask them who they employ, how long they have been in business, what hours they will work, their cost per hour, and how long their contract will run, for a beginning. Remember, they must be available on a schedule to fit your needs.

Figure 12–4 may give you some suggestions as to frequency of cleaning and general housekeeping. Keep the initial contract for services short so that you can check the performance of the cleaning service.

Be especially alert when you are adding new programs. In addition to the cost of the room and equipment, be sure that you have set aside sufficient money to provide a safe, clean, and comfortable environment. Although this is especially true when adding an infant/toddler room to your school, it is important to any addition. The staff, parents, and children will notice the difference. In some surveys, cleanliness (in rather broad terms) is the most requested and looked-for item when parents are seeking child care.

Teachers question the degree to which they should be involved in routine cleanup procedures. There is no doubt that, if teachers keep their rooms tidy dur-

REPAIR AND REPLACEMENT RECORD					
Item	Repair	Replace	Repaint	Date Requested	Date Completed
Classrooms					
Tables					
Chairs					
Shelves					
Book cabinet					
Hollow blocks					
Floor blocks					
Record player					
Sand table					
Play Yard					
Swings					
Sandbox					
Sand					
Wheel toys					
Planks					
Boxes					
Jungle gym					
Playhouse					
Storage					
Office					
Typewriter					
Duplicator					
Adding machine					
Paper cutter					
Desk					
Chairs					
Bookshelf					
Computer					
Printer					
Grounds					
Driveway					
Parking lot					
Walks					
Garden					
Lawn					
Other					

Figure 12–3   Sample repair and replacement services form.

ing the day, cleaning needs will be significantly less. In the normal course of the day, teachers should not feel that their first duty is orderliness in the classroom. A short period of tidying up at the end of the day or the lesson helps. (A discussion of the special requirements in an infant/toddler room is found later in this chapter under HEALTH.) Children should participate in putting away materials. Learning to store objects in their proper places is part of the maturing process. Extreme disorder is not conducive to learning or pleasure for most children or teachers.

INVENTORY

Prepare an inventory of all physical equipment in the school over a specified dollar value. Start this list when the school begins and update it yearly. Record-keeping of this type is necessary for tax purposes, if for no other reason. Depreciate each

HOUSEKEEPING SCHEDULE					
Task	Daily	Weekly	Twice Weekly	Monthly	Comments
Bathrooms					
Toilets sanitized	X				
Washbowls cleaned	X				
Floor mopped	X				
Mirrors cleaned			X		
Towels refilled					As needed
Walls wiped				X	
Classrooms					
Floors wet mopped	X				
Floors waxed				X	
Carpets vacuumed			X		
Wastebaskets					
Emptied	X				
Washed			X		
Windows washed				X	
Stove cleaned				X	
Refrigerator					
Cleaned			X		
Defrosted				X	
Hallways					
Vacuumed		X			
Offices					
Vacuumed		X			
Dusted		X			

Figure 12-4   Sample housekeeping schedule.

piece of equipment on a fixed basis. Consult with a tax adviser as to the precise time span. If you are not using a computer inventory program, track each piece of equipment with a 3 x 5 card as shown in Figure 12–5. Store these cards in a safe place and keep them permanently.

SAFETY

Licensing guidelines and local building and safety codes are designed to ensure the safety of children in group settings. Be sure you know what is required and guarantee that your school always meets the specifications. Fines often are levied when codes are violated; in the extreme, your school could be closed until the violations are rectified. This can certainly be an expensive proposition and one to avoid whenever possible.

A safe school will also lessen the possibility of injuries to children that can result in costly litigation with parents. Young children notoriously do things no adult would ever think of doing. They may swallow small objects, taste a wide variety of

EQUIPMENT INVENTORY RECORD			
Item: _____ Date Purchased _____ Price_____			
Dates Inventoried	Accumulated Depreciation	Depreciation Current Year	Insurance Value

Figure 12–5 Sample equipment inventory record form.

play materials, and test their physical skills by trying somewhat dangerous feats. Awareness of children's behavior will help to prevent accidents. Periodic safety checks will further ensure the safety of your school.

Some suggestions for making your school as safe as possible will serve as reminders when you do safety checks.

Indoors

Include the following in your safety checklist:
• Eliminate any sharp corners or edges on furniture.

- Select furniture carefully, choosing an appropriate size for the children who will use it. When chairs and tables fit the children, accidents occur less frequently.
- Choose the best quality of any furniture or equipment that you can afford. Quality items have often been tested for safety and durability.
- Examine all toys carefully to be sure there are no small parts children can swallow or injure themselves with in any way.
- Place child-proof locks on any cupboards where hazardous supplies are kept. This includes cleaning supplies, medicines, and household paints.
- As a temporary measure, cover all electrical outlets with safety caps. Replace outlets with specially designed receptacles that make them permanently safe.
- Make sure that each classroom has two exits with doors that are easily opened. Check the placement of furniture so there is easy access to the exits.
- Place smoke detectors in each room and properly maintain them. There should be an appropriate hand-held fire extinguisher in each room.
- Use flame-retardant floor coverings and draperies.

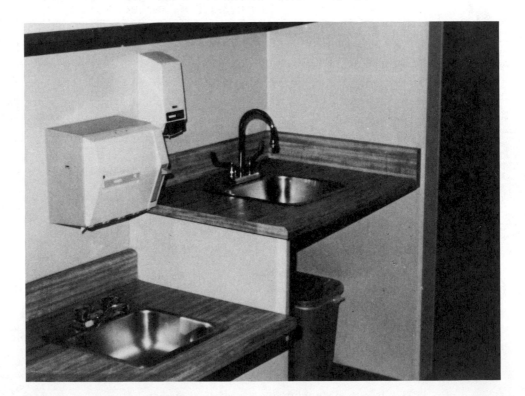

Figure 12–6   A clean school.

- If you have an infant/toddler room, further fire precautions will be necessary. Have one crib that will fit through an exit doorway. Mark it clearly. In case of fire, the nonwalking children can be put into the crib and wheeled out of the room.
- Plainly post directions for emergency shut-off of gas, electricity, and water.
- Use only safe, nontoxic paints, glue, play dough, or any other materials children might put in their mouths.
- Alert staff to possible safety hazards within the classroom. For instance, all staff should know that spills on vinyl floors are to be wiped up immediately or covered with a rug or towel.
- Keep hot water temperature below 120°F.

Outdoors

Children are more active outdoors than they are indoors. Therefore, careful safety inspections of all playground areas are extremely important. Staff must be constantly vigilant to foresee hazards and prevent accidents from happening. Add the following things to your safety checklist:

- Use safe materials for the surfaces under swings and climbing equipment. Check licensing requirements for what is acceptable.
- Make sure that all fences are at least four feet high and have securely latched gates.
- Select play equipment that is sturdy and free of sharp edges or splinters.
- Anchor all play equipment securely into the ground.
- Choose equipment that is developmentally appropriate for the children who will use it (no higher than 5 feet).
- Regularly maintain the play yard. If there is grass, keep it cut. Keep walkways clean and free of debris. Remove broken toy parts. Inspect all equipment regularly and repair as needed.
- Have clear rules about what children can and cannot do on the playground. Be sure that all staff know the rules and consistently enforce them.
- Train staff to prevent injuries by closely supervising outdoor play.

First Aid

Every school should have at least one major well-stocked and freshly renewed first aid kit. There should also be at least one adult who has taken the American Red Cross First Aid course. If possible, store smaller first aid kits in each classroom, with antiseptic and Band Aids™ as minimal contents.

Permanently affix a list of emergency telephone numbers for fire, police, and utilities near the first aid kit. Post copies of these in each room as needed. The school physician's (or nurse's) phone number should be readily available. Also, post the number of the nearest emergency room, hospital, or paramedic unit. All other information should be centralized so that staff can deal with emergencies expeditiously.

Figure 12–7   Outdoor equipment must be sturdy and solid.

For the central first aid kit, consider stocking the following:

adhesive tape ($1/4$" and 1")	hot water bottle	splints
alcohol	ice pack	thermometer
Band Aids™, assorted	needle, sewing	tongue blades
blanket	safety pins	towels
cotton balls	scissors, blunt	triangle bandage
flashlight	soap, liquid	tweezers
gauze pads, assorted	spirits of ammonia	Vaseline™

Accident Management

Develop a standard procedure for managing any accidents that happen at school or when children are in transit. A brief list may help you to develop your own plan:

- Each child's file should contain a form signed by the parents authorizing emergency medical treatment.
- Have a standard form on which pertinent accident information can be recorded. Complete it as soon as possible after the accident (see Figure 12-8 on page 243).
- Call paramedics or take the child to the nearest emergency room as required by the nature of the accident.

ACCIDENT REPORT FORM

Name of School _____ Date of Report _____

Child's Name_____ Sex M   F   Birth Date_____

Parent Name_____ Phone Number _____

Home Address____ _____

Date of Injury   _____ Time_____AM PM

Location Where Injury Occurred _____

Teacher in Charge _____

Present at the Time of Accident_____

Type of Equipment Involved _____

Description of How Accident Happened _____

_____

_____

_____

Action Taken:_____

First Aid Treatment_____
                            (Name of person administering)

Taken to Doctor_____
                                   (Name of doctor)

Taken to Hospital _____
                                  (Name of hospital)

Refused Treatment _____
                            (Name of person refusing treatment)

Parent Notification:

Was Parent Notified?   Yes   No   Time of Notification _____

How Was Parent Notified?_____

Comments from Parent_____

_____

_____

Witnesses to Accident _____

_____

Director's Signature _____

Figure 12–8 Accident report form.

- *Telephone the parents* as soon as possible. If the child is to be taken out of the school, ask that the parents meet you at the hospital.
- If the injury seems minor and does not require emergency care, the parents should *still be notified*. You and the parents can decide if the child should stay at school or be taken home.
- If the child stays at school, make sure that teachers watch for any further signs of difficulty during the day.
- Answer any questions the other children may have as completely and honestly as you can. Reassure them that the injured child is receiving care.

Disaster Plans

You may be required by your state's licensing regulations to develop a disaster plan. Even if not mandated, *preparation for disasters* such as fire, flood, hurricane, tornado, and earthquake should be made *before* any children enter a child care facility. Every staff member must be familiar with procedures for evacuating children or moving them to safe places in the building. *An evacuation route plan* should be displayed prominently in each room and at the entrance of the school. Fire alarms, fire extinguishers, and emergency exit lights should be clearly visible and checked regularly. *Schedule drills frequently* so that children have a chance to practice and staff have an opportunity to evaluate whether the plan needs any changes. *Notify parents of your plans*, including alternative shelters where children might be taken.

Designate one staff person to summon emergency help and see that the building has been completely emptied. That person will also contact parents. A final check of the building should be made to turn off any equipment, shut off gas lines (important in earthquakes), or any other measures that are necessary in your particular facility.

Store emergency supplies in evacuation areas within the building, packed in easily movable containers so they can also be taken to the alternative shelter when necessary. Include in your emergency kit:

- First aid supplies.
- Blankets.
- Water for at least one day's supply.
- Nonperishable food.
- Flashlights.
- Battery-operated radio.
- Children's books, games, crayons, paper, small toys.

Transportation

A discussion of safety would not be complete without considering measures to be observed when transporting children by car or bus. This is especially important today when many child care centers or preschools provide a pick-up service. Even schools that do not offer that convenience occasionally take children on field trips.

The driver of any vehicle must be properly licensed. The person should also be responsible and able to manage a group of children. Some training may be necessary to provide that capability. Parents should know the person who transports their children to school in order to feel more confident. A written permission form should be on file at school.

Sometimes teachers may be used as "substitute" drivers. Be particularly sure in such cases that the teacher has been given the same training and is licensed the same as the regular vehicle driver. People operating in a different environment are often susceptible to accidents.

All vehicles used to transport children should be equipped with restraints appropriate for the age of each child. You need infant beds or carriers for the youngest, and car seats and harnesses for the preschoolers. Older children can use seat belts and shoulder harnesses. A hard and fast rule should be that each child is buckled in for every trip, no matter how short.

Maintenance of all vehicles used for children is extremely important. Follow periodic inspections with any necessary repair work. Place a fire extinguisher near the driver so that it is easily available when needed. Purchase adequate liability insurance to cover the vehicle, driver, and the maximum number of passengers.

In some schools, parents transport children on field trips. Take precautions to ensure children's safety at these times as well. Make sure there is a safe place for cars to park when loading and unloading children. Remind parents to use restraints and watch when closing doors. Remember, although you are not liable when parents transport their own children, you may be liable when they carry other children on a field trip. Make certain your insurance will cover such an eventuality. A last precaution: Use parents for field trips as infrequently as possible. It is risky.

HEALTH

Alison Clarke-Stewart, in an article that appeared in *Parents* magazine (September 1982), published a checklist that parents could use to assess the quality of day care settings. Health and safety was the first section on the list. Other items covered were physical space, materials, staff, and parent contacts. Reviewing previous research on the effects of day care, Clarke-Stewart found that children's social and intellectual skills are enhanced by attending a good preschool. She also found that children may get a greater number of infectious diseases than children who stay at home.

On the other hand, Mary Howell presents a different viewpoint in "Is Day Care Hazardous to Health?" published in *Working Mother* (July 1983). She said that twenty years of research does not show there are any increased risks to children in day care. She adds that all children under the age of ten years have frequent illnesses. Even when exposed only to older siblings or other children in the home, children will frequently "catch" something. She also is reassuring when she says that a child who has more illnesses between two and three is probably building up an immunity so that there will be fewer illnesses later.

What we can glean from conflicting research results, or even our own experience, is that very young children are prone to a lot of illnesses. It then becomes an important task of the preschool or day care center staff to do everything possible to lessen the frequency of occurrences. In the case of infants and toddlers, the responsibility is even greater since for them some illnesses can actually be life-threatening. Before setting policies regarding health care of children in your school,

Figure 12–9   In a day care center, children brush their teeth.

draft some health goals. Once you have these, you can develop your policies in a more organized and efficient manner.

HEALTH GOALS

Design health goals for either a preschool or day care program to improve the health and functioning of individual children. These goals should be the basis for health policies and procedures in your school. However, implementation of the goals will have a much wider impact than just changing the health status of individual children. When individual children are healthy, fewer illnesses may be passed around in the school. The families will certainly benefit, especially working mothers who will miss fewer work days because their children are ill.

Some sample goals to guide you in developing your own list are:
- Assess the child's current health status and recommend treatment of existing problems.
- Suggest treatment for conditions that are progressive.
- Identify and suggest treatment for conditions that may interfere with how the child functions in school.
- Institute practices that prevent future illnesses.

Assessing Current Health Status

When a child first enters your school, whether for part of the day or all day, you must know the status of the child's health. You need to know in general whether the child is capable of participating in all the activities of the school or if there should be some restrictions. Most schools require a preenrollment physical examination. The physician's report will certify that the child is free of communicable diseases, describe any abnormal conditions, and include a record of immunizations.

Further assessment may include a discussion with the child's parents in which you take a brief developmental history. In some cases, it may be important to know about the mother's pregnancy and the circumstances of delivery. Additional information may include allergies, previous illnesses, hospitalizations, and any accidents the child has experienced.

Health screening tests are used in some schools, particularly those that receive government funds such as Head Start. Children may receive hearing or vision tests in addition to medical and dental screening. Some may receive general motor coordination tests.

Observations by teachers are also useful in discovering a child's health problems. They see children for many hours during a week and can often detect problems that may not have been previously noticed. They may notice behavior that points to hyperactivity, hearing and vision impairment, or poor motor coordination. Poor nutrition may be seen as a reason for the child's listlessness or withdrawal from group activities.

FYI

Children face significant health risks in the next decade.
1. *The World Health Organization predicts that by the year 2000 HIV will infect ten million children worldwide. Pediatric AIDS research cannot be the same as for adults. Drugs that work with adults may not work with children. Conversely, drugs that do not work for adults may help children.*
2. *In 1991, a study done by the Centers for Disease Control in nine major cities in the United States found that only 10 to 42 percent of children starting preschool had received appropriate vaccinations.*
3. *There has been a resurgence of preventable childhood diseases, including mumps, measles, whooping courgh (pertussis), and rubella.*

Treating Progressive Conditions

Certain health conditions will become progressively worse if left untreated. They may have a lasting and irreversible effect upon the child's health and ability to function in school. Examples are excessive tooth decay or strabismus (crossed eyes) and amblyopia (lazy eye). Malnutrition may permanently disturb the child's growth pattern. Behavior problems may affect learning and may become increasingly difficult to treat successfully as the child grows older. Often, though, it is hard to find the best sources of help, and they are likely to be expensive when found.

Comprehensive healthcare provided by some publicly funded preschool and day care programs covers the cost of treating progressive conditions. In Head Start centers, a Health Coordinator works with the Community Involvement Worker to facilitate health referrals for medical or dental care when necessary. A Head Start Nutrition Committee, made up of parents, plans monthly menus and assists in conducting nutrition activities for children. This committee also plans and conducts nutrition activities with the parents.

Schools that do not have the support of public funds may have to find other ways to work with families to treat progressive conditions. Some individuals among the parents may be able to provide help. For instance, a parent knowledgeable in nutrition may work with the staff to increase children's awareness of good nutrition. Along with staff members, this parent may also help to draft a list of lunch-box suggestions that can be given to all parents. A nurse or physician may be able to recommend community sources of help for families needing referral for medical or psychological help.

Talk to the parents of children in your school. They can probably tell you which pediatricians are best when interacting with both parents and children. They may know the dentists who can really "handle' young children as well as treat their dental problems. Talk to other directors and agencies in your community to find sources of psychological help for families. When you or your staff have identified a need for assessment or treatment, you can be ready with several suggestions where parents might look for help.

If you are the director of an employer-supported school, another option may be open to you. The business or industry that supports your school may be associated with a healthcare organization that can provide health services. Your role then is to suggest that the parents make appointments with the appropriate departments of the health organization. Hospitals that support a day care center obviously have their own built-in services that are probably available to parents.

Only a few programs can afford comprehensive healthcare services. Therefore, your responsibility is to identify the need for healthcare and to refer families to appropriate sources of help.

Identifying Conditions That Interfere with Learning

Often, conditions that interfere with learning never become identified until the child reaches elementary school. By then, a lot of time in which the difficulties could have been corrected has been lost. The preschool or day care center can be instrumental in preventing this delay.

The most obvious *vision* problems usually are recognized, but only a very alert adult will recognize other conditions. Teachers should watch for the child who has difficulty with eye-hand coordination or is awkward in games. The child who avoids close work or assumes an abnormal posture when doing it may also have poor vision. Complaints about inability to see or lack of curiosity about visually interesting objects may indicate vision problems.

Children's speech is often a good indicator of *hearing disabilities*. The teacher may be the first person to recognize a difficulty because parents are so accustomed to understanding the child's particular speech pattern. Hearing loss in young children is fairly frequent, sometimes due to the recurring middle-ear infections suffered at this age. Some indications of hearing problems that teachers should be aware of are listed here:

1. Limited use of speech.
2. Lack of response when spoken to.
3. Consistent lack of attention during group activities.
4. Talking very loudly or very softly.
5. Asking for a repetition of what has been said.
6. Watching intently when being addressed.

Speech difficulties may occur without hearing loss but will have an equally severe impact upon a child's learning. Language skills are intimately related to the development of cognitive skills. These problems range from *delayed speech* to *indistinct articulation*.

Delayed speech may stem from a wide range of causes. A neuromuscular disorder such as cerebral palsy or simply shyness and lack of environmental stimulation may lead to limited speech.

Articulation deviations are common in young children. Many children find it easier to say "b," "d," and "g" at the beginning of words and often end words with "p," "t," and "k." Double consonants such as "sp" and "tr" are also difficult. If only a few words are unintelligible, you can expect that the child will be able to say words more clearly with time. On the other hand, if all the child's words are unintelligible and the child is older than 3 or $3^1/_2$, professional help is indicated. A speech therapist should evaluate the child and possibly institute a remedial program.

Children who have delayed speech may be helped through special activities at school and at home. Both teachers and parents can encourage children to talk by listening carefully to what they have to say. Adults should ask questions that encourage children to use sentences rather than a single word. Most importantly, children should have interesting experiences they can talk about.

Certain *behaviors* may interfere with the child's ability to take advantage of the curriculum of the school. These may range from very mild patterns to severe disabilities.

Mild patterns of behavior that limit the child's learning capability sometimes go unnoticed by parents. In school, though, the behavior is usually noted. In this category are such things as extreme shyness that prevents the child from participating in group activities or making friends. Also included is the limited ability to stay with an activity long enough to finish. Then, there is the child who only wants to play with one toy or one activity. Each of these behaviors interferes little with other children's rights, but if left unchanged, that behavior will limit what the child will gain from a preschool experience.

More severe patterns of behavior are easily identified by both parents and teachers. These are the behaviors that infringe upon others' rights. The child who hits or bites is noticed by everyone around him, at home or at school. The child who constantly moves around, creating havoc everywhere he goes, also does not escape

---

RECOMMENDED IMMUNIZATION SCHEDULE

This table is based on recommendations by the American Academy of Pediatrics and the Centers for Disease Control of the U.S. Public Health Service.

Vaccine	2 months	4 months	6 months	12 months	15 months	4-6 years
DPT	DPT	DPT	DPT		DPT	DPT
Polio	Polio	Polio			Polio	Polio
MMR					MMR*	MMR
HIB**						
Option 1	HIB	HIB	HIB		HIB	
Option 2	HIB	HIB		HIB		

DPT: Diphtheria, Pertussis, and Tetanus vaccine
Polio: Live Oral Polio Vaccine Drops (OPV) or killed (inactivated)
Polio: Vaccine shots (IPV)
MMR: Measles, Mumps, and Rubella vaccine
HIB: Haemophilius b conjugate vaccine

·In some areas, MMR is given at 12 months. Many experts recommend that it be given also at entry to middle school or junior high school.

·· HIB is sometimes administered under two additional options:
    Option 3: birth, 1–2 months, 6–18 months
    Option 4: 1–2 months, 4 months, 6–18 months

Figure 12–10 Recommended immunization schedule.

notice. Severe temper tantrums long past the time when most children have found other ways of expressing frustration can also be considered serious.

Behavior deviations can often be assessed correctly by experienced teachers. They will know that some behaviors are part of a child's normal developmental progression. Others are personality characteristics. Refer children with other behaviors, particularly those that persist or severely limit the child, to appropriate professionals. A detailed discussion of behaviors is not appropriate here, but suggested sources for further information appear at the end of this chapter.

Although many disabilities and problems can be helped through participation in a good preschool program, you and your staff have to decide whether your school can accommodate these children. "Mainstreaming" is the word used to describe integrating handicapped children into a program designed for the nonhandicapped. Additional staff, materials, and perhaps modifications in the physical environment may be required. Those schools that do make the effort often find it an extremely positive experience for all concerned.

Children with handicaps such as mental retardation, visual or hearing limitations, and physical disabilities can be managed fairly easily in the regular classroom. On the other hand, a child with emotional problems may be a disruptive influence in the classroom that many teachers do not have the skills to manage. One disruptive child can make it impossible for all the other children in the group to gain as much as they might from their preschool activities.

Before you consider accepting a handicapped child, discuss it with your teachers. Let them observe the child before deciding. Enroll the child only if it can be a positive experience for the child, other children in the group, and the teachers.

Preventing Future Illnesses

Each person involved in an early childhood program should be concerned about the problem of illnesses in children in their care. Young children are especially vulnerable to a variety of infections and communicable diseases. This vulnerability is due to some special characteristics of this age level. Young children:

1. Have not developed immunity.
2. Have a small body structure. The distance between the nose and throat area and the middle ear is especially small. Respiratory infections are the result.
3. Are in close contact with other children while playing, eating, toileting, and diapering.
4. Use their mouths as an additional way to find out about the world around them.
5. Fall frequently, getting bumps and scrapes that can become infected.
6. Do not know how to protect themselves and have not developed routine hygiene procedures.

One way to minimize occurrences of illness in your school is to develop procedures for care of the *environment*. Since the requirements for infants and toddlers are somewhat more extensive than those for older children, you might find it helpful to look at these separately.

General precautions to prevent the spread of diseases in a child care environment are the following:

1. Clean rooms on a regular basis, including floor scrubbing and carpet cleaning.
2. Wipe tables with detergent and water after a play activity.
3. Clean and disinfect toys, utensils, or any objects that children handle or put in their mouths at least once a week. Wash in a dishwasher or dip in a bleach

solution ($1/4$ cup household bleach and 1 gallon of water prepared fresh each day).

4. Clean and sanitize bathrooms daily using a bleach solution.
5. The entire play area should be routinely cleaned and disinfected on a daily basis.
6. Clean sleeping cots or mats at least once a week. Each child should have a cot or mat with a sheet or blanket. Wash sheets or blankets each week.
7. Whenever possible, cleaning should be done with paper towels rather than cloth towels.
8. Encourage children to wash their hands after toileting, before eating, and before participating in a cooking activity.
9. Encourage children with "runny" noses to use a tissue and then wash their hands afterward.

The incidence of AIDS and other serious infectious diseases that affect children makes it necessary for staff members to take additional precautions when handling any body fluids (urine, feces, vomit, blood, saliva, or discharges from the nose, eyes, or draining sores). Important measures are the following:

1. Staff should wear latex gloves when cleaning up any of the above fluids. Gloves should be used once, for only one incident, then discarded.
2. Staff should wash their hands after handling any of the above-mentioned fluids, whether they were wearing latex gloves or not.
3. For spills of vomit, urine, or feces, staff should clean and disinfect the area, including floors, walls, bathrooms, and table tops.
4. Blood-contaminated material should be disposed of in a plastic bag with a secure tie, and placed out of the reach of children.
5. If any staff member has any known sores, or breaks in the skin, on his or her hands, particular care to wear gloves should be taken when handling blood or body fluids containing blood.
6. Staff who may be exposed to Hepatitis B or to contaminated blood should be informed about immunization.

The requirements for an *infant and toddler room* are more stringent because of the kinds of activities that go on there. Children crawl on the floor, are diapered, and put almost all objects in their mouths. So, in addition to the general room cleaning that is done, some special procedures can increase the safety of this area of your school. They are the following:

1. Vacuum carpeting daily and wet-mop vinyl floors with detergent and disinfectant. Clean all floor surfaces thoroughly on a regular schedule.
2. Wipe cribs and mattresses with a disinfectant regularly. Change the sheets whenever wet or soiled. Wash sheets weekly, or as needed.
3. Cover the diapering table with paper towels when being used; however, wipe it with a disinfectant after each use.
4. Dispose of soiled diapers or hold for a laundry in a closed container.
5. Rinse the potty chair cup after each use, and spray the seat with a disinfectant.

6. Wash all toys with a disinfectant at the end of each day. Put them in a mesh bag, dip them in a disinfectant solution, and hang them to dry.

7. Spray with disinfectant and wipe any large pieces of equipment that children climb.

8. Disinfect food containers and utensils regularly.

9. A solution of one ounce of chlorine bleach in a gallon of water is an adequate disinfectant for most cleaning purposes.

10. All caregivers in the infant/toddler room should automatically wash their hands after diapering and before feedings or preparing food for children.

11. A last precaution for caregivers: Cleanliness is important in this area of the school but should not present an obstacle to interactions with children. Cleanliness should become so automatic that children can be attended to while also having as safe and disease-free an environment as possible.

A discussion of preventing unhealthful conditions should include *management of the sick child*. Each school should have a child inclusion/exclusion policy statement stating when children should be kept at home and under what conditions a child will be sent home. Such a policy might state that children will not be denied admission nor sent home unless:

a. their illness prevents them from participating in activities

b. their illness results in need for more care than the staff can provide without jeopardizing the health or safety of other children.

Children should be sent home and kept home as long as the following conditions exist or until medical evaluation deems it safe for the child to return:

1. Oral temperature 101 degrees F or greater; rectal temperature 102 degrees F or greater; armpit temperature 100 degrees F or greater, accompanied by changes in behavior or other signs of illness.

2. Symptoms and signs of a severe illness: coughing, wheezing, lethargy, irritability, crying.

3. Vomiting: two or more episodes in the previous 24 hours.

4. Uncontrolled diarrhea.

5. Rash, along with a fever or change in behavior.

6. Mouth sores accompanied by drooling.

7. Purulent conjunctivitis (pink eye).

8. Tuberculosis.

9. Strep throat or other streptococcal infection.

10. Scabies, head lice, or any other infestation.

11. Impetigo.

12. Chicken pox, until six days after onset of the rash or until all sores are dry and crusted.

13. Mumps, until nine days after the onset of gland swelling.

14. Pertussis, until five days of antibiotic treatment have been completed.

15. Hepatitis A virus, until one week after the onset or as directed by health authorities.

16. Rubella, until six days after onset of rash.

17. Measles, until six days after onset of rash.

The first step is to train teachers and caregivers to recognize early signs of a sick child. The most obvious symptoms are a runny nose, red throat, sneezing, and coughing. Diarrhea and vomiting also are quickly associated with a possible illness. Less apparent signs may be "glassy" or watery eyes and a general listlessness. Irritability, fatigue, or loss of appetite might also not be recognized as portending an illness. Several staff members should know how to take children's temperatures and to interpret the reading. (An oral temperature over 99.4 degrees Fahrenheit or an axillary reading over 98 degrees Fahrenheit accompany many childhood illnesses.

The next step in managing the sick child is to decide what to do when you discover the child is ill. If it is the beginning of the day and the illness is noticed at the morning inspection routine, you can send the child home. If the illness becomes apparent only as the day wears on, you have to make other kinds of decisions.

The ideal would be to have a portion of the school environment set aside for the care of sick children. Here children could stay and be taken care of until the end of the day when the parents can come to pick them up. Some programs do offer this kind of service. The school must have a planned environment that allows the children to be in a less stimulating setting than their regular classroom. There also should be medical services available by telephone as needed. The Fairfax-San Anselmo Children's Center in Fairfax, California, provides this kind of service. One of the classrooms is called the "get well" room. Staffed by regular child care workers who have had specialized training, the room can accommodate six children. Parents let the staff know about the child's evening and morning symptoms. Staff keep careful records of the child's day for parents' information at pick-up time.

Some day care centers provide care for a sick child within the regular classroom. The Frank Porter Graham Child Development Center in Chapel Hill, North Carolina, has operated such a program for more than ten years. Children with minor illnesses are allowed to attend school and stay in their regular classrooms. Children with contagious diseases such as measles and chicken pox are excluded, but because so many children are immunized, few have been kept home. The usual caregivers take care of the children, but medical assistance is nearby when necessary. The designers of this program reason that the child is most contagious long before recognizable symptoms appear, so there is little reason to exclude children once the illness has been identified. Children in this program do not become ill more frequently than in other programs, and the diseases are no more severe.

Another kind of service for sick children is a day care center totally devoted to their needs. An interesting child care center aptly named Chicken Soup in Minneapolis, Minnesota, is the first school in America licensed to care only for children who are moderately ill. The program accommodates children from six months to twelve years who have colds, flu, or even chicken pox. Children are separated according to their illnesses, and nurses are available to care for them. Although this is a relatively expensive kind of child care, it is probably a bargain to the parent who might otherwise miss a full day's pay by staying home to care for the child.

As you help parents struggle with the problem of caring for a sick child, consider the foregoing options. If you are lucky enough to be starting a new program, perhaps you can plan this kind of innovation from the start. Even if you are operating a profit-making school, care for sick children may be the one thing that will make your school competitive with others in your area. So consider it in your planning sessions.

Including sick or recovering children in your regular classroom may mean that staff will have to be responsible for *giving medication* during the day. This should be done only with signed permission from both parents and the children's physicians. Keep medicines in a separate place, either on a high shelf or in the refrigerator. Maintain careful records of the time a dosage was given, the person who gave it, and the amount given. Parents and caregivers should confer daily as to the continuance of the medication.

One further way to prevent future illness is *immunization*. This practice protects children against many of the preventable childhood diseases including rubella, mumps, measles, polio, whopping cough, diphtheria, and tetanus. Many parents have their children routinely immunized from an early age. Others are seemingly unconcerned because they do not recognize that some of these conditions are life-threatening to young children. Others think these diseases have been eliminated and, therefore, their children need not be subjected to the procedure. A few worry about the side effects of immunization.

Immunization is required before entering public school in all states and the District of Columbia. In states where the requirement for preschools and day care centers are not similar, many teachers, directors, and others responsible for policies have opted to require immunization as a condition of entrance.

When, in spite of all preventive measures, a child in your school has contracted ones of these illnesses, it is your responsibility to see that the parents of all children who might have been exposed are notified. A simple form can indicate that their child has been exposed to such-and-such illness. You might also want to include information about the incubation period and possible signs and symptoms.

Children should not be allowed back into the classroom until their physician certifies that they are free of contagion. This will protect staff, children, and parents in the best possible way.

Including Children with HIV/AIDS

The Children's Defense Fund reports that in 1987 HIV infection was the ninth leading cause of death among one- to four-year-olds. Despite the fact that evidence indicates these children can attend child care programs without harm to other children, many child care professionals are concerned. In actuality, HIV children themselves are at risk of contracting other childhood diseases because their immune systems do not develop antibodies to combat them. In order to relieve anxieties by staff members and parents, it is important to become educated about what the disease is, how it is transmitted, and what precautions can be taken to prevent spread.

FIRST PRESBYTERIAN NURSERY SCHOOL OF SANTA MONICA
POLICY OF INFECTIOUS DISEASES

I.   BACKGROUND

The growing number of individuals who have been diagnosed as suffering from AIDS or who are infected with the HIV virus makes it desirable for the nursery school to adopt a policy and guidelines which is in keeping with the philosophy of respect for the dignity of each individual as a worthwhile person loved by God.

II.   POLICY

In formulating policy the nursery school will rely upon guidelines from the American Red Cross and U.S. Public Health Service, the American Academy of Pediatrics, the Surgeon General's report on AIDS and the InterFaith Ecumenical Guidelines for children with AIDS in nursery school.

School personnel will receive current information on AIDS and appropriate information regarding any precautions for cleanup of blood spills or body fluids.

The school will deal with the children who are victims of AIDS on a case-by-case basis. Therefore, it is possible that a child and/or personnel with AIDS or HIV Virus may be included in the nursery school program.

III.   GENERAL GUIDELINES

Medical decisions related to attendance by students and/or staff will be based on the best medical evidence available.

Each case will be evaluated on an individual basis.

Infected individuals may or may not be identified to all school personnel. Therefore, it is important that proper measures for preventing the spread of all infectious diseases be practiced by and for all students and staff.

IV.   PROCEDURES FOR CHILDREN/EMPLOYEES

Procedures related to children:

1.   Each child will be evaluated on an individual basis to determine the benefits and risks.

2.   Most children with AIDS will be able to attend school without endangering others. "Not one case of AIDS is known to have been transmitted in a school, day care, or foster care setting. AIDS is not spread through the kind of contact children have with each other, such as touching, hugging, or sharing meals and bathrooms. This is supported by long-term studies of family members of both adults and children with AIDS. Not one household member has become infected through routine, non-sexual contact with a family member with AIDS." (AIDS AND CHILDREN: Information for Teachers and School Officials, published by American Red Cross and U.S. Public Health Service.)

3.   A decision related to attendance in nursery school will be based on:

   a) Risk to the child and his/her physical condition, immune status, stamina, degree of any handicap, and need for any special environment or physical care.

   b) Possible risk to others—open lesions, infections and inimical behavior (biting, spitting, fighting, mouthing toys).

   c) Environmental needs in terms of age, maturity level, neurological status, including control of body functions and degree of handicap.

Each decision will be made in conjunction with the child's private physician(s) who can provide information on the ability of the child to attend school, any risk factors and any special needs for school environment and physical care.

4. Confidentiality is a medical and in some cases, a legal requirement. Personnel who are informed about a child's health condition will be limited to those who have a compelling need to know.

5. The child's progress must be monitored and open communication maintained between the nursery school and the private physician, especially after an absence due to illness.

6. Physical care of the student at the school site must include precautions for the clean up of blood spills/body fluids.

7. All immunocompromised children, including those with AIDS, may need to be removed from school, with the physician's knowledge, if exposure to communicable disease (such as chicken pox or measles) becomes a factor.

Procedures related to employees:

1. Each employee will be evaluated on an individual basis to determine any risk to self or others. All employees must be physically and mentally able to perform the duties of their position and be free of any condition or disease detrimental to their health and safety or to the health and safety of other persons.

2. Each employee will be evaluated by the Nursery School Committee. A decision regarding an employee's work assignment will be based on:

a) Risk to the employee's physical condition, immune status, stamina, degree of any handicap and ability to perform related duties in the assigned environment.

b) Possible risk to others, behavior, open lesions, infections.

3. Each decision will be made in conjunction with:

a) The employee's private physician(s), who can provide information on the ability of the individual to perform assigned duties in the assigned environment, any risk factors and any special needs.

b) The Nursery School Committee.

4. Confidentiality is a medical and, in some cases, a legal requirement. Personnel who are informed about an employee's health condition will be limited to those who have a compelling need to know.

5. The employee's progress must be monitored and open communication maintained between the Nursery School Committee and the private physician(s), especially after an absence due to illness.

6. Physical care of the employee at the work site must include precautions for the clean up of blood spills/body fluids.

In adopting these guidelines, the nursery school recognizes that the state of medical knowledge about AIDS is changing and will update the policy statement in light of significant new information on the disease.

(The above policy was discussed and approved at the October 1987 meeting of the Board of Directors.)

Figure 12–11 First Presbyterian Nursery School of Santa Monica Policy of Infectious Diseases. (Reprinted with permission.)

Children with HIV have been infected by their mothers during pregnancy or through receiving a contaminated blood transfusion. Adults acquire the disease by sexual contact involving secretions and sperm, infected blood, and contaminated needles. It is *not* transmitted by casual contacts such as sharing food, dishes, drinking glasses, toilets, pools, clothing, or toys. You cannot get it from hugging, kissing, or touching. Children with HIV can go to school, play with friends, and participate in out-of-school recreational activities without risk to other children. The Centers for Disease Control (CDC) and the Pediatric AIDS Foundation of Santa Monica, California, recommend that children be kept out of group activities *only if they have bleeding or open sores* that might expose other children to risks. When children are included in school, the precautions listed in this chapter should be strictly adhered to, especially when cleaning up any blood or blood-contaminated fluids. It is recommended that schools and child care centers *draft a policy on infectious diseases, including HIV*, that is distributed to all staff members and parents. For further information about HIV, contact the Centers for Disease Control of the U.S. Public Health Service.

Another excellent source of information regarding health and safety of children in group care can be obtained from the National Association for the Education of Young Children It is called *Model Child Care Health Policies* and is available on a computer disk, either IBM-compatible or Apple/Macintosh. Topics covered include admissions policies, supervision, discipline, care of ill children, health plans and services, emergency plans, transportation of children, sanitation and hygiene, food handling, sleeping, and staff policies. The publication can be obtained by writing to:

NAEYC
1509 16th Street, NW
Washington, DC 20036-2460
202-232-8777; 800-424-2460; Fax 202 328-1846
Ask for NAEYC #717; specify computer type.

Recordkeeping

Although the matter of adequate records of children's health has been touched upon, it is important enough to be covered more extensively. Adequate records are the basis for planning for individual children, for developing policies and procedures, and for checking the attainment of your health goals. Each child should have a file that contains information about health before entering school and during the time of attendance.

Each child's file should contain the following information.

HEALTH

Physician's examination prior to entrance including general health status, any conditions that might interfere with functioning at school, immunizations, conditions the school should be aware of, such as seizures and allergies

Health screening tests or observations by teachers

Continuing healthcare—illnesses, surgery, injuries, current medications

CHILD DEVELOPMENT

Information concerning the mother's pregnancy

Developmental history from birth to school entrance

Profiles done by teachers on a periodic basis

FAMILY INFORMATION

Application form including residence, place of work of both parents, family members

Emergency information including persons to contact in case the child is hurt or ill

Release for emergency medical treatment

Persons authorized to take child from school

Authorization for use of child's photo or voice recording for educational purposes

Permission to take child on trips away from school

Financial arrangements for payment of tuition

Health and safety of their children when being cared for by someone else is probably the greatest concern of working parents. A well-maintained, safe, and healthful environment is worth all the staff effort and time that it takes. Make your school a model, and you will be repaid by the gratitude of parents. You will probably find there is a financial benefit as well. A safe, well-maintained, and attractive school will bring a more stable enrollment and a more consistent income.

SUMMARY

Do not overlook the physical environment of the school in planning or execution. It bears equal weight with educational programs.

Maintenance consists of major projects; operations are the day-to-day tasks required to keep the school functioning hygienically and attractively.

Take an inventory of all buildings and equipment at least annually. Keep accurate records.

Licensing guidelines and local building and safety codes are designed to ensure the safety of children in group settings. Know what is required and comply at all times. In addition, make regular safety checks of all equipment both indoors and outdoors.

Have a well-stocked first-aid kit. At least one person on staff at all times should be Red Cross certified to administer first aid.

Develop a disaster plan for meeting emergencies such as fires, floods, hurricanes, or earthquakes. Post an evacuation route in each classroom and in entry areas. Schedule drills frequently so staff and children know what to do in the event of a disaster.

Every early childhood center should have a set of health goals designed to promote the health and well-being of children. These goals should be the basis for health policies that guide preventive practices.

Health goals should address children's health status and include means for alleviating conditions that prevent children from learning. Health goals should also address the prevention of future illnesses.

Prevention of future illnesses is facilitated by maintaining a clean and sanitary environment. In addition, staff must take additional precaution when handling body fluids.

Each school should have a child inclusion/exclusion policy stating when children should be kept at home and under what conditions children will be sent home.

The inclusion of children with HIV/AIDS is an issue that needs to be addressed in child care. All staff members and parents should become educated about the causes of AIDS, how it is transmitted, and what precautions can be taken to prevent spread. It is important to keep accurate records of children's health. Include information regarding the child's general health status, developmental information, and family information.

SELECTED FURTHER READING

American Academy of Pediatrics, Committee on Early Childhood. 1987. *Health in Day Care: A Manual for Health Professionals*. Elk Grove Village, Il: American Academy of Pediatrics.

Aronson, S., M.D. 1991. *Health and Safety in Child Care*. New York: Harper Collins.

Aronson, S., M.D. 1986. "Exclusion Criteria for Ill Children in Child Care." *Child Care Information Exchange* 49 (January), 30–35.

Aronson, S., M.D. 1987. "Health Update: AIDS and Child Care Programs." *Child Care Information Exchange* 58 (November), 35–39.

Deitch, S.R. 1982. *Health in Day-Care: A Manual for Health Professionals*. Elk Grove Village, Il: American Academy of Pediatrics.

Fredericks, B., Hardman, R., Morgan, G., and Rodgers, F. 1986. *A Little Bit Under the Weather: A Look at Care for Mildly Ill Children*. Boston, MA: Work/Family Directions.

Kendrick, A., Kaufmann, R., and Messenger, K., eds. 1988. *Healthy Young Children—A Manual for Programs*. Washington, DC: National Association for the Education of Young Children.

Marotz, L., Rush, J., and Cross, M. 1993. *Health, Safety, and Nutrition for the Young Child*, 3rd ed. Albany, NY: Delmar Publishers Inc.

NAEYC Information Service. 1989. *Child Care and Ill Children and Healthy Child Care Practices*. Washington, DC: National Association for the Education of Young Children.

Sleator, E.K. 1986. *Infectious Diseases in Day-Care*. Urbana, Il: Eric Clearinghouse on Elementary and Early Childhood Education.

STUDENT ACTIVITIES

1. Draw the floor plan of a classroom you know. How would you replan it after having read this chapter? What are your reasons for the changes?
2. Visit a school for young children. Observe the playground for an hour. What changes would you make if you were in charge? Why?
3. What methods are used to clean your school? Are they adequate? Why?
4. Visit the health department of your community. What services are available to children? Who can use them?
5. Look in the telephone book under the listing for physicians. How many pediatricians are there?
6. Where is the closest emergency hospital to your school? Is the phone number posted? Do you know the most direct route?

REVIEW

1. Why is the physical appearance of a school more than cosmetic?
2. List safety precautions that should be taken when transporting children.
3. What kinds of information are included in a disaster plan?
4. List items that should be included in a disaster kit.
5. List five general precautions to prevent the spread of diseases in a child care environment.
6. What special precautions should be taken when handling any body fluids?
7. How do physical defects interfere with a child's ability to learn?
8. Under what conditions should children be sent home and be kept at home?
9. What are the current recommendations for including children with HIV/AIDS in child care?
10. What are the three categories of information that should be in a child's health file?

GLOSSARY

AIDS   Acquired Immune Deficiency Syndrome

Disaster plans   detailed plans for evacuating children and managing a disaster.

Maintenance   major expenditures on the physical plant: painting, alterations, repair.

Operations   recurring, day-to-day activities involved in the upkeep of a school.

13

Food and Nutrition Services

OBJECTIVES

After studying this chapter, the student should be able to:
- Explain why good nutrition is important in an early childhood center.
- List several principles of menu planning.
- Describe some of the mechanics of food service.

Proper nutrition is vital to the development of young children. What children eat during the years of rapid growth between birth and five years can affect their development for years to come. Improper nutrition may delay or permanently stunt physical growth. A child who is ill or lethargic because of poor nutrition will certainly have less interest in learning. An irritable child is likely to have problems in social situations. So, as more children spend longer hours in group settings, the adults who care for them must assume greater responsibility for seeing that they get an adequate diet.

CAREGIVER'S ROLE

The caregivers or teachers who are with children during most of their waking hours must closely observe their eating patterns. They should be aware of children's food likes and dislikes, the amount each child consumes, and any changes in food habits. At times, you use this information to reassure parents that their child is eating well at school. At other times, you must alert parents to changes in a child's eating "habits."

Caregivers must also know what changes to expect in children's food consumption at each stage of development. During periods of rapid growth, children eat well. When growth slows down, they automatically consume less. Unless the adult is knowledgeable enough to see this as a normal change, parents may be needlessly anxious or pressure their children to change.

Current recommendations for good nutrition should be a part of the caregiver's knowledge. As research reveals more about what the body needs, ideas about what constitutes a proper diet have also changed. For instance, in the past, solid foods were introduced to infants as early as five to six weeks. In 1981, the American Academy of Pediatrics recommended that breast-fed babies do not need supplementary foods until six months of age. Bottle-fed babies may need some vitamin supplements. At about six months, the ability to chew, swallow, and process solid foods is more developed. At that time, parents can gradually add cereal, fruits, vegetables, meat, and fish. By the end of the first year, children should be consuming a variety of foods from the four food groups.

Caregivers should know how to encourage children to make appropriate food choices. When given choices of food, children should be able to select those that will contribute to their well-being. Teachers should foster positive attitudes toward food. Children should view eating as a necessary and enjoyable part of their daily routine. In addition, children should be able to participate in the fun of planning and preparing good food.

MENU PLANNING

As director of your school, your responsibility will be either to plan menus or to oversee someone else who does the planning. If your school is open all day, you may serve breakfast, lunch, and two snacks each day. This constitutes a large portion of the child's daily intake. Therefore, you must know how to plan meals that include as much of the child's daily requirement as you can.

Start by checking your state licensing requirements. They will vary from state to state, but are based on the number of hours a center is in operation. In general, guidelines specify the following:

- If your center is open three to four hours, serve a midmorning or afternoon snack no closer than two hours before the next meal.
- If your center is open five to eight hours, food service should provide one-third to one-half of the daily requirement.
- If your center is open nine hours or more, serve at least two-thirds of the total daily requirement.
- If your center includes infants, they will have individualized eating plans and schedules.

Some child care programs receive funding under the Child Care Food Program. This provides reimbursement for meals in child care centers and for the cost of labor and administration. Money comes from the Food and Nutrition Service of the U.S. Department of Agriculture and is administered through state departments of education. Guidelines specify nutritional standards and serving sizes for children from birth to age twelve. Head Start centers also have their own nutritional standards and serving-size regulations.

Organize your menu planning so that it is efficient. Lynn Marotz and her co-authors of *Health, Safety, and Nutrition for the Young Child* recommend the following materials to help in menu planning:

- Menu forms.
- A list of foods on hand that should be included.
- Recipe file.
- Old menus with notes and suggestions.
- Calendar.
- Grocery ads for short-term planning.

Start with the main dishes to be served for lunch. Include protein foods or substitutes. Then list the vegetables and fruits to be served. These can be as salads, with the entrée, or as dessert. Enriched or whole-grain breads or cereal products come next. Finally, add a beverage, usually milk. Plan snacks and breakfast to round out the daily requirements.

Figure 13–1 Children enjoy preparing their own snacks.

Consider having cyclic menus. Make out several weekly menus; test them out to see if the children will eat the food. Make any necessary changes, then recycle them every month or so. This has a decided advantage since it allows you to order larger quantities of some foods, thus saving money. It will also save the time it can take to prepare new menus every week. Children like familiar foods and do not mind having the same things every few weeks or so. Once you have some basic menus, you can make changes using seasonal fruits or vegetables easily.

Include some ethnic or regional foods. This will help children from different backgrounds feel more comfortable. It will also introduce all children to the concept of cultural differences or similarities.

Some schools have instituted the idea of "special day foods." These foods do not appear on your cyclic menu, but are served on special occasions. The "party" atmosphere of a day such as this may encourage children to try foods they would ordinarily reject. Examples might be a "smorgasbord" of out-of-the-ordinary fruits or vegetables that the children can taste-test at snack time. Another might be an "upside-down day," such as whole-wheat pancakes with fruit toppings for lunch or cheese sandwiches for breakfast. The idea is to make tasting foods an adventure.

GUIDELINES FOR MENU PLANNING

Some further guidelines may be helpful to you as you develop a series of menus to use in your school.

Work within the framework of the basic four food groups. This is a simple division of foods into four categories: vegetables and fruits, milk and milk products, breads and/or cereals, and meat and/or an alternate. Each day's food consumption should include foods from each of these groups. Familiarity with the foods that are included in each of these groups will allow you to make appropriate choices and supply alternates when necessary. A new way of looking at daily nutrition requirements was suggested by the U.S. Department of Agriculture in 1992. A Food Guide

FOOD GROUP	NUTRITIONAL NEEDS	FOOD
Vegetables and Fruits	Vitamin C, Vitamin A, Iron	Green and yellow vegetables; all fruits and melons; dried fruits; beans—green, wax, lima
Milk and Milk Products	Calcium, Riboflavin, Protein Calories	Milk, cheese, ice cream, cottage cheese, yogurt, butter
Breads and/or Cereals	B Vitamins, Minerals, Protein Calories	Whole grain or enriched bread; biscuits, muffins, crackers (whole wheat flour); cookies made with whole grains; enriched or whole grain cereal
Meat and/or Alternate	Protein, Iron, B Vitamins	Meat, poultry, fish, cheese, eggs, peanut butter, beans, peas

Figure 13–2 The four food groups.

Pyramid includes the four food groups, but recommends different quantities from each group. Figure 13–3 shows the Pyramid. However, the quantities as indicated have not been adjusted to fit the needs of young children. Therefore, menu planning for early childhood centers is best done using the Basic Four Food Groups.

Choose foods children like. Children are sensitive to the four basic tastes— salty, sweet, sour, and bitter. Because of this enhanced taste awareness, they are more conservative in their approach to foods. Most have a very limited number of foods they like. They will often reject foods that are strong in flavor or heavily spiced. They often reject new foods before they even taste them. Children do not like their foods mixed in casseroles or stew. Most want their food to be easy to manage, in bite-sized pieces or as finger foods. So develop a list of the proven favorites to use in your basic menus. New foods can gradually be added to broaden the children's diet.

Plan menus that can be prepared and served using the kitchen equipment you have available. When you are preparing food for large numbers of people, one of the problems often incurred is that there is not enough oven space or large pans. Know what is in your kitchen, and anticipate what you will need to prepare the food. Consider, too, what you will need to serve the food. As an example, prepare a finger food for dessert if all the small bowls are to be used for the meal.

Consider the number of personnel available for preparing and serving food. If your school is very large, you may have both a cook and an assistant. Meals are likely to be different in this kind of school than in one where there is only a part-time cook. In a family day care home, where the owner-operator does all the cooking, meals must be extremely simple and easily prepared.

Include foods that provide appetite appeal. Remember the old saying "We eat with our eyes as well as our mouths." Vary the color of foods served. A meal of mashed potatoes, fish, and cauliflower will hardly be appealing. Change the shape of familiar foods. Cut sandwiches in triangles, circles, or slim rectangles. Include several different textures: crunchy, soft, chewy.

FYI

One in five school-age children is classified as obese according to research done by William H. Dietz, M.D. and Ph.D., an associate professor of pediatrics at Tufts University School of Medicine. A child is considered obese when he or she weighs 25 percent more than the ideal weight for his or her height or age.

Some children are heavy because their parents are heavy (inherited). Others are overweight because of inactivity or because they eat high-fat foods like burgers, fries, and sugary cereals. Children can be helped to maintain a desirable weight by being in an environment where balanced, low-fat meals are served, where they learn to substitute low-calorie foods for high-calorie foods, and where they are encouraged to increase their activity level.

Food Guide Pyramid
A Guide to Daily Food Choices

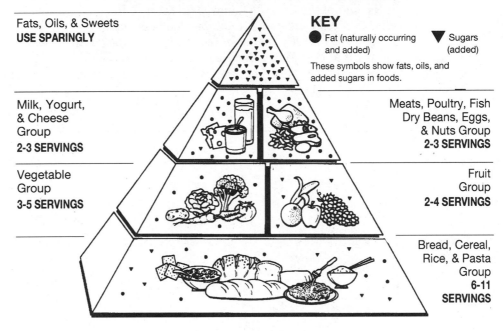

Fats, Oils, & Sweets
USE SPARINGLY

KEY
● Fat (naturally occurring   ▼ Sugars
   and added)   (added)

These symbols show fats, oils, and
added sugars in foods.

Milk, Yogurt,
& Cheese
Group
2-3 SERVINGS

Meats, Poultry, Fish
Dry Beans, Eggs,
& Nuts Group
2-3 SERVINGS

Vegetable
Group
3-5 SERVINGS

Fruit
Group
2-4 SERVINGS

Bread, Cereal,
Rice, & Pasta
Group
**6-11
SERVINGS**

Figure 13–3   Food Guide Pyramid.

Introduce a new food along with a familiar and accepted food. If you want the children to try a new vegetable, serve it with their favorite chicken. Or if you want to serve a carrot salad for the first time, schedule it for a day when spaghetti is also on the menu.

Consider dessert as an integral part of the meal, not a special treat when other foods are eaten. Serve only desserts that contribute to the daily food requirement. Fruits, cakes made with whole-wheat flour, cookies with nuts or raisins, or milk puddings are all examples. Children also enjoy ice cream or fruit sherbets, which contribute to good nutrition.

Broaden children's learning by including them in planning their own meals and snacks. When given limited choices, preschoolers and school-age children can plan some of their own meals and snacks. Obviously, they cannot be given total freedom since they might well choose a meal of potato chips, ice cream, and chocolate cupcakes. But if they are given information about the food groups, they should be able to plan a meal using foods from each. So let them plan lunch once a week, once a month, or as often as you can.

PARENTS

Don't forget the parents of children in your school as you plan foods to be served. One of the first questions many parents ask when they arrive to pick up their child at the end of the day is "Did my child eat well today?" Parents are concerned that their children eat the right foods in adequate amounts.

Post your weekly menus in an easily seen place so parents know what was served that day. When they see a food they know their child likes, they can feel more confident. At home, the evening meal can then supplement whatever the child had at school.

PATTERN	CHILDREN 1 TO 3	CHILDREN 3 TO 6	CHILDREN 6 TO 12
Breakfast			
Milk	1/2 cup	3/4 cup	1 cup
Juice or fruit	1/4 cup	1/2 cup	1/2 cup
Bread	1/2 slice	1/2 slice	1 slice
Cereal	1/4 cup	1/3 cup	1/2 cup
Snack			
Milk	1/2 cup	1/2 cup	1 cup
Bread or substitute	1/2 slice	1/2 slice	1 slice
Juice	1/2 cup	1/2 cup	3/4 cup
Lunch or Supper			
Milk	1/2 cup	1/4 cup	1 cup
Meat or alternative—One of the following combinations to give equivalent quantities.			
Meat, poultry, fish	1 ounce	1 1/2 ounce	2 ounces
Egg	1	1	1
Cheese	1 ounce	1 1/2 ounce	2 ounces
Cooked dry beans	1/4 cup	3/8 cup	1/2 cup
Peanut butter	2 tablespoons	3 tablespoons	4 tablespoons
Vegetables and/or fruit (2 or more to total)	1/4 cup	1/2 cup	3/4 cup
Bread or alternate	1/2 slice	1/2 slice	1 slice
Butter or margarine	1/2 teaspoon	1/2 teaspoon	1/2 teaspoon

Figure 13–4   Serving portions for children ages 1 to 12.

Use your parent newsletter to provide information about appropriate food choices for young children. Share with parents information from your own reading about nutrition, or get articles from your local library. Summarize the articles or reprint them in totality for parents. If the children in your school bring breakfast or lunch from home, suggest nutritious foods. Tell parents how to avoid the "television advertising trap"—those appealing ads that make children demand the foods in their lunch boxes. Only clever substitutes will satisfy many children. Your newsletter might also give suggestions for nutritious birthday treats that parents may bring to school.

Keep parents informed about their child's food intake. Some schools have a form that is filled out by teachers each day indicating how much the child ate. If your school does not use a form, tell teachers to be alert to each child's consumption so that parents' questions can be answered.

Develop a partnership with parents of infants and toddlers to plan food choices. The diets of these young children need to be carefully thought out to avoid food allergies, digestive upsets, and poor nutrition. Pediatricians have traditionally worked with parents to avoid these problems. Now the school must be included in the planning. Compounding the difficulty is the fact that babies react in different ways to new situations, including new foods. Caregivers need to be aware of those habits so they can avoid rejection of food the child needs. Many toddlers have particular ways in which they want their food prepared or presented. No other way will do. So it is essential that the school have a close alliance with the parents to ensure that these youngest children are eating an adequate diet.

Make sure that all parents inform you of their child's allergies. A large number of preschool children have allergic reactions, although not all are to food. The

Figure 13–5 Lunch is a time to socialize.

common food allergens are chocolate, milk and milk products, wheat, and eggs. When you plan a menu item using these foods, be sure there is a substitute that can be served to the allergic child. Some schools ask parents to supply alternate foods on these days. Other schools keep foods on hand to use at these times.

Provide parents with recipes of school foods that children especially like. Many children talk about a popular menu item and want Mom to prepare it at home. So translate your quantity recipes to smaller portions and have copies available when parents ask. Just as serving home-like foods at school brings home and school closer together, the opposite will bridge the gap as the child reenters the home routines.

FOOD SERVICE FOR CHILDREN

The best-planned menus are of no use unless children eat the food. So put a great deal of thought into ensuring that the atmosphere in which food is presented encourages the children to consume an adequate amount.

Straighten the classroom before mealtime. Many teachers involve children in this task. It can also be done while the children are outdoors or having a story in another area. Put toys that might create a distraction out of sight. Clear away any clutter on shelves or floors.

Make tables as attractive as possible. A centerpiece of flowers or something made by the children will add interest. Children can make their own personalized

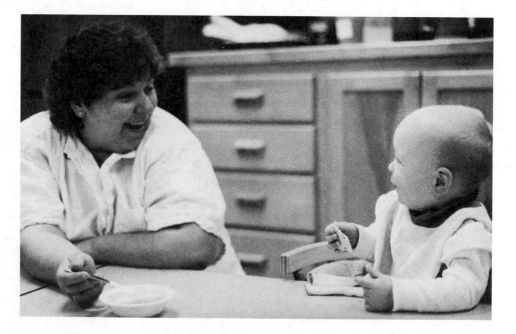

Figure 13–6   Snack time in the infant room.

	MONDAY	TUESDAY	WEDNESDAY	THURSDAY	FRIDAY
BREAKFAST	1/2 an orange 1/4 cup shredded wheat cereal 3/4 cup milk 1/2 cup milk	1/2 cup tomato juice 2 4"-pancakes 2 Tbsp. applesauce 1/2 tsp. margarine 1/2 cup milk	1/2 cup sliced peaches 1/3 cup oatmeal 3/4 cup milk	1/2 a banana 1/4 cup shredded wheat cereal 3/4 cup milk 1/2 slice toast 1/2 tsp. margarine	1/2 cup orange juice French toast 1/2 slice bread milk egg powdered sugar 1/2 cup milk
SNACK	1/2 cup milk 2 graham crackers	1/2 slice cheese 4 small whole wheat crackers	1/2 cup yogurt with fruit 2 whole wheat crackers	1/2 slice cheese 1/2 apple	1/2 cup apple juice 2 graham crackers
LUNCH	1/2 cup milk 2 fish sticks 4 carrot sticks 1/2 slice bread 1/2 tsp. margarine 1/3 cup applesauce	1/2 cup milk 1 oz. meat loaf 1/4 cup peas 1/4 baked potato 1/2 tsp. margarine 2" square of spice cake made with w.w. flour	1/2 cup milk 1/2 cup spaghetti 1/4 cup meat sauce 1/4 cup green salad 2 orange wedges	1/2 cup milk 1/2 cup macaroni & cheese 1/4 cup string beans 1/4 cup string beans 1/4 cup Apple Betty w/ wheat germ topping	1/2 cup milk 1/2 tuna sandwich 1/4 cup carrot & raisin salad 1/2 cup ice cream
SNACK	Assorted raw vegetables Sour cream dip 1/4 slice whole wheat bread 1/2 tsp. margarine	1/2 cup yogurt with fruit 1 graham cracker	1/2 peanut butter sandwich 1/2 cup milk	WW raisin cookies 1/2 cup milk	1/2 cup milk 1/2 warm tortilla 1/2 tsp. margarine or grated cheese

Figure 13–7 Sample menus for a day care center.

placemats. Cover the mat with clear contact paper for durability. Set the table in an orderly manner with napkins, utensils, and plates carefully placed and convenient to the children's reach. Special occasions such as holidays or birthdays call for special table decorations.

Mealtime furniture should be appropriate for the age level of the children. Consider, for instance, whether you want to use tables or highchairs for toddlers. Magda Gerber, Director of Resources for Infant Educarers, believes that highchairs are confining. As soon as babies can crawl and sit up, Gerber says they can get themselves to a table that is only a few inches off the floor. At the other extreme, school-age children need larger chairs and higher tables than preschoolers.

Children should participate as much as possible in the routines of mealtimes. They can certainly set the table before the meal begins. Allow each child to serve himself or herself from serving bowls rather than having each plate already "dished out" before it comes to the table. At the end of the meal, children can scrape leftovers from their own plates and put their utensils in a container.

Teachers and caregivers should eat with the children at mealtimes. Seeing adults enjoying food serves as a role model for the development of appropriate attitudes and behavior in the children. Mealtimes should also be a time when children and adults have a chance to talk quietly to each other. It certainly should not be a time when table manners are stressed or pressure exerted for "clean plates."

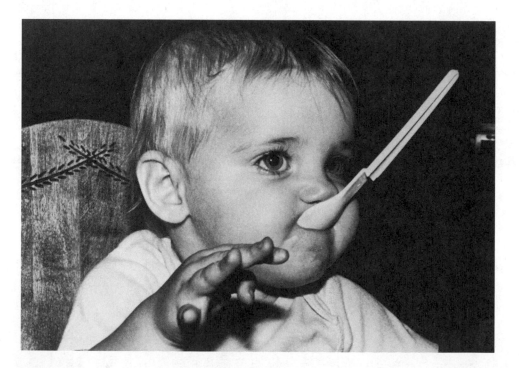

Figure 13–8   Learning to feed yourself can be fun.

COOKING EXPERIENCES FOR CHILDREN

As you consider the total process of food service in your school, do not forget to plan for cooking experiences for children. Children should prepare their own meals or snacks frequently as a part of the curriculum of each classroom. You may have to be the motivating force to encourage teachers to become involved. Some teachers love to cook and enjoy sharing their skills, interests, and knowledge with children; others see it as a chore.

Include your staff in discussions of menus and invite their suggestions for things they can prepare with the children. Starting with snacks is the easiest, since many can be done without much preparation or cooking. Even two-year-olds can spread peanut butter on a cracker with a plastic knife. Preschoolers can make a fruit shake in a blender or cut their own hard-cooked eggs with an egg slicer. School-age children, obviously, are capable of preparing a variety of nutritious snacks for themselves.

At staff meetings, discuss how teachers can set up a cooking experience so there is little danger that children will get hurt. Many adults shudder at the thought of three- and four-year-olds using a knife or an electric frying pan. Careful planning is essential. If an activity is set up properly and supervised adequately, teachers should have few problems. A wide variety of books can help you and your staff plan cooking in the classroom. See the list below for some suggestions.

Instead of whole milk: use dry nonfat milk, cottage cheese, mild cheddar cheese, ice milk.

Instead of expensive cuts of meat: use less tender cuts, stewing chickens, fresh fish in season, home-cooked meats.

Use dried beans, peas, lentils, peanut butter.

Fruits and vegetables: buy fresh fruits and vegetables in season.

Breads and cereals: use whole-grain or enriched flour, home-made cakes and rolls, whole-grain crackers.

Use brown rice and enriched spaghetti and noodles.

Figure 13–9 Inexpensive substitutes with more food value.

There are many good cookbooks for children designed to teach them to cook:

Ackerman, D. *Cooking with Kids*. Mt. Rainier, MD: Gryphon House, 1981.

Catron, C., and Parks, B. *Cooking Up a Story*. Minneapolis, MN: T.S. Dinison and Company, Inc., 1986.

Cristenberry, M., and Stevens, B. *Can Piaget Cook?* Atlanta, GA: Humanics, Limited, 1984.

Jenkins, K. *Kinder Krunchies*. Pleasant Hill, CA: Discovery Toys, 1982.

McClenahan, P., and Jaqua, I. *Cool Cooking for Kids: Recipes and Nutrition for Kids*. Belmont, CA: Fearon Pitman, 1976.

Stori, M. *I'll Eat Anything If I Can Make It Myself*. Chicago, IL: Chicago Review, 1980.

Wanamaker, N., Hearn, K., and Richarz, S. *More Than Graham Crackers: Nutrition Education and Food Preparation With Young Children*. Washington, DC: National Association for the Education of Young Children,

Warren, J. *Super Snacks/Sugarless*. Everett, WA: Warren Publishing House, Inc., 1982.

Wilms, B. *Crunchy Bananas*. Salt Lake City, UT: Gibbs M. Smith, 1984.

Zeller, P.K., and Jacobson, M.F. 1987. *Eat, Think, and Be Healthy!* Washington, DC: Center for Science in the Public Interest.

MECHANICS OF FOOD SERVICE

With the cost of food constantly rising, you will need to become a wise shopper when buying food for a large school. Your goal will be to serve high-quality meals at a cost your budget can afford.

Purchase

Check your community for food service companies that supply restaurants and institutions. They offer large-quantity packaging, often at a lower cost than the local supermarket. If you are a nonprofit institution, they may even give an additional discount. Some deliver, but check on the cost of that service. The cost may be too high, or completely justified when weighed against your time to shop for the food.

Read newspaper ads for the weekly specials and also for fruits and vegetables that are in season. Markets feature items that are in large supply and lower the cost to attract buyers. You can save money by filling out your cyclic menus with whatever fruits and vegetables are on sale.

Choose the quality of food that is best-suited for its purpose. Top quality, and therefore, probably a higher price, is not always necessary. Read labels and check grades of food before deciding. A can of peaches to be used in a cobbler for dessert does not have to be the best but can be a lesser grade, for instance.

When buying perishable foods, buy only enough that can be used quickly. Meats, fruits, vegetables, and milk products fall into this category. Judge how much children are eating at meals and adjust the quantity you order to correspond.

Preparation

The best planned meals will not be eaten if they are not prepared properly. Food can be overcooked or undercooked. Nutrients can also be lost in the cooking process so that the food contributes little to the children's health.

It is your responsibility to see that appropriate guidelines are followed by who-ever prepares food at your school. This includes teachers in the preschool or after-school care rooms who help children with cooking. It also covers the person in the kitchen who puts together meals for the entire school. Some simple precautions may be in order.

Blender Beaters
   Yogurt, fruit, honey
   Yogurt, banana, canned crushed pineapple
   Milk, nonfat dry milk, berries
   Yogurt, frozen fruit (berries or cherries), honey

Yogurt Yummies
   Plain yogurt with any combinations of the following:
      maple syrup, honey, brown sugar, molasses
      wheat germ
      applesauce, apple butter
      raisins, nuts
      peaches, pineapple, blueberries, strawberries
      chocolate syrup, vanilla, cinnamon

Pancake Parade
   Whole-wheat pancakes with any of the following:
      apple sauce, apple butter, peach butter
      crushed berries, sour cream
      maple syrup, honey, molasses
      mashed bananas with lemon juice, honey, cinnamon
      mashed canned apricots combined with apple sauce
      berries, plums, or pears blended with pineapple juice
      crumbled bacon mixed into batter

Snazzy Sandwiches
   grilled cheese
   grilled cheese and tuna
   open-faced: pizza sauce, grated cheese
   refried beans, cheese in a soft tortilla
   pita bread stuffed with chopped tuna
   pita bread, scrambled egg, mild salsa

Figure 13–10   Better breakfasts.

- Prepare ahead only those foods that can safely be held under refrigeration: puddings, Jello™, and spaghetti sauce are some.
- Plan so that all foods finish cooking at about the same time so that none are held too long or reheated.
- Use cooking methods that preserve as many nutrients as possible. Do not soak vegetables for long periods of time in water or cook them in large quantities. Do not overcook vegetables.
- Prepare foods in ways that will be appealing to children. Add a touch of color sometimes with a sprinkling of paprika or parsley. Put a dab of jelly on vanilla pudding to make it more appetizing.

- Prepare food that is easy for children to manage. Cut meat into small pieces. Quarter sandwiches or cut them into interesting shapes. Vary the way fruits and vegetables are cut: Oranges can be in slices or wedges; carrots can be sticks or "pennies."

Peanut butter with
  raisins or dates
  apples or banana
  apple sauce
  chopped celery or shredded carrots
  graham crackers
  nonfat dry milk and honey
Cheese balls—form balls with softened cheese and roll in chopped nuts
Nut bread with cheese spread
Celery stuffed with peanut butter, cheese spread
Pizza—use pizza dough or English muffins
Tacos or burritos—fill with cheese, leftover meat, or finely shredded carrots or zucchini
Cottage cheese with fruit
Yogurt with fruit
Ice cream in milk shakes, with fruit, or in make-your-own sundaes
Deviled eggs
Wheat toast topped with tuna salad or cheese, boiled to melt
Tiny meatballs on toothpicks
Orange sections
Banana slices—dip in honey, roll in nuts
Watermelon wedges—try seedless melons
Peaches
Apple slices, dip in orange juice to prevent browning
Granola or grape-nuts sprinkled on yogurt
Assorted raw vegetables with seasoned cottage cheese dip
Fruit shakes—blend fruit and nonfat dry milk in blender with a few ice cubes
Fruit kabobs—banana wheels, pineapple chunks, cherries, strawberries, orange wedges
Fresh fruit juice gelatin cubes

Figure 13–11 Scrumptious snacks.

Safety

The safety of food served to children in a preschool or day care setting should be of primary concern to all of us. Take every possible precaution to see that food is stored properly and prepared safely. All preparation and serving areas should be clean. Teachers, kitchen staff, and any others who handle food should observe good hygienic practices.

Food handlers must maintain the strictest standards of health practices. They should undergo periodic medical evaluations to determine their general health status and that they are free of tuberculosis. Anyone suffering from an illness should stay at home until recovered.

Food handlers must maintain strict standards of personal hygiene. This includes wearing clean clothes and washing hands frequently. Hair should be tidy or contained under a net. Food preparers should refrain from smoking.

Food handling should ensure that food is clean and free of contamination or spoilage. When food is delivered, inspect it for spoilage. Wash all fruits and vegetables thoroughly. Immediately put away foods that need refrigeration or are frozen. Put bulk foods such as flour or rice into air-tight containers.

Food storage should provide optimum conditions for preserving the safety and nutritive value of food. Refrigerators should maintain a temperature of 38 to 40 degrees Fahrenheit. A freezer for long-term storage should be at 0 degrees Fahrenheit. Foods on the shelf should have an even, cool, dry temperature. All containers should be stored off the floor.

Never save leftover food that has been served but has not been eaten. The only exception might be fruits and vegetables. These can be washed and saved for serving at a later time. Food that has been left in the kitchen and held at a safe temperature can be covered and put into the freezer for later use. These foods will still be safe if hot foods have been held at 160 degrees Fahrenheit; cold foods must be held at below 40 degrees Fahrenheit.

Seeing the children in your school are well-nourished, healthy, and developing positive attitudes toward eating is just as important as making certain that they acquire appropriate cognitive skills. Sadly, though, some directors see it as far less critical. Make it a goal in your school, and you will find that staff, parents, and children will benefit.

SUMMARY

Caregivers or teachers must have an adequate knowledge of nutrition that enables them to be sensitive to children's dietary needs and behaviors.

Menu planning or supervision is an important part of a director's schedule.

There are several principles to observe in planning menus:
- Use the four basic food groups to your advantage.
- Choose foods children like.
- Plan menus within the capabilities of your kitchen.
- Fit menus to personnel available to cook and serve.
- Include food that has appeal.
- Introduce new foods along with familiar ones.
- Consider dessert as an important part of the meal.
- Integrate meal planning into part of the child's learning.

Ordinarily, parents are very concerned with their child's eating habits; include parent information about food and eating habits, along with other disclosures.

The eating environment and atmosphere are important. Classrooms used as dining rooms should be neat and attractive, furniture should be comfortable, children should participate in setting and serving, and teachers should eat with their charges.

Children should be exposed to cooking experiences that are appropriate to their developmental level.

Give a good deal of thought and enterprise to the mechanics of food procurement and preparation. Purchasing must be done along thrifty lines. Food poorly prepared is often wasted. Food should be easily handled and appealing to children.

Food must be prepared and served under strict sanitary conditions. All food handlers should be free of infectious disease. Take care against spoilage in handling and storage.

The development of good attitudes toward food is as worthy a goal as the acquisition of any other socially desirable trait. The preschool has an important role to play here.

SELECTED FURTHER READING

Committee on Nutrition, American Academy of Pediatrics 1986. "Prudent Life Style for Children: Dietary Fat and Cholesterol." *Journal of Pediatrics* 12: 521–25.

Kendrick, A., Kaufmann, R., and Messenger, K., eds. 1988. *Healthy Young Children—A Manual for Programs*. Washington, DC: National Association for the Education of Young Children.

Marotz, L., Rush, J., and Cross, M. 1993. *Health, Safety, and Nutrition for the Young Child*, 3rd ed. Albany, NY: Delmar Publishers Inc.

Rogers, C., and Morris, S. 1986. "Reducing Sugar in Children's Diets." *Young Children,* 41 (5) 11–16.

Weiser, M. G. 1990. *Group Care and Education of Infants and Toddlers*. Columbus, OH: Merrill/Macmillan.

STUDENT ACTIVITIES

1. Prepare a poster for school-age children that shows the basic four food groups. Include suggestions for snack foods from each of the groups.

2. Plan a series of three lessons designed to teach four-year-olds about nutrition. Present the lessons to a group, then evaluate its effectiveness. Did the children understand the concepts you presented? Were there any perceptible changes in their attitudes toward any of the foods you discussed?

3. Observe two meals in a child care center. Evaluate them using the following rating:

	Excellent	Good	Fair	Poor
Attractiveness of setting				
Cleanliness of setting				
Comfort of seating				
Appearance of food				
Child-size portions				
Teacher participation				
General atmosphere				

4. List the foods you liked as a young child. Why do you think these particular foods were favorites? Was it the taste, color, or ease of eating? Or were they favorites because of some association with pleasant experiences? What does this tell you about serving food to children in a child care setting?

REVIEW

1. Why is it important to see that young children receive adequate nutrition in child care?
2. If a center is open nine hours or more, what proportion of a child's daily minimum nutritional requirement should be provided?
3. Name the four food groups.
4. Which foods are at the top of the Food Guide Pyramid?
5. State five suggestions for encouraging children to eat nutritious foods.
6. In what ways can a school establish and maintain a partnership with parents regarding their child's nutritional needs?
7. How can a director encourage teachers to plan cooking experiences for children?
8. Suggest some ways to decrease the cost of purchasing foods.
9. List several snacks that can easily be prepared for a group of preschool children.
10. Food storage should preserve the nutritional content of food and ensure safety. At what temperature should the refrigerator be kept? What is the optimum temperature for long-term storage in a freezer?

GLOSSARY

Allergens   environmental substances or foods that cause a reaction such as asthma, hives, or hay fever.

Food Guide Pyramid   new recommended daily servings of food developed by the U.S. Department of Agriculture in 1992.

Part V

Environment

14

Space: The Preschool

OBJECTIVES

After studying this chapter, the student should be able to:
- State general considerations for organizing space.
- List and describe specific activity areas.
- Discuss adaptation of the environment for children with special needs.

Environment changes our moods and receptivity. In a pleasant setting, we feel content; in an unpleasant one, unhappy and eager to leave. One setting can soothe us; another can stir up a myriad of feelings that make us uneasy. We can concentrate and learn in the quiet atmosphere of a library, but we might find it hard in the clamor of an airport.

So, too, does the classroom environment affect the way children feel, how they behave, and what they learn. If we want children to feel competent, we must provide a setting in which this can develop. If we expect cooperative behavior, we must create an atmosphere where this is possible. If we want children to learn, the environment must invite them to explore.

Your role as director of a school is to help your staff arrange the best possible setting for the children you serve.

Some guidelines will help you in this task.

GENERAL CONSIDERATIONS FOR ORGANIZING SPACE

Reality

Every director and probably most teachers have a picture of the ideal school. It has lots of open space with rooms that are clean and bright. Each room has a bathroom and sinks with hot and cold running water. There are spaces where teachers can relax and where they can prepare materials. Other space is available to provide privacy for parents and staff to talk. For most of us, that is just a dream.

The reality is that most directors and staff find themselves in space that has either been planned by someone else or that has been used for another purpose. That space has to be adapted to fit their school's requirements. In an existing school, the kinds of changes that can be made may be limited. When you adapt space used for another purpose, such as a residence or commercial building, the cost of renovation may be high. So the ideal school always has to be weighed against what is possible and the demands of your budget.

It may be impossible to make drastic changes in an existing school where rooms and supporting space have already been designated. However, you can make changes within rooms or even consider using rooms for new purposes. Start by asking your teachers to make detailed plans of their indoor and outdoor space. Locate indoor electrical outlets, doors, windows, and any fixed objects. Outdoors, include placement of trees, walkways, and gates. In a series of meetings, ask your staff to consider ways their space can be changed, keeping in mind the considerations listed in the following sections.

If you are starting a school in space that has been used for another purpose, you will have to visualize how the space can be divided. You may have to add or take out walls, add bathrooms, or cut new doors. To minimize the cost, get as much information as you can before deciding on your final plan. Visit other schools to see how they utilize space. Talk to other directors. Refer to child development textbooks that deal with planning space. Consult an architect.

Regulations

Check the licensing requirements in your area for any regulations that might affect plans for your environment. There will probably be statements regarding the amount of space required for each child. Regulations may also provide for the number of bathrooms, space for sick children, and areas for adults. You will be required to fence outdoor areas and possibly put in certain kinds of surfacing or include shaded areas.

Check also with your city departments. You may need to meet certain requirements. Building codes may specify the kinds of changes you can make to indoor space. Health departments may have requirements for storage of food or cleaning supplies. The fire department may require fire walls and doors. Be familiar with the regulations and be sure to include them in your planning.

Goals and Objectives

Both indoor and outdoor space should reflect the goals of your school. You and your staff should examine the basic educational purposes of your program and consider ways in which they can be furthered through a planned environment.

As an example, one of the goals of your program may be to encourage children to take responsibility for themselves and their belongings. Think of all the ways this can be accomplished. You might include some of the following:

- Cubbies for each child's belongings.
- Areas for performing real tasks such as woodworking and cooking.

- Child-sized tables and chairs.
- Learning centers that require no assistance from adults.
- Faucets and drinking fountains at children's level.

One of your goals might be to encourage children's social skills. If so, you might provide space for the following:

- Spaces where children work together on a common project.
- A block area that will accommodate a group of children.
- A housekeeping center.
- An art area where several children can work together.
- Outdoor dramatic play area (playhouse, store equipment, gas pumps and signs).

Program Type

The kind of school you are operating will have an impact on your overall design. An all-day school must provide areas for the physical care activities that are less important in a half-day school. You must allow space for children to eat their meals, take a nap, and care for their physical needs. Few schools have the luxury of

Figure 14–1   The environment is planned for independence.

a separate nap or lunch room. These functions must be carried on in the same classroom where all the other activities take place. If your school serves meals, provide enough seating space for each child. You may want additional small tables so that children can serve themselves buffet style or clean up their dishes when finished. Cots must be stored within the classroom in a manner that makes it easy to take them out when needed. Bathrooms need places for children's toothbrushes and washcloths.

An all-day school should plan areas where children can be alone. The stimulation of being in a group for long hours during a day can be stressful for some children. They need a quiet place where they can be by themselves or where they can work individually.

A parent cooperative or a laboratory school must consider a place for adults as well as for children. Rooms have to be large enough to accommodate the adults who participate during the course of the day. A laboratory school will be enhanced by the addition of an observation room and a place where students and instructors can meet.

Age level

Environments should be appropriate to the age level of the children who will use them. Very young children have different requirements than do older children. For instance, two-year-olds seem to feel more secure if their indoor and outdoor space is not too large or does not have too much equipment in it. On the other hand, four-year-olds need lots of space for strenuous physical activities. They need places to ride their trikes, climb, and run.

If the age level is mixed, the problem is a little more difficult. The environment must provide challenges for the oldest children while still being safe for the youngest. In this kind of setting, equipment should be changeable and moveable rather than fixed in place. Indoors, provide enclosed spaces with partitions for some of the youngest children. Provide places for them to play on the floor rather than at tables. Outdoors, use moveable barriers to allow some children more active play while protecting the younger ones. Equipment such as boxes, boards, tires, and inner tubes can be used by many different age groups.

Traffic Flow

When planning space, consider traffic flow. Examine where doors are placed and imagine the ways children and adults are likely to move through the room to enter and exit. Now decide if you want to allow direct access or if you want to divert the flow somewhat. Large pieces of furniture or equipment will change the way people move from one place to another.

Place furniture so that activities are not interrupted by children moving about the room. A reading corner can provide a cozy place for quiet contemplation if others are not tramping through it. A block area will be used more extensively if buildings that the children make are protected from traffic paths.

Consider the safety of children as you plan the placement of outdoor equipment. Children are more active outside, running or riding their bikes. They can be

Figure 14–2 Learning centers allow children to explore.

oblivious to possible safety hazards, so place swings and climbing equipment away from the traffic flow. Do provide interesting walkways that invite children to explore their environment on foot or on bikes. A path with a slight incline or a bridge is much more enticing than a straight, flat one.

Noise Level

A room full of preschoolers can get pretty noisy at times, causing tension and irritation to both adults and children. When planning space, consider the noise levels of different activities. It is best not to have two noisy activities side by side. Block play and dramatic play are examples. Separate them into different areas of the room.

Separate noisy activities from those that require the children to pay attention and concentrate. Set up science activities in a quiet area of the room. Enclose a reading or music area with shelves or cupboards. A quiet area might also be designed into a structure within the room. For instance, some schools build a loft structure inside. In the upper level, children can play without interruption from activities below. In the lower level, there might be cozy spots where children can be alone.

Outdoors, set aside areas where children can run vigorously, jump, or climb. Other areas should accommodate more quiet play with sand, dolls, and manipulatives. Use hills, plants, large boxes, and pieces of equipment to separate these areas.

Storage

Provide adequate storage in all areas of your school. A central storage area is essential. It should allow for storage of supplies such as paper, paint, and glue. In addition, there should be room for teaching materials that can be shared by more than one classroom. Boxes that contain special science or math projects can also be placed here. Extra props for dramatic play might also be included. This should be a place where teachers can come to find new materials to enrich their daily classroom activities.

Outdoors, there should be a place to store bikes, sand toys, and other moveable equipment at the end of the day. A large outdoor shed, where dramatic play and art materials can be kept will be a tremendous asset to your school.

In the classroom, allow space for curriculum materials. Provide closed cupboards where teachers can store materials that they take down as needed. Use open shelves for materials that children are allowed to get out for themselves. These should be placed close to where the materials will be used. Children will not carry a puzzle across the room to a table. If there is no table nearby, they will use the floor. Often the result is that puzzle pieces get lost.

Hard and Soft Areas

The preschool classroom should include both hard and soft spaces. Children respond to tactile stimuli, so provide some objects that are soft and pliable to the touch. Rugs, pillows, soft furniture, finger paints, and clay are some examples. Elizabeth Prescott of Pacific Oaks College has studied the effect of environments on children and concludes that soft objects "provide experiences where the environment responds to the child." Children can roll around on a rug, pound clay, and spread finger paint. Each object does what the child wants it to do.

In contrast, hard surfaces provide a different kind of experience. Tiled floors, wooden furniture, and asphalt playgrounds tell children that they must do what the environment requires of them. Prescott feels young children are not ready to abide by that message for long periods of time during the day. She says that, especially in a full-day program, inhibiting children's behavior through a hard environment is fatiguing and will lead to tension.

Provide hard and soft areas outdoors as well. Include soft areas for playing in sand and water, digging in the dirt, or gardening. Wood chips and grass are another way to provide soft play areas. Cemented or asphalt areas are hard surfaces where children can ride bikes, build with blocks, or play ball.

Aesthetic Appeal

Play areas for young children should be appealing. Children may not comment on the appearance of a room, but they do react to a pleasant environment. Use attractive colors in the classrooms, with well-designed basic furniture. Keep the environment simple and uncluttered. Remember that the children's eye level is very much lower than adults'. Keep furniture lines low so children can see over them. Place bulletin boards at the children's level so they can see them.

In outdoor play areas, trees, shrubs, and flowers add to the pleasure children get from their environment. Natural woods used in play equipment add another scope. Surfaces such as grass, dirt, redwood chips, and sand add to the interest of outdoor areas.

Diversity

In Chapter 5, you read about the importance of including concepts concerning diversity in the early childhood curriculum. You will remember that one goal is to

FYI

Current trends in population indicate that our nation is changing and that future adults will need to adapt to diversity.

• *By the year 2000, one-third of all people in the United States will be non-white. (Williams, C.G. 1986. "Population Trends Affect Education."* South Carolina School Board Association Journal.)

• *Nearly one of every four Americans is over 50 years of age. It is predicted that by the year 2030, one in three Americans will be over 50.* (Truth About Aging, 1986. Washington, DC: American Association for Retired Persons.)

• *Out of 100 poor children in America, 37 live in homes with a married-couple head of the family, 59 live in homes with a female head of the family, and four live with a male head of the family. (Children's Defense Fund.* The State of America's Children, 1992.)

introduce children to differences and similarities of ethnic and cultural groups. The second goal is to stress the importance of freeing children from gender stereotyping and preventing the development of biased attitudes toward persons who are differently abled. Activities and materials were suggested to create a diverse curriculum. In addition to the materials, *the total environment of an early childhood classroom should reflect an attitude of acceptance* of diversity as well as provide specific spaces for activities.

Furnishings and equipment in the classroom should include articles from different cultures. Examples are:
- A child's chair from Mexico.
- A bedspread from India.
- Tatami mats from Japan.
- A Chinese wok.
- Baskets from Guatemala.

Pictures displayed at activity areas should show:
- Persons of different ethnic/racial groups doing everyday tasks.
- A balance of men and women doing jobs both inside and outside the home.
- Images of elderly persons of various backgrounds doing different activities.
- Images of children and their families, showing a variety of configurations and backgrounds.
- Images of differently abled persons from different backgrounds doing work or in recreational activities.

Artwork that reflects the culture of the artist:
- Sculpture, wood carvings.
- Woven textiles.
- Ceramics.
- Paintings or prints.
- Folk-art objects.

Remember to plan for diversity in the outdoor areas as well.

Flexibility

An environment for young children should be flexible, not set in one pattern. Periodically, staff must assess what is happening within that environment and decide whether to change it.

Ask your staff to consider how the environment either fosters or deters goals. Questions they might ask are:
- Are children using the environment in ways that are achieving my goals?
- Are children using the environment in ways I hadn't thought of?
- Are there other ways I can arrange materials or equipment to further my goals?

Teachers can include children in a discussion of the environment. They can talk about the ways the space is being used and any problems that occur and question whether any changes can be made. Some brave teachers have even taken all the furniture out of a room and then asked the children to bring it back in and arrange it. It is certainly worth trying to stimulate new ways of looking at physical space.

SPECIFIC AREAS

Aside from the general considerations used when planning space, you might wish to consider ways to plan for specific activities. Most schools for young children have specific areas for blocks, dramatic play, creative activities, learning, and music or reading. The goals of your school may call for the inclusion of some additional areas.

Dramatic Play

The dramatic play area is often called the housekeeping center because the first play usually focuses on activities the children have experienced at home. They cook, put babies to sleep, clean the house, go off to work, and discipline the children. They may talk to each other on the telephone or visit for meals. It is an area where children can role play being an adult or a baby. They can use small-muscle skills to prepare meals or do cleaning chores. They also have many chances to increase their social skills and language abilities.

As children get older, dramatic play areas may include a doctor's office or hospital. Sometimes a restaurant, fire station, or gas station appears. This kind of play gives them additional opportunities to role play jobs and situations they have witnessed. Some of the play in these areas mimics situations they have seen on television.

To make dramatic play as satisfying as possible for children, they must have an appropriate setting and adequate props. Select props to put out at various times to further play already in progress or to stimulate new play.

The setting should:
- Be in a place free of traffic interference.
- Have enough space for several children.
- Include convenient storage space.
- Allow some privacy but also allow for adequate supervision.
- Be near related activity areas or be large enough so that the play can accommodate more than one dramatic theme. (Inside and outside the house, bike riding and gas station, cooking and sleeping.)

Props for dramatic play can include:

FOR HOUSEKEEPING

Child-sized furniture (stove, sink, refrigerator, table, chairs, beds, mirror)

Dolls representing a variety of ethnic groups: Black, Latino, Asian-Pacific, Native American, White (dolls can be home-made or bought, but should be reasonably authentic-looking)

Dolls that are both male and female, with an assortment of appropriate clothing articles

Dolls with different kinds of disabilities (can be bought or home-made)
Dishes, pots, pans
Empty food containers, including some that are typical of specific ethnic groups
Food models (plastic fruit or vegetables, meats, breads, eggs)
Dress-up clothes for both males and females, and representing both work and
     play activities
Cleaning equipment (broom, mop, sponge, bucket)
Tools that are used outside the house (rake, wrench, wooden hammer, flashlight)
Unbreakable mirror at children's eye level
Tools and equipment used by persons with special needs (canes, braces, heavy
     glasses, crutches, wheelchair, hearing aid)

FOR DOCTOR OR HOSPITAL

Cot or doll bed, blankets, small pillow
Stethoscopes
White jackets, nurses' caps, surgical masks
Band Aids™, pill bottles (use small cereal for pills)
Cotton balls, elastic bandages

FOR GAS STATION

Gas pumps, short hose lengths
Signs
Ramp for repair area
Tools and tool box (wrench, screwdriver, flashlight)

FOR FIRE STATION

Short fire hose lengths (1/2 inch hose)
Fire fighters' hats
Fire fighters' jackets
Fire-fighting tools (plastic hatchet, flashlight)

HAIRDRESSER

Curlers, hair clips
Combs, brushes, hand mirror
Makeup (face powder, lipstick, eyebrow pencil)
Soft whisk
Electric trimmer (remove cord)
Razor (remove blade)
Cloths for shoulder covers

The possibilities for dramatic play props are almost endless. Gather materials so they will be available as children's interests call for some new accessories to their play. These can be stored in your school's central storage area and shared by all the classrooms.

Block Area

Many teachers have said that if they had a limited budget to spend for equipment, they would still include a good set of blocks. This is because of the versatility of blocks. They can be used in many different ways and by widely divergent age

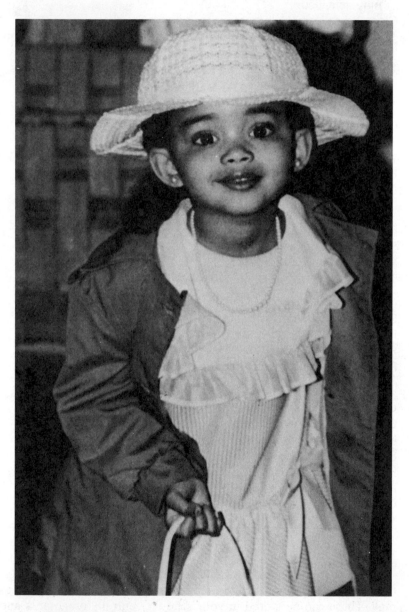

Figure 14–3 Dramatic play needs the right clothes.

Figure 14–3 (*continued*)   Dramatic play needs the right clothes.

groups. Blocks allow children to develop their fine- and gross-motor skills while working out problems of replicating their own experiences. Block play encourages the use of social skills as children work toward a common goal. They can learn mathematical concepts as well as increase their understanding of balance, spatial relations, size, and shape.

The setting should include:
- A large enough set of unit blocks to accommodate several children at the same time; arcs, ramps, cylinders are included in these sets.
- Shelves that are wide enough to accommodate the largest blocks;

Figure 14–4 A child explores with art materials.

- As needed by the children: cars, trucks, boats, planes, trains, road signs, rubber or wooden animals.
- A variety of hats.
- Flat boards, hollow blocks, colored blocks, trees, rocks, pieces of driftwood.
- People, both male and female, from different ethnic groups.
- To stimulate ideas, pictures of buildings, freeways, train tracks, boat dock, airport, farm, forest with wild animals, and men and women working at a variety of jobs.

Art Center

The freedom to explore and experiment in an art area affords children an opportunity to develop a variety of skills. Children can acquire fine-motor skills as they manipulate paint brushes, cut with scissors, use a paper punch, or paste small pieces on a collage. They use their whole arms when playing with clay or finger paints or when painting at an easel. This develops large-motor skills. Art materials allow children to feel successful at an activity of their own choice and so increase their self-image. An art area can be set up so that children work together strengthening their social skills. Some children use creative activities to express their feelings about themselves, their experiences, and their environment. Lastly, art experiences help children to develop an appreciation for color and form or, perhaps in a broader sense, beauty.

The setting should include:

- Easels, brushes of different sizes.
- Paints, including tan, brown, and black paint.
- Crayons that include skin-tone colors.
- Mirrors so children can look at their own appearance.
- Paper of different colors, textures, and sizes.
- Scissors, rulers, paper punch, stapler, tape, glue.
- Felt pens, crayons, chalk.
- Collage materials: fabric scraps, ribbons, glitter, beads, wood pieces, wrapping paper, etc.
- Styrofoam pieces, tooth picks.
- Textured materials—sandpaper, rubber, plastic.
- Sewing equipment—burlap, tapestry needles, buttons, embroidery hoops, yarn.
- Magazine pages, wallpaper pieces, tissue paper.

Add any other materials of interest to the children. The variety is endless.

Math and Science Center

This area should provide children many opportunities to explore and to test their own knowledge or skills. They should be able to increase their vocabulary of mathematical and scientific words. They can learn to count, sort, and classify objects. Children can judge and understand size, shape, and texture of objects. They should be able to learn about their physical environment, about matter and energy, and about living things. Activities in this area should provide many opportunities for children to use all their senses to consolidate their learning.

A math and science center can be set up in two ways. It can be arranged at a table so that several children can work at the same time on separate projects or together at a single project. It can also be placed in an area where children can work alone. Either way, it is important to place this center in a place where the children will not be distracted by noisy or active play from others. Some science projects may require the use of electricity, which further dictates where the center should be located.

Plan carefully how a science table or individual workplace will be set up. Consider using large trays to delineate each work space. Make the setup attractive so children will be motivated to explore this area. Let the arrangement tell children what to do with the materials.

The setting should include:
- Materials for counting, sorting, weighing, and measuring (beads, beans, small blocks, wood shapes, pegs and pegboard, empty egg cartons, measuring cups).
- Scales, magnifying glass, color paddles, thermometer, prism, magnets.
- Growing plants, animals.
- Large-dimensional numbers, letters of varied textures (sandpaper, cardboard, felt).
- Collections of birds' nests, eggs, insects, feathers, shells, rocks, crystals.
- Pictures, books on science-related topics.
- Books that require counting objects.

As with each of the areas described here, the variety of materials that can be included are not limited to those listed here. Many different kinds of materials can be used for counting, weighing, and measuring. The physical world provides countless objects and ideas for exploration.

Reading/Writing Center

This area should provide opportunities for children to acquire skills they will need in order to read and write. That includes an appreciation of books, the development of language skills, and fine-motor skills. Activities in this area should also help children to develop the ability to put events in proper order, to relate a story from beginning to end.

The setting should include a selection of story books that:
- Reflect diversity of racial and cultural backgrounds, ages, gender roles, and physical abilities.
- Show people of all groups working at daily tasks.
- Show different life-styles based on income level or family configurations.
- Reflect different languages (alphabet books, stories in different spoken languages, stories in Braille, or sign language).
- Large picture-card stories reflecting the same diversity as indicated above.

- Puppet stage and puppets (both male and female, different ethnic groups, special needs).
- Tape recorder and recorded stories (earphones for individual listening are recommended).
- Both soft places to sit and a small table and chair for writing.
- Writing materials (pencils, felt pens, paper of different sizes and colors).
- Felt board stories, felt board.

Music/Listening Center

The purpose of this center is to encourage children to listen for information and for enjoyment. Activities should increase their language skills as well. Children should have opportunities to create rhythms and their own dance movements.

The setting should include:
- Record player.
- Records, including music that reflects different cultures.
- Musical instruments, both home-made and commercial, including some that are typical of different cultures.
- Tape recorder, cassettes, ear phones.
- Tapes of children in the class singing, talking, or playing instruments.
- Film strips or video cassettes.
- Pictures of instruments and musical games.

Circle/Game Center

There are times during each day when most teachers schedule an activity involving all the children. Conversations can take place and children can share experiences. Group lessons can be given or plans can be made for future activities.

This setting should include:
- Quiet comfortable area, large enough for all the children.
- Carpet or other soft surface for sitting.
- Bulletin board, flannel boards.
- Freedom from other distracting materials.

Cooking Center

Cooking can be seen as a science activity, but it also incorporates many other learning opportunities; therefore, it is treated here as a separate center. Young children enjoy the real tasks involved in preparing their own snacks or meals. While doing so, they have an opportunity to use real tools, to play a role they have observed many times. In addition, cooking gives them a chance to see how matter changes under different circumstances. Social skills develop as children wait their turn or share tasks with others. Cooking activities can also provide children with some basic information about where food comes from and about nutrition.

This center should include:

- A table—limit the number of children at this center by the size of the table.
- An electrical outlet—place table so that children will not trip on the cord.
- Portable oven, frying pan, ice cream maker, popcorn popper, blender, mixer, food processor.
- Mixing bowls, spoons, measuring cups, knives—children can safely use short serrated knives with rounded ends.
- Large trays, chopping boards, baking pans.
- Recipe picture-books, flip-card recipes, pictures of food and food products.
- Sponges, buckets, soap for cleaning up.
- Aprons for children—for especially messy projects.

Computer Center

Computers can be used as another learning center in a preschool classroom. They should not replace the concrete, hands-on kinds of experiences, but they can supplement and reinforce learning activities. The key is in choosing appropriate software to achieve the goal you have in mind. Some programs allow a great deal of creativity and imagination, while others are designed to teach specific, limited skills.

What can preschoolers do with computers? They can use the direction keys, joy sticks, or a mouse to move objects right, left, up, and down to solidify their sense of direction. They can compare and match objects or discriminate between them. They can create shapes and then change them. Some programs require problem-solving skills or memory. They can play games that test their eye-hand coordination or the speed of their reactions. Programs like LOGO™ allow children to assemble their own figures on the screen, then move them in any direction.

Aside from the physical and cognitive skills that computer use can develop, there are some emotional and social benefits. Children will often stay at a computer center for long periods of time, exhibiting a high level of motivation. They obviously enjoy the sense of control over this adult tool. Researchers have also noted that rather than isolate young children, computers become a drawing point for social interaction among children. This social interaction leads to acquisition of new words and increases in language ability almost as a by-product.

This setting should:

- Be in an area away from light sources that will reflect on the monitor screen.
- Be in an area that is away from heat, dust, and magnetic fields created by television monitors, telephone bells, and vacuums.
- Be placed on a static-resistant mat if the area is carpeted.
- Contain a child-sized table with at least two chairs.
- Include a central processing unit, a monitor, and either a keyboard, mouse, or joystick.

- Be near an electrical outlet and include a power strip. (A power strip is a multi-outlet strip that includes a surge suppressor to protect from surges of electrical power).
- Be placed so the on/off switch is easily reached.
- Have pictorial labels on switches and disk drives showing the sequence of actions to be followed. (Include a chart of the sequence of steps if desired).
- Include a place to store and display software conveniently. (Label software programs with a picture for children who cannot read the name.)

Outdoor Space

Plan outdoor play spaces as carefully as you do indoor areas. This space may be less flexible because large pieces of equipment are permanently in place. However, you can add items to suggest new activities or new ways of using the existing equipment.

Outdoors, children have an opportunity to develop their large muscles, to run, jump, climb, swing, and ride bikes. Vigorous physical play allows them to burn off excess energy that may have been kept under control while indoors. Dramatic play outside can take on new dimensions that range over a wider space or incorporate two widely separate areas. It can move from the bike-riding area to the sandbox, then to the playhouse. The variety of textures, sights, smells, and sounds that are part of the outdoors will stimulate children to use their senses to explore.

This setting should include:
- Pathways, clearly defined areas for each activity.
- An easily accessible source of water and a drinking fountain.
- Spaces for woodworking, art activities.
- Different surfaces—sand, grass, cement, wood chips.
- Shaded areas and sunny ones.
- Hilly areas and flat surfaces.
- Basic equipment that can be used for more than one purpose (climbing equipment, sandbox).
- Shovels, hoses, buckets, dishes for sand play.
- Innovative additions to basic equipment—rope ladders, ropes, pulleys, tires, inner tubes, plastic-covered pillows, boards, saw horses, hammock.
- Props that can be used for dramatic play—hoses, signs, hats, tools, housekeeping furniture.
- Storage area for outdoor equipment.

ADAPTATIONS FOR CHILDREN WITH SPECIAL NEEDS

Many early childhood centers now incorporate children with special needs into regular classrooms. More will do so in the future. Some adaptations to the environment must be made to accommodate these children. The scope of this book does not, however, allow a detailed discussion of adaptations for special needs children.

The list below will give you some ideas. Refer to the reading list at the end of this chapter if you wish to obtain further information.

INDOOR ADAPTATIONS

Build ramps into the room and out to the playground

Widen doors to 32 inches or install offset hinges

Remove any barriers to free movement around the room

Install grab bars beside toilets

Provide easy access to cubbies from a wheelchair—position them at proper height for a seated child

Install a smoke alarm with a flashing light

Store materials where they can be easily seen or reached

Label areas in Braille, with different textures of fabric, or with pictures

Set up areas in such a way that children easily recognize the routine—place bright aprons at entrance to art area to remind children to put them on before painting

Provide easels, tables, and a water table that can accommodate a child in a wheelchair

Purchase wheeled equipment (scooter boards, wagons) for children who navigate by crawling

Display books on slanted shelves or hanging in clear plastic pockets—more easily read by visually impaired children

Build a low platform or use futons or low couches in the reading area—children on scooter boards or in motorized carts can easily move to them for comfortable reading

Provide table-top easels for children who wish to read seated in their wheelchair

Secure any loose rugs or use carpet and non-skid floor covering

Purchase an overhead projector for enlarging pictures

OUTDOOR ADAPTATIONS

Provide wheelchair-accessible pathways from one area to another

Build a table-high sand box

Place extra railings and handles on climbing equipment

Provide bucket seats with safety belts on swings

Include grassy areas where wheelchair-bound children can be out of their chairs and feel the grass

Include plants that have a fragrance—bamboo or trees that make sounds in the wind

Delineate pathways with low-growing plants that have interesting textures

Include plants that attract butterflies or birds

Use planter boxes or containers for vegetable gardens

Figure 14–5 Swinging burns up excess energy.

Remember, as well, that the environment "tells" both children and adults how to behave there. If you want a well-functioning, effective program with reasonably content inhabitants, start with a well-planned physical plant. Assess it periodically to determine whether it continues to meet your expectations. If not, change it. The physical space, equipment, and materials of your school are your most important asset. Visitors notice and assess the environment long before they understand the intricacies of your curriculum or the skill of your staff. So it is important to make the environment as attractive as possible, while also conveying what your school is all about.

SUMMARY

Environment affects the way children feel and behave. The ideal environment is one in which children feel calm, competent, and cooperative. The reality is that often directors and teachers must settle for less than an ideal physical space, and must be creative in adapting it to suit the needs of children.

Physical space for early childhood centers is subject to licensing regulations and fire and safety codes. The goals and objectives of a school also dictate how space is used. An all-day school has different space requirements than one open only a few hours each day. The age of the children utilizing the environment will also dictate its characteristics.

There are additional considerations to take into account when planning a preschool environment: traffic flow, noise level, storage, hard and soft areas, aesthetic appeal, cultural diversity, and flexibility.

Specific areas to include are: dramatic play, blocks, art, math and science, reading/writing, music/listening, circle/games, cooking, and computer centers.

Outdoor space should be planned as carefully as indoor space, including pathways, water, areas for specific activities, hilly and flat areas, basic equipment, and storage facilities.

As more children with special needs are incorporated into early childhood centers, directors must become knowledgeable about how to adapt the environment. *Indoors*, build ramps, widen doors, remove barriers, install grab bars, label areas in Braille or pictures, and make furniture accessible to children in wheelchairs. *Outdoors*, build wheelchair-accessible pathways, build table-high sandbox, provide bucket seats on swings, include a grassy area, and use plants that attract butterflies and birds, or that have a fragrance or make sounds.

SELECTED FURTHER READING

Gibson, D.F. 1987. "Down the Rabbit Hole: A Special Environment for Preschool Learning." *Landscape Architecture.* 68 (3) 211–216.

Jordan-Bloom, P. 1987. *A Great Place to Work: Improving Conditions for Staff in Young Children's Programs.* Washington, DC: National Association for the Education of Young Children.

McCracken, J.B. 1990. *Playgrounds: Safe and Sound.* Washington, DC: National Association for the Education of Young Children.

Miller, J. 1990. "Three-Year-Olds in Their Reading Corner." *Young Children*, 46 (1) 51–54.

Moore, R. 1986. *Childhood's Domain*. Berkeley, CA: MIG Communications.

Morris, L.R., and Schulz, L. 1989. *Creative Play Activities for Children with Disabilities: A Resource Book for Teachers and Parents*, 2nd ed. Champaign, IL: Human Kinetics Books.

Strikland, D.S., and Morrow, L.M. 1989. *Emerging Literacy: Young Children Learn to Read and Write*. Newark, DE: International Reading Association.

Witherspoon, C., ed. 1986. *Designing Space for Young Children*. Nashville, TN: Tennessee Department of Human Services.

Wortham, S.C., and Frost, J.L., eds. 1990. *Playgrounds for Children: National Survey and Perspectives*. Reston, VA: American Alliance for Health, Physical Education, Recreation and Dance.

STUDENT ACTIVITIES

1. Obtain the licensing requirements from the appropriate agency and list them. Visit the local building and safety department to determine their requirements. Check with the fire department to find out if they have special requirements for preschools. Summarize all these findings and report them to the class.

2. Plan a playground for a group of three-year-olds. Draw the plans, placing all equipment in appropriate places. Indicate any moveable or changeable equipment.

3. Draw a plan of the classroom in which you are now teaching. Indicate doors, windows, electrical outlets, and water sources. Show current placement of furniture and activity areas. What changes can be made to improve this environment? Cite sources from this chapter.

4. Create an interest center for a group of four-year-olds. List all the materials you would need and describe several arrangements.

5. Visit a preschool that has a computer in the classroom. Observe the way the computer center is arranged. Does the center attract the children? If so, why does it work? If the children are not working there, is the physical arrangement unsatisfactory? How can it be changed for the better?

6. Examine the outdoor arrangement of your school. List the ways it would have to be changed to meet the needs of children in wheelchairs. For children who are blind?

REVIEW

1. What factors affect the achievement of an ideal physical setting for young children?

2. Give an example of how goals dictate the design of physical space.

3. How are the space requirements of an all-day program different from one that is in session only four hours each day?

4. Give some examples of how pictures can be used in an early childhood setting to convey attitudes toward diversity.

5. List props that can be added to a dramatic play area to expand children's awareness and acceptance of diversity.
6. List items that should be included in a reading/writing center.
7. Describe a cooking center for a group of three-year-olds.
8. List the kinds of cognitive skills children might acquire through using a computer.
9. State ways in which indoor space can be adapted to fit the needs of children with special needs.
10. This chapter suggested several ways to use plants to enhance an outdoor environment for special needs children. What were the suggestions?

GLOSSARY

Aesthetic appeal   pleasant appearance derived from a well-designed environment.

Flexibility   ability to change or be modified.

Scooter board   a 12-inch plastic or wooden square, with swivel casters. (Commercially produced plastic boards are equipped with handles on the side.)

15

Space: Infants and Toddlers

OBJECTIVES

After studying this chapter, the student should be able to:

- Discuss general considerations when planning space for infants and toddlers.
- List and describe specific areas.
- Discuss the inclusion of infants and toddlers with special needs.

Although many mothers remain at home when their children are under the age of five, a large percentage are forced to return to the work force soon after their babies are born. In 1990, the *National Child Care Survey* prepared by the National Association for the Education of Young Children indicated that 19 percent of children under age three were in family day care and 18 percent were in early childhood centers. Good programs for children from birth to age three differ from all other types of programs. They are not just scaled-down versions of preschool programs, but are planned specifically to meet the needs of babies and toddlers.

GENERAL CONSIDERATIONS FOR INFANTS AND TODDLERS

Licensing

Your state may not have added regulations for infant and toddler programs to the guidelines for preschools and day care centers. Be sure to check, though, to determine if regulations exist and what they are.

In areas that have implemented infant and toddler program guidelines, there are usually some general categories of requirements. One category may cover the sanitation of the building, playground, bedding, food areas, and toys or equipment. Concern for health may be reflected in requirements that all surfaces, including flooring, be washable. Specifications might stipulate that all toys be washable and free of small parts children might swallow. There may also be suggestions for cleaning and sanitation procedures for caregivers to follow.

Regulations will likely cover the arrangement of indoor space. It might be necessary to provide sleeping space separate from indoor activity space. There may be statements requiring safe places for babies to crawl and explore. Guidelines might suggest that the environment contain pictures, books, and other objects that invite children to explore.

Requirements for outdoor space may also be covered in the regulations for your area. You will be required to fence in your outdoor area and make sure it is safe from anything that is a potential hazard. You may be required to provide both a shaded area and a sunny one. Crawling babies may be required to be in playpens or in an enclosed area safe from the more vigorous activities of the toddlers.

Goals

Review the overall goals for your school to determine whether they fit the specific needs of infants and toddlers. If not, develop separate goals that reflect their developmental stage. Remember that infants and toddlers need the following:
- Opportunities to experience their environment through their senses—seeing, hearing, smelling, tasting.
- To move around as freely as possible when they become mobile.
- To interact with adults in order to develop trust and security.
- To interact with other infants and toddlers in order to develop self-esteem.
- Acquire independence skills such as feeding, dressing, toileting.
- Develop language so they can communicate their needs and interact socially with others.

Each of these needs can be expressed as a goal and implemented when planning the environment. An appropriate goal might be "The child will be able to use all his senses to explore and learn about his environment." In order to implement this in your physical environment, include many opportunities for sensory input. Floor coverings can vary from soft or rough carpeting to smooth, hard vinyl flooring. As babies crawl from one to the other, they experience two different sensations. Hang bright, different-textured fabrics at the children's level so they can touch and look. Include different sounds in the room environment: soft music, voices, wind chimes, or toys that make sounds. A corner of the room might have soft pillows covered in vinyl and in a washable fabric. Vary the intensity of light in the room during the day, sometimes bright and at other times subdued.

Safety

Take extra precautions to see that the infant/toddler environment is safe and free from all hazards. This age level is known for its active exploration, poking, pushing, and pulling on objects to find out what will happen. Therefore, the elimination of all possible dangers is extremely important. Secure heavy pieces of furniture or

Figure 15–1   The furniture fits the size of the infant.

equipment so they don't topple over. Cover all electrical outlets, and pad the sharp edges of furniture. Check all furniture to be sure there are no braces on legs that might entrap a baby's head. Protect babies from injury under the rockers of a rocking chair by keeping toddlers out of these chairs. (They may not notice crawling babies underneath.) Provide them with their own child-sized rockers. Another way to have rockers in the room, but protect the babies, is to place the rockers outside of the babies' crawling area.

Use gates or grates to close off any areas that might be hazardous to infants or toddlers. Secure stairways, air conditioning or heating vents, and kitchen areas. Consider half-doors into the classroom as another safety measure. Leave the upper half open so that anyone entering the room can see whether a small child is close by before opening the door. A telephone or intercom in the room will also allow help to be summoned in case of an emergency.

Developmental Appropriateness

The infant/toddler room should be appropriate for the age level of the children using it. Toys and activities should reflect their interests and capabilities. They should be neither too simple, nor too complicated. For example, at six months, babies can usually sit up and use their hands and arms to manage objects. They will enjoy having toys they can poke, bang, and shake. Manipulative boards and push-and-pop toys are popular. If the toys make sounds, that is even better. At 15 months, most children are walking and love to push or pull toys as they wander around. At this age, children are ready to climb simple structures as well. Vinyl-covered mats and cubes of different sizes can provide a safe climbing area.

Outdoors, there should also be areas and equipment that are appropriate for the age level. Provide soft areas where babies can explore freely and safely. Simple, soft ramps might provide places where they can use their large muscles. Hammocks or fabric swings and tunnels might offer additional interest areas. More active toddlers need to have separate places to play. Use low fences to provide areas where they can ride their trikes, run, and play ball. Low-climbing equipment and a sandbox might also be in this area.

Rest, Solitude

The infant/toddler environment should provide areas where children can rest or where they can retreat to be alone. There should be a separate sleeping area for the babies who nap frequently during the day. A walled-off area within the classroom will serve this purpose. Consider using clear Plexiglas™ for large areas of the wall. In this way, staff can view the babies, or babies can watch activities in the room if they wish. Within the classroom, also provide hiding areas behind low screens, under tables, or in large boxes. Crawling babies or walking toddlers can withdraw there when group stress gets too much for them. Outdoors, a sandbox, large packing boxes, tunnels, and climbing structures can offer hiding areas. Another way to provide privacy for children, either indoors or outdoors, is to respect their right to play by themselves. A toddler may want to play in the small sandbox all alone for a while or to be the only one in a large crate.

Ethnic and Cultural Relevance

During the first three years of life, children lay the foundation for their sense of

Figure 15–2   The sandbox encourages toddlers' play.

identity. Their cultural or ethnic heritage is an important part of "who they are." Therefore, the infant/toddler room should encourage and support the cultural background of each child's family. Consult with parents to find out the kinds of furniture or play objects the children might have at home. Where appropriate, include those in the infant/toddler room. Provide books and display pictures of babies and families from different backgrounds. Decorate the room with colorful objects or fabrics that are culturally based. Play ethnic music or sing folk songs.

Sensory Input

Infants and toddlers use all their senses to explore their environment and to organize information about the world around them. Therefore, provide them with an environment that is rich in sensory diversity. There should be things they can look at, listen to, smell, feel, and taste.

Some ways to add sensory stimulation to the environment of these youngest children are:

FOR LOOKING

Provide windows so that children can see outside
Optionally provide skylights in the room for adding brightness

Figure 15–3   Washing up just like Mom does.

Choose pleasant colors for walls of the classroom
Add colorful curtains, objects, blankets, toys
Place pictures at the children's eye level
Attach an unbreakable mirror to the wall at eye level
Place an enclosed fish tank on a low shelf
Hang a mobile over a crib; change at frequent intervals
Include books with brightly colored pictures
Hang a large ball, balloon, or mobile from the ceiling

FOR LISTENING

Provide pieces of crumpled, heavy foil, parchment paper, tissue paper, colored
    paper used for wrapping produce
Play soft music at rest time
Hang wind chimes near the door
Include a music box or Jack-in-the-box
Include squeeze toys that squeak, rattles

FOR TOUCHING

Use both carpet and vinyl flooring
Have grass or a wooden deck outside
Place soft pillows in a corner
Include cuddly toys
Include large plastic beads or plastic keys
Include a collection of fabric pieces with different textures; pieces of fur
Provide a sensory enclosure large enough for a baby or toddler to sit in and fill
with plastic or cotton balls
Provide a large tub for holding cooked spaghetti or warm, soapy water

FOR TASTING AND SMELLING

Serve foods with pleasing odors and tastes (avoid the strong odors and tastes
that most children dislike)
Place fruit or flowers that have intense fragrances in the room
Make sure the room always smells clean and fresh
Choose cleaning and disinfectant materials that have a mild odor

Flexibility

Because infants and toddlers are growing and changing so rapidly, keep their environment flexible. Use moveable partitions with plexiglass windows to change the configuration of the room as needed. Have all indoor equipment on large casters for easy moving. Use large mats, cubes, and ramps for building indoor climbing equipment. Consider tables that can be raised or lowered easily. Use them as low as six inches off the floor for the babies and then raise to fit the toddler-sized chairs when needed.

SPECIFIC AREAS

An infant/toddler room may not have the clearly defined activity areas that are found in a preschool classroom. Crawling babies and toddlers tend to move about the room carrying their toys with them. Nevertheless, staff should think in terms of equipping areas of the classroom where specific activities will take place.

When planning activity areas, keep in mind one other consideration. In the preschool, a wide variety of materials can be put on the shelves so children can make choices. When they are finished, they return their materials and take out others. This does not work in an infant/toddler room. Staff and children would find the floor hopelessly littered with toys. Therefore, choose a limited selection of materials to display at any one time. Change the selection frequently so children have new experiences.

ROUTINE AREAS

A large portion of the day in an infant/toddler room will be filled with routine tasks: feeding, changing diapers, or sleeping. The areas for these activities must be planned so they can be both used and maintained easily by staff members, and also meet the needs of the children.

FOOD PREPARATION AND EATING

The eating area of an infant/toddler room has two parts: a place where food can be stored and prepared, and a place where babies can be fed and toddlers can feed themselves. Babies and toddlers seldom eat at regularly scheduled times and therefore, staff must be able to provide nourishment quickly without waiting for food to come from a kitchen. Also, many babies have their own formulas or special foods that parents bring from home. These need to be close at hand.

The food storage and preparation area should include:

- A counter and sink.
- Refrigerator and microwave oven.
- Utensils for preparing food (pans, spoons, tongs).
- Unbreakable dishes, bottles and nipples provided by parents.

Figure 15–4   Snack times can encourage social interaction.

- Equipment used for washing and sterilizing dishes and area—keep in a high cupboard, inaccessible to children.
- Bulletin board for posting instructions for each child's food intake and schedule—it should also include a place for recording actual amounts each child consumes each day.

When babies and toddlers are eating, social interactions can take place. Children can see each other; adults and children can talk or listen. Set up the eating area to foster as much interaction as possible. Some ways to do this are:

- Provide highchairs or low tables and chairs—chairs with curved backs are ideal for toddlers and babies who are able to sit up.
- Arrange tables and/or highchairs so children can see each other.
- Have rocking chairs so adults may nurture bottle-fed babies during feeding—add large, soft pillows for babies who attempt to hold their own bottle while being assisted by an adult.

SLEEPING

The sleeping area should be partitioned off from the play area. It should also be easily supervised by staff members. The furniture needed will depend on the age of the children. This area might include:

- Bassinets for the youngest infants; cribs for older infants.
- Cots or individual mats for toddlers—each child should have a separate sleeping place not shared with others.
- Rocking chair or other comfortable chair.
- At least one crib on wheels for transporting babies in case of an emergency.
- Shades on windows so the room can be darkened.
- Clean sheets and blankets for each crib.
- Sturdy mobiles hung over the cribs—place them where the youngest babies can see them and where slightly older babies can kick or hit them.
- Space of at least 24 inches between each of the cribs to protect against transmission of germs.

DIAPERING

A well, set-up diapering area will allow the task to be accomplished easily but will also foster a lot of social play and interaction. Set up the diapering area with:

- A table that is a good height for the adults.
- A cupboard for all the supplies that are needed: lotion, ointment, wipes, paper covers for table, paper towels, germicidal spray.
- A sink with a foot-operated faucet.
- A storage can for storing used diapers.
- A mirror where babies can see themselves and caregiver.
- Mobiles hung from the ceiling near the area.
- Sign reminding staff to wash hands.

FYI

Research studies show that infants and toddlers in center care often score higher on tests of their cognitive development. In 1981 Rubenstein, Howes, and Boyle found that children who had been in centers as infants had more complex speech and higher scores on the Peabody Picture Vocabulary Test.

In 1982 Trickett, Apfel, Rosenbaum, and Zigler studied 17 children who had been in child care from birth. They found that the children scored higher on IQ tests and later on school performance.

*Source: Howes, C. 1986. Keeping Current in Child Care Research, an annotated bibliography. Washington, DC: National Association for the Education of Young Children.

TOILETING

During the second year, some toddlers begin to indicate they are ready to use the toilet. Provide facilities away from the play area for the children to develop independence in caring for their own needs.

- Low toilets, potty chairs, or toilet seat adapters (disinfect after each use).
- Low sinks.
- Steps for toilets or sinks if needed.
- Soap dispensers and paper towel holder.
- Covered pail for used disposable diapers.
- Low mirror over the sinks.

COGNITIVE AREA

A section of the room should provide a safe and interesting environment where both infants and toddlers can develop their cognitive abilities. The youngest babies need to be in a protected area where they can see and hear activities in the room or explore a few simple toys. As they get older, they want to be able to crawl about freely and explore wider sections of the room. Toddlers are mobile and need space to move about and to engage in social interactions. Therefore, depending on the the age levels of the children involved, an infant/toddler room might have two cognitive areas.

FOR INFANTS TO ONE YEAR

- A large playpen or other enclosed space with a mat, rug, or blanket—this space should be large enough to include an adult or several babies.
- Clear view of adults and children within the room.
- Pictures at floor level.
- Texture boards, texture quilts, or wall quilts.
- Mobiles—some that make sound, some that move—or balls hung from the ceiling.

- Unbreakable mirror mounted at floor level.
- A few colorful, soft, washable toys—make sure there are no small parts that may come off and be swallowed.
- Cloth or cardboard books.
- Rattles, nesting toys, balls.
- Mechanical toys that make sounds: Jack-in-the-box, pounding toys.

FOR TODDLERS

- Vinyl flooring or large plastic sheets to cover the carpet.
- Low table and chairs.
- Large trays or tubs for floor activities.
- Low shelves containing a variety of manipulative materials: large beads, stacking cones, large Legos™, simple puzzles.
- Tubs to fill with dry rolled oats, rice, beans, soapy water, and cooked spaghetti—add scoops, measuring cups, pans, sponges, or dolls as needed.
- Variety of mechanical toys that can be pounded, poked, or pushed.

FINE-MOTOR AREA

This area should include a variety of materials children can use to strengthen their fingers and hands. Many commercial materials are designed specifically for this purpose. You can also look around your house to find many items that infants and toddlers love to play with.

Define the work area, if you wish, by using a low table. If children prefer to work on the floor, consider placing large trays on the floor. Encourage the children to take their material to a tray and work there. You can also place a mat or large piece of cloth nearby to indicate that this is where the materials are to be used.

This area might include:

- Shelves for conveniently storing a selection of materials.
- Clear plastic boxes or bins to hold the materials.
- A selection of materials: large pop beads, nesting cups, small blocks, large Legos™, simple puzzles, form boards, stacking toys, linking loops, large pegs and pegboard, form box, pounding toys, plastic lock box.
- Large plastic curlers, plastic clothespins, plastic containers.
- Large plastic or metal mixing bowls, wooden spoons.
- Magazines with colorful pictures that children can use for turning the pages or tearing off pieces.
- Plastic bread baskets that can be used for putting things in, and dumping them out.

Look at catalogues from companies that supply educational toys. You will find a wide choice of materials.

LARGE-MOTOR AREA

One of the main tasks for children during the first two years is to develop their motor skills. They are eager to try new things and to repeat or practice things they have already learned. So the large-motor area will be a much-used part of both the indoor classroom and the outdoor play area of an infant/toddler program. Through large-muscle play, these children have an opportunity to develop their posture and

Figure 15–5   Barriers should be low so children can see over them.

balance. They gain a sense of security as they learn to control their own bodies. They can learn to integrate both sides of their body, sometimes using alternate sides for tasks.

As you plan these activities, keep in mind the safety of all the children in the room. Protect crawling infants from any equipment that might injure them, but allow them access to any that are safe. For instance, if you have a rocking boat in the room or outside, infants should not be able to crawl nearby. On the other hand, if you use large foam mats and cubes for a climbing activity, some babies may be able to manage safely.

Indoors, this area might include:
- Large vinyl-covered mats, cubes, ramps.
- Rocking boats, rocking chairs, rocking horse, rolling trikes.
- Vinyl-covered foam tunnels.
- Low climbing structure with a low slide and steps.
- Large pillows, bean bags, buckets.

Outdoors, this area might include:
- Low climbing structures.
- Large boxes, either wooden or cardboard.
- Buggies, wagons, bikes.
- Wide walking boards, steps, large boxes, ramps.
- Bounce mattresses, barrels, tunnels.
- Large blocks, hollow blocks.
- Rubber tires, inner tubes.
- Sandbox, shovels, pails, cups, pots, pans.
- Large balls.
- Wading pool or large tub for water.
- Tire swings, swings with safety belts.
- Push toys, buggies.
- A variety of surfaces, such as wood, grass, sand.
- Hilly and flat areas for walking, running, or rolling.
- Low slides.

LANGUAGE AREA

By the end of the first year, infants are able to understand a great deal of the language they hear. During the second year, they learn to use words themselves to express ideas, thoughts, and feelings. An infant and toddler program should encourage language skills as adults speak and listen to children. A language activity area can provide additional stimulus for language development.

The language area should:
- Be in a secluded area, away from distractions (enclose a corner with shelves).
- Have large, soft pillows or a low couch where children can sit.
- Include a collection of cloth, cardboard, or plastic books that the children can look at and touch.
- Include tape recorders, record players, and musical instruments.
- Include albums with photos of the children and their families.
- Include pictures at the children's eye level.
- Include books that adults can read to or share with children.

PSYCHOSOCIAL AREA

A psychosocial area of an infant/toddler room should provide for interactions between adults and children and among the children themselves. This area should allow children to learn about themselves and to develop relationships with adults and with their peers.

An area for learning about themselves might include:
- Nonbreakable mirrors attached to the wall at both crawling and standing height.
- Small unbreakable mirrors that children can pick up and use.
- Pictures of babies and children displayed at eye level.
- Places for being alone—tunnels, blocked-off areas, large boxes.
- Individual storage spaces for their belongings.

An area for developing relationships with adults might include:
- Comfortable, low places for adults to sit while observing or interacting with children.
- Rocking chairs where an adult can comfort an infant, and soft chairs where an adult and toddler can sit together.
- Low barriers—some of plexiglass—so adults and children can see each other.
- Changing tables and feeding areas that are comfortable for adults and children, thus fostering interaction.

An area for developing relationships with peers might:
- Include low tables where toddlers can stand to play.
- Provide enough duplicate toys so toddlers can play near each other with the same toy.
- Have low barriers, shelves, or equipment so infants and toddlers can be together.
- Provide padded areas where toddlers can jump and play together safely.
- Provide safe places where babies can crawl together.
- Provide a place for dramatic play—table, chairs, stove, dishes, pots, pans, dress up clothes, dolls, mirror.

The addition of an infant/toddler room to your school can be a tremendous asset. You will provide a much-needed service to parents. You will also have a "built-in" enrollment for several years into the future. If parents are satisfied with your program when their children are infants, they will continue with you for many years. Your school can become an "extended family" for working parents.

ADAPTATIONS FOR SPECIAL NEEDS INFANTS AND TODDLERS

Infants and toddlers with special needs can benefit from being mainsteamed into regular child development programs. Although all-day care for these children may not be needed and may not be advisable, part-time participation can optimize their development. In addition, parents find help and support for the sometimes difficult task of caring for their children. Anyone who considers accepting these infants should seek out community resources and consultation before planning an environment or a program.

A basic need for all children during the first two years, and especially important to children with disabilities, is to gain control over themselves and their environment. In order to achieve mastery, the environment should:

- Be appropriate for each child's capabilities.
- Offer challenges while also ensuring some successes.
- Be safe, free of any objects or obstacles that could be harmful.
- Provide appropriate sensory stimulation—the visually impaired infant provided with assortments of tactile materials, the physically limited child provided visual or auditory materials, and so on.
- Include orthopedic chairs, table, or other specially designed structures for making infants comfortable.

SUMMARY

Good programs for infants and toddlers are different from all other types of programs. They are not just scaled-down versions of preschools, but are designed specifically to meet the needs of babies and toddlers.

The environment of the infant/toddler room should meet all licensing regulations for your particular area and should reflect the goals of the program. Safety is a primary concern since infants and toddlers engage in active exploration of their surroundings.

A developmentally appropriate environment will include materials and equipment that fit the stages of development from crawling and sitting to walking and climbing.

Infants and toddlers need places where they can rest and be alone. Indoors, provide a sleeping area and hiding places. Outdoors, include a sandbox, large boxes, tunnels, and climbing structures.

Children lay the foundation for their sense of identity during the first three years of life. Ethnic and cultural heritage is an important part of "who they are." Therefore, include objects, colors, and music that are culturally based.

Young children learn through exploring their environment using all their senses. An infant/toddler room should include many things to see, hear, smell, feel, and taste.

Infants and toddlers are growing and changing rapidly so their environment needs to be flexible.

Specific areas for an infant/toddler room include:

- Routine areas—eating, sleeping, diapering, toileting.
- Cognitive area.
- Fine-motor area.
- Large-motor area.
- Language area.
- Psychosocial area.

Infants and toddlers can benefit from part-time mainstreaming into regular child development programs. A few adaptations will allow them to gain control over their environment.

SELECTED FURTHER READING

Bailey, D.B., and Wolery, M. 1992. *Assessing Infants and Preschoolers with Handicaps*. Columbus, OH: Merrill Publishing Company.

Dittman, L., ed. 1984. *The Infants We Care For*, rev. ed. Washington, DC: National Association for the Education of Young Children.

Gerber, M., ed. 1979. *Manual for Resources for Infant Educarers*. Los Angeles, CA: Resources for Infant Educarers.

Godwin, A., and Schrag, L. 1988. *Setting Up for Infant Care: Guidelines for Centers and Family Day Care Homes*. Washington, DC: National Association for the Education of Young Children.

Gonzalez-Mena, J., and Eyer, D. 1993. *Infants, Toddlers, and Caregivers*, 3rd ed. Mountain View, CA: Mayfield Publishing Company.

Gonzalez-Mena, J. 1992. "Taking a Culturally Sensitive Approach in Infant-Toddler Programs." *Young Children*, 47 (2), 4–9.

Ross, H.W. 1992. "Integrating Infants with Disabilities: Can 'Ordinary' Caregivers Do It?" *Young Children*, 47 (3), 65–71.

STUDENT ACTIVITIES

1. Visit an infant/toddler program. Are there any potential safety hazards in the room? If so, what changes would you make?
2. Make a list of ten pieces of equipment that might be included in an infant/toddler room. Defend each of your choices based on developmental appropriateness.
3. Observe a group of toddlers for at least an hour. List and describe any sensory activities they engaged in during this time.
4. Draw a floor plan of an infant/toddler room. Include the specific areas that were discussed in this chapter.

REVIEW

1. Licensing requirements for infant/toddler programs have some specific areas of focus. What are they?
2. One developmental need of toddlers is to acquire independence skills in toileting. How can the environment support this need?
3. What special safety precautions must be taken in an infant/toddler room?
4. List some ways the environment can provide visual stimulation for an infant.
5. Describe the arrangement of a food storage and preparation area.
6. How can a toileting area be designed to encourage independence in toddlers?

7. Describe a cognitive area for infants to one year.
8. List the kinds of equipment, structures, or natural areas that might be included in an outdoor area.
9. List furniture and equipment that might be in a psychosocial area to promote development of relationships with peers.
10. In what ways can the environment be adapted so that children with limited abilities may gain mastery?

GLOSSARY

Flexibility   ability to be changed as needed.

Psychosocial area   space that is planned to encourage interactions between adults and children, and among the children themselves.

Sensory input   objects and experiences that stimulate the senses.

16

Space: School-Age Children

OBJECTIVES

After studying this chapter, the student should be able to:

- List general considerations when planning space for older children.
- Discuss overall design of indoor and outdoor space.
- Devise ways to share indoor and outdoor space with another group.
- List activity areas to be included.

Space for school-age children, both indoors and outdoors, should be designed specifically for their needs. Ideally, this means having "dedicated" space not shared by any other part of your program. This is not always feasible, and often school-age programs are housed in shared space, or in space that was designed for other uses, such as a multipurpose room or gym. This chapter will present general considerations to keep in mind when planning space for older children and give you some suggestions for sharing space with other parts of your program.

The same principles apply when planning space for older children as for pre-schoolers, but how they are implemented will differ. School-age children need to be physically active following a day sitting in the classroom. They need space to move about and to sharpen their physical skills. They want to socialize with a few friends, or be a part of a small group or club. They have a wide variety of interests and are able to prolong their involvement in any one activity for long periods of time.

GENERAL CONSIDERATIONS

Licensing

Just as with infant programs, regulations in your area may not have caught up with the trend toward adding school-age child care to existing preschools. Check with your state licensing agency to find out if guidelines exist.

Where school-age regulations have been adopted, several categories may be covered. One may require the separation of older children from younger ones within the preschool setting. Outdoors, you can accomplish this by using low fences, establishing a separate play area, or scheduling use of outdoor space at different times. Indoors, older children should be separated from preschoolers for unstructured play activities. Use moveable walls and partitions. Each can use a room at different times. During structured activities, older children and preschoolers can often work together effectively.

Regulations will probably specify that you must provide toilets with separate stalls for individual privacy. You may need to have a separate bathroom for boys and for girls.

Even in areas where regulations for school-age child care have been adopted, they are likely to be less stringent than for younger children. Older children are less vulnerable to physical hazards than infants and preschoolers. Since regulations address the physical environment primarily, you will find fewer for after-school programs. This does not mean you should be unconcerned. Remember that regulations are minimum standards. Your school should provide the best possible environment for the children you serve.

Goals

Throughout this text, you have read that goals are the basis for planning all aspects of a facility for young children. Review your school goals before deciding how to plan space in the school-age section. Although the overall goals for your school may include statements that can be applied to the school-age program, you will probably need to have others that are specific for that age group. Some examples will help to illustrate. You want children to be able to:

- Sustain cooperative efforts and involvement in activities over a long period of time.
- Gain greater control over their bodies through participation in individual activities and organized games.
- Develop independence in caring for themselves.

Each of these goals requires provisions for space or materials. In order to carry out the first goal, you must provide a place where several children can work together on a project. There also must be a place where they can store their work safely until the next day or the next week. The second goal indicates a need for outdoor play areas where children can participate in activities like skating, ride bikes, practice "shooting baskets," or playing organized games. One way to achieve the third goal is to have the children plan and prepare their own snacks. This calls for a food preparation area or a cabinet that contains kitchen equipment they could use to prepare food for snack time.

Safe Yet Challenging Environment

The school-age period is a time when children are rapidly developing their physical skills. They are capable of performing almost any motor skill, and can challenge themselves and each other to reach higher levels of mastery. Some of this testing can put them into dangerous situations. Picture the eight-year-old walking along the top of a narrow, high wall to test his balance, or an eleven-year-old plunging off a ramp on his skateboard. The physical skill that allows children to perform these feats is there; the judgment to assess the danger may be lacking.

Children should be able to test their physical abilities as far as possible in after-school programs, but they should be protected from serious injury while doing so. Provide space only for those activities that the children are developmentally capable of performing. Make sure that areas for active play are separated in distance from quieter pursuits. Inspect and maintain all playground areas and equipment periodically. Teach children ways to use equipment safely, and supervise closely at all times. Provide, as well, space and opportunity for sewing, knitting, painting, or preparing food.

Figure 16–1   School-age children build on skills.

Homelike Atmosphere

The setting for after-school child care should be quite different from the typical schoolroom environment. At school, children have to sit on hard chairs at desks or

Figure 16–2   Both preschoolers and older children can use this playground.

tables. The environment tells them how to behave. In child care, they should be able to sit in soft chairs, lie on a couch, or loll on the floor. Therefore, the child care environment for older children should be more like home than school.

You can accomplish a homelike atmosphere by including some of the following:
- Couches or soft, easy chairs.
- Large pillows, bean bag chairs, soft mats.
- Appropriately sized tables and chairs.
- Places for children to store their school books, lunch boxes, and jackets.
- Places to store their ongoing projects such as stamp collections or woodworking projects.
- Places to store games children bring from home.
- Places to be alone—boxes, lofts, tents, screening.
- Broom, dustpan, bucket, mop, sponges for cleanup.

Flexibility

Space for school-age children should be flexible and easily modified. Children change over a period of time, so what was suitable in September may not fit their needs in May. Also, the age span in an after-school program may be from six to twelve years. Physical space must accommodate the different interests of children at these widely diverse ages. Make space flexible by:

- Providing a variety of spaces—large open ones, or small ones designed for specific functions.
- Having mobile dividers to create work spaces.
- Having plenty of things that can be moved around to create spaces the children can design themselves—boards, crates, large building blocks, ladders, platforms, blankets, tires, ropes.
- Providing a variety of surfaces that can be used for different activities—blacktop, grass, sand, hills, dirt.
- Allowing access to water for sprinkling on hot days, playing in water, gardening, playing in the sandbox.
- Creating spaces for privacy for individuals or small groups—loft, tree house, hammock, rocking chair.

Size

School-age children need furniture and equipment that is appropriate for their size. If you must use a classroom that is used by preschoolers at other times of the day, be sure there is at least one larger table with proper-sized chairs. Older children can use the table for working on projects, doing homework, or eating snacks. Some areas can be used by both age levels. The preschool classroom may have large pillows or bean bag chairs in a reading area. Older children can use this area as well. Additions for the older children might include a workbench for woodworking and an adjustable easel for painting. Trays or mats can designate places for games or other activities to be done on the floor.

Outdoor equipment should allow for the kinds of activities older children enjoy. Include trees to climb, swings, a high jungle gym, a horizontal ladder. A blacktop area will provide space for organized games.

Aesthetically Pleasing Space

Space for all ages should be pleasing to the eye. Use color on the walls or furniture, pictures, and interesting objects to make the environment cheerful. Frame and hang the children's art work.

FYI

According to U.S. Census data, in 1992, three-fourths of all married women with school-age children worked outside the home. The Children's Defense Fund predicts that by 1995, there will be nearly 35 million working mothers with children between the ages of six and seventeen. A large percentage of these children care for themselves after school.

SOURCE: The State of America's Children, 1992. Washington, DC.

Allow the children to suggest ways to make the environment cheerful. They may wish to paint posters, put up signs, or bring objects from home to add interest and beauty. Where it is possible, allow them to paint a mural on a wall. The most important thing to remember is that the *environment should be pleasing to the children.*

Storage

If storage of equipment is convenient, children will have more time to spend at activities and play. There should be plenty of space for the ongoing projects school-age children enjoy. At this age, children have the attention span to work on long-term projects. They like to put together collections of stamps, insects, rocks, shells, etc. They may start a woodworking project that will take a week or two to finish. They must have safe places to store these materials from one day to the next. If they share space with younger children, secure these cupboards from interference.

These children should have a place to put their school belongings—their books, lunch boxes, and jackets.

SPECIFIC AREAS FOR SCHOOL-AGE CHILDREN

Quiet Corner

After a long day at school, many children need to have a quiet time to "unwind" before being involved again in group activities. Some may want to rest, read, or just sit by themselves. Others may want to sit quietly and do their homework. Some children will use this space for meetings of "secret clubs" or as a place to talk to a special friend.

Allow this kind of respite by providing:
- Enclosed corners created by shelves or dividers—furnish with rugs, large pillows or bean bag chairs, or sofa.
- Extra space for being alone such as stairways, closets, offices.
- A book corner with a selection of appropriate books.
- A music corner where a child can listen to music with earphones.
- A comfortable table or desks and proper lighting where children can do their homework.

Creative Area

Creative materials can provide children a release from some of the tensions left over after a day at school. Make a variety of materials available to children along with an adequate place to work. Furnish this area with some of the following:
- Paint—finger paint, tempera, watercolors, brushes of all sizes.
- Wide variety of paper—colored, parchment, oatmeal, etc.

- Play dough, clay, papier-mâché.
- Crayons, chalk, marking pens.
- Colored sand, glue.
- Scissors, paper punches, staplers.
- Ice cream sticks, coffee stirrers, styrofoam pieces.
- Weaving materials, small looms.
- Yarn, knitting needles, crochet hooks, tapestry canvas.
- Tissue paper, struts for kite making.
- Fabric and materials for tie dying, batiking.
- Collections of materials for collage—wood pieces, fabric, ribbons, beads, shells, rocks.
- Fabric markers, puff pens.
- Large pieces of fabric for making costumes.

Games and Manipulatives

School-age children enjoy the challenges provided by games, puzzles, and other kinds of manipulative materials. Many of the materials that are used in the pre-school can also be fun for this age level. Set aside a space where these activities can take place—either at a table or on the floor. Have a shelf conveniently nearby where children can get the materials and return them when finished. Some things to include in this area are:

- Playing cards for games such as concentration, go-fish, war, rummy, hearts, solitaire.
- Board games such as Monopoly™, Scrabble™, Life®, Clue®, checkers, Chinese checkers, jackstraws, bingo, tic-tac-toe.
- Marbles, jacks.
- Magnetic marbles, magnetic building sets, magnetic designers, magnetic mazes.
- Legos™, Lego™ accessories.
- Parquetry-design blocks, design cards.
- Large jigsaw puzzles, small 100–500 piece jigsaw puzzles.
- Plastic building sets, Tinker Toys™.

Woodworking, Cooking

School-age children enjoy the independence that comes from being able to use real tools to perform real tasks. Set up these activities in an area free from traffic flow and away from any quiet areas. Take safety precautions to make sure that children don't trip on electrical cords or get burned by hot appliances. Explain to the children safety rules for the use of woodworking tools.

Equip a woodworking area with:

- A sturdy workbench.
- Saws, hammers, screwdrivers, drills, pliers, clamps, level, tape measure.
- A variety of sandpapers, nails, screws, nuts, bolts.
- Sheets of wood, small wood pieces, wooden spools, wheels.
- Varnish, paint, brushes.

Equip a cooking area with:
- A table to work on, either at sitting or standing height.
- Pot holders, aprons.
- Water and cleaning supplies nearby.
- A variety of cooking tools—mixing and measuring spoons, measuring cups, cookie cutters, graters, rolling pins.
- Cutting board, knives.
- Several size pans and mixing bowls.
- Cookie sheets, muffin tins, baking pans, pots.
- Hand or electric mixer, blender.
- Popcorn popper, electric frying pan, ice cream maker, small over, waffle iron, toaster.
- Cookbooks written for children or other cookbooks containing "easy to prepare" recipes.
- Fire extinguisher.

Dramatic Play

Through dramatic play, children can imitate adult role models, play out their fantasies, or relive childhood experiences. Some children will use dramatic play to relieve stresses they encounter at school or at home. As children in this age range get a little older, they use dramatic play materials for producing their own plays or skits.

Equip a dramatic play area with:
- A full-length mirror.
- A variety of clothes for dress up, an assortment of hats.
- Washable face paint or makeup.
- Scarves, jewelry, plastic or silk flowers.
- Puppet theater, assortment of puppets.
- Stethoscope, gauze, splints, Band Aids™.
- Workmen's tool carrier, tools, old shirts, flashlight.
- Theatrical or Halloween costumes, wigs.

Block Building

Children at widely different age levels can use blocks. If your after-school program is housed in a preschool classroom, use the blocks that are already there. Place the block area where buildings will not be toppled by other children moving about. Having a hard surface to build on is ideal, but children can also build on a carpeted floor. Encourage the children to add to the basic materials to create their own play activities.

Some of the things that might be in a block area are:
- Wide shelves to hold the blocks—if the shelves are on casters, they can be moved if needed.
- Containers for accessory materials such as dolls, cars, trucks, boats, trains, airplanes, animals.

- Colored blocks, sheets of Masonite™, or thin plywood.
- Large hollow blocks, large cardboard blocks.
- Giant lock bricks, waffle blocks, giant Legos™.

Figure 16–3   School-age children can create elaborate block structures.

Discovery Center

A discovery center for school-age children should supplement the kinds of learning children are exposed to at school. However, present activities in such a way that children do not feel pressured to participate, but can follow their own interests. This area can promote children's natural curiosity and ability to pursue topics over a period of time.

Equip the discovery area with the following:
- Magnets, electromagnetic kit.
- Simple microscope, collection of prepared slides.
- Magnifying glasses, insect collections.
- Aquarium, books on tropical fish.
- Ant farm, ants.
- Bug house, bug-catching containers, butterfly net.
- Collections of shells, rocks, fossils.
- Sun-sensitive paper.
- Prisms, gyroscopes, color wheels.
- Small animals, cages, incubator for hatching eggs.
- Seeds, potting soil, small pots.
- Binoculars, bird books.
- Selection of books with project ideas and science information.
- Things to take apart—clocks, small appliances.

Language Center

Even though language development is very much a part of the elementary class-room, children can also enjoy participating in this kind of activity in the child care center. As with the discovery center, there should be no pressure to participate, and the activities should be fun.

The language area might include.
- A table and chairs or soft pillows and bean bag chairs.
- A selection of books.
- A tape recorder, recorded stories, ear phones, microphone, blank cassettes.
- Stamp pads with letters—both uppercase and lowercase.
- Poster boards of different colors.
- Word puzzles, crosswords, games such as Scrabble™.
- Word-matching games, word lotto, letter dice.
- Individual chalkboards, chalk, wipe-off board, marking pens.
- Paper, pencils, pens.
- Typewriter.

High-Tech Center

School-age children enjoy the challenge of operating equipment that is part of contemporary society. They get excited when they can master a computer, use a calculator, or write on a typewriter. If you can afford it, set up a center where children can experience using this equipment that is part of the grown-up world.

Include in this center:
- A table and chairs at a comfortable height.
- Computer, rack for software, bulletin board or book with instructions for use, printer (more detailed suggestions for setting up a computer center are found in Chapter 14).
- Calculator, paper, pencils.

- Typewriter, paper.
- Filmstrip projector, filmstrips.
- VCR, selected cassettes.

Clubroom

During the school-age period, children develop strong relationships with their peers and begin to group themselves according to shared interests. These friendships and interests are fostered through the formation of clubs, allowing groups to pursue topics in depth or sustain an interest over a period of time. Typical topics that appeal to children are photography, calligraphy, ceramics, computers, cooking, magic, collecting (rocks, shells, stamps), dance, drama, ecology, stitchery, space, sports, and woodworking.

A clubroom might include:
- A table and chairs or bean bag chairs and soft pillows.
- Shelves or a cabinet for storing materials.
- A sign and decorations made by the children.
- A bulletin board for posting rules, outline plans, or presenting a display.
- Specific materials or equipment needed for special interests.

Sharing Indoor Space

Your school may not have the luxury of having a separate room for your school-age children. This group may be required to share space with another age level, or use space that was designed for another purpose. With a bit of imagination, you can still create an environment that fits their needs. You and your staff could:
- Set up interest centers each day. Store all the materials necessary for an activity in large boxes, shoe boxes, baskets, or five-gallon ice-cream cartons. Label each container, and list the materials contained in each.
- Put large casters or wheels on cupboards, bulletin boards, or dividers that can be used to designate activity areas. Label the cupboards according to contents and apply locks.
- Choose furniture that can be used in more than one way. Examples are cupboards with doors that can also be used as bulletin boards or chalkboards. Attach hooks to the side of cupboards so that a screen or divider can be attached to create an enclosed space.
- Use large pegboards, framed and mounted on casters, for hanging wood working tools, art supplies, or cooking equipment.
- Have large pillows or bean bag chairs to create a quiet corner, or for being alone.
- Involve the children in setting up the environment each day or in finding new ways to use the area. They are the ones who will use the space and often have creative ideas about ways to adapt it to their own needs.
- Purchase adjustable equipment that can be raised when used by older children—tables and easels are examples.
- Utilize extra space such as hallways or special rooms for small group projects;
- Place stackable containers on a wheeled platform for use as individual cubbies for the children.

- Provide carpet squares or mats for designating areas for floor activities.
- Use large cork boards or foam boards mounted on wheels to display children's art work or project displays.
- Most importantly, encourage all staff members who share space to work together to make the arrangement mutually satisfying. It will take patience, flexibility, and time to develop ways to share space without problems.

Outdoor Environment

After being confined in the elementary school classroom all day, children need the opportunity to be outside, engaging in active play. Although a preschool play area will contain some equipment that older children will enjoy, some additions or modifications are necessary. An outdoor environment for older children should include the following:

- Single and multipurpose equipment—swings, sandbox, jungle gym, parallel bars, climbing rope, swinging bridge.
- Storage area for additional equipment as needed—balls, racquets, hoops, hockey sticks, jump ropes, tumbling mats, horseshoes, yo-yos, batons.

Figure 16–4 A sandbox stimulates a wide variety of play activities.

Figure 16–5   Parallel bars are a single purpose equipment.

- Space for special activities—hard surfaces for skateboarding or roller skating, covered area for creative activities, blacktop area for dodge ball, kick ball, jump rope, basketball court, baseball diamond or soccer field, and swimming pool.
- Adventure play area where children can build their own structures using—large blocks, boards, cartons, cable spools, sawhorses, tires, inner tubes, logs, pieces of wood or cardboard.
- Garden area with storage shed for necessary equipment—water outlet, shovels, hoes, trowels, small pots, potting soil, seeds.
- Different levels for climbing and for hiding under—hilly area, ladder, tents, benches, large pipes, low tree branches, or a fallen log.
- Shaded area for resting or reading—large tree in a grassy area, hammock.

Sharing Outdoor Space

It is often difficult for staff members in school-age programs to plan shared outdoor space with younger children. Many directors solve the problem by scheduling groups to use the play areas at separate times, but that does not completely address the needs of children at disparate age levels. The following suggestions may help:

- Provide adequate supervision of all areas of the playground.
- Establish clear rules so that older children know what they can and cannot do when younger children are present.
- Encourage older children to help younger children.
- Use movable equipment (see suggestions in the previous section) that can be brought out when younger children are not present.
- Set aside some areas for the exclusive use of older children, using movable barriers or fences.
- Schedule times that older children can use community facilities such as a park, a baseball diamond, a basketball court, or a swimming pool.
- Plan joint activities with another school-age program that has its own outdoor area.

SUMMARY

Space for school-age children, both indoors and outdoors, should be designed specifically for their needs. Ideally, this means having "dedicated" space, not shared by other parts of the program.

General considerations for planning space for older children are similar to those used for younger age levels, but they are implemented differently. Basics for planning space are:

Licensing requirements: may require separation of older children from younger children in instructional and play areas, and separate toilet areas.

Goals: Overall school goals may apply to older children, but there should also be goals specific to *that* age level.

Safe yet challenging environment: older children are physically capable and want the opportunity to test their skills. They need a safe environment for their activities.

Homelike atmosphere: after-school setting should be different from the typical schoolroom environment by allowing children to engage in active play or to sit in soft chairs, lie on a couch, or loll on the floor.

Flexibility: space for school-age children should be changeable, allowing children to modify their environment to suit their changing needs.

Size: school-age children should have furniture and equipment that is appropriate for their size.

Aesthetically pleasing: the environment should be colorful and children should be allowed to decorate their own room.

Storage: should be convenient and provide a safe place where children can store their long-term projects and collections.

Specific areas in a school-age environment include the following:
- Quiet corner.
- Creative area.
- Games and manipulatives.
- Woodworking, cooking.
- Dramatic play.
- Block building.
- Discovery corner.
- Language center.
- High-tech center.
- Clubroom.

When space for a school-age program must share indoor space with other age levels, planners must be creative. The suggestions include:
- Use casters or wheels on furniture to make it movable.
- Choose furniture that can be used in more than one way.
- Provide adjustable tables and easels.
- Store materials in boxes for ease in moving.

School-age children need to be physically active after sitting in a classroom all day. Therefore, their outdoor environment should include the following:
- Single- and multipurpose equipment.
- Storage area for additional equipment to be brought out as needed.
- Space for special activities.
- Adventure play area where children can build their own structures.
- Garden area with storage shed for tools.
- Different levels for climbing or hiding.
- Shaded area for resting.

When a school-age program must share outdoor space with other age levels:
- Provide adequate supervision.
- Establish clear rules.
- Encourage older children to help younger children.
- Use movable equipment when younger children are not present.
- Set aside some areas for the exclusive use of older children.
- Schedule times that older children can use community facilities.
- Plan joint activities with other child care centers.

SELECTED FURTHER READING

Bender, J., Elder, B., and Flatter, C. 1994. *Half a Childhood: Time for School-Age Child Care*. Nashville, TN: School-Age NOTES.

Click, P. 1994. *Caring for School-Age Children*. Albany, NY: Delmar Publishers Inc.

Greenman, J. 1988. *Caring Spaces, Learning Places: Children's Environments That Work.* Redmond, WA: Exchange Press, 1988.

Haas-Foletta, K., and Cogley, M. 1990. *School-Age Ideas and Activities for After School Programs.* Nashville, TN: School-Age NOTES.

Richard, M. 1991. *Before & After School Programs: A Start-Up and Administration Manual.* Nashville, TN: School-Age NOTES.

Wheeler, K. 1993. *How Schools Can Stop Shortchanging Girls (and Boys): Gender-Equity Strategies.* Wellesley, MA: Center for Research on Women.

STUDENT ACTIVITIES

1. Obtain several catalogues from companies that supply materials for school-age children. Choose three items that you would use in a classroom of eighteen children ranging in age from six to eleven. Defend your choice in terms of the development of children during middle childhood.

2. Visit a park that attracts school-age children. Observe their play activities and make a list of those that could take place in a child care setting. Describe the space or equipment that would be needed.

3. Plan and conduct one indoor and one outdoor activity for a group of six eight-year-olds. Evaluate the success of the activities. How long did the children stay involved? What comments did they make? Would you change either the materials you provided or the way in which the activity was conducted? If so, in what ways?

4. Write several paragraphs describing the kinds of play activities you enjoyed during middle childhood. Which of the interests inherent in these experiences have you continued to pursue at the present time?

REVIEW

1. How do licensing requirements for school-age programs differ from those for younger children?

2. State one goal that is applicable to a school-age program.

3. List several ways to make space flexible.

4. Name five items that could be included in a woodworking center.

5. What is the purpose of a discovery center in a school-age child care?

6. List nine items that can be used to stimulate children's language development.

7. State six ways to adapt indoor space when it must be shared with younger children.

8. What kinds of items might be found in an adventure play area?

9. How can you provide different levels for climbing high or hiding underneath?

10. Describe ways that outdoor space can be successfully shared with other groups.

GLOSSARY

Dedicated space   space that is not shared with any other part of a child care program.

Multipurpose equipment   equipment that can be used in more than one way.

Adventure play areas   outdoor areas where children can use a variety of materials to build their own structures.

Part VI

Beyond the School Itself

17

Parent Involvement, Eduation, and Public Relations

OBJECTIVES

After studying this chapter, the student should be able to:
- Discuss the changing roles of parents and preschools.
- List some ways that parents may participate in the school.
- State some possible goals for parent education.
- Cite several ways a school may help parents learn.
- Itemize some activities that can publicize your school.

Traditionally, parents have been responsible for rearing children, and schools have had the task of educating them. Recent years have brought about some changes in these two roles.

CHANGING ROLES

Changing family life has forced modification of the traditional role of parents. In the United States, more than half the mothers of children under the age of six work outside the home. Children no longer stay home until they go to elementary school at five or six. Many children start in day care as babies and continue until or even through adolescence. As a result, parents no longer have sole responsibility for rearing their children. This task is shared with teachers or caregivers.

Those who are with the child while parents work are forced into new roles as well. Teachers can no longer focus only on teaching. They have to help the child through each developmental stage, be concerned about his health, and provide the nurturing that once was done by parents.

This merging of responsibilities for rearing and educating the child has caused both parents and teachers to realize that their responsibilities overlap and that they must work closely together. This is especially true when infants are involved. Parents are understandably anxious about placing their baby in someone else's care. They want caregivers who will listen to their concerns and who will follow their suggestions about feeding, sleeping, and toileting. On the other hand, the school needs that kind of input to plan for the appropriate care of the baby. This need to work together changes in character but continues even when the child is a preschooler and older.

PARENT INVOLVEMENT

Even when children are in day care, research consistently shows the enormous influence parents still have on their children. They remain the primary support for the child as teachers and caregivers change. Parent involvement in the school becomes essential for the optimum development of the child. Follow-up research on children who attended Heart Start shows, for instance, that the children who had lasting gains had parents who were closely allied with their school.

Many parents and teachers who took part in the early cooperative schools found their involvement brought unexpected benefits. The parents learned a good deal about their own children. They also learned some basic principles of child development. They gained comfort by finding that other parents had similar problems. In fact, they learned that some problems were merely stages in a child's growth. The school provided a support system sometimes lacking in many communities. A few parents gained enough inspiration to become teachers when their children got older.

Beginning in the 1960s, some parents began demanding a more active role in the education of their children. It was a time of social unrest, marked by the civil rights movement. Some of the demands arose from criticism of schools in general. More specifically, the grievances were aimed at the "failure" of educational systems to understand minority needs. Some people felt schools were unresponsive and bureaucratic. The Head Start Project was one result of all this turmoil.

However, early attempts to involve parents in Head Start projects were difficult for the parents and the schools. Parent participation was "built into" the legislation. But parents sometimes felt insecure in the presence of the authority symbol of the teacher. On the other hand, teachers were reluctant to include parents for fear they might dominate the program. The partnership that was mandated in Head Start guidelines took time to implement.

Today, in the successful Head Start centers, parents and professionals seem to be working together harmoniously. Parent representatives serve on advisory committees. Parents have a high degree of input into curriculum. Some serve as aides in the classroom helping the teachers directly. Parents are taught how to enhance learning through activities at home.

For some time, nonprofit schools have used parents in fund raising, recruitment, and public relations activities. However, the attitude that educational aspects should be left to the school staff persisted. Now, schools are finding that parents have many skills they are willing to share for program enrichment.

FYI

The standards for accreditation of early childhood education programs developed by NAEYC include a staff-parent interaction component. The inclusion was based on the belief that children's needs cannot be adequately met without the active involvement of their families. The standards specify that high-quality programs should include the following:

- *Information about the program's philosophy and procedures given to all prospective families.*
- *A procedure for orienting children and families.*
- *Communication between staff and parents regarding childrearing practices.*
- *Open door policy allowing parents to visit at any time.*
- *Verbal and written system for sharing day-to-day happenings that affect the children.*
- *Conferences held at least once a year or as needed.*
- *Parents informed through regular newsletters, bulletin boards, notes, or telephone calls.*

SOURCE: Accreditation Manual, *National Academy of Early Childhood Programs.*

So, too, have proprietary schools found that parents are willing to take part in many ways. Parents with a profession offer their skills as consultants; others use special abilities to enrich subject matter. Satisfied parents are more willing to help the school broaden its recruitment activities.

As already noted, the steadily increasing number of day care programs has altered the picture. When children spend many of their waking hours in school, the relationship between home and school has to be even closer. Directors must be instruments for change in this situation. Parents and teacher, guided skillfully by the director, share the responsibility for determining the best environment for the child's physical, social, and intellectual growth.

The kind and extent of parent involvement depends on the program offered by the school. As in Head Start, parent participation may be mandated with specific guidelines. Little deviation is allowed.

The extent of parent participation where there are no specific written agreements will depend on the philosophy and attitudes of the school. In centers where director and staff fully realize the importance of parent presence, the involvement may be broad and almost unlimited.

Parental Roles

Parents may participate in the school in several ways. They may sit on policy-making committees, play a supportive role, act as aides in the classroom, or be trained as teachers of their own children at home.

The rationale for involving parents stems from the belief that people feel a commitment to decisions in which they have had a part: the Y theory of management. In the long view, for children to benefit from their school experience, their parents must feel an integral part of it, too. And, in practical terms, many tax-supported programs depend on active community support for renewal of funds.

Further rationale for involving parents comes from the belief that development of decision making and other skills will help in other aspects of their life. Learning that their personal input can influence the school encourages self-growth and further participation outside the school.

In a *policy-making role*, parents may take part in planning a new program by suggesting goals. They may be asked to join in operational aspects such as hiring or helping to evaluate staff. They may also suggest topics for parent education activities.

Some policy-making functions for parents might be:

- Serving as members of an advisory committee or council.
- Representing parents on the board of trustees.
- Helping to set policies concerning finance and personnel.

Some parents may fulfill *supportive roles*. These are tasks the parents can sometimes do at home or outside of the school. They are designed to aid or supplement educational functions. Some tasks parents may perform in a supportive role are to:

- Provide parts of major maintenance projects.
- Act as clerical support.
- Plan and carry out fund raising.
- Be responsible for social activities.
- Provide baby-sitting or car pool services.

The real purpose of a supportive role for parents is to fulfill a mutual need; the school and parents both want the best for the children. The school may desperately need some services parents can provide.

The supportive role may help some parents begin involvement at a level of their own comfort. Not everyone is ready or able to invest as much time and effort as is necessary to become competent in policy making or serve as an aide.

When they do work as *aides in the classroom*, parents must learn some of the duties and skills of a teacher in order to be effective. As aides, parents may do some of the following:

- Perform tasks assigned by the teacher, such as helping with large group activities or working with individual children.
- Prepare materials, arrange the room, and keep records of children's progress.
- Supervise small groups of children during specific times.

In some programs, participation of parents as aides is part of the "career ladder" concept. This may be the first rung in the progress toward paid employment. Head Start and many day care centers train mothers for jobs in schools for young children.

Parents may be trained to become *better teachers of their own children*. In this role, parents do the following:

- Learn to recognize the child's readiness for learning.
- Learn the value of a variety of learning experiences to further the child's development.
- Make use of common materials found around the home to enhance the child's learning.

Figure 17–1 Dads should be included!

Head Start has met this need by providing Home Visitors who work with families in their homes. Together the Home Visitor and parents plan activities for the child and determine what the child is ready to learn. Common and inexpensive household materials are used for activities. All family members are encouraged to participate. Schools other than Head Start can also provide this kind of training in other ways. As parents become more competent, they are encouraged to become more involved in their child's school. Training parents as teachers of their own children is discussed in more detail later in this chapter.

Limits on Involvement

Each community and the schools within it have their own particular characteristics. The appropriate kind of parent involvement must be tailored to fit the situation to be effective. Factors to be considered are (1) number of working parents, (2) ethnic group values, (3) stability of the community, (4) size of the community, and (5) physical setting of the school.

The number of working parents, especially mothers, certainly determines the amount and time of involvement. Obviously, in a day care school where almost all the parents are working, few parents can serve as aides. It is possible that some parents may work part-time or on a flexible schedule that would allow them some limited participation. Most parents cannot do this. The school must realize that the working schedule of parents determines involvement.

However, some ways in which fully employed parents can be involved in the education of their children are to:

- Participate in decision making at convenient times.
- Provide support by doing work at home or after work.
- Be involved in training as teachers of their own children at home.

You must realize, and your staff should be reminded, that a working parent often has little surplus energy. Reluctance to become involved in the school may be just plain fatigue, not an indication the parent is not interested.

Values, attitudes, and traditions of the parents in your school should be carefully considered. These vary from community to community. You will be more effective in reaching out to parents if you understand these belief systems:

- Is it acceptable for the mother to be solely involved in school activities, or should the father be included?
- Is the school still seen as the absolute province of the professionals?
- Do the families see the school and home as entirely separate entities?

The stability or mobility of the community from which the school draws children also determines the degree of parent participation:

- If the population is largely transient, involvement that takes a long time to develop will not be possible.
- If the community is relatively stable, parents can take the time to develop decision-making and teaching skills.

The size of the community in which the school is based will also determine parent involvement:

- If children are bussed to school from distant areas, it may be harder to find ways to involve parents.
- A school located within walking distance may naturally become a center for varied activities.

The physical limitations of the school may restrict involvement by parents:

- If the school is small and space is at a premium, many parents may feel "squeezed out."
- If certain areas can be set aside and scheduled for parents' use, they may feel more welcome and free.

Initial Contact

Parents' first visits to your school after enrolling their children are the most important for setting the tone of future contacts. As parents walk into your school, will they feel welcome? Come in the entrance of your building and look around through the eyes of a parent. Are there ways in which the environment says "Parents are welcome, too?" Do you or some other staff member greet parents when they enter? Does your school have an "open-door" policy in which parents are welcome to visit at any time?

Some schools opt for an open house to set the tone for parent relationships. Often scheduled just before the school year begins, an open house gives parents an opportunity to meet all the staff and get to know other parents.

Figure 17–2   Parents can use their special abilities to enrich the curriculum.

Every contact staff members have with parents is important. Teachers should be as responsive to the parents as to their children. Even during brief meetings when the child is delivered or picked up in the evening, teachers should be sensitive to parents' feelings. In other words, parents should feel that the school people are as interested in them as they are in their child.

A physical space reserved for parents is important. If a room can be used as a parent-teacher lounge, or a place for the parent to feel at home, big dividends will accrue. A bulletin board for parents used to announce parent meetings, community lectures, fund raisers, books of interest, etc., is useful. You could also post the weekly food menu. A newsletter for parents will keep them informed and emotionally involved with the school.

Encouraging Participation

After you make the initial contact with parents, the task of encouraging continued participation begins. The primary responsibility is yours. As leader, your first task is to *create the climate* in which staff members work. Staff members who have high morale and who feel secure in their jobs will feel more positive toward both parents and children.

A second task as leader is to *implement a program* in which home-school relations is an important part. Teachers may need encouragement to involve parents in their classroom activities. Suggest ways they can use parents as aides or in supportive roles. Let them know which parents have talents or skills they might call on for help.

The third important task for you is to *act as coordinator* for a program of parent involvement. Busy teachers may need help in arranging times and other specifics of getting parents to help with classroom activities. As coordinator, you can also offer positive reinforcement for parents who have participated.

The process of involving parents in the education of their children has some "built-in" obstacles. Parents and teachers often deal in stereotypes of each other. This makes working together difficult. The parent may see the teacher as an "expert" and, therefore, critical of parents. This may make the parent feel uneasy and unwelcome while visiting the school. As a result, the parent avoids contacts with the school.

Teachers, on the other hand, may feel the parent has unrealistic expectations for what the school should do. When these expectations are not reached, the teacher feels under attack. Again, there is avoidance, this time from the teacher.

Parents' attitudes toward school are often based on their own experiences. If they hated school, they may need a great deal of encouragement to participate in their child's school. On the other hand, some parents loved school and are only too ready to participate when asked.

Inexperienced teachers often feel they have enough to do learning to work well with children. Having to be concerned about parents is an added burden. Some may have tried to get parents involved but have been unsuccessful. It then is easier to justify not including parents by feeling that these parents do not care enough about their children. Even experienced teachers may be influenced by negative contacts with parents.

Some teachers fear that parents may not regard them as knowledgeable because they do not have children of their own. A few parents do say, "You don't know what it's like being with a child 24 hours a day." Even when it is not said, some teachers feel parents will think it.

Lack of training in working with parents may also create problems. Working with adults does require special skills and adroitness. Teachers often do not understand and, therefore, are critical of the feelings parents have about their children. Teacher training programs often fail to help the beginning teacher develop greater empathy for parents.

Some teachers seem to be able to involve parents more easily than others. Use these teachers to help other teachers. Schedule times when beginning teachers can observe more experienced teachers working with parent volunteers. Plan follow-up staff meetings where you can discuss their observations.

Incentives for Sustaining Involvement

It is often as difficult to sustain parent interest and participation in your school as it was to acquire it originally. But the most important incentive for parents is, of course, their children. Parents want their children to be successful in school. Feedback on children's progress in the school helps. They also want to know how to be better parents. Build upon these needs to foster parent involvement. If they believe they are helping their children, they will freely help your school.

Few schools can pay parents with money. A few publicly funded programs can offer reimbursement for out-of-pocket expenses. But mostly encouragement, knowledge, and positive reinforcement are the coin of repayment. Some employer-sponsored schools may offer limited released time away from the job to help in the school. Or in day care centers, dinner meetings may be arranged just after the close of school with free child care time.

Parents' interest can be aided by promoting personal growth. In some programs, contact with the school is the first or only activity tried by parents outside home or work. If they feel successful, their feelings of worth will increase. It may be the first step to broader community activities.

Social relationships that are developed through parent involvement are also important in continued interest. Single parents, especially, may find friendships that become an important part of their lives. New associations with other adults offer a single parent a broader outlook than a strictly child-centered world.

You can safely institute programs that are geared solely to adult needs. Classes in nutrition or family finance might be successful rallying points. If there is room and these classes meet at the school, parents have an additional inducement toward belonging. Even broader excursions such as trips to museums, art galleries, or theaters may broaden parents' experiences and enhance friendships.

Recording Parent Involvement

You should keep records to show the extent of parent involvement in your school. In some publicly funded programs, this is necessary to stay within guidelines. In any case, the records may prove valuable when you are attempting to evaluate the program and to determine if changes may be made. The following records may prove useful:

- List of current committee members.
- Minutes of all meetings involving parents.
- Attendance records at committee and board meetings.
- Copies of resolutions involving parents' work.
- Correspondence relating to parents' efforts.
- Evaluation of parent involvement.
- Records of any citations or awards made.

To think of the parents as part of a team made up of the school and the home is most productive. The teacher and parents have similar aims that are sometimes frustrated by false impressions. One of the major aims of parent involvement is to break through these barriers in order to give the children a superior education. Consider teacher, director, parent, and community as a unit. Without this sense of wholeness, there are sure to be gaps in the child's attainment.

PARENT EDUCATION

While the aim of parent involvement is to establish a partnership for the care of the child at school, parent education is designed to help parents be better informed about childrearing and family life. As director of your school, it becomes your responsibility to formulate the structure for a parent education program. In your leadership role, you will want to encourage teachers to participate as fully as possible. It might be easier to do all the parent education work yourself, but your staff will gain by taking part.

Start by formulating some goals. You may work on several simultaneously or concentrate on one goal for a period of time. Goals, though, should form the base for planning parent education activities.

Goals for Parent Education

Although all the following may not be completely applicable, they may give you some ideas for developing goals. It is most important that you have goals that are consonant with your general philosophy of the total school.

Establish a partnership with the family for the education and care of the child. Convey the attitude of partnership to each staff member. It begins when a parent first walks into the school and talks to the secretary or director. To convey this attitude is especially important during the time the child and parent are adjusting to school attendance.

Help parents to recognize and respect their own abilities. Most parents do a good job of rearing their children. They sometimes feel inadequate. An important part of parent education is to help them realize their own strengths and trust their own feelings about what is right for the child.

Provide parents with factual information about child development. Many parents have limited experience with young children and may feel that some of the things their children do are unusual. A knowledge of child development will help them to view behavior as developmental stages.

Explain the school curriculum and planned activities. Parents should know why you provide certain activities and materials. They should understand why the teacher presents the materials in a specific way. They need to understand the value of free play and what is gained in group participation.

Help parents understand the ways that children can learn. Some parents believe that learning takes place only when the instructor is teaching. They may not remember that children are actively learning when they are playing. Children learn in different ways. Parents can be encouraged to recognize experiences at home that may be important.

Introduce the parents to a wide variety of educational materials and experiences. The family can be helped to make use of readily available materials for the child's learning experiences. Offer guidance as to the sources and values of toys, books, paper supplies, puzzles, and other aids such as how-to-do-it books and games. The appropriate materials for the child's age level is recommended to encourage creativity and self-growth.

Activities

An attractive parent education program will have a wide variety of activities and methods from which parents may learn. Some are planned and structured; others occur spontaneously. An effective program may use some of the following formats.

One of the first opportunities for a parent to learn in the school setting is the orientation meeting. This meeting is usually held early in the school year. It is a chance for parents and staff to meet informally. This is probably the first opportunity to present information important to parents. Some of the purposes of the orientation meeting are to:
- Welcome parents formally.
- Introduce staff.
- Explain purposes and goals of the school.
- Outline essential parts of the curriculum.
- Acquaint parents with rules about clothing, toys, and snacks.
- Describe methods of introducing children to classroom.
- Answer parents' questions.
- Set friendly tone for including parents in school.

Some schools have found it helpful to record some of the information given at the orientation meeting. For example, you might show a slide presentation covering the curriculum and save it for parents who cannot attend. Written information compiled in a parent handbook is another way of presenting this information to parents. In addition to discussion at the orientation, parents can take the handbook home for later review.

Observation is an important avenue for learning. Parents can see how the school operates and see the interaction between teachers and children.

Observations may be casual and unscheduled. Each time a parent is in a classroom is an opportunity to observe. If a school has one-way screens into the classroom, the parent may observe without intrusion. This type of observation may be especially helpful for parents who are having separation problems with their children. The parent can see that the child almost always stops crying when the teacher diverts or comforts the child. This may help immensely in guilt reduction.

The one-way screen offers anonymity to the parent. Often the child acts differently when the parent is present. This is a rare chance to see the child more objectively. Within the school's child-oriented environment, the child is often different from the person seen by the parent at home.

Casual observation also has its pitfalls. The parent may see something that is not entirely understood. Either the teacher or director should be available to explain the child's part in the total group. Many times parents have questions most easily answered by you, as a "neutral" observer.

Scheduled observations of demonstration activities also help parents learn. Their attention can be directed to specific activities. They can be coached as to what to look for and what not to expect. They may also be asked to note the way the teacher varies activities of the group and of each child.

If a group of parents observes, hold a discussion after each session to clarify and reinforce learning. As in any endeavor, each person sees slightly different aspects of what happened. Sharing and comparing observations may be an exciting way to learn.

Group discussion even without observation is another important parent project. The opportunity to share experiences and feelings common to all parents is invaluable. Parents learn that their child is not so different from other children. They also may learn that it is not uncommon to have conflicting emotions about their own children.

Group discussions can also provide an opportunity to talk about each child's place in the group. Parents gain insight into developmental levels of children. They can begin to understand some of the underpinnings of the curriculum. They can learn ways that teachers (and parents) can be most effective with children.

Lectures or panels are additional teaching methods. Ask experts in various fields to speak at parent meetings. Take care to find an interesting as well as an informed speaker. Nothing can be so deadly to a parent education session as a long, dull speech, especially if it is given after working hours. Something of this sort not only can induce sleep, but also can seriously derail the entire effort.

Choose lecture topics with care. Some topics create anxiety rather than promote knowledge. Controversial topics attract interest but should be handled skillfully. Present both sides of an issue.

Films, slides, and tapes help parents learn. Many informative and interesting films and video tapes are geared to parents of young children. You should preview each tape or film before showing it. Make notes while viewing for use during the discussion period that follows.

Films or videotapes made at the school should illustrate the activities and materials used in everyday teaching. Videotapes made at intervals may show language development during the year. The same holds for other kinds of ventures. Art, music, and science all hold developmental promise. Take care to edit tapes carefully so that nothing embarrassing to any child will appear.

Workshop participation can offer information about the curriculum. Parents may participate in the same activities as their children do. They may finger paint, work with wood or blocks, and sing. This gives them a first-hand feel of what the child is doing.

Another kind of workshop is one in which parents can make learning materials to use at home with their child. This can be a game, a piece of equipment, or a learning kit. This kind of workshop for parents can have a twofold benefit: (1) they have made something for their child, and (2) they have explored the potential of materials.

Parents can learn through participation in the classroom. Many parents have special skills or training that can be useful on a short-term basis in the classroom. Help them to feel free to share these with all the children. It is a welcome change of pace to have a parent read a story, lead a music activity, or share a cooking experience. Some parents may be able to share stories and objects from their own ethnic backgrounds. This can be an effective way of bringing an added dimension to the classroom.

If parents show some desire to serve as aides on a longer-term basis, the hurdle of training may appear. This will vary with each individual, but a brief overview, followed by on-the-job instruction will probably suffice. Volunteers must understand the special goals of the school, if any. They need to know the rudiments of interacting with young children in a group. They should begin by working under the close supervision of the regular teacher and progressing to individuals or very small groups.

Saturday or holiday sessions of a school give fathers an opportunity to participate. Some schools schedule this kind of activity at least once a year. With both father and mother now working, this type of scheduling is gaining in popularity.

All communications with a parent have an educational potential. Regard any phone call to or from a parent as part of the parent involvement/parent education program of the school. Phone calls made when a child is home sick are especially important to remember. It tells the parent that the teacher cares. It may also give the parent a moment to talk to the teacher about the child.

Daily contacts, though routine, are important. The way the teacher answers a parent's questions about the child establishes feelings. A simple question such as "Did Johnny eat?" may be answered in some detail or with a colder "Yes." Parents want reassurance that the teacher knows and cares about what the child did during the day. When that kind of feedback is given, the result can be greater trust and confidence in the school. The little things do count.

Conferences are probably the most efficient way a school can help parents learn. A one-on-one meeting between the teacher and the parents, or occasionally the parent and the director, is the time that the child's progress can be fully explored. This is also the time that shared problems can be stated. It is probable that a child's difficulties in the home are carried over into the school.

Figure 17–3   Sometimes parent conferences are informal.

Make conferences more effective by adopting some or all of the following suggestions:

- Examine the content of the conference beforehand.
- Start and end the conference on a positive note.
- Encourage the parents to discuss concerns or ask questions. It is important to listen.
- Take care to ensure that teachers avoid making the parent feel guilty or anxious. (Occasionally, this is unavoidable. When it is necessary, get the family to seek help for the child).
- Guide parents toward finding their own solutions to their problems.
- Tell teachers not to be afraid to admit that the school does not have all the answers.
- Guarantee that the conference is free from interruptions.
- Allow enough time to cover necessary items adequately, but do not let the discussion drag on into inconsequence. It is not necessary to solve all problems in one conference.

- Definitely slate another conference if needed.
- Whenever possible, end a conference with a summary of what has been discussed and accomplished.

Convey information for parents through a parent library, a periodic newsletter, or a bulletin board. Some parents may prefer to increase their knowledge by reading. Others may resist this fiercely. But the school should make available some books on child development—the best in the field. If your budget will not allow outright purchase, a reading list of good resources at the local library may suffice. Already mentioned, the newsletter may keep parents informed of what is happening at the school and in the field of child development. You can try your hand at writing an article aimed at your parents! Ask your teachers to draft articles as well. A centrally located bulletin board, attractively arranged, can serve as a center of interest near an exit or entrance. Be sure that the board is well maintained and up to date.

An integral part of early childhood education is the enlightenment of parents. The school has the children for only a part of each day. For each child's education to be consistent, the parents must carry the same goals into the home. To make this possible, the school must make a concerted effort to present itself to the parents. Parent education is really a cooperative enterprise on the part of the school and parents to make the child's education truly unique and whole.

THE SCHOOL AND THE PUBLIC

Schools must actively promote themselves in order to remain competitive. No one requires very young children to go to school. When parents choose to put their children in school, they sometimes make choices capriciously. The school is located near the home or work place. It is convenient to transportation. It is inexpensive. The motivations are many and varied. The schools with full enrollment and waiting lists have made earnest efforts to promote themselves.

Probably the best form of public relations is good parent education and intense parent involvement with your school. One of the most sincere forms of advertising is word-of-mouth testimony of satisfied customers. Parents who are satisfied are good promoters.

A few schools have adopted easily recognized symbols to promote themselves. Kinder-Care® uses a red tower in all its buildings and as a logo on printed material. It is not necessary to compete on this level, however. There are common, everyday ways of making the school known in the community, and even outside it.

As usual, you must assume the responsibility as public relations director in addition to your other duties. To be effective, go about this self-promotion in an organized and thoughtful way. Isolate areas over which you have some good measure of control and pursue these before launching something such as a paid campaign. Give some thought to: (1) the exterior appearance of the school, (2) telephone-answering procedures, (3) visitor utilization, (4) brochures and pamphlets, (5) open houses, and (6) community activities.

Appearance of the School

You may have become habituated to the appearance of your school. The casual passerby has not. Evaluations are frequently formed from first impressions. The next time you enter your school, try to adopt the attitude of a total stranger. What do you see outside? Peeling paint and fading signs or an attractive color and well-kept entrance?

Look at playground areas that are visible from the outside. What kind of equipment can be seen? Is it being used? Does it look sturdy and well maintained? Is the equipment designed to appeal to children or only to adults? Are there open places for children to play?

Enter the building. What do you see first? Is the entrance arranged so that someone will greet you? Is there a place to sit down? Is the reception area pleasant looking? Are there things that interest parents? Is the area clean and free of unpleasant odors? Sensory impressions are important in setting the tone for first visitors. Within the physical limits of what you now have, be sure you are making the most of it.

Figure 17–4 A good secretary is vital to public relations.

Telephone-Answering Procedures

Many first contacts and first impressions are made over the telephone. The person answering the telephone becomes a front-line public relations person.

Often this person is your secretary. Parents telephone for information regarding price, hours, age range, and other variables. To ease the burdens on your time, train your secretary to give this kind of routine information about the school. Provide forms for recording names, addresses, and telephone numbers. Establish a procedure for following an inquiry with written information. Also, train your secretary to know when to refer calls to you. You may want to answer questions about policy, curriculum, or goals yourself.

Caution your secretary to be pleasant and polite when answering the telephone. Encourage the use of clearly enunciated speech. An unrushed and unhurried manner may reassure a parent who already has a doubt or two.

Visitors

Parents of children already enrolled in your school should feel free to visit at any time. Set aside specific times for other visitors. Consider planning one or two days a week when you can be free to accommodate prospective parents, community persons, or others wishing to see your school. Plan what the visitors will see and prepare any written materials that will be helpful. Don't forget to tell teachers they will have visitors in their classrooms.

After a short orientation, take the visitors to a classroom. Introduce them to the teacher. Seat them well away from the center of activity of the children. Thirty minutes is about the maximum time for visitors to spend in the classroom.

Allow another half an hour to an hour for a discussion after the observation. Encourage visitors to share what they have seen, or to ask questions. If disparate interest groups, such as visiting teachers and prospective parents, are touring the school, meet with them separately. Their questions and observations may be quite different.

Try to schedule visitors for times when interesting activities are taking place. Let them see children working at learning centers or involved in a group activity. Your discussion with visitors can focus on how the lessons further the goals of the school.

The Brochure

A brochure should be a succinct portrayal of your school. It should be attractive and in good taste. You may want to use colors, but avoid gaudiness.

Send it out in response to a telephone call or give it to parents who stop by. Distribute it at professional meetings. Send it out into the community. It is your small ambassador.

The effectiveness of the brochure depends on how carefully you prepare it. A poor brochure is worse than none at all. A good one has few rivals for good publicity. Be sure to survey your staff members for those with special art or writing abilities to help in the production. Don't overlook parent volunteers with special talents either.

Many people don't read brochures carefully. For that reason the information should be condensed, not detailed. The essential facts should be clear when the document is skimmed.

It must contain all pertinent information. It should be of a size and weight that can be mailed for minimum first-class postage. The paper used should have a good "feel." Twenty-weight coated stock is often used in an 8 1/2 x 11 format, folded three times. Look to mailing the brochure without an envelope; it is less costly.

Although you must study total cost, it is not wise to count pennies. The addition of cuts for pictures and of some color costs more. But selective bidding by printers and a judicious selection may partially compensate. Perhaps fewer brochures for limited and controlled distribution would be better if quality suffers.

In planning a brochure, be sure to include:
- Name, address, and telephone number of school.
- Sponsorship (if any) of school.
- Hours school is in session. Days of the week and months of the year might also be helpful.
- Procedure and cost of enrollment. If enrollments are taken only at specific times, state when.
- Ages of children served.
- Tuition and other fees. (You may decide to use a separate sheet for tuition and fees. It is less expensive to reprint when costs change.)
- Brief statements of philosophy—in terms everyone can understand.
- Short description of program(s) of school.
- Description of unique features.
- Name of person to contact for enrollment.
- Affiliations or accreditations.

See Figure 17–5 for a suggested brochure layout.

Open House

An open house can be the vehicle for publicizing the best features of your school. This can be especially effective when you are just opening a new school. There are really two parts to it: preparation of the school itself and publicity to lure the community to attend.

Try to involve as many staff members as possible in planning and preparing for the open house. Aim at the more dramatic and graphic aspects of your educational program. Classroom displays with children's art work will show creativity. Block buildings, pictures, story books, and varied constructions all lend themselves to self-advertisement.

Room arrangements should be attractive. A story corner can be set up as though children were expected. A table set for snack time shows that proper nutrition is a vital part.

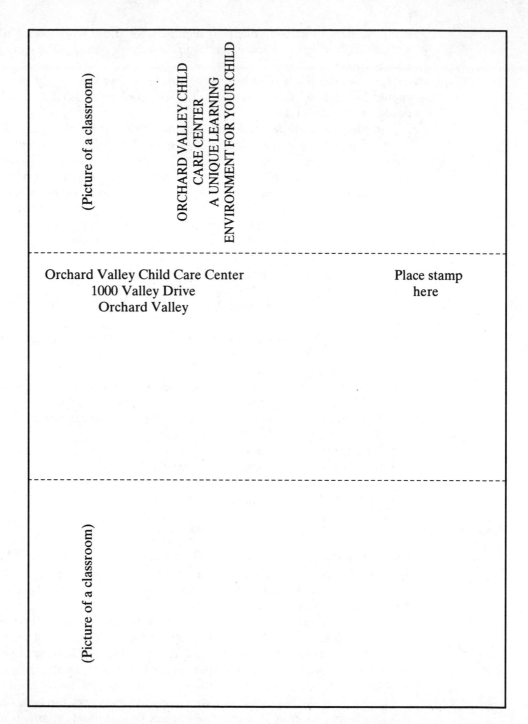

Figure 17–5   Sample brochure.

PROGRAM

Orchard Valley Child Care Center is committed to providing an optimum environment for children while they are in our care. Our philosophy and goals are used to plan and implement all aspects of our program.

We believe:

- Each child is unique and deserves opportunities to make choices, to develop independence, and to receive reinforcement when successful.
- In providing a physical environment in which the child can be safe, can explore, and can be challenged to develop optimum motor skills.
- All teaching staff should be role models for children and should plan learning activities appropriate for each age level.
- Parents are the most significant adults in a child's life and should be included as partners in planning for the child's growth and development while at school.

(picture of a child)

ENROLLMENT

New enrollments are accepted at any time there are openings available. Application must be made in person. For an appointment, please call:

Mrs. Mary Anton
555-3014

A $35.00 nonrefundable registration fee is charged at the time of initial enrollment and at the beginning of each new enrollment year.

AGES

Our infant/toddler program accepts children at six weeks.

Children between ages two and five can be enrolled in our preschool program. A kindergarten classroom is available for those who are ready for a more academic program.

A before- and after-school service meets the needs of children from age six to twelve. If required, our school van will take these children to their elementary school in the morning and pick them up again in the afternoon.

HOURS

Orchard Valley Child Care Center is open from 6 A.M. until 6 P.M. Monday through Friday.

FEES

Fees are payable at the beginning of each month and are based on the number of hours the child attends. A child may be enrolled for a half or full day, two to five days each week. A fee schedule will be sent to you upon request.

(Picture of a child)

Orchard Valley Child Care Center is a member of the Preschool Owners Association.

In 1988, the school was accredited by the National Association of Schools for Young Children.

After visiting the classrooms and displays, the visitors should have ample opportunity to ask questions. Staff members should be available to talk about the program or to answer questions. Have a guest book near the entrance. Ask guests for their addresses, telephone numbers, and comments. These names can then be added to the general mailing list.

Display your brochures in a prominent place. If you don't have a brochure, pre-

Figure 17–6　A school shows its best at open house.

pare a simple one-page statement of philosophy and goals. Either document should include school name, address, phone number, and contact person.

The finest open houses are somewhat wasted efforts if attendance is light. Although individual notices may be sent to people on the mailing list, a more general outreach is required. Simple posters may be placed in local stores. The community newspaper may run a feature, or you can place an ad. Local service clubs may make an announcement. One hint is to start early with your publicity efforts—several weeks is not too long.

Community Activities

Involvement in community activities is another way to make your school known. Some schools are planned to serve as part-time community centers, with adjacent meeting rooms. Others may gradually evolve into centers because of the variety of services offered. Either way, the school becomes known in the community for its openness and friendliness.

You can find ways to bring the community into the school. Services for parents, older people, and older children are recommended. Lectures, films, and discussions centering on childrearing will be attended by community folks as well as parents if they are given ample publicity. Rummage sales, art sales, and used book sales attract people of all ages. You can offer Saturday art classes and general recreational activities for older children.

Plan fund raisers to publicize the school as well as to collect funds. The publicity and program should include facts about the school and stimulate further interest.

Encourage each staff member to join one of the community organizations open to them. Consider such groups as the Chamber of Commerce, community child care task forces, women's organizations, and parent groups. Staff members should do this consciously as school representatives. In reality, it often falls to you, as the director, to carry the major load of community activity. You must not isolate yourself in the school.

You and your staff should also participate in professional meetings, conferences, and workshops. This leads to the exchange of ideas within the early childhood group. Try your hand at writing an article for a magazine for parents or a professional journal. Even though these methods do not reach the public directly, they can be a way of letting others know about your school. Other directors and teachers may have opportunities to refer parents to your school.

You should be aware of free mention or presentation on radio or television if you have innovative programs, or anything new and different. Be aware that media people are constantly searching for human interest stories, and few topics are as intriguing to the public as young children's activities. But you must go to them and sensitize them to the many possibilities open. A news release to the local media (you should have a list) is the first step. A telephone call is often necessary as a follow-up.

Some directors find promotion of their school to be somewhat distasteful. When you have a high-quality program, you should have no regret in sharing it with your community. Good publicity must be worked for diligently. Bad publicity may come unbidden. If the positive factors have been emphasized over the years, the negative may not matter. Effective public relations are another one of your almost endless jobs. The final motivation is that it is absolutely essential as part of running a successful business.

SUMMARY

As the role of the parent has changed, so has the role of the school varied to compensate.

Parent involvement in the school yields benefits to the school and to the parent.

The ways in which parents may become part of the school are many and varied.

There are also limits on what the school may expect of the parent.

Techniques for encouraging participation are limited only by the ingenuity of the school; they may begin with initial contact.

Sustaining interest is as difficult as stimulating it. A major incentive and focus is the welfare of the child.

One of the major aims of parent education is better understanding of the child and of themselves.

State specific goals for parent education that are consonant with the total philosophy of the school.

A great many specific activities lead directly to a greater understanding of the child: orientation meeting, child observations, lectures or panels, films and tapes, workshops, and active classroom participation.

Use routine conferences as a primary means of parent education.

One of the best forms of public relations is a group of satisfied parents. However, other methods of advertising may be used effectively.

The physical appearance of the school should be as attractive as possible.

Telephone answering, especially with regard to first contact, must be as pleasant as can be managed.

Preparation for visiting groups should expose them to the best the school has to offer. The open house as a variant on this can be used effectively.

A tasteful brochure can serve as a fact-filled ambassador.

Involvement with community activities works two ways: Staff members should be involved locally and the community should feel at home in the school.

SELECTED FURTHER READING

Albrecht, K. 1991. "Helping Teachers Grow: Talking with Parents." *Child Care Information Exchange*, 82, 45–47.

Berger, E.H. 1991. *Parents As Partners in Education: The School and Home Working Together*. Columbus, OH: Merrill Macmillan.

Brazelton, T.B., M.D. 1986. *Toddlers and Parents*. New York, NY: Dell Publishing.

Bundy, B.F. 1991. "Fostering Communication Between Parents and Preschools." *Young Children*, 46 (2), 12–17.

Galinsky, E. 1988. "Parents and Teacher-Caregivers: Sources of Tensions, Sources of Support." *Young Children*, 43 (3), 4–12.

Gelfer, J.I., and Perkins, P.G. 1987. "Effective Communication with Parents: A Process for Parent/Teacher Conferences." *Childhood Education*, 64 (1), 19–22.

Honig, A.S. 1975. *Parent Involvement in Early Childhood Education*, rev. ed. Washington, DC: National Association for the Education of Young Children.

Powell, D.R. 1989. *Families and Early Childhood Programs*. Washington, DC: National Association for the Education of Young Children.

Stone, J.G. 1988. *Teacher-Parent Relationships*. Washington, DC: National Association for the Education of Young Children.

STUDENT ACTIVITIES

1. Discuss the degree of parent involvement that you think is appropriate for your school. What factors are important in determining this?
2. Talk to some parents in a Head Start program in your community. How do they feel about involvement?
3. Plan a parent education activity for your school. Use an evaluation form to check its effectiveness.
4. Interview several directors of different kinds of schools. How do their goals for parent education differ?
5. Obtain brochures from at least three different schools in your community. Compare and evaluate.
6. Write a two-paragraph news release concerning a recent event at a preschool.

REVIEW

1. Describe the changing nature of school and home since the end of World War II.
2. What are some of the benefits to the child that parent involvement entails?
3. Are there unreasonable demands that the school may make on the average parents? What are they?
4. What are some of the ways that the school can encourage parent participation?
5. What is the major goal of parent education?
6. What is one of the most tangible forms of public relations?
7. Why is the physical appearance of the school important?
8. List some of the facts to include in a brochure.

GLOSSARY

Parent conference   one-on-one meeting between teacher and parents to discuss child's progress or to resolve problems.

Parent education   activities designed to help parents become better informed about child rearing and family life.

Parent involvement   sharing in the education of their children through participation in school activities.

18

Regulations and Child Abuse Laws

OBJECTIVES

After studying this chapter, the student should be able to:
- State the reasoning behind state regulation of preschools.
- Tell what is generally covered by licensing regulations.
- Describe the accreditation process.
- List several categories of child abuse.
- Explain how child abuse may be prevented.
- Cite a few laws pertaining to child care.

Throughout this book we have referred to the increasing numbers of children who spend their days in family day care homes, preschools, or day care centers. Many children enter a child care setting in infancy and continue well into the elementary school years. This fact makes the subject of regulation of these programs a fitting topic for the final chapter. Regulation is primarily achieved through licensing, but other laws and ordinances apply as well.

Parents who look for day care should feel secure that there are regulations designed to protect their child. The National Association for the Education of Young Children, in their "Position Statement on Licensing," advocates regulation of all forms of out-of-home care. There are several reasons for that position. First, children usually do not tell about neglect or maltreatment they receive while away from home. Either they are afraid, or they have no basis for judging what is good care, and what is not. Second, children are extremely vulnerable. During the early years, when they are developing physically, emotionally, and cognitively, poor conditions can adversely affect them for the rest of their lives. Lastly, children cannot form a powerful lobby to stand up for their rights. Others must do that for them.

Unfortunately, the existence of licensing guidelines does not always ensure that the best possible conditions for children will be provided. Lack of money to monitor programs properly is a serious defect in the system. Most schools are visited once a year, if that often. During the rest of the year, infractions can exist without anyone knowing about them. Parents can help to prevent that by knowing what the regulations are in their state and reporting any deviations.

While a primary concern should be to keep children safe, businesses and organizations that provide child care also have a right to protection from unwanted intrusion. Regulations should not be so stringent that it is difficult or impossible to operate. There must always be a balance between protecting the rights of children, and the rights of legitimate operators of businesses.

REGULATION THROUGH LICENSING

Licensing regulations provide a baseline for acceptable care of children. They are meant to be minimum standards below which no program should operate. All states within the United States have licensing regulations, but they vary widely in scope.

Why Regulation?

Licensing requirements should achieve their primary purpose of ensuring adequate, safe care of children. Each state, though, determines what the actual acceptable level should be. Variation from state to state comes from differing community needs. Some differences, however, result from disparate perceptions of what children need, or lack of official recognition of the importance of quality care. Over the years, however, licensing agencies have worked with professionals in early childhood education to raise the standards of acceptable care.

A good regulatory system will benefit those who provide care as well as the children they serve. A license carries with it an official recognition of the importance of the job. It can also be an advantage when recruiting children. Families will feel more secure placing their child in a licensed facility. Parents may benefit in another way because of licensing. Licensing agencies can provide parents with information about standards for quality care that is helpful when they choose a place for their child. On the other hand, facilities can more readily justify the high cost of quality care when parents understand the standards.

Who Is Covered?

Not all programs are covered by licensing. There are some exceptions. In general, those programs that are covered by other regulations do not have to be licensed. Exempted programs might include those covered by state education codes such as the children's centers within public school systems. Laboratory schools in public colleges or universities also fall into this category. Head Start and other federally funded programs have their own standards that are usually higher than the licensing requirements.

Licensing regulations also do not apply to those who care for children of family members in their home. Even family day care homes that care for nonfamily members may not be regulated. Some states register family day care homes rather than include them in licensing procedures. Where this is true, inspection is not required before registration, and the programs are not monitored. Parents are informed of standards and are encouraged to inspect or monitor for themselves.

All other programs must obtain a license before they can begin operation. If you operate a private for-profit school, a church-related program, an employer-sponsored day care center, or a cooperative, you must have a license. Each school within a corporate chain must have its own license. Licenses are awarded for a specified period of time and must be renewed before their expiration date.

We suggested in an earlier chapter that when you first begin planning your "ideal" school you contact your state's licensing agencies. You will be given a copy of the licensing guidelines and an application packet. The guidelines provide you information to use as you design your school and choose an appropriate building. The application packet includes all the paperwork that must be completed.

The application process entails obtaining clearances for your building, getting staff fingerprinted, and compiling records. You should allow three to six months to complete these tasks. When you have completed all these requirements, the final step before opening your school will be to submit the application. An on-site inspection will be made to determine whether you have met all the specifications. If not, a period of time will be allowed for you to do so.

Licenses are usually awarded for a year. Another on-site visit will be made before a new license can be given. In addition to renewal, most licensing regulations include methods of enforcement. If the licensing agency makes an unannounced visit to your school and finds infractions, you will receive a notice of noncompliance. You as the licensee will be given a period of time to rectify the problems. If they have not been rectified when another inspection is made, a fine can be levied. Schools that do not obtain a license, or operate with an expired license, may be closed by legal means.

What Is Covered by Licensing?

In general, licensing regulations are directed toward conditions that affect the health and safety of children. Statements tend to be broad and general in content to fit a variety of situations. Schools and day care centers can be found in converted warehouses, storefronts, churches, or residences. It is unrealistic to expect that requirements that are too specific could apply in all these settings. With general statements, those who monitor programs can interpret the regulations to fit the needs of each school.

In general, licensing regulations in your area may cover some or all of the following topics:

- *Admission procedures and enrollment records*.
- *General administrative procedures*.
- *Amount of physical space*, both indoors and outdoors.

- *Equipment*—usually general statements requiring that it be appropriate for the age and number of children and that it provide for their developmental needs.
- *Food services and nutrition*—requiring that children be served nutritious meals that are prepared under safe conditions.
- *Health procedures*—requiring that preadmission health reports of children be on file, that health records are maintained, that sick children be isolated, that emergency medical care of children is provided.
- *Safety procedures*—providing for the safe storage of cleaning supplies or any other harmful materials, safe maintenance of equipment and building, fire and disaster procedures.
- *Program*—requiring that the daily schedule offer opportunities for children to engage in activities that promote their growth and development, that there be time for rest and taking care of their physical needs.
- *Staff*—specifying the number of staff required for the number of children served, the qualifications of all staff members, personnel procedures and records.
- *Discipline*—prohibiting certain kinds of punishment, encouraging the use of positive means of disciplining children.
- *Transportation*—requiring safe maintenance of vehicles used to transport children, methods to ensure children's safety while in transit, and the qualifications of drivers.
- *Parent involvement*—requiring that parents be included in planning for their children, serve on advisory boards, be given materials and information about the program's goals and policies, have contact with staff through conferences.

Some states have now included additional guidelines for those who care for infants and elementary school children. Many of the same topics as those already listed will be covered, with specifications suitable for these ages levels.

For infants, the following areas may be added:
- Specifications for sleeping equipment.
- Provision for storage, preparation of food, feeding procedures.
- Provision for diapering, including equipment needed and procedures to follow.
- Specifications for general sanitation procedures.
- Procedures for meeting children's developmental needs—toilet training, introduction of solid foods.
- Inclusion of parents in planning.

For older children:
- Specification of a play area separate from the younger children in a school.
- Special equipment or furniture appropriate for older children.
- Safety procedures for swimming pool activities and field trips.

Related Regulations

As part of the licensing process, many areas require that schools, day care centers, and family day care homes comply with some local ordinances. Your school may need to meet *building and fire safety requirements and sanitation codes* before a license can be awarded. Each of these may be administered by different departments of local government, requiring separate visits from inspectors. In addition, *zoning regulations* limit the areas in which a school or family day care home can operate.

UPGRADE OF THE QUALITY OF PROGRAMS

Once your school is in operation, one of your basic functions as manager of your school or day care center will be to monitor and control the quality of your program. Licensing guidelines are a base, a minimum standard. You may wish to go beyond the minimum. In 1982, the National Association for the Education of Young Children (NAEYC) instituted an accreditation service to facilitate the process.

Accreditation of Schools

The NAEYC set up the National Academy of Early Childhood Programs to administer the accreditation process. Any group program serving children from birth through the elementary years can be accredited. Programs already accredited or in the process include: half-day or full-day church-related programs; parent cooperatives; public school prekindergartens and kindergartens; Montessori programs; Head Start centers; laboratory schools; for-profit child care centers; and hospital-affiliated centers.

The system is voluntary and involves a three-step process: self-study by the director, teachers, and parents; validation visits by trained professionals; and an accreditation decision by a team of early childhood experts. Schools can pace the length of time involved in completing the process, but it usually takes from four to eighteen months.

The self-study step is the critical element of the accreditation process. After paying a fee and receiving the Accreditation Manual, the director, teachers, and parents rate the quality of the program in ten different categories. Upon the completion of the self-study, a final report is prepared and the results are reported to the Academy. Academy personnel review the materials to determine whether the information is complete or whether further material is needed.

The categories of center operations that are covered by the accreditation process are the following:
- Interactions among staff and children.
- Curriculum.
- Staff-parent interactions.
- Staff qualifications and development.
- Administration.
- Staffing patterns.
- Physical environment.
- Health and safety.

- Nutrition and food service.
- Evaluation processes.

When the director feels the center is ready, an on-site validation visit is requested. One or more validators appointed by the Academy may visit a site depending on the size of the center. The purpose of the visit is to verify that the day-to-day operations of the center are as described in the self-study report. Validators meet with the director, observe in classrooms, and interview staff. At the end of the visit, validators and the director meet to discuss the results of the validation. At this time, the director can submit additional information concerning any nonvalidated criteria.

The final step involves an Accreditation Commission consisting of three people chosen from a diverse group of early childhood professionals. The commission reviews the information provided by validators and can decide to grant accreditation, or to defer it until further improvements are made. If deferment is decided, reasons are given for deferment and specific recommendations are made. Deferred centers can appeal, and if there is just cause, another commission will be assigned. Accreditation is valid for three years. During this time, centers must submit annual reports. Before expiration, centers must repeat the evaluation process.

Those who have already been involved in the accreditation process report that the expense and time involved are worth it. Directors point to the improvement in staff development, morale, and communication among staff members. Parents seem to feel a greater sense of trust in the school after having been involved in the accreditation process. In some situations, accreditation is being used as a selling point for funding requests. Even if you know your school already has a high-quality program, accreditation can help to achieve recognition in your community.

Information about accreditation can be obtained by writing to:

National Academy of Early Childhood Programs
1834 Connecticut Avenue, NW
Washington, DC 20009-5785
(202) 328-2601
(800) 424-2460

Accreditation of Teachers and Caregivers

Upgrading the quality of programs can also come about through the credentialing of teachers and caregivers. The Child Development Associate credential is a nationally recognized credential for early childhood personnel. It is based on the achievement of a series of competencies and is available to those who work in centers or in family day care homes.

For more information about the CDA credential, contact:

Council for Early Childhood Professional Recognition
1718 Connecticut Avenue, NW, Suite 500
Washington, DC 20009-1148
(202) 265-9090
(800) 424-4310

CHILD ABUSE

Spectacular stories of children being abused in their preschools or day care centers have sharpened the public's awareness of this problem. As a result, many parents express fears for their children and may be reluctant to place them in a school. In addition, teachers and caregivers have become afraid to touch, hug, or hold children for fear they will be accused. These fears are unfounded. Studies show children are much more likely to be molested or abused in their own homes than in an organized child care setting.

All states have laws relating to child abuse. These are designed to protect both children and adults who care for children. If you don't know the laws in your state, contact the attorney general's office. Be informed yourself and educate your staff.

Several categories of abuse are recognized:

- *Physical abuse*—a child is physically injured by other than accidental means. Severe corporal punishment may be classified as abuse.
- *Physical neglect*—failure to provide a child with adequate food, shelter, clothing, protection, supervision, and medical or dental care.
- *Emotional abuse*—excessive verbal assaults, continuous negative responses, and constant family discord may add up to emotional abuse. These cases are extremely difficult to prove and to prosecute.
- *Emotional deprivation*—deprivation suffered by children when their parents fail to supply normal experiences that help children to feel loved, wanted, and secure.
- *Sexual abuse and exploitation*—any sexual activity between an adult and child. When the activity occurs between blood-related persons, it is called incest. Included in sexual abuse is the use of children for making pornographic pictures or films.

Causes of Child Abuse

Although it is often believed that most child abusers are poor, uneducated, or emotionally disturbed, this is not true. Studies show that only one in ten abusers can be classified as "disturbed." Most abusers are not very different from any other parents. They love their children and want what is best for them, but something happens to trigger abuse.

According to several studies, adults are more likely to abuse children when the following factors exist:

- If they were abused as children themselves.
- If they are young—abuse is more frequent when the parents are under age twenty.
- If they are isolated from others, with few friends or nearby relatives.
- If they are victims or perpetrators of spouse abuse.
- If they use drugs or are alcoholics.
- If they have experienced stress caused by family problems, divorce, loss of a job, unwanted pregnancy.

- If they live in crowded conditions, with little privacy.
- If they have low self-esteem.
- If they have difficulty controlling anger.
- If they have unrealistic expectations for children's behavior.

Recognition of Abuse

Both parents and early childhood professionals must learn to recognize the signs of abuse. Because the idea of any kind of mistreatment of children is so repugnant, there is a tendency to overlook the indications. Yet, children say and do things that should warn us. Often, though, it is only after abuse is finally recognized that we can look back and say, "Yes, I did see some things that made me wonder." You and your staff should be familiar with signs that may indicate a child has been physically, emotionally, or sexually abused. Parent education programs should provide the same kinds of information to parents.

Your state attorney general's office or licensing agency can probably supply you with information about what might be suspicious. If not, the following summary should be helpful.

Physical Abuse

Physical abuse might be suspected when you see the following injuries on a child:
- *Burns*—burns in places that would not be expected as the result of accident (e.g., buttocks, shoulder blades, abdomen).
- *Linear marks*—wrap-around marks made by a strap, belt, or electrical cord.
- *Bruises*—multiple bruises with different colors indicating various stages of healing, bruises on many parts of the body including the genitals.
- *Lacerations*—multiple wounds or locations of wounds in unexpected places. Mouth lacerations, for instance, may indicate a bottle nipple has been jammed into the baby's mouth.
- *Fractures*—any fracture in an infant under twelve months should be suspect.

FYI

In 1989, 2.4 million children were reported abused or neglected. This is a 10 percent increase over 1988 and nearly 150 percent since 1979. The National Committee for Prevention of Child Abuse links substance abuse, poverty, lack of medical care, homelessness, and domestic violence to the increase in abuse of children.

Source: The State of America's Children, 1991. *Children's Defense Fund.*

One of the most important grounds for further investigation is when a child tells you "My daddy hurt me" or "My mommy spanks me with a belt." Take what the child says seriously.

Physical Neglect

Physical neglect is the failure of a parent or caregiver to provide adequate care and can be suspected when:
- There are unsanitary conditions in the home or child care site.
- There is inadequate heat or there are potentially unsafe conditions.
- Food is inadequate or not sufficiently nutritious.
- The child lacks proper clothing for the weather, or clothing is unclean.
- The child lacks proper medical or dental care.
- A young child is left at home or unsupervised for any period of time.

Emotional Abuse

Although some of the signs of emotional abuse are the kinds of behavior you occasionally see in all children, the extent, the frequency, or the duration of the behavior should alert you. Abuse might be suspected if any of the following behaviors continue for a long period of time, or are the only ways that a child behaves:
- The child is withdrawn, depressed, or apathetic.
- The child "acts out" or is often disruptive.
- The child is overly rigid, is afraid to misbehave, or fails to do what is expected.
- The child shows signs of emotional disturbance such as repetitive movements, lack of verbal or physical communication with others.

Children sometimes reveal emotional abuse when they comment on their own behavior. They may say "My mommy tells me I'm bad" or "My daddy says I can't do anything right." Listen. Take the child seriously.

Emotional Deprivation

Emotional deprivation is the most difficult to judge, but should be suspected if you see the following:
- The child refuses to eat, or eats very little.
- The child is not able to do things that would be expected of the age level—walking, talking.
- The child may have exaggerated fears.
- The child is frequently aggressive or shows other antisocial behaviors.
- The child is abnormally withdrawn or sad, or does not respond to others.
- The child constantly seeks attention from any adult, even strangers who come into the school.

Sexual Abuse

Children go through periods of being curious about their own bodies and those of others. They have times when they masturbate or ask about how you get babies. Teachers and parents are often embarrassed by this behavior. They don't want to see or hear it. As a result, signs of sexual molestation sometimes go completely unrecognized. Children, too, learn to be secretive about what happens to them when they see how others react. In addition, abusers often frighten children by telling them that terrible things will happen to them if they tell anyone.

Sexual abuse can remain hidden for a long time. It should be suspected, though, if you see the following signs:

- The child has bruising or inflammation of the anus or the genitals.
- There is a discharge or blood in the child's underwear.
- The child has unusual interest and awareness of sexual activities. Sometimes young children play out sexual scenes in the dramatic play area.
- The child is particularly seductive with adults, touching their breast or genitals.
- The child seems fearful of an adult or is afraid to talk about that adult.
- The child is the victim of other kinds of abuse.

Children probably least often reveal sexual abuse by talking about it. They may not even have the words to express to others what has been done to them. If they have been threatened by the abuser, they will be even more reluctant to tell their secrets. Responsive adults who are willing to let children reveal their stories in their own way can find out a great deal.

When to Report Abuse

Teachers and others who have close contact with children are in a unique position to see signs of abuse. Because of this, they are legally mandated to report suspected incidents. They are not required to prove abuse and, if none is found, are protected from any retribution. On the other hand, if mandated individuals know of abuse and fail to report it, they may be liable for fines or imprisonment.

The law is clear, but the moral dilemma facing a teacher who suspects abuse is not always clear. Suspicion of abuse can be extremely upsetting for parents or for school personnel. The normal reaction is to become angry, to feel guilt, or to want the perpetrator to be punished immediately. Everyone involved must remain calm. When adults overreact, harm to the child may be intensified. The opposite reaction may also occur. Adults can convince themselves that they must have been wrong, that nothing really happened. Nothing is done, and that may lead to further harm to the child.

So how do you know when to report? Do not report every time you see some signs of disturbance in children. Many times that is normal, transitory behavior. *Do report* when you have enough evidence to convince yourself that there is reasonable suspicion to warrant further investigation. Obviously, if there are signs that a child's life may be in danger, don't wait. Report it immediately.

When you see any of the signs listed in previous paragraphs, make a record. Write down what you observed, what the child said, or what the parent said. If you see bruises, burns, or lacerations on a child, take a picture of them. Photographs can be taken without the parents' consent as long as they are not used for any other purpose.

If the injuries you observe don't meet the usual criteria for abuse, keep a record anyway. Over time, you may find that the same kind of injuries keep recurring. A pattern of abuse may emerge that can be reported.

If you are not sure, talk to others. Teachers should talk to their director; directors can check with the teachers' observations. You can also call a child abuse agency or hotline in your area. They can often help you to sort out your impressions. Call the child protective agency in your area, as well. Workers there can often tell you if what you have seen is a reportable offense.

When you are ready to report, telephone the local child protective services, the sheriff's department, or the police department. Be prepared with the information that will probably be needed. You will have to have the following information:

- Child's name, address, and age.
- Where the child is at the present time.
- Your observations, descriptions of injuries.
- Information that led you to believe abuse has occurred.
- Parents' names, address.
- If the child is in immediate danger, make that clear to the person to whom you are reporting.

You will probably be required to follow your verbal report with a written report within a specified period of time. Forms for the report will be available from law enforcement or protective services agencies.

Many teachers and directors ask whether they should tell the parents about the report. Opinions vary. If someone other than the parents is the abuser, the parents may be relieved that you have discovered what has been occurring. They will welcome your support and concern for their child. If one of the parents is the abuser, you are likely to be the target of tremendous anger. There may also be denial at first and even accusations that the abuse occurred at school, not at home. The parents may immediately withdraw the child from your school. Be prepared for any of these reactions.

The discovery of abuse is a traumatic experience for parents, teachers, and child. You, as director, will have to remain calm and sympathetic. It may lessen the trauma for everyone involved if you can do this. The child will need to know that others understand, that they will be supportive. Whether the parents are the abusers or not, they, too, need to have your support through this experience. Also, you can see that the family gets support from others in the medical, legal, and child advocacy systems.

Your staff will probably need help in dealing with the abuse. They must be cautioned to respect the privacy of the child and family. Information about the abuse should never be discussed with anyone not directly involved in the incident. They should try not to be judgmental toward the parents.

Staff may also need an opportunity to talk about their own feelings of anger or guilt. If the child remains in your school, staff may react by being overprotective. They should be cautioned that the child will recover more quickly if helped to follow regular routines. Your sensitive handling of an abuse situation will help everyone involved to recover.

Unfortunately, because of the upheaval discovery causes, a large number of child abuse cases never get reported. Encourage your staff to see that it is their moral, as well as legal, obligation to protect children. When cases are not reported, there is the possibility that other children will be victimized.

Abuse Allegations at School

You may be faced with having one of your staff members accused of abuse. Reports may come from parents or from other staff members. If the report first goes to the licensing agency, it will be referred to the police department. If the police department receives the first complaint, they will report to the licensing agency.

The two agencies will work together to complete an investigation of the report. The staff member should receive appropriate legal representation before being interviewed by the police. Although no one is required to answer questions, encourage your staff to cooperate. In this way, a quicker resolution to the problem can occur.

Prevention

Schools can play a vital role in the prevention of abuse.

First, you can do a great deal to lessen the possibility of abuse by staff members by:

- Developing hiring procedures that carefully screen applicants—most states require a fingerprint check.
- Checking the person's references carefully.
- Planning and implementing in-service training for new employees, ongoing staff development for others.
- Adequately supervising staff, pairing new employees with experienced ones.
- Holding regular staff meetings to discuss problems with children and parents, or among staff members.
- Developing clear personnel policies regarding methods of disciplining children.
- Allowing staff members the means for alleviating fatigue and burnout. (Give adequate breaks, have reasonable staff/child ratios, pay adequate salaries, give positive reinforcement.)

Second, your school and your staff can be extremely effective in helping parents manage the stresses of parenthood that might lead to abuse. Some of the things that can be done to help parents are the following:

- The school or day care center can become part of an "extended family" that provides support.
- Teachers and caregivers can educate parents about what to expect of children at different age levels.
- Teachers and caregivers can act as models to help parents find more effective ways of interacting with their children.
- Teachers and caregivers can provide an outlet for parents to express some of the frustrations involved in parenting.
- Teachers and caregivers can share with parents the joys of watching children grow and change.

Third, you can do a great deal to lessen the chances of misunderstandings that lead to accusations of abuse at school. In your work with parents, the following will be helpful:

- Educate parents about child abuse—what causes it, signs that may indicate abuse.
- Establish an open-door policy in your school—welcome parents' visits at any time, without an appointment.
- Share your schools' discipline policies with parents.
- Establish a caring relationship with parents—listen to parents' concerns, answer parents' questions.

Prevention of child abuse is certainly a preferred tactic to reporting and punishing abuse. As more and more children are in group settings at earlier ages, the role of the school becomes vital to prevention. Educate yourself, your staff, and your parents. Although there is no sure cure for child abuse, the knowledge and skills of those who care for children can help.

LAWS PERTAINING TO CHILD CARE SETTINGS

Most child care centers must meet federal, state, and local laws pertaining to employer/employee relations. Some small schools may be exempt, but it is a good idea to comply wherever possible. In that way, it is easier to expand the school in the future. If your school contracts with federal, state, or local government agencies, you may have to comply with some special requirements.

Educate yourself as much as possible about laws with which you must comply. Write to appropriate agencies for information. Consult an attorney to find out about state and local laws. The scope of this book cannot thoroughly address every geographical area. The following information is a broad outline of the issues.

Personnel Policies

Good personnel policies, as discussed in Chapter 7, are necessary to ensure the smooth operation of a school. In addition, personnel procedures may be covered in some laws. Some areas that are covered by federal laws are:

- Equal Pay Act of 1963 requires equal pay for men and women performing similar work.

- Fair Labor Standards Act of 1938 (1972 Amendment) sets a minimum wage, equal pay, and recordkeeping requirements.
- Civil Rights Act of 1964—Title VII (amended in 1972) prohibits discrimination because of sex, race, color, religion, or national origin.
- Rehabilitation Act of 1973 prohibits job discrimination because of a handicap. It further requires affirmative action to hire and advance handicapped workers.
- Vietnam Era Veteran's Readjustment Assistance Act of 1974 prohibits job discrimination and requires affirmative action to hire and advance qualified Vietnam veterans.
- Executive Orders 11246 and 11375 require an affirmative action program for all federal contractors and subcontractors whose contract exceeds $10,000.
- The Age Discrimination Act of 1967 (amended in 1978) prohibits discrimination against persons forty to seventy years of age in hiring practices for any employment.

Salary Procedures

Some laws require or prohibit certain procedures related to employee salaries. Refer to the following:

- Federal Wage Garnishment Law restricts the amount of an employee's wages that may be deducted in any one week for garnishment procedures. It further restricts the amount that can be deducted when an employee is discharged because of garnishment.
- Social Security Act of 1935 and Federal Insurance Contributions Act provide for retirement, disability, burial, and survivor benefits to eligible employees. They require deductions from salary plus matching contribution from employer.
- Federal Income Tax Withholding requires the employer to collect employee's income tax and deposit it in a federal depository. Failure to comply with this law is a criminal offense.

On-the-Job Safety

Federal Law regulates any conditions that might affect the safety and health of employees:

- The Occupational Safety and Health Act of 1970 requires employers to provide a safe place to work.
- Most states require employers to carry Worker's Compensation Insurance to ensure injured workers will receive necessary medical care and be compensated for loss of income.

Sources of Information

For more information regarding laws that may affect your school, write to the following:

U.S. Equal Employment Opportunity Commission
2401 E Street, NW
Washington, DC 20706

Employment Standards Administration
Office of Federal Contract Compliance Program
Third and Constitution Avenues, NW
Washington, DC 20210

United States Social Security Administration
6401 Security Boulevard
Baltimore, MD 21235

U.S. Department of Labor
Occupational Safety and Health Administration
Room S-2315
200 Constitution Avenue, NW
Washington, DC 20216

U.S. Department of Labor
Employment Standards Administration
Wage and Hours Division
Washington, DC 20210

Posting Employee Information

Certain information must be posted in conspicuous places used by employees.
Both federal and state laws govern the kinds of information needed. Check with
your attorney for compliance within your state. Federal laws require the following:

- Minimum wage and maximum hours—obtain from U.S. Department of
  Labor, Wage and Hours Division.
- Equal employment regulations—obtain from nearest branch of Federal Equal
  Employment Opportunity Commission.
- Age discrimination laws—obtain from nearest branch of Federal Equal Em-
  ployment Opportunity Commission.
- Annual summary of specified injuries and illnesses—obtain information from
  U.S. Department of Labor, Occupational Safety and Health Administration.

U.S. Census figures show that within a few years there will be 23 million children
under the age of six. As more and more mothers enter the work force, there must
be places to care for these children, yet quality child care is already in short supply.
As the nation tries to fill the gap, careful thought must be invested in the issues of
regulation. Children must be adequately protected, and quality care must never be
sacrificed for other considerations. On the other hand, potential operators must not
feel overly constrained with laws and regulations. It requires a delicate balance.

SUMMARY

Licensing regulations issued by the various states are designed to protect children
enrolled in out-of-home care.

Almost all programs are covered by licensing; the major exceptions are laboratory schools, child care centers in public schools, and Head Start and other federal programs.

Licensing can be a fairly lengthy and complex process; it is also for a specific period of time. In general, licensing covers admissions, administrative procedures, allotted physical space, equipment, food service, health and safety, staff, discipline, transportation, and parent involvement. Licensing for infant and older children programs includes other facets.

An accreditation (certification) process has been initiated by the National Academy of Early Childhood Programs. The voluntary process consists of self-study, a visit by a professional team, and a written evaluation.

Prominent press coverage has highlighted child abuse recently. Abuse can be of several kinds: physical abuse and neglect, emotional abuse and deprivation, or sexual exploitation. There are many causes.

Certain physical or emotional results occur after abuse. Your staff should be able to recognize each kind. It is often difficult to determine whether to report child abuse. It is always acceptable and reasonable to keep a record.

Since much emotion is encountered in child abuse situations, the most consistent attitude to take is one of calm objectivity.

There are proven ways to prevent child abuse in a preschool. It is the responsibility of the director to inform the staff.

Many federal, state, and local laws pertain to child care. There are numerous sources, and most of them are listed here. It is, again, the responsibility of the director to inform the staff and parents of these laws.

SELECTED FURTHER READING

Bredekamp, S., ed. 1991. *Accreditation Criteria & Procedures of the National Academy of Early Childhood Programs*. Washington, DC: National Association for the Education of Young Children.

Finkelhor, D., Williams, L.M., and Burns, N. 1988. *Nursery Crimes: Sexual Abuse in Day Care*. Newbury Park, CA: Sage Publications.

Morgan, G. 1983. "Child Day Care Policy in Chaos." In E. Zigler, S. Kagan, and E. Klugman, eds. *Children, Families, and Government: Perspectives on American Social Policy*, 249–265. New York: Cambridge University Press.

Phillips, C.B. 1990. "The Child Development Associate Program: Entering a New Era." *Young Children*, 45 (3), 24–27.

Pizzo, R.D. 1993. "Parent Empowerment and Child Care Regulation." *Young Children*, 48 (6), 9–12.

Whitebook, M., Howes, C., and Phillips, D., eds. 1989. *Working for Quality Child Care*. An early childhood education text from the child care employees project. Berkeley, CA: Child Care Employee Project.

STUDENT ACTIVITIES

1. Contact the licensing agency in your state and request guidelines for starting an early childhood center. Review the regulations to find out if the areas covered are similar to those discussed in this chapter. Are regulations for infant/toddler programs and after-school care included?
2. Schedule a visit to an accredited center in your community and an interview with the director. Ask the director to describe the accreditation experience and its effect on staff and parents. Was it a positive experience? What changes were undertaken as a result?
3. Write a short paper on child abuse. Focus on whether media coverage of high-visibility cases has changed attitudes of early childhood personnel. Are they more cautious about how they interact with children? Are they more aware of the signs of abuse in children in their care?
4. Visit an agency in your community that works with families where abuse has occurred. What is the agency doing to help families?

REVIEW

1. In what ways do licensing regulations benefit early childhood centers and families?
2. Which of the following child care facilities must be licensed?
    a. Child care centers in public schools
    b. Family day care home
    c. Head Start centers
    d. Private for-profit school
3. List the topics that are covered under licensing guidelines.
4. Accreditation involves a three-step process. What are the steps?
5. What is the Child Development Associate credential?
6. What are the causes of child abuse?
7. List the five kinds of child abuse.
8. Describe the procedures for reporting child abuse.
9. Discuss the role of a school in preventing abuse.
10. Name and describe three federal laws that pertain to employees in child care centers.

GLOSSARY

Accreditation   national program for validating the quality of early childhood programs.

CDA   Child Development Associate credential that certifies the holder has achieved a level of competency.

Child abuse   serious harm to children in the form of physical, emotional, or sexual mistreatment.

Appendix A
Computerized Data Management

Since the last edition of this text, there has been a substantial increase in the number of early childhood centers that have instituted computerized record management systems. The most significant reason is a *pressing need to become more business oriented* in order to keep up with inflationary costs and economic hard times. Directors of programs have to continually weigh expenses in relation to the amount of income that is generated. This means keeping an accurate account of money that comes in and where it is spent. This can certainly be done more quickly and efficiently when records are computerized. Secondly, *many schools are part of a system*, operating more than one facility. Computers can link one center to another, facilitating enrollment and financial record keeping. Thirdly, there are *more choices of software programs* from which to select a package that suits the needs and pocketbook of each center. New programs have been developed and there are updates of earlier ones. Perhaps, the last reason is a *greater acceptance of computers as a necessary tool* for managing information.

Throughout the text there was frequent reference to the use of a computer for several purposes: budgets, correspondence, enrollment records, etc. Any computer will do these tasks, but when the decision to purchase a computer is finally made, often the first question that is asked is "Should I buy an Apple/Macintosh or an IBM?" There is no easy answer except to say that at this time there are more child care center management software systems written for the IBM than for the Apple products.

An explanation of the differences will be helpful. First, programs written for an Apple/Macintosh will not operate on an IBM-type computer and vice versa. Although the cost of computers has decreased considerably in the last few years, usually Apple computers are more expensive than IBM. The reason for this is that Apple is the sole manufacturer of this computer. The IBM-type has many makers, including the IBM Corporation. Compaq, Hewlett-Packard, AST, Tandy, and literally dozens of foreign manufacturers produce the so-called IBM clones. They compete with each other fiercely, and as a result, lower prices considerably. Visit computer stores and test computers of several manufacturers. You will probably find that you prefer one over another. Next, investigate software packages before deciding which of the two computer types to purchase. List the kinds of files you want to create. Financial records, enrollment lists, staff attendance, and menu planning are a few possibilities. After you complete your list, contact the software companies. Discuss with them what their program package includes and the costs to install. All but one of the software programs reviewed in this section are marketed as modules. You purchase only the modules you need for your individual operation. You can add other modules as needed. In addition, if you need multi-user and/or networked systems, there are other modules. Evaluate programs before you buy—take advantage of the 30-day or longer money-back guarantee.

Many software companies offer hardware packages as well. If you are a novice to computer use, this may be the way to go. You will know that the hardware and software are guaranteed to work well with each other. This approach is generally more expensive, but it removes much of the hassle from the seemingly awesome task of choosing the hardware. These companies often also provide training at additional charge. However, training may not be necessary if you can spend a period of time learning the program by using the manuals that come with it.

Before making a decision about which software or hardware to choose, there are several categories of information you should gather from each software vendor. They are:

- Ease of use—How much time must be invested to learn to operate the software? Can a novice computer user understand the manuals, or is a training course required before you can even begin? If training will be needed, do they conduct training courses in your area?
- Updates—How often has the program been updated in the past? Will you be informed of updates and how much additional cost you will incur? How successful have updates been, or have there been problems? Will it be necessary to update your hardware each time a program update is purchased?
- Support—What type of support system will the company provide to answer questions? Are there technical persons who are knowledgeable in the use of the program available by telephone? Is telephone support free? Is there an 800 number, or must you pay long-distance telephone charges each time you call?
- Understanding of your business—Do they really understand the unique needs of child care centers? Is their product being used by other centers in your area?
- Expandability—Is the package in modules that can be purchased as needed? What is the cost of a basic package, and then, of each additional module?
- Flexibility—How much flexibility is built into the program? Can you only use forms and information as programmed, or can you change specifications as needed?

During the course of revising this text, I looked at programs that are either nationally advertised for use in schools and child care centers, or were featured at conferences for persons involved in early childhood education. There may be others, but I did not find them. The five IBM-type and one Apple/Macintosh programs are listed alphabetically. All of the software packages provide for the following:

Child/Parent Information. A data base provides for the child's and parent's (guardian's) name, address, phone, Social Security numbers, etc. It also provides capabilities for entering medical information (doctor, dentist, insurance, immunization schedules, and allergies).

Emergency Information. Persons authorized for child pick-up is included. Enrollment, disenrollment, classes, groups, and birthdays as well as any special information can be accommodated. Rate schedules (hourly, daily, weekly, or other), sliding-scale fees, and third-party co-payers can be recorded. This information, once entered, automatically attaches to the areas identified and does not require reentry. Pertinent information can be accessed as needed.

Scheduling and Attendance. Provides for permanent record of contracted and actual attendance. The check-in/check-out times automatically post actual attendance to this module. Postings to accounts receivable are also automatic. Special events and school holidays are accommodated here. This module simplifies planning and recording of all your resources including employee assignments, late pick-ups, and/or additional hours.

Check-in/Check-out. A time clock is provided to record the child's and employee's check-in and -out times. This information may be automatically transferred to the areas where needed. It can contain provision for parent's *Personal Identification Number* (PIN) to replace cumbersome sign-in/sign-out sheets. This time clock can be either within the computer itself, or an add-on unit connected remotely to the computer. Add-on units are at extra cost, but the computer is then freed for use by authorized personnel only.

Meal Planning. Meal planning and food program reporting capabilities are included in these systems. This module covers food purchasing as well as dispensing. You can track meals served to each student or staff member. A food purchasing list can be generated from a menu and the number of children of various ages to be served for a given period of time. Some programs actually print out USDA forms that can be used for reimbursement claims.

Accounting Features. Accounts Receivable, Accounts Payable, and General Ledger are part of these systems. Information from the other modules is automatically entered into the appropriate account. Any of these may be viewed or printed when needed. Most programs will print checks and post to the appropriate account.

Personnel Management Features. In addition to the standard name, address, Social Security number, and other personal information for employees, this module keeps track of wages and benefits, schedules, leave, and time keeping. Provision is made for employee observation and evaluation as well. Employee development, such as education and certification, is another provision.

Payroll. All payroll information is kept in this module. All that is required of the administrator is to enter the hours worked—the system does the rest. The system will calculate all deductions and taxes, print paychecks. W-2 forms, Social Security forms, and others.

Letter Writing/Mailing Labels. A word processing module allows for letter writing, bulletin preparation, and other needs such as notices, reminders, announcements, etc. It allows preparation of standard letters and automatically merges the names with the letters to personalize each one. It has capabilities for preparing mailing labels for any group listing.

Reports. Various kinds of reports may be produced. In addition to the standard accounting information: family and child history reports, receipts, shopping lists, menus, tax statements for the center as well as the parent, and attendance reports, etc. These reports can be produced daily, weekly, monthly, or as needed.

The software programs available at this time are the following:

CCM-Turbo, version 4.0, is reviewed in this section. **CCM-Turbo Plus** will be available in the near future. The company promises unlimited user support at absolutely no additional charge.

Available from:
Personalized Software, Inc.
P.O. Box 66
Ashland, OR 97520
1-800-553-2312

Child Care 2000, version 2.0, is the program reviewed in this section. A unique feature of this program is a *bar-code reader* for quick check-in/check-out cards for children. Each person authorized to drop off or pick up a child is issued an encoded card. A simple "pass of the card" and the information is automatically recorded by the computer.

Available from:
Care Systems, Inc.
P.O. Box 1530
6543-C Commerce Parkway
Dublin, OH 43017-1530
1-800-875-5002

Child Quest, version 2.0. This is the only system reviewed that includes all modules at just one price. This certainly makes the package less expensive than the others; however, as a new product on the market (at this writing), it does not have a "track record." The company does, however, offer a 30-day, money-back guarantee. This system also offers an optional keypad check-in system used for time clock functions for both staff and children. The program is available with either a single user or multiuser license, making it possible to link several computers together. Users are invited to suggest improvements for future releases.

Available from:
Yore Software Systems, Inc.
P.O. Box 277
Pinellas Park, FL 34664-0277
1-800-220-9673

EZ-CARE, version 13. This system is flexible since it comes with customized entry screens that match your application forms. The program is easy to use and requires no previous experience or training. (There is also **MacCare** for an Apple Macintosh computer, but I did not review it.)

Available from: SofterWare, Inc.
                               540 Pennsylvania Ave., Ste. 200
                               Fort Washington, PA 19034
                               1-800-848-3279

Maggey, version 3.2, was reviewed. The outstanding feature of Maggey is the integration of a special keypad and monitor devoted exclusively to a time clock function. It can be positioned in the entrance area of a school for quick check-in and check-out of children. The dealer will sell complete systems (hardware with software programs already installed).

Available from: Childcare Management Services, Inc.
                          2532 E. Fountain
                          Mesa, AR 85213
                          1-800-462-4439

Private Advantage, version 1.6L, was reviewed. This is the only program designed solely for an Apple/Macintosh computer. This version indicated that some of the modules such as a time clock, a flexible schedule manager, a finance manager, and a meal manager were not available at this time but were planned to be released in the near future.

Available from: Mt. Taylor Programs
                          1305 Dutton Ave.
                          Santa Rosa, CA 94501
                          1-800-238-7015

The above accounts are based on data furnished by the manufacturers at my request, as well as a personal examination of their demonstration programs. Most of these programs would be an acceptable, though expensive, beginning for a computer-oriented start. One recommendation would be to purchase each module separately, starting with the basic child record-keeping one. Not only would this greatly simplify your paperwork, but also would give you an almost painless introduction to working with a computer.

All these programs have elements in common. They substitute cost for expertise. This means that if a user had some in-depth knowledge of computer systems, he or she could convert or write a software program with the same capabilities of these programs at far less cost. But that is true of all computer programs. You pay for someone else's knowledge. In using these preplanned systems, there are trade-offs. The programs use preset forms which you must use. There is some latitude or flexibility in most of them that allows the user to customize most of the forms. The programmer has presumed to know your needs and has furnished them (or not furnished them). Because these programs are written by professionals in the field of child care, they usually provide what you need, and for the most part, are easy to use.

Directors should realistically assess what their own time is worth and how much of it they put into "time-wasting" paperwork. An administrative computer can free valuable time for working with teachers, parents, other staff members, and children. One final word: Do not be persuaded by salespersons to buy the most advanced computer hardware on the market, even though prices have fallen recently. You do not need the very latest, nor the fastest computer, but neither should you buy obsolete equipment. Today's prices for a state-of-the-art, 80486 IBM-compatible computer are no more than the 8088 model sold eight years ago and now obsolete. We would recommend that you consider a laser or an ink-jet printer. They are practically noiseless, and the quality produced is definitely superior. Do not feel alone and helpless, either, when you buy your first computer. There are free or low-cost classes offered for first-time users at most adult schools, community colleges, or university extension centers. Most likely your community has its local "Computer Users' Group" that meets monthly and offers free help and free software to members. Ask at the local library or computer store. If all else fails, the market is flooded with self-help books on how to "get started" in computing. Try Van Wolverton's *Running MS/DOS* from the Microsoft Press for starters.

I hope I have directed you somewhere along the path that leads to "happy computing." Once you get started, you will marvel at having been anywhere else.

—Phyllis Click

Appendix B
Organizations and Sources of Information

Action for Children's Television
46 Austin Street
Newtonville, MA 02160

Administration for Children, Youth and Families
Head Start Division
P.O. Box 1182
Washington, DC 20013

American Academy of Pediatrics
141 Northwest Point Road
Box 927
Elk Grove Village, IL 60007
(800) 433-9016

American Association for Deaf Children
814 Thayer Avenue
Silver Spring, MD 20910
(301) 585-5400

American Foundation for the Blind
15 West 16th Street
New York, NY 10011
(212) 620-2000

American Montessori Society
150 5th Avenue, Suite 203
New York, NY 10011
(212) 924-3209

American Speech-Language-Hearing Association
10801 Rockville Pike
Rockville, MD 20852
(800) 638-8255

Association for Childhood Education International
11501 Georgia Avenue, Suite 315
Wheaton, MD 20902
(800) 423-3563

Association for Children with Learning Disabilities
4156 Library Road
Pittsburgh, PA 15229

Association Montessori International
170 W. Cholfield Road
Rochester, NY 14617-4599
(716) 544-6709

Bank Street College of Education
610 W. 112th Street
New York, NY 10025

Capital Children's Museum
800 3rd Street, NE
Washington, DC 20002

Centers for Disease Control & Prevention
1600 Clifton Road, NE
Atlanta, GA 30333
(404) 639-3534

Child Care Law Center
22 2nd Street, 5th Floor
San Francisco, CA 94105
(405) 495-5498

Child Welfare League of America
440 1st Street, NW
Washington, DC 20001-2085
(202) 638-2952

Child Care Information Exchange
P.O. Box 2890
Redmond, WA 98073

Children's Book Council, Inc.
67 Irving Place
New York, NY 10003

Children's Defense Fund
25 E Street, NW
Washington, DC 20001
(202) 628-8787

Council for Early Childhood Professional Recognition
1718 Connecticut Avenue, NW, Suite 500
Washington, DC 20009-1148
(800) 424-4310

Council for Exceptional Children
1920 Association Drive
Reston, VA 22091-1589
(703) 620-3660

Day Care and Child Development Council of America
1602 17th Street NW
Washington, DC 20009

Director's Network, Child Care Information Exchange
P.O. Box 2890
Redmond, WA 98073-2890
(800) 221-2864

Ecumenical Child Care Network
1119 Daphne Street, #5
New Orleans, LA 70116

ERIC Clearinghouse on Elementary and Early Childhood Education
University of Illinois
805 W. Pennsylvania Avenue
Urbana, IL 61801-4897
(217) 333-1386

ERIC Clearinghouse on Handicapped and Gifted Children
Council for Exceptional Children
1920 Association Drive
Reston, VA 22091-1589
(703) 264-9474

High/Scope Educational Research Foundation
600 N. River Street
Ypsilanti, MI 48198-2898
(313) 485-1169

The Jean Piaget Society
113 Willard Hall Building
College of Education
University of Delaware
Newark, DE 19711

National Association for Child Care Management
104 Sweetwater Hills Drive
Longwood, FL 32779
(305) 862-7825

National Association for the Education of Young Children (NAEYC)
1509 16th Street, NW
Washington, DC 20036
(800) 424-2460

National Association for Family Day Care
725 15th Street, NW, Suite 505
Washington, DC 20005-2201
(202) 347-3356

National Black Child Development Institute
1023 15th Street, NW
Washington, DC 20005
(202) 387-1281

National Center for Clinical Infant Programs
2000 11th Street N., Suite 380
Arlington, VA 22201-2500
(703) 528-4300

National Coalition for Campus Child Care, Inc.
P.O. Box 258
Cascade, WI 53011
(414) 528-7080

National Down Syndrome Society
141 Fifth Avenue
New York, NY 10018
(212) 460-9330

National Institute of Child Health and Human Development
National Institute of Health, Public Health Service
U.S. Department of Health and Human Services
Bethesda, MD 20014

Parents Anonymous
Identification-Treatment-Prevention of Child Abuse
7120 Franklin Avenue
Los Angeles, CA 90046

School-Age Child Care Project
Center for Research on Women
Wellesley College
Wellesley, MA 02181-8201
(617) 283-1000

Society for Research in Child Development
5720 S. Woodlawn Avenue
Chicago, IL 60637
(312) 702-7470

Southern Association on Children Under Six
P.O. Box 5403, Brady Station
Little Rock, AR 72215
(501) 663-0353

United States National Committee of OMEP
World Organization for Early Childhood Education
1314 G Street, NW
Washington, DC 20005-3105
(800) 424-4310

Work/Family Directions, Inc.
930 Commonwealth Avenue, West
Boston, MA 02215
(617) 278-4000

References and Additional Resources

CHAPTER 1: THE DIRECTOR: A BROAD VIEW

Eiselen, S. 1985. *The Human Side of Child Care Administraton*. Washington, DC: National Association for the Education of Young Children.

Hammon, M. 1981. "Women as Directors—Reactions to the Role." *Child Care Information Exchange*, 22, 5–9.

Hildebrand, V. 1993. *Management of Child Development Centers*, 3rd ed. New York, NY: Macmillan Publishing Company.

Jones, E., ed. 1993. *Growing Teachers: Partnerships in Staff Development*. Washington, DC: National Association for the Education of Young Children.

Taylor, B.J. 1989. *Early Childhood Program Management: People and Procedures*. Columbus, OH: Merrill Publishing Company.

CHAPTER 2: CHOICES: SCHOOLS AND PROGRAMS

Decker, C., and Decker. J. 1992. *Planning and Administering Early Childhood Programs*. New York, NY: Macmillan Publishing Company.

Sciarra, D.J., and Dorsey, A.G. 1995. *Developing and Administering a Child Care Center*, 3rd ed. Albany, NY: Delmar Publishers, Inc.

CHAPTER 3: BEGINNINGS; A NEW SCHOOL/A NEW YEAR

Allen, K. 1992. *The Exceptional Child: Mainstreaming in Childhood Education*, 2nd ed. Albany, NY: Delmar Publishers Inc.

Child Care Law Center. 1993. *Caring for Children with Special Needs: The Americans with Disabilities Act and Child Care, ADA Series*. San Francisco, CA.

Fauvre, M. 1988. "Including Young Children with 'New' Chronic Illnesses in an Early Childhood Education Setting." *Young Children*, 43 (6), 71–77.

Widerstrom, A. 1982. "Mainstreaming Handicapped Preschoolers: Should We or Shouldn't We?" *Childhood Education* (January/February), 172–178.

CHAPTER 4: SETTING GOALS: PLANNING AND EVALUATION

Bredekamp, S., and Rosegrant, T., eds. 1992. *Reaching Potentials: Appropriate Curriculum and Assessment for Young Children*, Vol. 1. Washington, DC: National Association for the Education of Young Children.

Hendrick, J. 1986. *Total Learning Curriculum for the Young Child*. Columbus, OH: Charles E. Merrill Publishing Company.

Lawton, J. *Introduction to Child Care & Early Childhood Education*, 1988. Glenview, IL: Scott, Foresman and Company.

CHAPTER 5: PLANNING: THE PRESCHOOL

Buckleitner, W. 1988. *Survey of Early Childhood Software*. Ypsilanti, MI: The High Scope Press.

Erikson, E. 1950. *Childhood and Society*. New York, NY: Norton.

Fein, G., and Rivkin, M., eds. 1986. *The Young Child at Play: Review of Research*, Vol. 4. Washington, DC: National Association for the Education of Young Children.

Heller, W., Caldwell, B., and Rutten, R. 1982. "Ethnic and Cultural Diversity in Day Care Programming." In D. Streets, *Administering Day Care and Preschool Programs*. Boston, MA: Allyn and Bacon, Inc.

Holder-Brown, L., and Parette, H.P., Jr. 1992. "Children with Disabilities who use Assistive Technology: Ethical Considerations." *Young Children*, 47 (6), 73–77.

Hoot, J.L. 1986. *Computers in Early Childhood Education: Issues and Practices*. Englewood Cliffs, NJ: Prentice Hall, Inc.

Katz, L., Evanelou, D., and Hartman, J. 1990. *The Case for Mixed-Age Grouping in Early Childhood*. Washington, DC: National Association for the Education of Young Children.

Lawton, J. 1988. *Introduction to Child Care & Early Childhood Education*. Glenview, IL: Scott, Foresman and Company.

Lay-Dopyera, M., and Dopyera, J. 1986. "Strategies for Teaching." In C. Seefeldt, ed. *Early Childhood Curriculum: A Review of Current Research*. New York: Teachers College Press, Columbia University.

Pugmire-Stoy, M.C. 1992. *Spontaneous Play in Early Childhood*. Albany, NY: Delmar Publishers, Inc.

CHAPTER 6: PLANNING: INFANTS AND TODDLERS

Berger, K. 1993. *The Developing Person Through the Life Cycle*, 3rd ed. New York, NY: Worth Publishers, Inc.

Bredekamp, S., ed. 1986. *Developmentally Appropriate Practice in Early Childhood Programs Serving Children Birth Through Age 8*. Washington, DC: National Association for the Education of Young Children.

Cataldo, C. 1986. "Infant-Toddler Education: Blending the Best Approaches." In J. Brown, ed. *Administering Programs for Young Children*. Washington, DC: National Association for the Education of Young Children.

Erikson, E. 1950. *Childhood and Society*. New York, NY: W.W. Norton & Company, Inc.

CHAPTER 7: PLANNING: SCHOOL-AGE CHILDREN

Blakely, B., et al. 1989. *Activities for School-Age Child Care: Playing and Learning*, rev. ed. Washington, DC: National Association for the Education of Young Children.

Cherry, C. 1990. *Creative Art for the Developing Child*, 2nd ed. Belmont, CA: David S. Lake Publishers.

Milford, S. 1990. *Adventures in Art: Art and Craft Experiences for 7–14-Year-Olds*. Charlotte, VT: Williamson Publishing.

Click. P. 1994. *Caring for School-Age Children*. Albany, NY: Delmar Publishers, Inc.

Gardner, R. 1985. *Science Around the House*. NY: Julian Messner.

Stangl, J. 1986. *Magic Mixtures*. Belmont, CA: David S. Lake Publishers.

Stassevitch, V., Stemmler, P., Shotwell, R., and Wirth, M. 1989. *Ready-to-Use Activities for Before and After School Programs*. West Nyack, NY: The Center for Applied Research in Education, Inc.

Wolff, M. 1985. *The Kids' After School Activity Book*. Belmont, CA: David S. Lake Publishers.

CHAPTER 8: STAFF SELECTION/PERSONNEL POLICIES

Caplow, T. 1986. "How to Be an Effective Supervisor." *Child Care Information Exchange* (January), 3–6.

Hendrick, J. 1986. "Starting from Scratch: Coping with 'Green' Employees." *Child Care Information Exchange* (May), 3–6.

Jorde-Bloom, P. 1988. *A Great Place to Work: Improving Conditions for Staff in Young Children's Programs*. Washington, DC: National Association for the Education of Young Children.

Murray, K. 1986. "Legal Aspects of the Selection Process." *Child Care Information Exchange* (January), 27–30.

Robinson, R. 1988. "Vanishing Breed: Men in Child Care Programs." *Young Children*. 43 (6), 54–58.

Staley, C.C., Jr., Ranch, E.R., Pereault, J., and Neugebauer, R. 1986. "Guidelines for Effective Staff Selection." *Child Care Information Exchange* (January), 22–26.

CHAPTER 9: STAFF SUPERVISION AND TRAINING

Bredekamp, S. 1992. "Composing a Profession." *Young Children*, 47 (2), 52–54.

Child Care Employee Project. 1992. "On the Horizon: New Policy Initiatives to Enhance Child Care Staff Compensation." *Young Children*, 47 (5), 39–42.

Daniel, J. 1990. "Child Care: An Endangered Industry." *Young Children*, 45 (4), 23–26.

Greenman, J. 1989. "Diversity and Conflict: The Whole World will Never Sing in Perfect Harmony." *Child Care Information Exchange* 69, 11–13.

Jones, E. 1991. "Do ECE People Really Agree: Or Are We Just Agreeable?" *Young Children*, 46 (4), 59–61.

Jones, E., ed. 1993. *Growing Teachers: Partnerships in Staff Development*. Washington, DC: National Association for the Education of Young Children.

Kostelrick, M. 1982. "A Practical Approach to Resolving Inter-Staff Conflicts." *Child Care Information Exchange* (July/August), 7–12.

Phillips, C.B. 1990. "The Child Development Associate Program: Entering a New Era." *Young Children*, 45 (3), 24–27.

CHAPTER 10: STUDENT TEACHERS/VOLUNTEERS

Albrecht, K.M. 1985. "Monitoring, Measuring, and Evaluating Teacher Performance." *Child Care Information Exchange* (March), 8–10.

Harris, R. 1985. *How to Select, Train, and use Volunteers in the Schools*. Lanham, MD: University Press of America.

Rogers, D.W., Waller, C.B., and Perrin, M.S. 1987. "Learning More About What Makes a Good Teacher Through Collaborative Research in the Classroom." *Young Children*. 42 (4), 34–39.

CHAPTER 11: BUDGET

Decker, C., and Decker, J. 1992. *Planning and Administering Early Childhood Programs*, 5th ed. New York, NY: Macmillan Publishing Company.

Godwin, A., and Schrag, L. 1988. *Setting Up for Infant Care: Guidelines for Centers and Family Day Care Homes.* Washington, DC: National Association for the Education of Young Children.

Gross, M., and Warshauer, W. 1983. *Financial and Accounting Guide for Nonprofit Organizations.* New York, NY: John Wiley and Sons.

Neugebauer, R. 1987. "Child-Care Center Management Software Buying Guide Update." *Child Care Information Exchange* (November), 43–47.

Sciarra, D.J., and Dorsey, A.G. 1995. *Developing and Administering a Child Care Center,* 3rd ed. Albany, NY: Delmar Publishers, Inc.

Willer, B., ed. 1990. *Reaching the Full Cost of Quality in Early Childhood Programs.* Washington, DC: National Association for the Education of Young Children.

CHAPTER 12: MAINTENANCE, HEALTH AND SAFETY

Aronson, S., M.D. 1986. "Exclusion Criteria for Ill Children in Child Care." *Child Care Information Exchange* 49 (May), 30–35.

Aronson, S., M.D. 1992. "Health Update: Coping with the Physical Requirements of Caregiving." *Child Care Information Exchange* 55 (May), 39–40.

Dixon, S. 1990. "Talking to the Child's Physician: Thoughts for the Child Care Provider." *Young Children,* 45 (3), 36–37.

Hrncir, E., and Eisenshart, C. 1991. "Use with Caution: The 'At Risk' Label." *Young Children,* 46 (2), 23–27.

Meddin, B., and Rosen, A. 1986. "Child Abuse and Neglect: Prevention and Reporting." *Young Children,* 41 (4), 26–30.

National Association for the Education of Young Children, 1987. *Child Care Center Diseases and Sick Child Care: NAEYC Resource Guide.* Washington, DC: NAEYC.

Weiser, M. 1990. *Group Care and Education of Infants and Toddlers.* Columbus, OH: Merrill/Macmillan.

CHAPTER 13: FOOD AND NUTRITION SERVICES

Lovato, C., Allensworth, D., and Chan, F. 1989. *School Health in America: An Assessment of State Policies to Protect and Improve the Health of Students,* 5th ed. Kent, OH: American School Health Association.

Rothlein, L. 1989. "Nutrition Tips Revisited: On a Daily Basis, Do We Implement What We know?" *Young Children,* 44 (6), 30–36.

Warren, J. 1992. *Super Snacks.* Everett, WA: Warren Publishing House.

Zeller, P., and Jacobson, M. 1987. *Eat, Think and Be Healthy!* Washington, DC: Center for Science in the Public Interest.

CHAPTER 14: SPACE: THE PRESCHOOL

Bryan, F. 1986. *A Garden for Children.* London, England: Michael Joseph, Ltd.

Burns, M.S., Goin, L., and Donlon, J.T. 1990. "A Computer in My Room." *Young Children,* 45 (2), 62–67.

Diamond, K., Hestenes, L., O'Connor, C., and Berk, L. 1994. "Integrating Young Children with Disabilities in Preschool: Problems and Promise." *Young Children,* 49 (2), 68–74.

Dinwiddie, S.A. 1993. "Playing in the Gutters: Enhancing Children's Cognitive and Social Play." *Young Children,* 48 (6), 70–73.

Jones, E. 1977. *Dimensions of Teaching-Learning Environments: Handbook for Teachers.* Pasadena, CA: Pacific Oaks College

Jones, E., and Villarno, G., 1994. "What Goes Up on the Classroom Walls—And Why." *Young Children*, 49 (2), 38–40.

National Association for the Education of Young Children, 1991. *Facility Design for Early Childhood Programs: An NAEYC Resource Guide*. Washington, DC: NAEYC.

Readdick, C.A. 1993. "Solitary Pursuits: Supporting Children's Privacy Needs in Early Childhood Settings." *Young Children*, 49 (1), 60–64.

Shaw, L.G. 1987. "Designing Playgrounds for Able and Disabled Children." In C.S. Weinstein and T.G. David, eds. *Spaces for Children: The Built Environment and Child Development*, 187–213. New York, NY: Plenum.

Smith, P.K., and Connolly, K.J. 1980. *The Ecology of Preschool Behavior*. Cambridge, England: Cambridge University Press.

CHAPTER 15: SPACE: INFANTS AND TODDLERS

Greenberg, P. 1991. "Do You Take Care of Toddlers?" *Young Children*, 46 (2), 52–53.

Infant/Toddler Caregiving: A Guide to Setting Up Environments, 1990. Sacramento, CA: California State Department of Education.

Prescott, E. 1984. "The Physical Setting in Day Care." In J.T. Greenman and R.W. Fuqua, eds. *Making Day Care Better*. New York, NY: Teachers College Press.

Seefeldt, C., and Barbour, N. 1986. *Early Childhood Education, An Introduction*. Columbus, OH: Charles E. Merrill Publishing Company.

Winter, S. 1985. "Toddler Play Behaviors and Equipment Choices in an Outdoor Playground." In J. Frost and S. Sunderlin, eds. *When Children Play*. Wheaton, MD: Association for Childhood Education International.

CHAPTER 16: SPACE: SCHOOL-AGE CHILDREN

Baden, R., Genser, A., Levine, J., and Seligson, M. 1982. *School-Age Child Care: An Action Manual*. Boston: Auburn House Publishing Company.

Bender, J., Edler, B., and Flatter, C. 1987. *Half a Childhood: Time for School-Age Child Care*. Nashville, TN: School-Age Notes.

Click, P. 1994. *Caring for School-Age Children*. Albany, NY: Delmar Publishers, Inc.

Haas-Foletta, K., and Cogley, M. 1990. *School-Age Ideas and Activities for After School Programs*. Nashville, TN: School-Age Notes.

"Creating Environments for School-Age Child Care." Superintendent of Documents. Washington, DC. (#S/N 008-000-00375-1).

Morris, L., and Schulz, L. 1989. *Creative Play Activities for Children with Disabilities: A Resource Book for Teachers and Parents*. Champaign, IL: Human Kinetics Books.

CHAPTER 17: PARENT INVOLVEMENT, EDUCATION, AND PUBLIC RELATIONS

Albrecht, K. 1991. "Helping Teachers Grow: Talking with Parents." *Child Care Information Exchange* (November/December), 45–47.

Berger, E.H. 1991. *Parents as Partners in Education: The School and Home Working Together*. Columbus, OH: Merrill/Macmillan Publishing Company.

Bundy, B.F. 1991. "Fostering Communication Between Parents and Preschools." *Young Children*, 46 (2), 12–17.

Clay, J.W. 1990. "Working with Lesbian and Gay Parents and Their Children." *Young Children*, 45 (3), 31–35.

Davidson, D.H. 1990. "Child Care As a Support for Families with Special Needs." *Young Children*, 45 (3), 47–48.

Galinsky, E. 1990. "Why Are Some Parent/Teacher Partnerships Clouded with Difficulties?" *Young Children*, 45 (5), 2–3, 38–39.

Galinsky, E. 1988. "Parents and Teacher-Caregivers: Sources of Tension, Souces of Support." *Young Children*, 43 (3), 4–12.

Hendrick, J. 1992. *The Whole Child*, 5th ed. Columbus, OH: Merrill Publishing Company.

Kagan, S.L. 1989. "Early Care and Education: Beyond the School House Doors." *Phi Delta Kappan.* 71 (2), 107–112.

Swick, K. 1984. *Inviting Parents in the Young Child's World*. Champaign, IL: Stipes Publishing.

CHAPTER 18: REGULATIONS AND LAWS

Bulkley, J., Ensminger, J., Fontana, V., and Summitt, R. 1983. *Dealing with Sexual Child Abuse*. Chicago, IL: National Committee for Prevention of Child Abuse.

Faludi, S. 1988 "Are the Kids Alright? The Truth Behind the 'Day Care Is Bad for Your Child' Hype." *Mother Jones* (November).

Lawton, J. 1988. *Introduction to Child Care & Early Childhood Education*. Glenview, IL: Scott, Foresman and Company.

Murray, K., Esq., ed. 1987. *Child Care Center Legal Handbook*. San Francisco, CA: Child Care Law Center.

Musick, J.S., and Weissbourd, B. 1988. *Guidelines for Establishing Family Resource Programs*. Chicago, IL: National Committee for the Prevention of Child Abuse.

Nelson, M., and Clark, K. 1986. *The Educator's Guide to Preventing Child Sexual Abuse*. Santa Cruz, CA: Network Publications.

Powell, D.R. 1988. *Parent Education As Early Childhood Intervention: Emerging Directions in the Theory, Research, and Practice*. Horwood, NJ: Abliex Publishing Corporation.

Glossary

Accreditation   national program for validating the quality of early childhood programs.

Adventure play areas   outdoor areas where children can use a variety of materials to build their own structures.

Aesthetic appeal   pleasant appearance derived from a well-designed environment.

AIDS   Acquired Immune Deficiency Syndrome.

Allergens   environmental substances or foods that cause a reaction such as asthma, hives, or hay fever.

Anti-bias curriculum   an approach to planning curriculum that includes not only cultural aspects, but gender and physical ability differences.

Attachment   strong bond between an infant and caregiver.

Authoritarian manager   those administrators who make decisions and determine policies for others.

Budget   a statement of goals for one year stated in financial terms.

Budget calendar   a schedule for compiling budget data.

Caregiver   one who provides a caring, nurturing environment for children who spend long hours away from home.

CDA   Child Development Associate credential that certifies the holder has achieved a level of competency.

Child abuse   serious harm to children in the form of physical, emotional, or sexual mistreatment.

Church-sponsored school   a child care center or preschool organized as an extension of the educational program of the church.

Clique   a group formed by school-age children as a means of strengthening bonds with peers and to be free from adult supervision.

Concrete materials   objects that children can touch, taste, smell, hear, and see.

Contract   written agreement between a child development facility and the employee that promotes job security.

Controllable expenses   those which vary and over which the director has some control.

Cooperative school   nonprofit enterprise, owned by all the parents who currently have children enrolled in the school.

Corporate school   business corporation operating multiple schools at different sites.

Creativity   a unique way of reacting to a situation, not just imitating what others have done.

Critical job elements   things which, if they were not done, would seriously impede the total teaching practice.

Dedicated space   space that is not shared with any other part of a child care program.

Democratic manager   those administrators who involve others in decisions and policy-making processes.

Developmental appropriateness   based on a knowledge of universal sequences of growth and change and of each child's individual pattern and timing.

Developmentally appropriate program   curriculum based on a knowledge of the physical, emotional, social, and cognitive abilities of the children served.

Disaster plans   detailed plans for evacuating children and managing a disaster.

Egocentric   children's inability to see things from more than one point of view.

Employer-sponsored programs   on-site or off-site child care facilities supported by a company or business.

Evaluation   process to determine if the goals of an early childhood center are being met.

Expendable supplies   items that are used up and have to be replaced.

Family child care home   child care service provided in a private residence.

Family group   children whose ages vary, sometimes by several years.

Fixed expenses   those that do not vary or change little over periods of time.

Flexibility   able to be changed or modified.

Food Guide Pyramid   new recommended daily servings of food developed by the U.S. Department of Agriculture in 1992.

For-profit/proprietary school   school owned by one or more individuals, established to provide a community service but also to make a profit for the owners.

Fringe benefits   mandated or voluntary benefits that are added to personnel expenses.

Goal   expected long-term changes in a child's behavior.

Industry vs. inferiority   Erikson's middle childhood stage during which children acquire skills needed for adulthood.

Knowledge   a familiarity with a particular subject or branch of learning.

Laboratory school   early childhood center that is part of the instructional program of a college or university.

Laissez-faire managers   those administrators who remain passive, often leaving decisions to others.

Maintenance   major expenditures on the physical plant: painting, alterations, repair.

Management skill   ability to coordinate all the parts of an organization to meet common goals.

Master teacher   experienced, model teacher who can provide a positive learning experience for student teachers.

Mentor   someone who can serve as a role model to help an inexperienced teacher gain new skills and knowledge.

Multicultural   a curriculum that introduces children to the similarities and differences among different cultures and ethnic groups.

Multipurpose equipment   equipment that can be used in more than one way.

Nonexpendable items   equipment and toys that last a long time.

Nonverbal messages   facial expressions, movements, and posture.

Objective   expected short-term changes in a child's behavior.

On-going costs   expected costs of operating a school.

Operations   recurring, day-to-day activities involved in the upkeep of a school.

Parent conference   one-on-one meeting between teacher and parents to discuss child's progress or to resolve problems.

Parent education   activities designed to help parents become better informed about childrearing and family life.

Parent involvement   sharing in the education of their children through participation in school activities.

Peer   a person of the same age as oneself.

Peer group   children who are close to the same age.

Philosophy   a distillation of ideas, beliefs, and values held by an individual, a group, or an organization.

Preschool period   the years before a child enters elementary school, either from two to five or three to six.

Probationary period   the time before the full contract goes into effect, usually from one to three months.

Psychosocial area   space that is planned to encourage interactions between adults and children, and among the children themselves.

Resource and referral service   information service for parents seeking child care.

Scooter board   a 12-inch plastic or wooden square, with swivel casters. (Commercially produced boards are equipped with handles on the side.)

Self-concept   children's understanding of their own characteristics.

Sensorimotor period   Piaget's first stage of an infant's development taking place from birth to one year.

Sensory input   objects and experiences that stimulate the senses.

Skill   an ability that comes from knowledge, practice, or aptitude. (Sometimes called competency.)

Start-up costs   Expenses incurred before a new school can open.

Statement of personnel policy   written document covering employer-employee relations.

Student teacher   college or university student who is enrolled in a practice teaching or field study course requiring placement in a school or child care center.

Supervision   overseeing staff members during the performance of their jobs.

Trust vs. mistrust   Erikson's first stage of an infant's development.

Volunteer   unpaid person who offers his services of his own free will.

Index

Figures are indicated by f

A

Abuse. *See* Child abuse
Accidents, 242–244
  reporting, 166
Accreditation
  of programs, numbers of, 80
  of schools, 368–369
  of teachers and caregivers, 369
Acquired immunodeficiency syn-
  drome (AIDS), children with,
  247, 252, 255, 258
Activities, school-age children,
  145–146
Activity level, preschool, 97–98
Advertising costs, 54
Advisory board, 18
Age Discrimination Act of 1967,
  377
Aggressive acts, preschool, 98–99
AIDS, children with, 247, 252, 255,
  258
All-day schools, 27–29
Allergies, to food, 269–270
American Association of Retired
  Persons (AARP), 214
Americans with Disabilities Act
  (ADA), 61
Anecdotal record method of eval-
  uation, 90
Apple/Macintosh computers,
  381–382
Art center, preschool, 294f, 295
Assessment information summary,
  93
Assistant directors, 10
Attachment, to caregivers, 126
Attendance chart, 62
Attention deficit disorder,
  preschool, 113
Authoritarian managers, 7–8

B

Behavioral objectives, 85–86
Behavioral problems, preschool,
  114
Behaviors, that interfere with
  learning, 249–252
Block area

preschool environment,
  292–295
school-age children environment, 329–330
Boards of directors
  communication with director,
  20
  duties of, 19–20, 21f
  types and composition of,
  17–19
Bodily fluids, precautions when
  handling, 252
Breakfasts, 275f
Brochures, 54–55, 356–357,
  358–359f
Budget, 218–233
  accountant services, 219
  analysis, 229
  average total cost per child,
  U.S.A., 229
  cycle, summary of, 226,
  228–229
  development of, 218–219
  expenses-controllable
    consultant or contract
    services, 220
    equipment, 220–221
    food, 221
    supplies and materials, 221
    transportation, 221
  expenses-fixed
    space costs, 221
    utilities/insurance/taxes/
    miscellaneous, 222
  expenses-personnel
    staff salaries, 219–220
    taxes and fringe benefits,
    220
  implementing the final budget,
  230
  income
    Federal, state, and local
    items, 223–224
    other sources, 223
    some intangibles, 224
    tuition, 222–223
  justification, 219
  keeping accurate records,
  230–231
  monthly financial report for

  budget tracking, 228f
  references and additional
  resources, 394–395
  sample budget form, 225–226f
  for a single for-profit school,
  227f
  trial budget, 224, 226
  using computer for, 219
  See also Finances
Building committees, 20
Bulletin boards, 354
Burnout
  causes of, 193–194
  prevention, 194–195
Bus service arrangements, 65
  See also Transportation
Buying a school building, 50
Bylaws, board of directors, 19, 21f

C

Caregivers
  accreditation of, 369
  interactions with children,
  124–125
  of school-age children, characteristics of, 146–147
  and teachers, compared, 96–97
CCM-Turbo software, 384
CDA National Credentialing
  Program, 174
Checking children in and out, 65
Checklists, for assessing child's
  capabilities, 91–92
Chicken Soup, Minneapolis, 254
Child abuse, 370–376
  categories of
    emotional abuse, 370, 372
    emotional deprivation, 370,
    372
    physical abuse, 370, 371–372
    physical neglect, 370, 372
    sexual abuse and exploita-
    tion, 370, 373
  causes of, 370–371
  prevention, 375–376
    pamphlets, 62
  recognition of, 371
  references and additional
  sources, 397
  staff members accused, 375

Child Abuse (*continued*)
when to report abuse, 373–375
Child Care 2000 software, 384
Child care centers, 36–37, 41f
Child Care Food Program, 263
Child Development Associate credential, 153
CDA National Credentialing Program, 174
Child Learning Center, philosophy statement, 78
Child Quest software, 384
Children's Defense Fund, 25
Children's World Learning Centers, 20
Children with AIDS, 247, 252, 255, 258
Children with special needs, 61–62
adaptations for
infant/toddler, 318–319
school-age children, 299–300
handicapped, 251
preschool, 113–115
Church-sponsored schools, 34–35, 40f
Circle center, preschool, 297
Civil Rights Act of 1964-Title VII, 377
Clubroom, school-age children, 332
Cognitive approach to learning, 77
Cognitive areas
infant to one year, 314–315
toddler, 315
Cognitive development
goals of, 82
preschool, 100
Committees, 19–20
personnel, 20
Communications
listening, 15
nonverbal messages, 13–14
preventing problems in, 14
verbal messages, 13
written reports, 15–16
Community activities, and public relations, 361
Competence development, infants/toddlers, 122–123
Computer center
preschool, 298–299
school-age children, 331

Computers, 12, 381–386
Apple/Macintosh or IBM?, 381–382
for budgeting, 219
establishing a data base, 59
information you need to ask vendors, 382
in preschool, 112–113
prices for, 386
printers, 386
reasons for using, 381
software programs available
CCM-Turbo, 384
Child Care 2000, 384
Child Quest, 384
EZ-Care, 385
Maggey, 385
Private Advantage, 385
what software packages should provide, 383–384
Conferences, with parents, 352–354
Consultant services, 54, 220
Contracts, staff, 164–165
Contract services, 54, 220
Cooking areas
for preschoolers, 297–298
for school-age children, 329
Cooperative schools, 34, 40f
Corporate schools, 31–32, 40f
Corporations, 21–22
Council for Early Childhood Professional Recognition, 174
Creative activities, school-age children, 145–146
Creative areas, school-age children, 327–328
Creative development, goals of, 82
Curriculum design, 88
sample weekly plan, 89f

D
Daily information sheet
for caregivers, 127f
for parents, 128f
Data management. *See* Computers
Day Care, and increased risk of illness, 245–246
Delegation of responsibility, 9–11
Democratic managers, 7, 8
Developmental delay, preschool, 113
Developmentally Appropriate

Practice in Early Childhood Programs Serving Children From Birth Through Age 8, 76
Developmentally appropriate programs
dimensions of, 76–78
infants and toddlers
attachment and separation, 126
environment, 128–130
goals, 123–124
interactions between children and caregivers, 124–125
language, 131
parent involvement, 125–126
play, 130–131
recordkeeping, 126–128
routines, 125
staff selection, 131–132
preschool
assessment, 103–104
children with special needs, 113–115
cognitive development, 104–106
creativity, 106
diversity, 107–109
goals, 103
grouping children, 101–102
parent involvement, 110
peer relationships, 111–112
prepared environment, 103
schedule, 102
staff interactions with children, 109–110
use of computers, 112–113
variety, 104
school-age children
friends, 145
goals, 142–143
independence, 143–144
pace, 143
parents, 145
skills, 144–145
Diapering areas, infant/toddler, 313
Director, 2–24
average salaries of, 8
as communicator
listening, 15
nonverbal messages, 13–14

preventing communication
problems, 14
verbal messages, 13
written reports, 15–16
and the corporation, 20–22
daily occurrences requiring
attention of, 3
evaluation of
assessing strengths and
weaknesses, 16
self-evaluation tools, 17
management methods, 7–8
management style, 4, 6–7
management theories, 9
as organizer
delegating responsibility,
9–11
organizing time, 11–12
planning, 12–13
references and additional
resources, 392
relation to boards of directors,
17–20
responsibilities of, 5–6f
skills and characteristics of, 3–4
and student teachers, 200–202
Disaster plans, 244
Discovery center, school-age children, 330–331
Dramatic play
preschool, 98, 290–291,
292–293f
school-age children, 329

E
E-Care software, 385
Education
of parents, 349–354
activities for, 350–354
communications with staff,
352
conferences, 352–354
films, slides, tapes,
351–352
group discussions, 351
lectures or panels, 351
observation, 350–351
orientation meetings,
350
parent library, newslet-
ter, or bulletin board, 354
participation in the
classroom, 352

workshops, 352
goals for, 349–350
of staff, 152–153, 188
Elderly persons, as volunteers,
207, 208, 214
Emergencies, handling, 11–12
Emotional development. See
Social/emotional development
Emotional problems, preschool,
114
Employees
behavior types, 9
See also Staff
Employer-sponsored programs,
32–34, 40f
Endowments, 223
Enrollment, 59–65
attendance chart, 62
bus service arrangements, 65
checking children in and out,
65
child abuse prevention pamphlets, 62
children with special needs,
61–62
establishing files, 62
family or peer grouping, 60–61
financial agreement form, 64f
identification and emergency
form, 63f
inquiry report form, 60f
parent messages, 65
permission form, 64f
Environment, 86
precautions to prevent the
spread of disease, 251–252
See also Space
Environmental approach to learning, 77
Equal Pay Act of 1963, 376
Equipment
appropriate size for school-age
children, 326
budgeting for, 220–221
Erikson, Erik
industry vs. inferiority, 140
initiative, preschool, 100
trust vs. mistrust, 122
Ethnic/cultural relevance,
infant/toddler environment,
308–309
Evaluating, applicants, 161–162
Evaluation sheet, 17

Executive committees, 19
Executive Orders 11246/11375, 377

F
Fair Labor Standards Act of 1938,
377
Family Connection, 49
Family day care home, 30–31, 40f
Family grouping, 60–61
Fantasies, preschool, 99
Fears, preschool, 99
Federal grants, 223–224
Federal Income Tax Withholding,
377
Federal Wage Garnishment Law,
377
Fees, budgeting for, 223
Field trips
school-age children, 146
staff training, 191
Files, 62
health information in child's file,
258–259
Films
parent education, 351–352
staff training, 190
Finance committees, 19–20
Finances
nonpersonnel budget items, 57f
ongoing costs, 55–57
building or rental fees, 56–57
potential income, determining, 55–56
salaries, 56
uncollectible tuitions, 56
start-up-costs, 51–55
advertising and publicity, 54
capital, 52–53
contract services and consultants, 54
fliers and brochures, 54–55
insurance, 55
legal services, 54
personnel, 53
renovation, 53–54
signs, 55
suggestions for, 69, 71
See also Budget
Financial agreement form, 64f
Fine-motor areas, infant/toddler,
315
First aid, 12, 241
kit, 242f

First Presbyterian Nursery School
of Santa Monica, policy of
infectious diseases, 256–257f
Fliers, 54–55
Food
    budgeting for, 221
    preparation and eating areas,
    infant/toddler, 312–313
    See also Nutrition services
Food Guide Pyramid, 267f
Food handlers
    qualities of, 155
    and safety, 276–277
Friends, and school-age children,
145
Fringe benefits, 166
Fund raising activities, 223

G
Games
    preschool, 297
    school-age children, 146
Goals and objectives
    curriculum design, 88
    developing objectives
        behavioral objectives, 85–86
        from goals to objectives,
        82–84
    distinguishing between, 79
    evaluating outcomes
        assessment information
        summary, 93
        checklists, 91–92
        collection of end products,
        93
        commercial tests, 90–91
        methods, 89–90
        observation, 90
        parent interviews, 92
        process, 88–89
        time sampling, 93
    formulating goals
        from areas of child's devel-
        opment, 82
        idea development chart, 81f
        what are they, 79
        who sets them, 79–80
        writing goals, 80–82
    general principles
        child's ability to achieve the
        behavior, 87
        child's ability to repeat
        familiar activities, 88

child's choice of experi-
ences, 88
child's feeling of satisfaction, 87
opportunities for child to
practice the behavior, 86–87
setting up the environment,
86
references and additional
resources, 392–393
sample weekly plan, 89f
Golden Preschool, philosophy
statement, 78
Governing board, 18
Gray Panthers, 214
Green Oaks School, philosophy
statement, 78
Group discussions
    with parents, 351
    staff training, 189–190

H
Half-day schools, 26–27
Handbooks
    for parents, 65–66
    for volunteers, 211–212
Handicapped children, 251
    See also Children with special
    needs
Head Start, 18, 37–39, 41f
    education of staff, 153
    Head Teacher, 39
    and healthcare, 248
    and Home Visitors, 344
    and multicultural diversity, 39
    and parental involvement, 39,
    341–342
    program goals, 38
    screening tests, 247
    teacher turnover, 162
Health, 245–259
    assessing current health status
    of child, 247
    day care and increased risk of
    illness, 245–246
    goals, 246–247
    identifying conditions that
    interfere with learning, 248–251
        behavior difficulties,
        249–252
        hearing disabilities, 249
        language difficulties, 249
        vision problems, 249

immunization schedule, 250f
management of the sick child
    early signs of a sick child, 254
    giving medication, 255
    immunization, 255
    including children with
    HIV/AIDS, 255, 258
    notifying parents, 255
    providing care at the center,
    254–255
    when to send child home,
    253–254
policy of infectious diseases,
256–257f
preventing future illnesses
    characteristics of young
    children, 251
    developing procedures for
    care of the environment,
    251–252
    precautions when handling
    body fluids, 252
    requirements for the infant/
    toddler room, 252–253
recordkeeping, 258–259
references and additional
resources, 395
treating progressive conditions,
248
Health and safety matters, of staff,
166–168
Hearing disabilities
    preschool, 114
    that interfere with learning, 249
High school students, as volunteers, 209
High-tech center, school-age children, 331–332
Home Visitors, 344
Homework, school-age children,
144

I
IBM computers, 381–382
Idea development chart, 81f
Identification and emergency
form, 63f
Illness. See Health
Immunization, 255
    schedule, 250f
Income
    federal, state, and local items,
    223–224

other sources, 223
some intangibles, 224
tuition, 222–223
Independence development
infants/toddlers, 122–123
school-age children, 139–140,
143–144
Individual education plan (IEP),
113
Individuals With Disabilities
Education Amendment of
1990, P.L. 101–476, 113
Indoor/outdoor adaptations, children with special needs,
299–300
Indoor space, school-age children,
332–333
Industry *vs.* inferiority, 140
Infants and toddlers, 119–136
daily information sheet
for caregivers, 127f
for parents, 128f
development, 119–123
appearance of language, 123
competence and independ-
ence, 122–123
learning to get along with
other children, 123
motor skills, 121–122
sensorimotor period,
120–121
strong attachments to
others, 122
trust *vs.* mistrust, 122
developmentally appropriate
program
attachment and separation,
126
environment, 128–130
goals, 123–124
interactions between children and caregivers,
124–125
language, 131
parent involvement,
125–126
play, 130–131
recordkeeping, 126–128
routines, 125
staff selection, 131–132
motor activities for, 133
references and additional
resources, 393

sensory activities for
hearing, 132–133
seeing, 133
touch, 132
social activities for, 133
Information sources, 387–391
Inspection, of the facilities, 71
Insurance
budgeting for, 222
costs, 55
Interacting with people, 4
Interactive approach to learning,
77
Interviewing, applicants, 158–161
Inventory, maintenance, 238–239
"Is Day Care Hazardous to
Health?", 245

K
Kinder Care, 20–21

L
Laboratory schools, 35–36, 41f
Language
development
infants/toddlers, 122–123
preschool, 100–101
school-age children, 138
difficulties, that interfere with
learning, 249
impairments, preschool, 114
Language areas
infant/toddler, 317
school-age children, 331
Large-motor areas, infant/toddler,
315–317
Laws pertaining to child care settings
on-the-job safety, 377
personnel policies, 376–377
posting employee information,
378
salary procedures, 377
sources of information, 377–378
Leadership ability, 4
Learning, conditions that interfere
with, 248–251
Lectures, for parents, 351
Legal services, 54
Library, for parent education,
354
Licensing requirements and regulations, 364–368

infant/toddler environment,
305–306
for menu planning, 263
preschool environment, 283
references and additional
sources, 397
regulation through licensing
related regulations, 367–368
what is covered?, 366–367
who is covered?, 365–366
why regulation?, 365
school-age children environment, 322–323
and zoning, 46–48
Listening center, preschool, 297
Location
buy, build, remodel, or rent,
48–51
advantages and disadvan-
tages of each, 51
community survey, 45–46
licensing and zoning requirements, 46–48
needs assessment questionnaire, 46
LOGO™, 112, 113, 298

M
Maggey software, 385
Mainstreaming, 251
Maintenance, 234–239
inventory, 238–239
operations, 235–238
references and additional
resources, 395
sample equipment maintenance
record, 236f
sample housekeeping schedule,
238f
sample repair and maintenance
form, 235f
sample repair and replacement
services form, 237f
Management
methods, 7–8
skills, 3
style, 4, 7
Master teacher
choice of, 202
responsibilities of, 205
Math center, preschool, 295–296
Medications, administering,
255

Mentor relationship, 187
Menu planning, 263–265
  guidelines for, 265–267
Montessori, Maria, 36
Motor activities, infants and tod-
    dlers, 133
Motor skills development,
    infants/toddlers, 121–122
Multicultural diversity
  and Head Start, 39
  and preschool environment,
    288–289
Music center, preschool, 297

N
National Association for the
    Education of Young Children
    (NAEYC), 55, 76
  and accreditation, 368–369
  Child Development Associate
    credential, 153
  guidelines, developmentally
    appropriate program, primary
    grades, 142–143
  personnel competencies, pam-
    phlet, 154
  "Position Statement on
    Licensing", 364
National Council on the Aging,
    214
Needs assessment questionnaire,
    46
Newsletters, 354
Noise level, 287
Nominating committees, 20
Nonprofit schools, 34–36, 40–41f
Nonverbal messages, 13–14
Numerical rating scale, 17
Nutrition services, 262–279
  better breakfasts, 275f
  caregiver's role, 262–263
  cooking experiences for chil-
    dren, 273–274
  food allergies, 269–270
  food service for children, 270,
    272
  inexpensive food substitutes,
    273
  mechanics of food service
      preparation, 274–276
      purchase, 274
      safety, 276–277
  menu planning, 263–265

basic four groups, 265–266
children planning their own
    meals, 267
consider number of person-
    nel, 266
dessert as integral part of
    meal, 267
foods liked by children, 266
foods with appetite appeal,
    266
introduce new foods, 267
the Pyramid, 267f
using available equipment,
    266
menus, samples of, 271f
and parents, 268–270
references and additional
    resources, 395
serving portions, ages 1 to 12,
    269f

O
Obesity in children, 266
Objectives. *See* Goals and objec-
    tives
Observation method of evalua-
    tion, 90
Open house, 357, 360
Opening of school, 58–59
Operations. *See* Maintenance
Organization of time, 11–12
Organizations, 387–391
Organizing ability, 4
Orientation
  meetings for parents, 66–67,
    350
  of new staff, 187
  of volunteers, 210–211
Outdoor space
  preschool, 299
  school-age children, 333–335

P
Parents
  education, 349–354
    activities for, 350–354
      communications with
        staff, 352
      conferences, 352–354
      films, slides, tapes,
        351–352
      group discussions, 351
      lectures or panels, 351

observation, 350–351
orientation meetings, 350
parent library, newslet-
    ter, or bulletin board,
    354
participation in the
    classroom, 352
workshops, 352
goals for, 349–350
references and additional
    sources, 396–397
handbooks for, 65–66
and Head Start, 39
interviews, 92
involvement, 125–126, 341–342
    changing roles, 340–341
    encouraging participation,
      347–348
    in food planning, 268–270
    incentives for sustaining,
      348
    initial contact, 346–347
    limits on, 345
    parental roles, 342–344
    recording, 348–349
    references and additional
      sources, 396–397
jealousy and competition with
    caregiver, 125
messages and notices to, 65
notifying about sick child, 255
orientation meetings, 66–67
and school-age children, 145
Pediatric AIDS Foundation, Santa
    Monica, 258
Peer grouping, 60
Peers, and school-age children,
    140
Permission form, 64f
Personnel. *See* Staff
Philosophy statement, 77–79
Physical development
  goals of, 82
  preschool, 97
  school-age children, 137–138
Physical impairments, preschool,
    113–114
Piaget, J., 36, 77, 120
Planning
  long-term, 12–13
  short-term, 12
Play, preschool, changes in, 98
Policy statement, 165

Portfolio writing, 189
Preschool, 96–118
  children with special needs,
    113–115
  development
    activity level, 97–98
    aggressive acts, 98–99
    fantasies and fears, 99
    of language, 100–101
    physical growth, 97
    play changes, 98
    self-concept of child
      defined, 100
    thinking changes, 100
  developmentally appropriate
    program
    assessment, 103–104
    cognitive development,
      104–106
    creativity, 106
    diversity, 107–109
    goals, 103
    grouping children, 101–102
    parent involvement, 110
    peer relationships, 111–112
    prepared environment, 103
    schedule, 102
    staff interactions with
      children, 109–110
    variety, 104
  references and additional
    resources, 393
  use of computers, 112–113
Printers, computer, 386
Priority setting, 11
Private Advantage software, 385
Private for-profit schools, 30–34,
  40f
Problem solving, among school-
  age children, 143–144
Professional meetings, 191
Profile, of the child, 93
Program committees, 20
Programs. *See* Schools and
  Programs
Psychosocial areas, infant/toddler,
  317–318
Publicity costs, 54
Publicly funded schools, 36–39, 41f
Public relations, 354–361
  appearance of the school, 355
  the brochure, 356–357,
    368–369f

  community activities, 361
  open house, 357, 360
  references and additional
    sources, 396–397
  telephone-answering proce-
    dures, 356
  visitors, 356

Q
Quality of child care, 25–26
  costs of, 56–57
Quiet corners, for school-age children, 327

R
Rating scale, 17
Reading center, preschool,
  296–297
Reading materials, staff training,
  191
Recordkeeping, 126–128
  file on health information of
    child, 258–259
Records, staff
  application materials, 168–169
  conferences, 170
  employment, 170
  evaluation, 170
  health, 169
  termination of employment,
    170
Regulations. *See* Licensing
  requirements and regulations
Rehabilitation Act of 1973, 377
Renting space, 49–50
Rest areas, infant/toddler environment, 308
Role models, 141
Role playing, staff training,
  189–190
Running MS/DOS, 386

S
Safety, 239–245
  accident management, 242–244
  accident report form, 243f
  disaster plans, 244
  of employees, federal laws per-
    taining to, 377
  first aid, 241
    kit, supplies for, 242
  in food preparation, 276–277
  indoors, 239–241

  infant/toddler environment,
    306–308
  outdoors, 241
  references and additional
    resources, 395
  transportation, 244–245
Salaries
  of directors, 8
  federal laws pertaining to, 377
  staff, 219–220
    determining, 56
School-age children
  activities for, 145–146
  development
    independence, 139–140
    language, 138
    peers, 140
    physical, 137–138
    role models, 141
    self-esteem, 140–141
    skills-industry *vs.* inferiority,
      140
    thinking, 139
  developmentally appropriate
    program
    friends, 145
    goals, 142–143
    independence, 143–144
    pace, 143
    parents, 145
    skills, 144–145
  references and additional
    resources, 393–394
  teacher/caregiver, characteris-
    tics of, 146–147
Schools, board-governed, 18
Schools and Programs
  references and additional
    resources, 392
  types of
    all-day schools, 27–29
    half-day schools, 26–27
  types of characteristics
    nonprofit schools, 34–36,
      40–41f
      church-sponsored, 34–35,
        40f
      cooperative, 34, 40f
      laboratory, 35–36, 41f
    private for-profit schools,
      30–34, 40f
      corporate schools, 31–32,
        40f

Schools and Programs (*continued*)
  employer-sponsored
    programs, 32–34, 40f
  family day care home,
    30–31, 40f
  publicly funded schools
    child care centers, 36–37,
      41f
    Head Start, 37–39, 41f
Science center, preschool, 295–296
Secretary, qualities of, 155
Self-concept, preschool, 100
Self-confidence, of the director, 4
Self-esteem
  attitudes and behaviors to
    observe, 84
  school-age children, 140–141
Self-evaluation tools, 17
Sensorimotor
  activities, infants and toddlers,
    132–133
  development, infants/toddlers,
    120–121
  stimulation, infant/toddler,
    309–311
Separation anxiety, 122, 126
Sick children, care and manage-
  ment of. *See* Health
Skill development, school-age
  children, 140, 144–145
Sleeping areas, infant/toddler, 313
Slides
  parent education, 351–352
  staff training, 190
Snacks, 143, 276f
Social activities, infants and tod-
  dlers, 133
Social/emotional development,
  goals of, 82
Social Security Act of 1935, 377
Software programs, 383–385
  CCM-Turbo, 384
  Child Care 2000, 384
  Child Quest, 384
  EZ-Care, 385
  Maggey, 385
  Private Advantage, 385
Space: Infants and toddlers,
  305–321
  cognitive area
    infants to one year, 314–315
    toddlers, 315
  fine-motor area, 315

general considerations
  developmental appropriate-
    ness, 308
  ethnic and cultural rele-
    vance, 308–309
  flexibility, 311
  goals, 306
  licensing, 305–306
  rest, solitude, 308
  safety, 306–308
  sensory input, 309–311
language area, 317
large-motor area, 315–317
psychosocial area, 317–318
references and additional
sources, 396
routine areas
  diapering, 313
  food preparation and eating,
    312–313
  sleeping, 313
  toileting, 314
special needs infant/toddlers,
  adaptations for, 318–319
specific areas, 311
Space: Preschool, 282–314
children with special needs,
  adaptations for, 299–300
general considerations for
organizing
  aesthetic appeal, 288
  age level, 285
  flexibility, 289
  goals and objectives, 283–
    284
  hard and soft areas, 287–288
  multicultural diversity,
    288–289
  noise level, 287
  program type, 284–285
  reality, 282–283
  regulations, 283
  storage, 287
  traffic flow, 285–286
references and additional
resources, 395–396
specific areas
  art center, 294f, 295
  block area, 292–295
  circle/game center, 297
  computer center, 298–299
  cooking center, 297–298
  dramatic play, 290–291,

292–293f
  math and science center,
    295–296
  music/listening center, 297
  outdoor space, 299
  reading/writing center,
    296–297
Space: School-age children,
  322–338
  general considerations
    aesthetically pleasing space,
      326–327
    flexibility, 325–326
    goals, 323
    homelike atmosphere,
      324–325
    licensing, 322–323
    safe yet challenging en-
      vironment, 323–324
    size of furniture and equip-
      ment, 326
    storage, 327
  references and additional
  sources, 396
  specific areas
    block building, 329–330
    clubroom, 332
    cooking, 329
    creative area, 327–328
    discovery center, 330–331
    dramatic play, 329
    games and manipulatives,
      328
    high-tech center, 331–332
    language center, 331
    outdoor environment,
      333–334
    quiet corner, 327
    sharing indoor space,
      332–333
    sharing outdoor space, 335
    woodworking, 328
Space costs, budgeting for,
  221
Special needs children. *See*
  Children with special needs
Speech
  delayed, 249
  impairments, preschool, 114
Staff
  first aid certification of, 12
  and the new year, 68–69
  records

application materials, 168–169
conferences, 170
employment, 170
evaluation, 170
health, 169
recommendations, 170
termination of employment, 170
substitute, 11–12
See also Staff practices; Staff selection; Staff supervision and development; Staff training; Student teachers; Volunteers
Staff practices, 163–168
advancement opportunities, 167
contract, 164–165
details of employment, 166
health and safety matters, 166–167
the job description, 167, 168f, 169f
physical environment, 166
statement of personnel policies, 165
termination of employment, 167
Staff selection, 57
application information, 157
infants/toddlers, 131–132
notification of employment or nonselection, 162–163
qualifications
education 152–153
experience, 153
knowledge, 154–155
personal characteristics, 153–154
required skills, 154
recruitment, 155–157
references and additional resources, 394
selection process
evaluating, 161–162
interviewing, 158–161
areas of inquiry to be avoided, 160
screening, 157–158
Staff supervision and development, 173–186
attendance, 186
evaluation of staff performance, 176–177

methods
observations, 180–181
performance elements, 179
questionnaire or checklist, 181
rating form, 180f
sampling of behaviors, 181
tests, 179
objectives, 177–178
standards, 178–179
use of, 181–182
learning styles, 186
place for training, 186
references and additional resources, 394
relationships
communication, 192
decision making, 193
size of groups, 184
skills application, 186
staff development, 182
staff interests survey, 185f
staff needs assessment, 183–184
stress and burnout
causes of, 193–194
prevention, 194–195
supervision of staff, 174–175
time for training, 185–186
Staff training
format for training sessions, 191–192
methods
college and university classes, 188
exchange observations, 190
field trips, 191
films, slides, and tapes, 190–191
group discussions, 189–190
mentor relationships, 187
orientation of new staff, 187
portfolio writing, 189
professional meetings, 191
reading materials, 191
role playing, 190
staff meetings, 188
team teaching, 188
workshops, 189
purpose of, 182–183
Standing committees, 19

Storage space
preschool children, 287
school-age children, 327
Stress
causes of, 193–194
prevention, 194–195
Student teachers
characteristics of, 199–200
master teacher
choice of, 202
responsibilities of, 205
orientation of, 203–204
reactions of, 205–206
references and additional resources, 394
role of the director, 200–202
Substitute staff, 11–12
Supervision. *See* Staff supervision and development
Supplies and materials, 69
budgeting for, 221

T
Taxes, budgeting for, 222
Teacher assignment chart, 57f
Teachers
accreditation of, 369
education, 152–153
Head Teacher, Head Start, 39
job description, 167, 168f
school-age children, characteristics of, 146–147
turnover rates, 162
vs. caregivers, 96–97
See also Staff; Student teachers
Team teaching, training, 188
Telephone-answering procedures, 356
Temper tantrums, 250
Tests
commercial, for child evaluation, 90–91
staff evaluation, 179
Thinking, development, school-age children, 139
Time samplings, 93
Toileting areas, infant/toddler, 314
Training, staff. *See* Staff training
Transportation
budgeting for, 221
bus services arrangement, 65
and safety, 244–245
Trust *vs.* mistrust, 122

Tuition, 222–223
    determining potential income,
    55–56
    uncollectible, 56, 224

U
Utilities, budgeting for, 222

V
Values, 77
Verbal messages, 13
Videostapes
    staff training, 190–191
Videotapes
    parent education, 351–352
Vietnam Era Veteran's
    Readjustment Assistance Act
    of 1974, 377

Visitors, 356
Visual impairment
    preschool, 115
    that interferes with learning,
    249
Volunteers, 207–214
    coordinator of, 208
    handbook for, 211–212
    intergenerational programs,
    films and videos of, 214
    orientation of, 210–211
    plan for services of, 207–208
    recognition of, 212–213
    records of service, 213
    recruitment of, 208–209
    references and additional
    resources, 394
    selection of, 210

supervision of, 212

W
Watson, 77
Woodworking areas, for school-
    age children, 328
Working checklist, 58
Working mothers, percentage of,
    326
"Workplace 2000", 9
Workshops
    for parents, 352
    staff training, 189
Writing center, preschool, 296–297
Written reports, 15–16

Z
Zoning regulations, 48